The Water Hustlers

The Water Hustlers

Robert H. Boyle

John Graves

T. H. Watkins

Sierra Club   San Francisco • New York

The Sierra Club, founded in 1892 by
John Muir, has devoted itself to the
study and protection of the nation's
scenic and ecological resources—
mountains, wetlands, woodlands, wild
shores and rivers. All club publications
are part of the nonprofit effort the
club carries on as a public trust.
There are 37 chapters coast to coast,
in Canada, Hawaii and Alaska.
Participation is invited in the club's
program to enjoy and preserve
wilderness everywhere. Address:
1050 Mills Tower, San Francisco,
California 94104; 250 West 57th
Street, New York, N.Y. 10019, or
235 Massachusetts Avenue N.E.,
Washington, D.C. 20002.

Designed and produced by Charles
Curtis, Inc., New York, and printed
in the United States of America.

Contents

Foreword

Once there was a time when the rain fell and trickled to the streams, and streams carried the water to the rivers and the rivers flowed unbroken to the sea. This was how Nature, God, The Great Spirit, Fate—take your pick—irrigated the land mass of the planet, kept it green and good for all living things. The giver of water, of course, was not impartial to all regions of the earth. Some areas received great quantities of water, others received little, a few received none at all. Where the rainfall was sparse, species adjusted accordingly, or expired. Where the rainfall was generous, life flourished in and beside the streams and rivers and lakes and estuaries. Only one standing-up species defied the natural order of things and ventured where—by biological laws—he did not belong. Man moved to the desert. And there, lacking the camel's hump but with profound ingenuity, he devised a manner of moving water from where it was to where it had never been before. Meanwhile, those who stayed behind in the lush rain-country were busy turning their streams and rivers into sewers, so that before long the water was unfit to drink and the people had to look elsewhere for new supplies. The search resulted in a manner of moving more water from where it was to where the people were. That is how water hustling came to be the second oldest profession in the world.

It is so ancient a profession that it may well have entrenched itself in our psyche, like a resident in-law in the attic apartment. All of us were, for a time in our youth, water hustlers. Writing of "The Plot to Drown Alaska" with a Rampart Dam on the Yukon River, author Paul Brooks observed:

> As any small boy knows, the presence of running water is a compelling reason to build a dam. Most boys when they grow up turn to other things, but a select few go on to join the U.S. Army Corps of Engineers. Here, under the heading of flood control, navigation, or power production, they build dams beyond the wildest dreams of youth. . . .

In the western states, a select few go on to join the Bureau of Reclamation of the U.S. Interior Department, whose marvels in concrete stand astride deep river canyons to dwarf the eastern colossi of the Corps. The employment opportunities do not stop here. There are power companies and flood control districts and boards of water supply, private, state and municipal, each with its own compelling reason to build a dam, dredge a canal, dynamite a mountain. The works are always justified because the "benefits" outweigh the costs or because some planner has projected for the future some need that is rooted in the experience of the past. The past teaches us that man multiplies both in numbers and in needs, that what suffices for 200 million people today may suffice for only half as many tomorrow when (the planners tell us) there will be twice as many people. And because it is easier to do things the way they have been done before than it is to refine alternatives, or to seek new solutions, the water hustlers of America are hustling from drawing board to construction site to impound or divert all the running water of this continent that has not already been dammed or ditched for some prior compelling reason.

Already, more than three-quarters of the major and secondary rivers of the United States have been manipulated in one fashion or another, so they are no longer wild or free. In many cases, manipulation has led to waste. The evaporative loss of surface water from large reservoirs throughout the country represents a volume more than enough to meet the municipal needs of all major U.S. cities combined. And behind the great high dams that impound these reservoirs the accumulating silt thickens. It is only a matter of time before we begin to see visible evidence that, whatever their failures, our engineers are supremely skilled in the construction of bogs.

The water hustlers do not take kindly to criticism, especially when it comes from persons who challenge their public works projects on environmental grounds. The hustlers regard themselves as representatives of the people and as custodians of the greatest good for the greatest number. Thus we hear from time to time the refrains of a curious Greek chorus, its theme being that conservationists value ducks more than people, or alligators more than people, or salmon more than people, depending on the particular habitat the hustlers would alter in the course of pursuing a mandate we never gave them. The fact is, those who oppose unnecessary water projects (and most of these projects today *are* unnecessary) do so because they value a life style that would preclude such simplistic *either-or* responses. It has been demonstrated, for example, that public works initiated to prevent flooding in south Florida have not only imperiled alligators and other wildlife in Everglades National Park but have also resulted in widespread ground fires and the threat of hyper-salinity encroaching on aquifers. These same aquifers supply south Florida cities with water. Those who speak for the alligator therefore also speak for the people. Parched landscapes do not enhance tourism, which happens to be Florida's leading industry; nor does salty water from the tap encourage sound health.

The flaw in the hustlers' philosophy is that man can and must conquer nature, especially if he holds a degree in engineering. Such thinking has led in this country to a multi-billion-dollar hydrological Maginot line—dams and levees designed to hold back the occasional flood and to encourage human habitation on the flood plains, with the implied promise of dry cellars in perpetuity. But nature doesn't work that way. As economist Kenneth Boulding has explained it:

> The truth is that what we call "flood control" means the eradication of little disasters every ten years or so at the cost of a really big disaster every fifty or 100 years . . . No flood-control program is able to protect a flood plain against the 100-year flood. After all, that is why the flood plain is there. . . .

Flood control is only a small part of the problem. The larger part involves the harnessing of rivers and streams to supply water for urban and rural uses, and to produce electric power (frequently for users far removed from the dam site). As a sop to the citizen, the hustlers throw in a bonus: recreation, generally of the still-water variety suitable for put-puts and such other appurtenances of our motor culture. Thus, in recent years, we have witnessed the erection of numerous dams, including an ecologically disastrous one at Glen Canyon on the Colorado. We have also witnessed some disasters averted through diligent public response, as in the case of the two dams planned for the Grand Canyon, the aforementioned Rampart project in Alaska, and the proposal to dam Kentucky's fabled Red River gorge. New battles are brewing: along the Snake and Salmon rivers of Idaho, at Tocks Island on the Delaware and in Quebec, where the provincial government proposes to dam ten wild rivers and divert five others in the James Bay watershed in order to sell megawatts to the extruded metropoli of the northeastern United States.

This endless proliferation of dams is bad enough. Enough of them on a single river or network of rivers can lay waste an entire watershed. What may be even worse is the practice of shuttling water from one watershed to another. Engineers call this an interbasin water transfer. Some other people we know call it robbing Peter to pay Paul. In a broad sense, it is what this book is all about.

Interbasin water transfers today are epidemic in the American West. One researcher, geographer Frank Quinn, counted 146 in the seventeen western states in 1965, involving an aggregate transfer of nearly 20 million acre-feet per year. Noting that most of the region's population growth since 1950 had occurred in Arizona, California, Colorado and Texas, "and, more specifically, in urban communities in the drier parts of these states," Quinn reported:

> . . . the popular mandate in the dry west seems to be founded on the logic that everyone gains—or at least no one loses directly— if unappropriated water can be found elsewhere . . . Today, one out of every five persons in the western states is served by a water-supply system that imports from a source a hundred miles or more away. . . .*

So there it is again, the old frontier ethic: *When it's all used up, there's more of the same over the next hill.* Or water-basin divide. Consider the pattern:

The Colorado River is overtaxed. Its allocations for withdrawal are spread among six dry southwestern states. Southern California looks enviously to the north. Arizona looks to California. California looks beyond its own plans and projects to the Columbia River, to the Snake-Colorado Project, to the modified Snake-Colorado Project, to the Yellowstone-Snake-Green Project, to the Western Water Project, and all of the western states, eyeing each other suspiciously, look finally to the grand flagon of them all, the North American Water and Power Alliance (NAWAPA), which even now, though we have not heard much about it lately, floats like the mirage of an oasis on the heat waves of our wildest technological dreams. *NAWAPA. Today, North America. Tomorrow, the world.* Or so it would seem, for NAW-

---

* Quinn, Frank. *Water Transfers: Must the American West Be Won Again?* The Geographical Review, LVIII, No. 1, New York.

APA, harnessing the headwaters of the Columbia, the Fraser, the Peace and Athabaska in Canada, and most of Alaska's major streams, including the Copper and Susitna, would redistribute these waters from a huge reservoir in the Rocky Mountain Trench of British Columbia to regions as distant as the Rio Grande Valley, the Great Lakes and Mexico. And then what? There's still a lot of water in Siberia. Trouble is, the Soviets have been mucking around with their rivers, too.

So have the Africans. With no small assistance from Western technocrats, the Africans have already provided the world with two classic demonstrations of how one can manage to cut off his economic nose to spite his ecological face. Both cases have been cited frequently in the recent literature of conservation, yet they bear repeating here, as lessons for those in this country who may still believe in the omniscience of technology or the infallibility of the dam-building engineer.

First, the Kariba Dam on the Zambesi River. This ambitious structure displaced some 29,000 farmers—a small matter inasmuch as the dam builders predicted that an increase in commercial fishery catches would offset the loss of flooded farmland. After an initial flourish, however, the catches of reservoir fish declined, stifled by a proliferation of algae and weeds (against a forecast of 20,000 tons of fish per annum, the actual catch averaged out at 2,100 tons). What's more, the eutrophying shallows provided excellent habitat for the tsetse fly, which promptly infected the displaced native livestock, not to mention a goodly number of natives.

Second, the Aswan High Dam on the Nile, largest structure of its kind in the world. The United Arab Republic anticipated a multitude of benefits: doubled production of electrical power, a significant increase in cultivated land, the impoundment of millions of cubic meters of water for irrigation. As it turns out, Aswan's giant Lake Nasser is a giant liability. It is rapidly filling with Nile silt. It is depriving the Nile Delta of rich nutrients essential to the web of marine life. The delta's once-flourishing sardine fisheries are on the decline, and there are fears that the harvest of shrimp may be similarly affected. No tsetse flies to speak of; just the continuing spread, through irrigation, of a snail-borne disease called schistosomiasis.

We are fortunate in these temperate United States. Ecological boomerangs turn around more slowly than they do in the tropics. How slowly? Who can say?

Who can say what the cumulative effect of a Texas Water Plan might be fifty years from now if, for example, the High Plains were to be irrigated with water transported from the Mississippi and all the state's Gulf-bound rivers were interdicted by a coastal canal? Who can say with any certainty that San Francisco Bay would not perish as an ecosystem if fresh-water inflows from the Sacramento-San Joaquin Delta were diverted to encourage crop surpluses in the Central Valley and urban necrophilia in the City of the Angels? And who can predict anything of the future of New York, where the unmetered use of water is still considered an inalienable right, and where the streams of the Adirondacks, the Catskills and Berkshires and Poconos are viewed as nothing better than extensions of the leakiest plumbing system in the world?

"Whatever shortage exists is not a shortage of water," science editor John Lear of *The Saturday Review* once observed, "but a shortage of human foresight."

A prodigious shortage of human foresight is chronicled in this book: the Texas Water Plan, the State Water Project of California, and a kind of Strangelovian scheme by the U.S. Army Corps of Engineers under which, as all roads once led to Rome, all waters would flow into New York City. Parts of these projects are already under construction or completed. A great many more remain on the drawing boards. So this is no post-mortem on rivers. The issues are very much alive. It is our hope that enough people, knowing about them, will somehow manage to keep the rivers alive, too, and in that process convince the water hustlers that the plans of nature are infinitely more compelling than their own.

The editors
Sierra Club Books

Part I
Texas

"You ain't seen nothing yet."

by John Graves

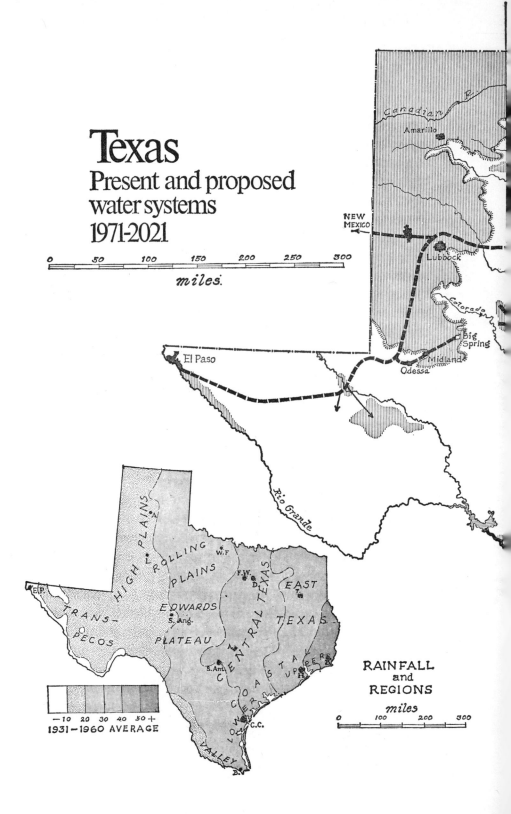

Texas
Present and proposed
water systems
1971-2021

0   50   100   150   200   250   300

miles.

NEW
MEXICO

Canadian R.

Amarillo

Lubbock

Colorado

Big
Spring

Midland

Odessa

El Paso

Rio Grande

HIGH PLAINS

ROLLING
PLAINS

W.F

F.W.
D.

EAST
T.

EDWARDS

S. Ang.

CENTRAL TEXAS

TRANS-
PECOS

PLATEAU

COASTAL

UPPER

S.Ant.

H.

E.P.

C.C.

VALLEY

B.V.

RAINFALL
and
REGIONS

miles

0   100   200   300

—10 20 30 40 50+
1931–1960 AVERAGE

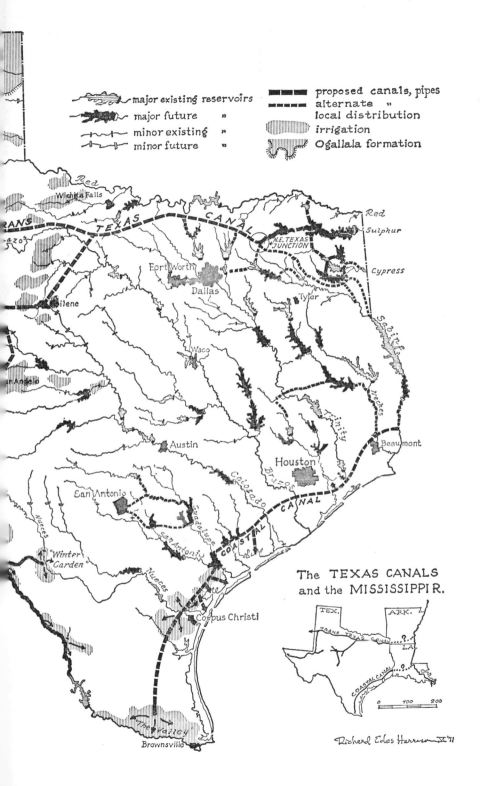

major existing reservoirs
major future   "
minor existing   "
minor future   "

proposed canals, pipes
alternate   "
local distribution
irrigation
Ogallala formation

Red
Wichita Falls
TRANS   TEXAS   CANAL
azos
Red
Sulphur
N.E. TEXAS
JUNCTION
Cypress
Fort Worth
Dallas
bilene
Tyler
Sabine
Waco
Neches
an Angelo
Trinity
Austin
Beaumont
Houston
Colorado
Brazos
San Antonio
Guadalupe
San Antonio
COASTAL   CANAL
Nueces
"Winter
Garden"
Nueces
Corpus Christi

The TEXAS CANALS
and the MISSISSIPPI R.

TEX.
ARK.
TRANS TEXAS CANAL
?
LA.
COASTAL CANAL
?
0   100   200

The Valley
Brownsville

Richard Edes Harrison   XI '71

I. East and West of Thirty Inches

As the world has been given to know from time to time, though less since Alaskan statehood became a fact, Texas covers a lot of ground. It covers quite a few types of country too, and despite modern homogenization a number of kinds of people who owe their lingering differentness both to heritage and to their conformity with the spirit and possibilities of those varying strips of country they inhabit. They have changed the country and diminished it, for except in a few patches of the harsh Trans-Pecos, Texas has little virginity left. But the country has changed them too. Even in the cities, stark and standard for the most part in their look and feel, these regional differences still show up in specific accents and outlooks and occupations, and in the smaller towns and the country they are strong. For better of worse many Texans, perhaps most, have not yet ceased to belong in the kind of country where they live.

No single influence has more to do with the way Texas regions vary than the distribution of water. Terrain and latitude and geology and history have some effect, but rain has far more. A precipitation map of the state is striped vertically with undulating isohyets ranging rather evenly from an average fifty-six inches per year along one part of the Louisiana border to less than eight inches at El Paso. Texas rivers, interstate and intrastate and international, run mainly south and east toward the Gulf, and tend to mirror in their respective volumes of flow these differences in rainfall, though the westernmost of them, the Rio Grande with its big farflung drainage basin reaching to the Rockies and the Mexican Sierra Madre, defies the pattern.

This wide variance in moisture distribution is based in a complexity of prevailing winds, of hurricanes, of blankets of Gulf-wet air wedged upward or shoved here and there by the big Plains "northers" of the cooler months, of dips and rises in the state's unemphatic topography. The thirty-inch isohyet wavers down the state back and forth across the ninety-eighth meridian, Walter Prescott Webb's old boundary between East and West, between a wet woodland-and-prairie way of being and a dry Plains way. In Texas, with its hot summers and big dry winds, this isohyet probably does roughly separate easterly regions where normal unirrigated farming is usually productive and flora and fauna are typical of temperate humid zones, and the western reaches of the state shading from subhumid into arid, where farmers often yearn for more water than the skies provide directly on their fields and grazing is the traditional major use of land.

On the moist side of the thirty-inch line are the well-watered East Texas forest regions with a lumber and pulpwood industry and along the abundant perennial streams good farmlands still in the process of recovery from hard early use, and people closer in type to those Faulkner wrote about than to the high-heeled, broad-swath western sort of thing. Here too are the sandy strips of hardwood scrub, erstwhile forests, that run south from the Red River, and the fertile loam prairies of Central Texas and the upper Gulf Coast, where almost anything can be made to grow well still, after more than a century of ungentle use. And because water is indispensable to big concentrations of people and the activities they engender, most of the state's main population centers and industries lie east of thirty inches as well.

Westward stretches drier country, varied too. There are the thorny-brush prairies along the lower coast and the Rio Grande, J. Frank Dobie's *brasada* where if you look in the right places you can still watch brown vaqueros ride out in the mornings long-stirruped and shielded in leather. There are the liveoak-cedar-grass savannas of the Edwards Plateau, perhaps the Texas heart-land, a rather beautiful but ungenerous expanse of dissected limestone whose German and Anglo ranchers nevertheless tend more sheep and Angora goats than are found in any other comparable region on the continent. North of the plateau lie the Rolling Plains, superb buffalo and cattle range in the early days and still productive where overgrazing and erosion have been slowed down or stopped. West and north of the Rolling Plains through most of the Panhandle are the scarp-edged flat High Plains, and west of everything is the generally desert country beyond the salty Pecos, a stream the epic old-time rancher Charles Goodnight once bitterly called "the graveyard of the cowman's hopes."

Though the less well-watered reaches of the state for the most part are still rather lightly peopled more or less in proportion to their dryness (Loving County on the Pecos boasted around 124 citizens in 1969), here and there petroleum, that widespread blessing and bane that has had so much to do with the whole modern Texas way of being, has fostered clumps of humanity that seem incongruous against the big empty country round-about. So has irrigated farming beside some rivers and in level places where major underground water occurs. One of the older and better known areas of irrigation is "the Valley," where al-luvial flats along the lower Rio Grande, seldom hit by freezes, have been turning out quantities of diverse comestibles and fibers since Spanish days, though the biggest development there has taken place during this century, with heavy promotional efforts to lure midwestern farmers and other winter-weary immigrants down among the palm and citrus trees, the subtropical birds, and the soft murmur of slurred border Spanish on the tongues of laborers traditionally content with very meager pay.

But activity in the Valley is dwarfed by what has happened lately on the tableland of the Panhandle High Plains, once an ocean of strong grass that paradoxically, for a time after buffalo and Comanche had been eliminated from it, was a barrier to stockmen in dry years because watering places were so few and far between. The windmill took care of that difficulty, permitting settlement by ranchers and dry-land farmers: "When I was little," an older Plainsman told me once, "any time my daddy walked up to a windmill he'd take off his hat and grin up at that fan going around. Just grin like an idjit." And in recent years—mainly since the 1940s—big modern pumps and engines sucking water out of a vast underground reservoir have converted the tableland into a checkerboard of thick-sowed fields of cotton, grain sorghum, wheat, alfalfa, and other crops, with huge machinery everywhere, enormous beef feed lots, and livewire growing communities speckled up and down where sun-dazed cow towns stagnated within recent memory. Around five and a half million acres are presently being irrigated there out of the Ogallala aquifer, which underlies nearly the whole Texas High Plains except where the Canadian River valley trenches across.

Even though the water Texas gets each year is unequally distributed, there is a lot of it. In a typical twelve-month period, something like 413 million acre-feet of moisture are dumped from the skies within the state's boundaries. If we want to make this look even more impressive, it adds up to some 134,638,000,000,-000 gallons, and if one could spread it evenly over the whole surface of Texas, which one can't, it would give every single region and subregion about twenty-eight inches of annual rainfall. Such a redistribution would make some Texans happy and thoroughly disgruntle others, but in time it would make all the regions resemble one another much more than they do right now. How one would feel about that would depend on how one feels about their differences as they are.

The great bulk of this received water evaporates back to the air from the surface of the land and from bodies of water, or after being used by plants, including crops, is transpired to the atmosphere by them. Eventually in the unending hydrologic cycle it comes back to earth or sea as rain or sleet or snow or hail or dew somewhere else, not necessarily within the purview of a Texas study. The one-tenth or so that escapes evapotranspiration seeks, as water does, the sea from which at one time or another it came. Some runs quickly overland to watercourses and down them; some soaks into the earth and sinks until it finds an impermeable layer along which to flow, then works its way down to lower river reaches or directly to the sea, sometimes taking years or even centuries to get there. (The mechanics of all this, it must be confessed, defy neat definition, for the deeper water formations do not necessarily respect state lines or even surface drainage patterns, so that some Texas ground water undoubtedly finds its way to air in Louisiana or Mexico or Oklahoma, just as some Texas spring water undoubtedly sank into the earth elsewhere.) And from the sea, of course, it goes sooner or later as vapor to the air again and is carried above the continents and renewed in purity falls again as rain or snow year by year, millennium by millennium, in a rhythm on which living things depend.

Men seize it for their various purposes as best they can in that interval between the time it falls and the time it finds the sea again. Where there is enough water and not too many men, they take it directly from streams or from shallow dug wells or from the springs where underground water surfaces on its journey. Where it is scarce or when there get to be too many people for however much there is, they punch wells down to deeper aquifers or build dams and other catchments to stay the vital fluid in its flow, and the more people there are the bigger and more sophisticated such measures are likely to be. Finally, when their demands outstrip even a thoroughly "developed" local supply, they grow less extravagant in their habits, or move elsewhere, or—often, in a day like ours—seek in technology still more sophisticated answers. Thus Los Angeles drinks rain that fell far to the north, and many a coastal chamber of commerce dreams dreams of infinite growth by way of desalted sea water.

Large technological dreams are stalking about Texas too. Traditionally its citizens have adjusted themselves to available supplies of water, the biggest adjustment being required of those who chose to inhabit the drier regions. Hence the sparse numbers of people in much of West Texas and the minimal, basic, domestic-and-livestock use they have customarily made of what water can be drawn from the ground or caught in cisterns and small impoundments. Many persons from that background, not necessarily far along in years, can remember their fathers hauling water for home use in barrels from muddy ponds or creeks maybe miles away, and have never quite grown used to turning on a tap and watching the clear miraculous liquid flow. Many others, in places where water from both ground and surface is tainted with various minerals left in the earth by ancient seas that repeatedly covered most of Texas, have perforce learned to tolerate or even to like its taste. I have one friend from the Rolling Plains—the so-called "Redbed Region" of salty seabottom clays—who claims that when he was growing up chiggers and ticks never bit people in his neighborhood because of the sulphur they had drunk. There are other old jokes too, like the one about the Pecos cowboys who had to carry salt shakers when they trailed cattle into strange country, to make the water taste right, and another about the old-timers who needed no standard curing brine for slaughtered pork but just used the local river's water.

Nevertheless, in the economy of abundance to which Texans along with other Americans and for that matter Europeans have been managing more or less to habituate themselves, copious, clean, sweet, cheap household water is mainly viewed as a need, not a luxury. And as the relationship of water in other, larger uses to abundance has become clear, there has been less and less stoic old-Texan acceptance of scarcity as foreordained, even in the more parched sections. Nor, with the quantities of Texans who exist at present (some eleven million by the 1970 count), the swarms expected as growth continues, and the fat life projected for them by those who project such things, does it appear that future scarcity is going to be as tolerable as traditional scarcity has been, unless technology or something else intervenes.

The most imminent shortages naturally loom west of the thirty-inch rainfall line. Surface water supplies have always been a little precarious in most of West Texas, and are much more so in relation to the spottily intense population build-up and the kinds of activity that are going on there now. Not only does less rain fall, but it tends to fall in big unmanageable gouts, and the beating sun and dry Chihuahuan winds characteristic of the region promptly snatch back a much bigger share of it than is subtracted by the atmosphere from East Texas's relatively abundant supply. In some dry places, net evaporation from the surface of a body of standing water like a reservoir amounts to eight feet or so per year, as contrasted to a foot or less in parts of far East Texas, and in such places the only way some streams can keep on running is underneath the protective sand and gravel in their beds.

Thus West Texans rely heavily on relatively deep underground water of the sort that made the Great Plains habitable once drilling rigs and windmills came into use. The only extensive regions that generally lack such a source are parts of the Rolling Plains and the Trans-Pecos, but in some other places the amount and mineral quality of the available ground water are problematic. In a few areas a combination of flat land, good ground water, deep-well pumps, and contemporary public farm and tax programs has led to such enthusiastic irrigation that a state of what hydrologists call "overdraft" exists. More water is being pumped out of the aquifers each year than natural processes are putting back in as recharge, and trouble has either already begun or is tiptoeing into view.

Trouble is biggest where irrigation is biggest—on that large segment of the High Plains, below the trough of the Canadian River valley, known sometimes prosaically as the South High Plains, and sometimes more ringingly as the Llano Estacado, or Staked Plain, a name of debated origin. (Did the old Spaniards put real stakes there to help them find their way home again, or did the palisaded escarpments on the New Mexico side suggest the name, or is *estacado* an evolved corruption of *destacado,* meaning isolated or detached, which that section of the Plains most clearly is? . . .) The water situation there is too extreme to be called typical, but it does illustrate the dilemma, and it adds up to a big enough problem all by itself to merit solid attention in any consideration of Texas water.

The High Plains as a whole, stretching northward out of West Texas and eastern New Mexico, are what is left of the original surface of a wide debris apron laid down by ancient, shifting, huge rivers. The rivers gushed off of the eastern slope of the Rockies in a time when those mountains were much higher than they are now and the rainfall they milked from windborne Atlantic clouds must have been enormous, as rainfall on the Andes' eastern slopes still is today. After the mountains were gnawed down by the elements and the climate changed, erosion of the debris apron by new streams in combination with other forces commenced, and in these lesser times the largest intact piece of the apron, the Llano Estacado of Texas and New Mexico, is a sort of lonesome table. It falls away sharply on the west and more gently on the south to the Pecos River drainage, on the north to the Canadian beyond which more High Plains continue, and on the east, by way of the canyoned Cap Rock escarpment, to the Rolling Plains.

The Ogallala water-bearing formation that underlies it is made up of coarser materials laid down beneath those ancient rivers' flood-plain silt. Like the Llano itself, that part of the Ogallala stands mainly above the eaten-away country roundabout. Hence any recharge water it receives cannot come seeping along side-wise and down from perhaps distant and better-watered porous areas, as recharge does in many other major aquifers, but derives solely from rain that escapes evapotranspiration and surface run-off on the Llano Estacado itself. Since that rainfall is not heavy—eighteen to twenty inches in a typical year—and only a tiny part of its total seeps down to the aquifer, mainly in abnormally wet seasons, the Ogallala's average annual recharge is very small. Most authorities put it at a quarter to a half of an inch, and some of them at as little as a twentieth.

The formation is capacious, up to 500 feet thick in places and having contained in a virgin balanced state immense amounts of water—perhaps 300 to 400 million acre-feet under Texas alone. Given its limited recharge, most molecules of that water have obviously been there for hundreds or even thousands of years—"fossil water," some people call it—and those who tap it are reaping the benefit of rain that fell in times before the continent itself, let alone the Plains, had felt a white man's foot. It is good water, though rather hard and in places heavily charged with natural fluorine. People from those places who have grown up drinking it often have big brown-mottled teeth strong enough to chomp railroad spikes, and you know when they smile where they are from.

The High Plains and the strata associated with them tilt slightly eastward, so that in Indian days the Ogallala's discharge of its annual surplus, in balance with its recharge, was mainly through springs below the eastern escarpment, with some brimming up into stream courses on the surface of the Plains themselves and some escaping westward and elsewhere. Some of the Cap Rock outlets were notable and are commemorated by place names like Roaring Springs and Big Spring. All had about them the miraculous feeling of bounteous cool water in dry country, and they were known and prized by wildlife and Indians and by settlers when they came. For a time their outflow made the roughish country below the Cap Rock much preferable to the lush short-grass plateau above as cattle range.

Tapping deeper levels of the aquifer, many of these springs still flow well, though hydrologists' opinions and old-timers' recollections often conflict sharply on this point. Regardless of the truth of that, it seems they are not destined to flow too much longer. For the Llano's Ogallala no longer has a surplus, and any water that escapes from it below the Cap Rock through the ancient orifices is now a drain on its capital accumulation, though tiny in comparison to the enormous upward drain through big-bore wells and pumps. Water from the formation is being sucked out for farming at an average rate of three to four feet or more a year in some sections. In effect, it is being mined.

Depth to the Ogallala's water is not the same everywhere, nor is its thickness, nor has the decline in its level been uniform throughout the Llano Estacado. In some places deterioration of the aquifer or increased pumping costs caused by the fall in the water level since the 1940s are making irrigators convert back to dry-land farming, dependent on rainfall. A 1970 agricultural survey of the whole area showed that an average irrigation well could be counted on to serve only 84 acres, as compared with 103 acres in 1960 and 140 acres in 1950. The margin of profit gets skimpier year by year, and throughout the region everyone knows that the end of the farming bonanza based on exploitation of the Ogallala is in sight. Cheaper pumping energy or fancier crops, if such were to present themselves, might make a difference for a time, but only for a time. Most informed persons think that in the immediate future—perhaps until about 1980—expansion of irrigated acreage on the smaller North High Plains of Texas, whose separate portion of the Ogallala began to get hard use much later, will more than offset in-state losses to the south, but that shortly thereafter the whole balloon will start wrinkling and collapsing.

If it does, the collapse may well create some noble ghost communities. For the thriving towns and cities of the Texas High Plains—Lubbock, Plainview, Amarillo, and the rest—are all at bottom dependent for their health on the crop production made possible by irrigation. Just about everyone in the region would feel the shock, whether or not they farm or sell things to farmers. Conceivably light industry and perhaps other activities, watered from what the irrigators leave of the Ogallala, could furnish a new basis for survival there, as could improved dry-land farming —agriculturalists believe, for instance, that the big Plains feed-lot industry could continue full-strength on the grain sorghums the region could produce without irrigation.

But it is not possible to find a High Plainsman who believes such substitutes would uphold anything like the fervid prosperity of the past quarter-century, or that the changeover would be anything but painful. "I grew up on that dry-land stuff," one farmer said with two cars in the garage of a good new house and a pickup and $7,000 tractor parked outside. "I watched my daddy fight it and I fought it with him. A little old cloud comes over and everybody sort of holds their breath and grunts, and it don't drop nothing and you just keep on watching the crops dry up. Uh-uh. When the water's gone I'm leaving too."

Wide reverberations from the boom's bust are foreseen by some savants, like Representative Bill Clayton of Springlake, who combines his legislative function with the executive directorship of a Plains promotional outfit called Water, Inc. Recently he intimated to a reporter that not only was Texas as a whole heavily dependent on Plains crop production but if the Plains went broke, indigent Plainsmen would swamp the welfare rolls of wetland Texas cities.

Nowhere else in Texas does the magnitude of a water problem approach what the High Plains have to face, though most of the other notable ones are linked, as there, with the same prodigal use of water for irrigation. In a part of the near Trans-Pecos and in the so-called "Winter Garden" far down the state southwest of San Antonio, and elsewhere, farmers have been treating their aquifers with the same exploitative vigor folks on the High

Plains have demonstrated, and with similar results. Areas that irrigate from major stream flows, like those found here and there along the Rio Grande from the lush region near its mouth all the way up to El Paso, have not been privileged to create quite such fat problems around their water resources, for you can't use up more of a river's water than its annual sustained yield; it simply is not there to use. Also Texas water laws, which we will have to glance at shortly, are fairly strict in rationing out surface water. Even so, more legally established "rights" for water use exist on the Rio Grande than can be satisfied in drouth years, and increased upstream use in New Mexico and in the republic across the river (one of whose streams, the Rio Conchos, dwarfs the hard-used Rio Grande at their confluence above Presidio in the Big Bend) is putting still more pressure on the situation. Furthermore, along the Rio Grande and elsewhere, there are large uncultivated or dry-farmed expanses of level land without attached "rights" that could be made to yield big profits if water could be found with which to dampen them. In harmony with the unstoic spirit of the times, potential irrigators and others are making this loudly clear. In the Lower Valley their plaints are the more poignant for being based in bilked hopes. There it had been believed that the yield from two big new international reservoirs upstream, Falcón and Amistad, was going to firm up the supply for present rights-holders and permit a great deal of new irrigation too, but an unexpected tangle of water-rights litigation has thwarted that dream thus far.

Most big Texas cities, as we have noted, are located in the humid regions, and to date have been able to cope fairly well with the water demands that go with expansion of population and industry, whose infinite desirability still goes largely unquestioned in the state. Mainly they have worked out a combination supply from ground water and from nearby reservoirs, sometimes community-built and owned structures but in recent years often federal multipurpose projects in which cities can buy a share.

Not that all is rosy all around. The heavy reliance of the

Houston megalopolitan complex, for instance, on the bounteous underlying Gulf Coast aquifer has caused some localized problems based on overpumping—land subsidence (buildings and pavements are Oz-ishly askew in certain suburbs), salt-water intrusion, declining water levels, and the like. San Antonio's long lyrical contentment with a pure, copious, handy supply of water from big springs and wells tapping the aquifer that lies along the Balcones Fault zone at the rim of the Edwards Plateau appears to be about to end, for if the city takes out much more than it has been taking, important damage to the aquifer is likely, including possible contamination with saline ground water and the drying up of some of the lovely and famous Balcones Escarpment springs like those at San Marcos, New Braunfels, and Austin. Eternally arid El Paso, dependent on what New Mexico bequeathes it of the upper Rio Grande's flow (less and less in recent years) and on a narrow deep aquifer, is beginning to foresee a conflict between municipal and agricultural demands for water.

And so on. Yet to date no major Texas city has come up against a crucial shortage of water, even if during the big drouth of the 1950s some of them had to scramble a bit, like Dallas, whose householders still remember the salty taste and corrosiveness of the Red River water that was piped across country to them for a while during that period. The main questions about municipal water supply, and the industrial requirements that are usually linked with municipal demands, have to do with what may happen in the future if growth keeps on spiraling. As do most of the other main questions of our time. . . .

Water supply and water quality are not separable considerations. No matter how much water you have around, if it is too foul or mineralized for what you want to do with it, it is no supply at all. In the past Texas, wide and mainly unindustrial, has tended to lag behind some other parts of the nation in the intensity and malignity of the pollution poured into its waters, but lately it has been striving hard to catch up. Sewage treatment-

plant effluents or plain picturesque sewage overfertilize and degrade varying stretches of streamway below most main Texas
towns and cities that have a stream to degrade. Oxygen deficiency,
stink, blue sludge, algae, and happy concentrations of bacteria
are some of the drearily familiar results known to anyone who
ever indulged himself in float trips on metropolitan rivers. Industry pours in its share of substances ranging from pulp-mill
wastes and poisonous heavy-metal compounds to chicken guts
and refinery discharges, with little restriction until lately. The
federally prodded process of discouraging all this is only now
getting weakly underway, hampered as it is everywhere else by
the political muscle of industry and the fact that communities are
often leery of giving offense to those who administer local pay-
rolls.

High-yield farming and farm-linked enterprises do their part
as well. Chemical fertilizers and persistent pesticides leach out
of the soil into streams or downward into ground water. Silt off
of sloppily farmed or grazed land clouds and chokes water and
smothers aquatic life. Feed lots bleed out the richness from
mountains of manure. "Return flows" from irrigation—the excess
water that runs or seeps back to rivers, often to be used over and
over again downstream—not only carry some poisons and fertilizers but also, through being evaporated down and passed
through several soils, may acquire enough dissolved natural minerals to make them unfit for municipal supply and damaging to
the land's own usefulness for farming. Common salt from the old
southwestern seas is probably the most troublesome of these
minerals. In places like the El Paso valley, irrigated from the Rio
Grande since early days, accumulations of it are making the soil
toxic to crop roots. It is a very ancient irrigation trouble, the bane
of many Old World farming civilizations in the past as well as
of a number of big American projects.

Salt is plentiful in Texas, and irrigation plays only a small part
in augmenting the quantities of it that sour some of the state's other
main rivers, including the Pecos, the Colorado, the Brazos, and

the Red. Much of this contamination is natural and longstanding, originating in the outflow of saline ground water here and there, the basis for the old wry jokes about cowboys' salt shakers and such things. Some also comes from oil-field operations that have tapped and released reservoirs of brine, which may go either directly into stream channels or into other underground formations containing good water. Quite a number of high-priced irrigation wells in areas all the way from the Llano Estacado to the coastal rice region have had to be abandoned for this cause, or sometimes because overpumping itself has brought about an intrusion of underlying salty water.

Besides being ugly and unsanitary and hard on aquatic life and plumbing and good farmland, pollution in its various forms scrambles and complicates the pattern of water use. If a town has a choice between drinking from a copious but filthy river, for instance, and an aquifer that will suffer from heavy use, its presiding elders are probably going to sink some wells regardless of the aquifer's welfare. Or they may condemn some valuable farms along a tributary creek and build a big preemptive reservoir that would not be needed if the town's own river were clean. And water-supply facilities themselves may succumb to pollution. Silt has already practically filled some reservoirs in Texas, like Lake Worth in Tarrant County, and the Trinity downstream from the Fort Worth-Dallas metropolis is so loaded with sewage nutrients that if it is not cleaned up, big main-stream reservoirs planned or already built far down the river are fated to undergo that form of rapid destruction known as "eutrophication"—the overfertilization and choking and sliminess that have infected Lake Erie.

If a certain fading engineering philosophy prevails, pollution can also lead to the construction of more and bigger reservoirs for pollution's own sake, with their heavy cost in money and land and the natural wholeness that uncluttered rivers and river bottoms help maintain. "The solution for pollution is dilution," one old saying has it, which means that if you maintain a big upstream reserve of stored water, you can release it into a river during periods of low flow and heavy organic loads to help the river digest those loads. The trouble with this approach is that, like "flood control" that aims to permit more construction and activity on a river's flood plain, it ultimately makes the problem worse by compounding its cause. . . . The cause of flood damage is people and their things on the flood plain where they are subject to damage. The cause of pollution is pollutants.

Within Texas, the final repository for most pollution is the state's coastal waters, including its string of estuarial bays that stretch along the Gulf shoreline most of the way from Louisiana to Mexico behind a barrier of low sandy islands and splayed peninsulas. They are a magnificent resource, shallow and brackish and marshy-bordered and rich with life, and great numbers of Texans and non-Texans are drawn there each year to participate somehow in that richness. The flat land runs to the flat bays, and beyond the flat sand islands is the blue flat Gulf, but it is dramatic enough for all that, because of the life that is there. Some of my own youngest outdoor memories are of going out at dawn with one of my hunting and fishing uncles to anchor on an oyster reef in Aransas Bay and cast into the swarms of speckled trout (the name for weakfish on that coast) that were slashing at shrimp and bait fish. Nearly any memory of that coast has in it a sense of teeming life. I can still manage a cringe recalling the time a friend and I, both young, sneaked up on a siene-bean pond near one of the bays to get ducks for a barbecue someone was having. Making a compromise between sport and meat, we agreed to shoot them on the rise, not sitting, crawled to within range on our bellies, and jumping up fired into an unexpected mass of frantic wings, for there were so many that they were as thick in the air as they had been on the water. The kill dismayed us—fifty-three—and I remember launching a stunned rhetorical question as to whether we had really shot that many.

"We sure as hell did," my practical friend replied. "And I'm sorry too, but let's load them up and get out of here before a game warden shows up." Not that they went uneaten, or that we had made a dent in the thousands that had risen. . . .

The bays matter supremely not only in the lives of shrimp and oysters and crabs and inshore wildlife but also in the spawning cycles of many fish that reach maturity in the open sea. People who ought to know have said that Galveston Bay alone, the biggest and most varied of the Texas estuaries, plays a direct part in the production of over 80 percent of the poundage taken by the state's commercial fishermen each year. The commercial harvest of fish and shellfish taken out of Texas and Louisiana (mainly the latter, one must unchauvinistically confess) amounted to 900 million pounds in 1968, or 22 percent of the total U. S. catch, virtually all of it dependent at some life stage on estuaries.

The phenomenal value of these bodies of water in a healthy state has been further dramatized in recent years by scientists investigating aquaculture and mariculture—water farming—which many think may become a prime tool for feeding Earth's growing billions of people as traditional dirt farming reaches its limits. Already a going business in places like Japan, it works best in rich ponds or under estuarial conditions, in the fertile, varying, but intricately balanced environment that has developed in those fortunate sheltered coastal places where fresh and salt water mingle into a nursery broth for many kinds of life. One recent set of experiments indicated that on expertly, intensively tended beds under ideal conditions it would be possible to harvest shellfish with an annual gross market value of around $26,000 an acre. Where is the farmland that will do that?

Texas bays cover about 1.3 million acres. Not all that acreage was prime estuarine habitat even under natural conditions, for fresh-water inflows may sometimes run too high at the mouths of the state's big eastern rivers, and often much too low on the dry coast to the southwest, where in drouth periods evaporation may make certain bays hyper-saline, saltier even than the Gulf outside the barrier islands. But fundamentally the Texas bays are estuaries, and they have that kind of value.

Yet like many other American estuaries—the Potomac downstream from Washington is a good graphic example, viewed by many—they have been abominably mistreated, and it is a measure of our American sang-froid that no one really knows yet how much damage has already been done, or how permanent it is, or how more damage might be averted. Where cities and clusters of industry stand close by and keep growing, the bays are used as sewers more casually than most rivers are. Galveston Bay, for instance, is fed not only by the over-enriched Trinity but by other tributaries draining metropolitan Houston, one of which, Buffalo Bayou, has been described by a federal water quality official as perhaps the worst polluted body of water in the entire world. Thermal discharges from increasing numbers of steam electric plants can upset nursery conditions in a thousand acres or more of water per plant. Pumped brine from oil and gas well-drilling operations flows in. Bulkheading and filling for resort or residential or industrial development does away with the bays' marshy borders, the most valuable of their varied nursery areas. Hurricane protection projects alter the regimen of inflows and outflows. Pesticides carried off of intensively farmed coastal prairies or washed down the rivers from other more distant areas build up in aquatic creatures' bodies. Investigators in 1969 found seven juvenile trout per acre in a part of the Laguna Madre where in 1966 there had been twelve, and in 1964 thirty, and the ovaries of adult female trout in the sampling area were heavily loaded with DDT. From fish the venom gets into other creatures like the brown pelican, down to considerably less than a hundred known individuals on the whole Texas coast, where a very few years ago it was one of the most common large birds around the bays and harbors. And it is of course common knowledge that these poisons go on out to sea as well, playing hell all the way— to the point, some scientists say, of killing off much of the plankton that is the basis of sea life and the origin of most of the cycled oxygen that air-breathing creatures, among them men, take into their lungs.

Wholesale hydraulic dredging of great deposits of oyster shell, used to make lime and cement and other things, chews up live oyster reefs and heaps spoil and silt widely over the bottom, smothering out much of the small animal life that holds the estuarial food chain together, clouding the water, even eating away at islands where seabirds nest or exposing them to the erosion of tides and waves and currents. Lately the National Audubon Society, on behalf of the whooping crane sanctuary near Aransas, tried to file suit against the state for permitting dredging in that neighborhood on the grounds that it was destroying the cranes' food supply, but the society was not allowed standing in federal court. This is only the latest in a long series of failures to discommode the dredgers, for dredging pays big money and has political ramifications. It is carried out under permits from the state, issued ironically through the department concerned with parks and wildlife. A few years ago it figured in one of the periodic upheavals in that agency when the executive head, a responsible man named Dodgen who did not believe that dredging and bays were necessarily a happy combination, was summarily canned by Governor Connally after a complexity of events that included Lyndon B. Johnson nabbed by a game warden in the Hill Country with a bag of doves, and other delights, but possibly all that is a bit far off the track of Texas water planning. . . .

Subtle, slow, but big and definite damage is being done to the bays also by the shrinkage of vital fresh-water inflows to them as water development takes place upstream on the rivers that feed them. In combination with pollution this subtraction is deadly, and particularly on the subhumid lower coast, where bay salinities were always higher and balances always more delicate, it has been making a noticeable difference in the species that thrive, and their numbers, oysters generally being the first to go.

I am aware that this is quite a large dose of material on the Texas bays with which to load an introductory chapter, but the bays matter greatly, and serve as a pretty fair example of where freewheeling growth is leading the state. The list of their troubles could be extended, as could the list of ills pertaining to the rivers and reservoirs and aquifers of Texas, all of them part of a whole thing, or a thing that was once whole. Clearly enough something needs to be done about Texas water, and just as clearly it needs to be different philosophically from anything large that has been done so far. Because the large things that have been done so far add up, philosophically and concretely, to all these troubles.

II. Of Plans and Planning

Historically, human use of water in Texas has grown in a happenstance way governed by natural and political conditions, whim, and available technology. This fact is reflected in a welter of water-oriented institutions, water developments, and water laws that can in all charity be best described as a mess.

Early Anglo-Saxons in the state brought with them, embedded in the web of precedence that constitutes the common law, the old humidland British concept of riparian rights, under which people who owned property along streams had a relatively unrestricted privilege to use the streams' water. It did not work perfectly even in wet country and has been subject to much modification by the courts. In dry parts of North America, especially where the enormously consumptive use of water for irrigated farming has been a part of the scheme of things, it worked so miserably that feuds and bloodletting were a common outgrowth of it. Hence a long time ago Texas law, like law in most of the other western states, began to include what has come to be called the doctrine of prior appropriation, whereunder—again within limits—the fellow who first starts using a stream's water has a favored legal claim on continued use of it, and anyone who gets there after the full supply is thus sewed up is more or less out of luck. Since then, the two doctrines have existed side by side in Texas law, often in conflict with each other. Prior appropriation has won most often, though modified to give preference to certain types of users—towns being privileged over farmers, for instance. At present the riparian right is usually construed to cover only a stream-side landowner's domestic and livestock-water needs (if you want to insist on your full due, you can water a vegetable garden but you can't sell anything out of it. . . .), but enough haziness still surrounds the subject to permit it to weave great legal tangles, as presently on the lower Rio Grande.

No rationality at all has managed to worm itself into the governance of ground water, concerning which medieval misconceptions about the hydrologic cycle have continued to rule, as medieval misconceptions are likely to do when someone gets a vested interest in them. In a day when practically all of Texas's aquifers, major and minor, have been studied to the point that scientists have some idea of their capacities, their extent, their percolation characteristics, the amount of recharge water they receive each year and where it comes from and therefore what a "sustained yield" withdrawal of their waters for use would consist of—in such a day, Texas law continues to regard most ground water as a mysterious separate blessing unrelated to other water and legitimately subject to capture and use in unlimited quantities by any property owner who digs or drills or drives a well. The law abounds in confusing and unscientific distinctions between "percolating ground water," "ground water in channels," "artesian waters," "diffused surface water," and the like, and it has led directly to such edifying spectacles as the mining of the Ogallala from beneath the Llano Estacado, where if you do not grab all the water you can from beneath your farm, your neighbors will legally grab it for themselves. It has also fostered some notable disruptions of surface-water rights, as when established irrigators near Fort Stockton in the Trans-Pecos, who had long used water from the big Comanche Springs, sued people whose new wells, drilled into the aquifer supplying the springs, had dried them up. Tough luck, said the court in effect; these are clearly two different kinds of water.

This shortage of rudimentary science in the legal framework makes adequate water planning in the state very hard at times, especially since about three-quarters of the water now used comes from underground. San Antonio's impending water problem was mentioned earlier. For some reason, perhaps age, this city is one of the less crassly commercial population centers of Texas. Commendably, those who guide its affairs do not want to abuse the Balcones Fault zone aquifer and dry up all those pleasant springs up and down the limestone escarpment where people have picnicked and swum and fished since the beginning of things, even though under state law they could go ahead and do so if they chose. According to testimony by a Bureau of Reclamation official at a hearing last year, one quite logical alternative would be for the city to drill a field of deep wells tapping the separate Carrizo-Wilcox aquifer which lies just to the south and could probably, used right, supply future needs. Yet the law would permit indiscriminate use of the aquifer by hundreds or thousands of irrigators too, and the city might well within a few years find itself with a multimillion-dollar investment in a set of dry holes, with appurtenant useless machinery and pipelines. Big industry has the same problem in relation to Texas ground water. On the High Plains, probable trouble with the Ogallala has driven some cities to buy water out of Lake Meredith on the Canadian, to the discontent of many citizens, for the Canadian water is hard on tastebuds, bowels, and pipes.

Early water development in the state was a local affair—individuals and companies and towns built dams and canal systems and such things for irrigation or municipal supply—and some development still is of this type. Cities, counties, and an amazing hodgepodge of legally established, variously intended, often overlapping "water districts" (no one seems to know just how many of these there are, but they add up to five or six hundred) all have wide powers to divert and control and use the water within their jurisdiction—or, by finding a comfortable niche in the vast cost-sharing apparatus of federal programs, to contract with national agencies for its development. Such piecemeal action, mainly uncoordinated with the needs of neighboring towns or districts, has led to a lot of unnecessary reservoir construction, misguided flood-control measures, loss of good bottom land productive of crops and wildlife, and sometimes a waste of water.

The first real attempt to deal with this fragmentation of effort and the resultant waste came in the 1920s and '30s when, under the stimulus of federal "regional" thinking of the sort that led to the Tennessee Valley Authority, several agencies were set up with basin-wide powers over water planning and development in the individual drainage areas of certain intrastate Texas rivers. The drainage basins were seen as separate natural units, to be handled as units. The agencies include such well-known bodies as the Brazos River Authority and the Lower Colorado River Authority, and the power they possessed to work out coordinated flood control, water supply, power generation, and other water-related programs within an entire river system was a step upward from the local scrambling that had prevailed before, although the latter still went on full force. Theoretically the river authorities (some of them called conservation and reclamation districts) inhabit a middle realm of government between state and local levels. In reality, some of them possess a sort of independence from state control based on their strong links with Congress and the federal government, whose agencies do much of their planning and construction work and push for their projects in Washington. This fact has lately begun to gravel officials of the new state-level water agencies with an interest in making development fit in with overall Texas needs rather than regional ones, and in maintaining Texas control over it.

Besides these intrastate authorities there are interstate bodies with federal participation, concerned with water in the streams Texas shares with neighboring states, and also an International Boundary and Water Commission that functions along the Rio Grande and has built the Falcón and Amistad reservoirs there.

In the past couple of decades federal agencies have made more than one bid to move strongly into the realm of overall Texas water planning and development. They have had less success than elsewhere in the West, but most of the elements suggested in federal studies have lodged themselves in state officials' thinking about water development and continue to crop up. One such element is the antithesis of the regional river-basin thinking embodied in the river authorities—the massive, orderly transfer of "surplus" water from humid river basins to regions of shortage. The first time it was eyed practically, as far as I have been able to learn (the progress of water planning in Texas is hard to see clearly at times, for there has been a reluctance on the part of successive groups of planners to admit that anyone else's study preceded theirs), was in a 1952 Bureau of Reclamation report called *Water Supply and the Texas Economy: an Appraisal of the Texas Water Problem,* the culmination of a study carried out by the bureau at the request of then-Senator Lyndon Johnson. The report caught the fancy of historian Walter Prescott Webb, who summed it up in a small pithy volume called *More Water for Texas.*

West Texans, the Bureau said (it was clear enough even then), were getting ready to use up all their water, and when they finished the job there was not going to be any economic way to continue big irrigation there. The Redbed Region, or Rolling Plains, could get a fair supply of less mineralized municipal water by building some dams. The Edwards Plateau was for sheep, goats, and cows, and for men who wanted to raise them. East Texas had no difficult water problems, but in fact a surplus of

water that ought to be put to use elsewhere, and the best place
to put it to use would be in the crescent of level land along the
Texas Gulf Coast from the Sabine to the Rio Grande, some 400
miles in length. This fortunate strip, the report averred, with its
fertile flat-lands, its minerals, its ample supplies of petroleum and
natural gas not only locally but out of pipelines running down
from the hinterlands, and its seaports, might feasibly be made into
an industrial and agricultural paradise by the expenditure of
about a billion dollars on a system of reservoirs and a large
interbasin aqueduct, running parallel to the coast and intersecting
all the Texas rivers to collect and distribute their water to dry
lower-coast sections as needed.

"Burleigh's Ditch," as the proposed coastal aqueduct has
sometimes been called, after the Reclamation official most closely
identified with it, Harry P. Burleigh, was the essence and gist of
the program, which was not rapturously acclaimed by the gen-
erality of Texans. The provincialism of Texas regions, for one
thing, has ever been a stumbling block in the way of statewide
schemes, especially when potential benefits were not widespread.
(Despite the state's range-cattle tradition and all those big hats
and belt buckles, for instance, no statewide brand-registration
law has ever threaded its way through the legislature, because of
East and Central Texans' distrust of the West Texas stockmen
who need such a measure.) Also, the intensely regional river-
basin concept of water and resource management, emphasized at
all levels of government in the thirties, had bred a philosophical
and statutory resistance to the idea of subtracting water from one
basin to add it to another, even though limited transfers of this
sort had been made.

Even stouter, though, was the philosophical resistance at the
level of state government to any federal control over Texas resources. The early and middle 1950s, if anyone remembers them
after the rapid-fire political changes of intervening years, were
a period of resurgent tub thumping for states' rights in Confed-
erate latitudes. Texas's governor from 1949 to 1957, Allan

Shivers, was one of the more energetic thumpers. The successful fight, mainly under his leadership, for retention of the state's ownership of oil-rich coastal tidelands fanned a lot of anti-federal feeling in Texas during those times, not that it had needed much fanning since Reconstruction times.

Furthermore, Bureau of Reclamation programs, unlike certain other federal water programs, have always had some fairly stout strings attached to them. The emphasis of the bureau's activities is on irrigation in the seventeen western states, and in the federal laws that guide it there is a basic rule that limits the land an individual landowner can irrigate with water bought from a bureau project to 160 acres. Though in practice a farmer and his wife can both sign for a share and irrigate up to 320 acres, and though there are certain other complex exceptions, the basic limitation has survived the assaults of big landowners and speculators and corporate agriculture since Teddy Roosevelt's day, and continues to reflect the old Jeffersonian, Populist bias in favor of family farms of moderate size.

But family farms of moderate size are not what some Texas interests have had in mind. It is a subject that will recur.

Trying again later in the decade of the fifties, L. B. J. and the federal establishment got authorization for a temporary federal agency called the "U. S. Study Commission—Texas," which conducted a comprehensive study of the eight intrastate Texas river basins from the Neches to the Nucces, formulated a wide plan, and presented it in a report to the president and the Congress in 1962. The commission's proposed fifty-year program, whose ultimate cost was reckoned at about $4 billion, covered all phases of water use and control and development and related land-treatment programs in the study area, which embraced about three-fifths of the state. Management was to be federal, though with state participation. The proposals included some eighty-three new major reservoirs, with interbasin transfers of water and the possibility of a "lower aqueduct" which was a form of Burleigh's Ditch. This new plan did not emphasize irrigation as heavily as the Bureau had, however, and passed over West Texas's looming hydrological catastrophe with the briefly stated calm assumption that irrigated farming in that region would fairly soon play out. The report filled three solid volumes, and nudged general thought about Texas water hard toward the concept of a Grand Plan, an overall detailed prescription for hydrologic bliss.

Though Texas representatives sat on the U. S. Study Commission—including its chairman George R. Brown, a Houston contractor and one of Lyndon Johnson's friends—Austin was uneasy about its implications. In the late fifties and early sixties a flurry of reorganization of the state's water planning and development apparatus reflected an awareness of the federal dragon's fiery breath. And in 1961, before the study commission's report came out, the Texas Board of Water Engineers (soon afterward known for a short time as the Texas Water Commission) issued *A Plan for Meeting the 1980 Water Requirements of Texas,* which was rather modest in scope and skeletal in structure but was nevertheless the first state attempt to undertake overall planning. It staked a claim, even if the subsequent federal commission report did make it look so ungrandiose that no state official ever urged its implementation.

A dearth of grandiosity has not in recent years been one of the defects critics attribute to the programs of the main federal water-development agencies—the Army Corps of Engineers, the Bureau of Reclamation, and increasingly of late the Soil Conservation Service. They do not need big state plans in order to function, and have been extremely active in Texas as elsewhere for decades now, selling dams and other items cheap or free. With their wide statutory authorizations and large quantities of Treasury cash, they have not had to exercise much salesmanship, for in Texas as in most of the West water development ranks with mothers and anticommunism as an automatically positive subject. Municipal and industrial and irrigation water, flood control, reservoir recreation, water quality improvement, the enhancement of farm and ranch production—all these and other benefits may attach to federal water projects, some of them reimbursable on easy terms by the beneficiaries, others paid for wholly or in part by Uncle.

In Texas at present there are around 180 reservoirs classifiable as "major" on the basis of a storage capacity exceeding 5,000 acre-feet. Of these over 50 hold more than 100,000 acre-feet, and a dozen or so hold more than a million acre-feet. The bulk of them have been built since World War II, with one federal agency or another having a hand in the construction of a majority of the bigger ones, all the super-bigs, and many of the others as well. Some have been badly needed, given the pace and pattern of postwar growth; there is no question, for instance, that places like Wichita Falls and Fort Worth and Dallas would be in trouble without the reservoirs that clutter the streams around them. A good many others were not all that clearly required except in the minds of the folks who instigated them for gain or glory, in the old American pattern of instigation of public works, which really hit its stride in the hardscrabble 1930s when anything that brought jobs and bustle to an area was a boon, and which has been striding along in big boots ever since. Politicians, chambers of commerce, river authorities, the big construction agencies themselves, vigorous individuals with influence, and other kinds of instigators have played a part in booming these projects, and most of them are undoubtedly able to feel an honest glow of pride when they look at the results. That connotation of virtue, coupled with the growth and impetus of the federal programs, the tidy profits to be had in real estate on lakes and alongside rivers dammed against flooding, and the ever-springing civic hope of growth, keeps leading onward to more and more construction, much of which has only a tenuous connection with human need.

Flood protection is a "need" that usually suffices when no other is in sight. Flood damages occur when people put houses and factories and other items of value on stream flood plains, where sooner or later they are going to get very wet, for it is in the nature of streams to run over their banks occasionally, and the flood plain is where they go when they do. People on flood plains at such times get wet too and sometimes drown—as about 500 have in Texas since 1908. This makes the subject an emotional one, and federal policies piecebuilt over the past few decades make structural protection at public expense rather easily available to areas hit by floods, or sometimes just in danger of being hit. This makes everyone feel the usual glow, especially real estate types and city governments relieved of the need for proper planning, but unfortunately such structural protection usually leads to a great deal more flood plain development. Since it is not economically or technologically possible to build protection against the greatest conceivable flood that might strike any given area, the certainty of much greater damages in the long run is established. Congress and other federals have been worrying over this for years now, and studying possible ways to make people start staying off flood plains again, as our ancestors did from necessity, but without much effect so far. Thus Texas, like a lot of other states, gets more and more flood-control dams each year, and the rivers in nearly all its cities (the original reason, usually, for the cities' being built where they were) have been straightened into ditches flanked by levees on which no tree is allowed to sprout.

This has been done to the Trinity in my own hometown, Fort Worth. Perhaps because of it, and because of pollution too, not many people under forty have a memory of the Trinity as the pleasant if rather scrawny meandering wooded stream it used to be. Which may have made it easier for another old booster's dream of instigation—its development for nagivation—to become a probability. . . .

When I was a boy there, the city had a sort of small-town wholeness and intimacy that have long since disappeared. Picturesqueness within limits was appreciated, and for a number of years before World War II one of the more picturesque figures was a big portly man who called himself Commodore Hatfield. When in town, the Commodore hung out principally in front of the Texas Hotel, but sometimes on other selected downtown corners, wearing a full beard, a large dirty Stetson, and occasionally a fringed buckskin jacket, though his hardihood was famous and he would often appear in shirt sleeves in the coldest weather. Reputedly once an oilman, he made his living in the days of my youth by selling mounted longhorn steer horns, displayed on a sidewalk rack. His voluminous conversation with anyone who paused, however, was more often on other subjects than horns, and of them all his favorite subject was his main passion, which was the navigation of the Trinity in a scow he called the *Texas Steer*.

Since the upper Trinity is only a trickle of water for some months during most years—though it was dear enough to us kids who fished and hunted and canoed along it—the Commodore was admired by some for his skill and doubted by others for his imagination, albeit seldom to his face. Whatever his gifts in this latter respect, he did make some notable voyages, once even getting as far away from Fort Worth as Chicago, by way of the Trinity, the Intracoastal Canal, and the Mississippi.

In some of this activity he was quietly subsidized by various backers in both Fort Worth and Dallas, and some of the trips got big press coverage, the idea being that if the Trinity's navigability were underscored emphatically enough, perhaps the federals would get interested in making it into a canal. And the idea of *that,* though seldom stated except by unboosterish skeptics, was not so much water transport as getting Fort Worth and Dallas declared port cities, which in the mystery world of governmental regulation would be a lever with which to get high railroad freight rates lowered. It is doubtful that the Commodore worried much about either of these ideas, being mainly interested in conversation, navigation, and the large festive free meals he got at riverside towns and farms. I am told by one old newsman who knew and liked him and sometimes cruised with him that there was a saying about the Commodore's appetite: "One chicken's not enough, but a turkey's a little too much." There is another newsmen's story about this hero, never published but apparently true, that concerns one of his epic arrivals at the up-river metropolis. Bearing a cargo of reporters, the *Texas Steer* had been making its way up the Trinity from the coast, with telephoned stories about its progress appearing on the front pages of the Fort Worth and Dallas papers every day or so. It was scheduled to arrive at a certain bridge—I believe the one on Belknap Street in Fort Worth—on the morning of a given day, and welcoming rites had been prepared. But on the day before that, a call from a point some distance below Dallas announced to the trip's sponsors that the *Texas Steer* had run out of river and was stuck. That night a large flat-bed truck was dispatched to pick the *Steer* up, under cover of darkness, and the next day at the bridge the Commodore aboard his refloated scow received hosannas and encomiums with the aplomb of a born winner.

Lately, though, navigation of the trickling Trinity has moved out of the realm of fun, the momentum of such ideas being terribly durable. After a study by the Army Corps of Engineers was presented to Congress, a billion-dollar project to fit the river for this purpose, with appurtenant reservoir storage and locks and pumping stations and raised bridges and straightened channels, was authorized more or less to the surprise of everyone except those who had kept pushing for it over the years. Construction funds have not yet been provided and may be a good while coming, but it appears quite possible now that the whole river will sooner or later be made over into a barge canal whose stair-step stretches of stilled water, if anything like present pollution continues, are going to be something to see and smell. They are also, if one believes what one reads, going to bring huge further growth to the Dallas-Fort Worth metropolis, though there are those around who doubt that further growth of a spraddle that presently holds well over two million people, in a state of fundamentally uncoordinated confusion, is what the spraddle really needs, or would ask for if it had a voice.

The Preliminary Water Plan of 1966

Texas officialdom did not seize eagerly on the plan presented in the 1962 *Report of the U. S. Study Commission—Texas*. Even in comments printed in an appendix to that same report, Governor Price Daniel and his water people rather peevishly criticized certain aspects of it, and when not long thereafter it was determined behind the scenes that a large measure of federal control was indeed envisioned with such a large and coordinated program, the chances of state approval of congressional authorization of the package dimmed, and the state's own planning apparatus shifted defensively into a higher gear.

At present Texas has three agencies—all fairly new or recently refurbished—with major statewide interest in water matters. These are the Water Rights Commission, concerned with who gets how much water and whence; the Water Quality Board, whose weighty burden is self-evident and does not grow lighter year by year; and the Water Development Board, which among other things buys storage space in federal reservoirs, collects hydrographic data, and draws up water plans. Some overlap exists among their functions, and other state agencies also have concern with water from one slant or another—among these are the State Soil and Water Conservation Board, the Parks and Wildlife Department, and the Railroad Commission. Resultant notable friction and confusions are supposed to be mitigated somewhat through a recent creation of the governor's office called acronymically PACT, the Planning Agencies Council for Texas, upon which representatives of all these and other agencies sit.

In 1964 Governor John Connally told his planners he wanted a state water plan that would not look feeble alongside what the federals had proposed—i.e., a Grand Plan. Thus enjoined, they labored and in May of 1966 gave birth to a shortish preliminary report called *Water for Texas: a Plan for the Future.* Examining rather sketchily present problems and projected future water needs to the year 2020, the report proposed some coordinated developments that were far from sketchy. Among them was a modification of the Burleigh's Ditch idea, whereby through a 980-mile conduit utilizing river channels, reservoirs, and stretches of built canal, water would be carried from the Sulphur, Cypress, and Red River basins of northeastern Texas by way of the Trinity, the Brazos, and the Colorado to the coastal prairies and the proposed Palmetto Bend reservoir on the Lavaca, and thence along a coastal aqueduct to the lower Rio Grande. Diversions to meet various local needs were scheduled all along the route. New major reservoirs and reservoir modifications proposed to serve this "State Water Project," as the conduit was called, plus others to satisfy demands in southeastern and central parts of the state, with a handful for near West Texas, totaled over sixty. The probable cost of these elements of the plan was computed and came to a healthy $2.7 billion.

To this point, the Texas preliminary plan differed from the 1962 U. S. Study Commission plan in certain definite ways, though many of the recommended reservoirs appear in both reports. The Texas plan took the whole state for its realm rather than just the eight intrastate river basins. It implied that development was to take place under Texas auspices, naturally with a good deal of federal help, and that its benefits were to be distributed by the state too insofar as that would fit in comfortably with such help. And its acceptance of the idea of large interbasin transfers of water, primarily through the big conduit but elsewhere too, was whole-hog, with heavy emphasis on the new and revived irrigation such transfers would facilitate on the coast and in the Lower Valley—an estimated one million acres or so.

This last departure from the Study Commission Plan is of special interest when viewed in the light of one criticism leveled at that federal plan by the Texas Board of Water Engineers and concurred in by Governor Price Daniel in Appendix I of the Study Commission's 1962 report:

> The proposed report does not provide data to demonstrate that a need for additional agricultural production presently exists which would warrant the authorization of the Lower Aqueduct to serve 750,000 acres of new land with water transported long distances from other river basins. In order to make the long range development of such a lower aqueduct feasible, it would require the State of Texas to reserve for the aqueduct a large portion of the surface-water resources of Eastern Texas, and withhold this reserved water from other development. The Board of Water Engineers recognizes that transbasin diversion of water is an accomplished fact in Texas, and under certain limitations is provided for in the Texas statutes. The Board does not approve of the reservation of a major supply of water at this time for a project of undetermined feasibility to supply a need which does not exist, and which may not exist for generations.

The federal dragon's hot breath, one surmises, had spurred them to start thinking a bit more amply in the intervening five years. . . . A few heads, for that matter, had rolled.

In addition to these concrete proposals, the 1966 preliminary state plan presented two additional elements without computing their costs. The first was a catchall category including navigation, nonreservoir flood and hurricane protection, upstream watershed improvement programs, control of heavily water-consumptive plants known as phreatophytes, and such things, most of them within the purview of existing heavily subsidized federal programs not considered hazardous to state autonomy. The other, however, was an attempt to grab hold of the cat-claw problem of providing enough water to allow West Texas to keep on irrigating full blast after its aquifers had been sucked out. This part of the preliminary plan, called Unit F, tended toward unconcrete phraseology and vague proposals, but at least did not seem to shut the door on West Texans' hope for rescue as the federal plan had done. In essence it said:

(1) There is not enough excess surface water in all the rest of Texas to furnish West Texas irrigators with what they would need to keep up their present practices. Even if there were, it would cost an estimated $168 an acre-foot to develop the supply in East Texas and deliver it on the Plains for use.

(It is perhaps worth parenthesizing here that this is eight or ten times what most authorities consider to be the maximum an average High Plains irrigator can pay for his water and still make a living.)

(2) We can study means of alleviating the problem somewhat by such measures as limited recharge of aquifers, desalination of salty ground water, improvement of surface water quality in certain areas, and importation of limited amounts of pipelined East Texas water for municipal and industrial use.

(3) We can also hope for and promote a giant-scaled federal multistate program of importing water to the Great Plains region from the Mississippi, the Missouri, or rivers to the northwest, through which West Texas might be able to obtain low-priced water in quantities that would not only maintain irrigated farming at present levels but spur further expansion of it.

Twenty-seven official hearings and three public meetings on the preliminary state plan were held in different parts of Texas during the summer of 1966. Various interested segments of the public voiced loud objections. Residents of the upper East Texas river basins showed a distressing unwillingness to give up their water for the benefit of coastal Texans and lower Rio Grandians, and were hostile toward parts of the huge plumbing job proposed in their valleys. Landowners with tracts lying within the numerous and often very large intended reservoir sites expressed disgruntlement. Environmentalists, growing in muscle in the sixties even in frontier-minded Texas, sided with East Texans on the matter of big diversions, pointed out the almost certainly catastrophic ecological effects of such large changes in the state's water regimen, and were vehement about the potential damage to the estuarial bays along the coast, much of whose indispensable inflow of fresh water would be grabbed away by the conduit and reservoirs of the proposed State Water Project—a subject on which the preliminary plan was rather casual. There were other objections based on the ruin of natural rivers, the flooding of scenic and historical and archaeological sites, and such things, besides some stout ones from people who thought that $2.7 billion was a lot of money to spend on water development.

West Texans with an interest in the irrigation economy tended more toward rage about the off-center way in which their problem had been viewed than toward edification that it had been included at all. It is told that after one High Plains hearing, at which Texas Water Development Board officials had reviewed for assembled locals the economic unfeasibility of a state project to bring outside water to them, an influential Plainsman cornered the Board's head spokesman and told him with western directness: "Look, we don't give a good God damn if it's feasible or not. You put us right in the middle of that thing or we're going to kill it for you, deader than hell."

The Texas Water Plan of 1968

Political feasibilities having been somewhat clarified, the state's planners sat back down, made studies and adjustments, and hired what one unsympathetic engineer has described to me as "some California word men" to wrap the whole thing up for them. The final result was issued in November of 1968 under an unequivocal title, *The Texas Water Plan*. This basic report consists of more than 200 pages of double-column text with numerous tables and attractive multicolored maps and graphs, and is backed up by other publications of the board. It is a distillation of years of varied hydrographic and hydrologic study by federal and state scientists and engineers, a projection of the most wishful dreams of the state's boosters and boomers and builders over the decades, and a rather slick sales package. It has dry stretches of economic and technical analysis, with occasional patches of phraseology like "possible dilution of conservative constituents to maintain the appropriate use-concentration spectrum." But in general it is readable for a reasonably willing layman, and is of interest not only for the nature and scope of its proposals but for the way those proposals relate to earlier ones, as well as for a number of things it leaves out.

The plan it presents is big enough to scare off dragons, big enough for anyone's fancy. "There is not," the report's foreword notes with satisfaction if with some rhetorical gracelessness, "a water resource plan of this magnitude or complexity in the world today or even in the planning stage. . . ." It is the grandest Grand Plan yet. It is also the state's official guide toward development of its water resources during the next half-century (forever, really, since the commitment of those resources is just about total) and toward the goals to be sought in the process of development.

Its major proposed element, supplanting the preliminary plan's "State Water Project," is a system of reservoirs and interbasin conveyance facilities to be called the "Texas Water System." One part of this system would be the coastal aqueduct, restored approximately to its original 1952 Burleigh's Ditch form and running over 400 miles from the Sabine to the Lower Rio Grande Valley. The other main part—West Texans having carried their point—would be a big Trans-Texas Canal dug mainly uphill from Northeast Texas to the High Plains, with one spur carried on to New Mexico and another down to the near Trans-Pecos, from which area a pipeline would carry supplementary municipal and industrial water to El Paso.

The water that would course liberally through these facilities —ultimately some 17.3 million acre-feet per year—would come in part from a welter of existing and proposed large reservoirs (most of them in the eastern and central reaches of the state) but mainly out of the Mississippi River, from whose annual flow 12 or 13 million acre-feet would be abstracted and transported across Louisiana by one route or another for delivery at the state line and introduction into the Texas Water System. There being an uphill difference in elevation between the state line and the High Plains of a good bit over 3,000 feet, power requirements for moving the water would be stiff—an estimated in-state total of around seven million kilowatts of new generating capacity, which is up toward 40 percent of what all Texas can presently muster for more modest and usual purposes.

In addition, a good many other big dams would be built here and there to take care of local problems, as would lesser inter-basin and intrabasin water-transfer canals and pipelines. In all, the Texas Water Plan of 1968 proposes the construction of about seventy new major reservoirs with a storage capacity nearly equal to that of all present reservoirs in the state, unspecified hundreds of miles of main canals not counting the one in Louisiana or straightened river channels (of which there are long stretches too, some rivers even being scheduled to run backward for a way), and an immensity of other components including irrigation distribution systems, small dams, levees, and pipelines. Flood protection, brush and phreatophyte control, water quality improvement, salinity alleviation, small watershed programs, wetland drainage projects, possible navigation systems like that authorized for the Trinity, water recreation, and other such matters all are given attention in the report and an implicit or explicit place in the Plan.

Contemplated costs naturally are large—two or three times as large, in fact, as any such set of figures that Texans have previously had to contemplate. Using "reconnaissance level methods" —i.e., broad estimates based on tentative data—the Water Development Board totted up costs allocable to reservoir flood control, water supply, irrigation distribution, and salinity control projects and emerged with a Plan price tag of $8,996,000,000.

This covers development only for these purposes (not for a number of the others listed above) within and for the state of Texas, and omits what New Mexico would be expected to chip in on the Trans-Texas Division in exchange for a share of irrigation water, as well as the inevitably huge price of facilities to deliver water from the Mississippi at the Texas-Louisiana line. (After publication of the report, the estimate was upped to $10 billion by a Water Development Board official, and since then it has been further upped by other people.)

Ultimate benefits attributed by the planners to their Plan are also large. They are based on the familiar assumption of ever-increasing growth tied to the conviction that if growth is supplied with enough raw materials—in this case water—it will be synonymous with prosperity and well-being. For the year 2020 and a projected Texas of some 30.5 million souls, the Plan avers it can ensure a firm supply of 32 million acre-feet of water per year. Of this more than 12 million would go to cities and industries, half a million or so to navigation and mining (including "secondary recovery" injection into old oil fields), 2.45 million to the estuarial bays for the maintenance of proper brackish conditions, and the remaining nearly 17 million acre-feet to irrigated farming. Total irrigated acreage in the state under the Plan in 2020 is put at 9,767,000, up from less than 8 million at present. The coastal aqueduct, in combination with ground and local surface resources, would ensure the irrigation of about 2.2 million acres along the coast and in the Lower Rio Grande Valley, while making water legally available from Amistad Reservoir far upstream to irrigate 254,000 acres in and near the Winter Garden. The Trans-Texas Canal—together with remaining ground water— would water over 6.6 million acres in North Central Texas, the High Plains, and the Trans-Pecos.

The economic and social and technical analyses and projections and breakdowns that underpin all these allocations in the Plan are formidable, and will deserve some attention later. . . . Cost-benefit ratios are computed by one of those procedures close to the hearts of project planners and legislative bodies and indicate, to no one's surprise who has ever before read a planning report, that the Plan is Economically Feasible, meaning that its overall dollar benefits outweigh its overall dollar costs. Perhaps because of the "reconnaissance level" of all these investigations, no detailed exploration is attempted of the relative parts of these dollar costs to be financed by the state and by the federal government. In relation to the Texas Water System package alone ($5.4 billion worth of reservoirs and canals and power facilities to shove water to West Texas and along the coast), the report does venture a guess that Texas's share would amount to between 20 and 35 percent, an estimate probably broad enough to be applied to the projected cost of the entire Plan. Furthermore, it is explicitly assumed that Uncle alone would finance the enormous ditch needed to bring Mississippi River water across Louisiana.

Uncle's share of the action being weighty, Uncle might be expected to want a weighty say in things, but the planners make it as clear as they tactfully can that they do not intend to let his say be any louder than it has to be. In a number of passages within the report, the idea of a "partnership arrangement" between Austin and Washington recurs, mainly in relation to the Texas Water System, which would need intricate management and supervision to function right—would indeed have been a total impossibility in the days before automation and computers. What partnership seems to boil down to is an extreme reinforcement of state autonomy—we tell you what we want; you build it and finance the biggest part; we run it and take in the money through which we will both be repaid.

That portion of the report's formal recommendations aimed at the president and the Congress asks that this approach be accepted, that the Plan be recognized as the prime guide to Texas water development (i.e., let us have no more federal plans), that the Texas Water System be congressionally authorized in toto, and that certain changes in federal policy be made to permit the Plan to achieve its goals. Among these recommended changes is the revision upward of Reclamation acreage limitations to allow bigger individual holdings to be watered out of federal projects, interest-free.

For most of the native objectors who surfaced at the 1966 hearings and raised one flavor or another of hell, the Plan has some sort of answers and adjustments. West Texas irrigators and their friends clearly have no kick left; their fondest hopes have been incorporated and given full weight and priority. Residents of the humid East Texas river basins are assured repeatedly and in detail that if they ever need their "surplus" water back again, it will be given to them. The coastal bays are being studied carefully, says the Plan, and the water they need to function well will be forthcoming. As for scenic natural river reaches and springs, valuable fish and wildlife habitat, and historical or archaeological sites, all these too will be studied and preserved if they turn out not to lie in the path of one of the Plan's developments.

For reservoir-site landowners no balm is offered, though a few sites have been changed since 1966. Eminent Domain is a potent and capricious god in a day when rural political strength is on the wane and even small-town chambers of commerce are aware of the profits attaching to lakeshore lots and influxes of pleasure-seekers. As for those environmentalists who had been outraged by the preliminary plan's massive ecological threat, and those tightwads who had called the price too high, the answer implied in the 1968 Texas Water Plan appears to be, You ain't seen nothing yet, for in the interim years both massiveness and costs have fattened grossly.

Throughout the Plan, bugle notes of urgency resound. Time is short, it says; these things need to be commenced now if Texas is not to be shut off from its true share of the ever-growing national wealth. Set us free to move and do and dig.

Old Governor John Connally, on his voluntary way out, and new Governor Preston Smith, on his voluntary way in, both hailed the Plan enthusiastically. Despite the large and basic difference of the Plan from the 1966 version, no new hearings were scheduled. Since the main thing required to set the Plan rolling was sweeping federal action through congressional authorizations, and since Congress was likely to be leery of a program whose total cost might run to $12 to $14 billion or more, unless the state showed itself eager and able to cough up its share, the big immediate need was money. In the spring of 1969 the Texas legislature expressed itself in favor of a $3.5 billion state bond issue for water development, with removal of an existing 4 percent ceiling on water-bond interest rates, to be submitted to voters for authorization in August as one of several proposed constitutional amendments. The measure made no commitment to the Plan as published, but only to water development in general. Such was the climate of acquiescence in the legislature that this bond issue, which has been called the largest in the history of the world, was approved for balloting with hardly any debate.

Plenty of debate, however, ensued elsewhere. Governor Smith, himself a High Plainsman from Lubbock, got his three predecessors in office—Shivers, Daniel, and Connally—to serve as cochairmen on his "Committee of 500," whose sole and avowed purpose was to get the amendment passed. Publishers, editors, lobbyists, local politicians, legislators, and bigwigs of all descriptions were drafted—including, it later emerged, some who had asked to be left out and many others who undoubtedly would have liked to ask the same thing had their interests and their obligations allowed it. The appeal launched by the committee was hyperpatriotic, in tune with bumper stickers that were red, white, and blue and shaped to suggest the Lone Star flag of Texas. So were the numerous newspaper pieces with which the committee members stumped for Amendment Number Two in the state's major journals.

The Plan's opponents—East Texan and environmentalistic and otherwise—were for the most part unmollified by its verbal bows in their direction. Made aware of one another during the earlier stages of fracas and presented with a very short time in which to act, they rallied together into a retaliatory Committee of 1000, overlapping with and reinforced by other organizations like the Sierra Club and the Texas Committee on Natural Resources as well as numbers of other citizens who may or may not have given a hoot one way or another about the Plan but did dislike the idea of being saddled with the biggest bond issue in the history of the world (whose actual extent of obligation, it was quickly noted, would be at least twice the stated $3.5 billion, after interest payable was included). These heterogeneous opponents had obviously shorter resources than the governor's people, no official status, and fewer outlets through which to tout their point of view. But in the short few months before August many of them worked nearly full time and the rest as much as they could, talking and writing letters to editors and articles for small conservation publications and other miscellaneous sympathetic organs, among which the small, potent, gadfly-liberal Austin biweekly called *The Texas Observer* was notable. They had a lot of arguments to voice, and most of these we will consider shortly.

They also won, barely. Maybe the defeat of Amendment Number Two on August 5, 1969—by a vote of 315,139 to 309,409—was based largely on that inescapable and horrific $3.5 billion figure, which the most torpid voter could see for himself. Maybe it was connected too with a light voter turnout—especially at the High Plains polling stations—and further influenced by the unpopularity of certain other amendments on the ballot. But almost certainly the defeat would not have occurred without the determined uproar created by those who disliked the bond issue and/or the Plan it was—apparently but not specifically—designed to subsidize.

"It was close enough to be spooky," one conservationist told me. "But it's the best thing that ever happened to people like us in Texas. We got together, and we found out we could swing some weight."

The Texas Water Plan itself had not been directly exposed

to the voters' caprice and therefore was not technically beaten, though it obviously emerged from the affray with some large red wounds. It remains the official declaration of the state's water-development aims, as was promptly pointed out by its architects and partisans when the results of the August balloting were known, and has been pointed out frequently since, mainly by West Texans like Representative Bill Clayton of Water, Inc. which has been understandably enthusiastic about the Trans-Texas Canal and Mississippi River water importation. Major piecemeal water development now taking place in the state, or imminent—individual reservoirs and also big basin-wide programs like the Sabine River Project—mainly fit in with the 1968 guidelines, and few observers doubt that, sooner or later, many or most or all of the Plan's primary concepts will surface again in big proposals for action.

III. An Examination

Because of general and legitimate public fascination with the crass dollar cost of things, much of the strongest criticism leveled at the Texas Water Plan and the presumably associated $3.5 billion bond-issue proposal has been economic in tone. The subject is fraught with wearying numbers. It has been pointed out that even at 6 percent interest (and no such ceiling was stipulated in the proposal), this bond method of financing the Texas share of the Plan's costs would add still another $3.5 to $4 billion interest burden on water users in paying off the bonds through water purchases, that taxpayers would be stuck with much of the cost during the long construction period before water user payments would start coming in, and—most emphatically—that despite the Plan's assignment of irrigation financing to the federals, there is no certainty that the Texas public would not end up largely subsidizing expensive irrigation water for West Texas and the coast and the Rio Grande. (Nor can one for very long at a time get away from the subject of irrigation in writing about the Plan, whose heart and soul it is.)

For one thing, whatever the Plan might say, the bond issue was not tied specifically to it but only to "water development," leaving the planners free to proceed as they might wish. For another, since the whole Texas Water System would be built mainly for irrigation, no real separation of state money from that use of water would be possible. For still another, the Plan is so loaded with oblique or direct references to the value of irrigated agriculture to the whole state's economy, that within the woodpile somewhere there lurks a rotund likelihood that along the line Texans in general are going to get a chance to help farmers pay Uncle for all that cotton and grain sorghum and vegetable water.

The last public estimate of the Plan's total cost I have seen—apparently including most intrastate elements this time—was $13.5 billion, which as someone has observed amounts to a third or more of all the money the federal government has spent on waterway construction since the year 1824. Assuming that this is an accurate approximation (not a good assumption at all, in view of the way early estimated costs of such projects invariably escalate in the performance, and the "reconnaissance level" of the planning), and that the $3.5 billion bond issue would more or less cover Texas's share, the contemplated contribution from the general American tax-paying public to Texas water development would be on the order of $10 billion in addition to what has already been spent on federal water projects in the state.

Plan critics with a flair for dealing with the engineers' own sort of economic and technical data have thought to discern rigged figures and inappropriate methods in the Plan's cost-benefit ratio calculations, as well as errors in labeling and computing such things as electric power requirements, ground water availability, and ultimate true irrigation requirements. Their accusations get off into such esoterica as whether the planners abandoned the preferred Separable Cost-Remaining Benefits (SC-RB) method of allocating costs in favor of the Alternate Justifiable Expenditures (AJE) method in order to cover up Plan deficiencies, and whether the planners knew the difference between static head and dynamic head or between kilowatts and kilowatt-hours or between their bellybuttons and a hole in the ground. To a dedicated noneconomist and nontechnician, these criticisms seem to add up to some probable slipshod effects of a "reconnaissance level" approach, and a good deal of self-serving hanky-panky aimed at making the Plan look better than it is. Such hanky-panky, unfortunately, is not an uncommon ingredient in project justifications.

Another body of criticism has bombarded the Plan's demographic and associated water-need projections. By this late date most of us know that our country's population, along with the world's, is moving on toward unmanageable proportions and may already have reached them. There is general awareness also that this poses social, economic, and ecologic problems of a sort man and his green planet have not faced before, and that it may not be altogether desirable. We even begin—wistfully, perhaps—to discern some signs that growth may be getting ready to slow down, and most of those who lead us have started to say publicly that it had better, including a couple of presidents and even on occasion Governor Preston Smith of Texas.

On the other hand, the Texas Water Planners consulted with the University of Texas's Bureau of Business Research, sent out questionnaires to Texas industries, and, emerging with the assumption that about 30.5 million Texans would be a good number to have around in 2020, set out to capture them by providing on paper all the water that could conceivably be needed by such a population in a hypothetical continuation and expansion of present activities and geographic preferences. The figure is not an estimate but a goal which water is supposed to help us reach; the Plan is designed to underwrite an approximate tripling of the state's population during the next fifty years and a continuation of present boom in exactly the same terms as today.

If the present birth rate continues, there are likely to be 16 to 18 million Texans in the year 2020, and in fact the birth rate has not been holding up but tending to abate. Even if Texans were immediately to be seized on by a breeding frenzy like that which followed World War II in the "baby boom" years, the state would still not attain the Water Plan figure by natural increase among its citizens, and no excess of immigration over out-migration is indicated in Census Bureau projections for the state. Some demographers, among them Dr. Hawley Browning, head of another University of Texas agency called the Population Reference Bureau (used officially by the state government but *not* consulted by the planners), have said that population projections for fifty-year periods are simply not possible, and that some strong evidence indicates Texas may have a good many fewer people by 2020 than either the Texas Water Plan or census trends suggest. One low estimate I have seen is 12.5 million.

If you want to play with statistics, it isn't hard to find support for almost any projection by picking a trend from some certain span of years. I lately saw it noted that by extending the trend in the U. S. birth rate between 1957 and 1968 (a steady decline from 25.3 per thousand to 17.4), you can prove that by 1990 our birth rate will be zero. The point is that the Texas Water Plan projection is both slapdash and saddening, not only ignoring professional data but through its improbable amplitude betraying the planners' nineteenth-century conviction that growth and expansion are of themselves high goals.

That conviction is reflected too in the use of water the planners expect all those Texans to engage in. Or something is. According to Plan figures, the total municipal and industrial use of water in Texas in 1960 was 2.6 million acre-feet, which comes to around 244 gallons per day for each of 9.5 million citizens. The Plan indicates that both cities and industries are expected to start making more efficient use of water. Yet in 2020 with 30.5 million paper Texans, the projected municipal and industrial use per annum is 12 million acre-feet—around 350 gallons per day per person. It looks as though someone may have told the planners that Americans are currently the heaviest per capita users-up of resources on the face of the earth, each of us consuming around thirty times as much natural riches as an average Indian. And again the planners seem to have answered, You ain't seen nothing yet. . . .

"Flexibility" has become a cultish word among project planners in the past few years, mainly because it was being used against them by people who objected to the disruption of landscapes and river-scapes and whole biological communities by the planners' large and often dubiously requisite creations. By adopting it and limiting their definition of it, they have sought to remove its sting.

The only true flexibility is technological and philosophical. It involves a recognition that new ways of doing things and new concepts of what ought to be done are emerging so fast these days that it is absurd to pin plans to presently available technology or presently apparent goals, except during the narrowest fringe of the future. It leaves scope for change, and as we of all people ought to know by now, change is inevitable—technological change, social and economic change, philosophical change in terms of people's values and the kind of life they want a chance to lead.

Philosophy and society aside for the moment, most presently available technology for water management differs only in scale from what the Mesopotamians knew. Besides wells, it consists mainly of reservoirs and canals—dams and ditches—and it has some great drawbacks. It is costly, not only in cash but in terms of the amenity, variety, and productivity of the only planet we mortals seem destined, despite astronautics, to be allotted for dwelling on. It is irreversible: its results are solidly and stolidly *there,* and through their presence farms and forests and swamps and rivers and populations of wild things and memorable or unique places are forever subtracted from the scheme of things. Its usefulness is less than ideal by a long shot, for its reservoirs lose vast quantities of water through evaporation and tend relatively soon to get choked with mud. And, perhaps worst of all, it has a murderous impetus, fed by new proliferating generations of engineers and construction firms and politicians and development agencies, all with a drive to keep on building dams and ditches, ever bigger and therefore presumably better. "The only way you could explain the water policy in this country," said economist Kenneth Boulding at a Conservation Foundation symposium a while back, "was the religious explanation that we worship the water goddess, and hence had to build all these pyramids—all these dams and temples. . . . I think we will go down in history as the age of the dam builders. The domination of almost all our resources policy by engineers and people of this kind is utterly disastrous."

Grand Plans by their very nature seize upon available technology and philosophy and seek to perpetuate them. They set out to hand down godlike dictums from off the mountain, and they do so in terms of what students of the subject call "linear projections"—single answers based on an assumption that while ways and goals may grow bigger they cannot really change. That stud buzzard of all Grand Plans, the Texas Water Plan, makes an early, *de rigueur* statement of its own flexibility, but after examination one is forced to conclude that this flexibility consists of little more than a degree of latitude in the scheduling, identity, and construction details of some of its reservoirs and conveyance canals—and even then mainly among those not tied in with the mighty Texas Water System. Its commitment to dams and ditches is all but total. It contains some rather good examinations of certain technological alternatives or adjuncts to dams and ditches, and says that investigations relating to them are continuing, but apparently includes them as Plan possibilities only to the extent that today's limited knowledge or political conditions could make them work. Aside from an announced intention to find ways to suppress evaporation in reservoirs, a proposed total war on water-using brush and phreatophytic vegetation like willows, cottonwoods, and salt cedars, and a slew of computers and automated controls, it is hard to find much in the Plan that is technologically new.

Thus desalinization, presently a rather expensive way of getting fresh water, is noted to be a feasible source of municipal but not irrigation supply for certain rather limited regions of the state, though an immense difference might result from new cheap energy sources or improved distillation methods or for that matter radical new forms of irrigation. Direct municipal recycling of waste-water gets shorter shrift, in accordance with the Plan's general tendency to tiptoe distantly around quality problems. So does weather modification—rainmaking, redubbed for deconnotation—though it is being researched seriously by both state and federal workers. Aside from technical difficulties it offers other problems both ecological and legal (the fundamental prickler being whether if you make rain drop in one place you can prove you're not robbing other places of its benefit), but if it were to become suddenly and predictably and acceptably workable under ordinary Texas conditions instead of only ideal ones as today, it could old-hat the Texas Water System's mighty conduits and many of its reservoirs overnight. No rancher or farmer doubts that who has glumly watched the deep-blue, wet Gulf clouds scud past his parched domain on their way to the hither Rockies, or shoved back southeastward by an uncatalytic norther, or just dangling sullen in the sky without turning loose any of their moisture. It is an old West Texas disease, dreaming about those clouds; as I write this paragraph in early 1971, a bad drouth time, residents of one county out there have kittied up $10,000 and hired an old-style rainmaker, with barrels of treated charcoal and high oratorical talk of "friction air" and similar phenomena, who has vowed to lay more water on the land of those who sweetened the kitty than on abstainers' places. . . .

The Plan report has an admirable section on the aquifers of

Texas, wherein what is known about them is laid out in layman's terms and their current mismanagement is noted if not deplored. The section implies too that proper management—by balancing withdrawals against recharge, spacing wells, inducing recharge by various means, protecting purity, and other procedures— would make them immensely more useful over the long haul of years than they are going to be if people keep on mining them. But it has no heart for a squabble with the medieval Texas legal concepts that make such proper management an impossibility, and hence cannot include wise ground water management as the basic Plan tool it ought to be. An intention is voiced to let some reservoir water go as recharge to the Edwards-Balcones Fault zone aquifer, a cavernous formation easily amenable to such treatment, and the report even implies that such recharge would necessitate some restrictions on pumping. But the document's general attitude toward ground water appears to be summed up in one of its "Planning Concepts"—a sort of circular statement somehow:

> Whenever feasible, ground water resources will be developed and used on a safe-yield basis. In ground water aquifers subject to overdraft, ground water pumpage will be reduced to safe yield as rapidly as possible by substitution of surface-water supplies.

In the set of recommendations addressed to the governor and the legislature, which includes some fairly sweeping items, no slight hint of a request for ground water law reform is enunciated.

Nor does the Plan leave room for unexpected new means of furnishing water, or unforeseeable new sources that might turn up. Not long ago, for instance, the Shell Development Company devoted some research to the possible use of superheated high-pressure ground water found while oil drilling along the coast at depths below 10,000 feet. The quantities of it are unknown but may be quite large, and the indications of the Shell experiments were that it could be used as steam for generating electricity at around a half-cent a kilowatt-hour, and the distilled by-product water sold to industry and towns for about forty cents a thousand gallons. As a source it remains to be fully evaluated, but who knows that deposits of this or some other kind may not turn up elsewhere in ten or twenty or forty years and obviate the need for reservoirs and canals in perhaps whole regions? The Plan seems to leave no place for that possibility or any other like it. Fifty years are a bloody great long time as technological time goes these days, as a glance at the past fifty will show. But dams and ditches, the planners indicate, were good for the Hebrew children, and they're good enough for us.

The technology of flood protection envisioned in the Plan is similarly lashed and knotted to current custom. The federal flood plain management program, established in 1960, which on request furnishes detailed studies of flood plain hazards to communities to aid them in planning to keep expensive and vulnerable development out of the way of possible floods—thus achieving "passive protection"—is cited approvingly. But no examination is attempted of the hodgepodge of programs and policies that often make it easier for a city to go ahead and let a flood plain get cluttered with housing and factories and other things, in the knowledge that big structural protection will be available from the Corps of Engineers or the Soil Conservation Service cheaply or free of charge. The Flood Plain Insurance Act of 1968, one overmild congressional attempt to start putting flood-protection costs where they belong—on those who choose to locate on a flood plain—is given one sole mention without discussion. In the major Texas reservoirs listed in the Plan report as already built or under construction, out of a combined total storage capacity of around 52.7 million acre-feet, 17.4 million acre-feet are earmarked for the purpose of floodwater interception. In the additional major reservoirs proposed by the Plan, with total storage of 49.9 million acre-feet, flood control is assigned 16.1 million—about the same proportion we now have. In other words, no intrusion of rationality in the form of flood plain management has been foreseen or allowed to creep into the planning. Levees, straightened stream channels with the trees all cut out, and other such wasteful structural methods of dealing with floods are included in similar huge measure.

Aside from engineers' deep attachment to procedures they have spent many years learning to handle and the inborn inflexibility of Grand Plans, one large reason that the Plan can ignore or slight new ways of doing things is the incorporation of twelve or thirteen million annual acre-feet of imported Mississippi River water as an element. For if you can count on that kind of augmentation of your supply, you don't have to worry much about really careful use of the water you can trap or tap within the irregular boundary lines of Texas itself. Adoption of the import concept must have bathed the board room with relief; everything now was possible, 30.5 million Texans and High Plains irrigation forever.

Somewhat unbelievably, the major part of the Plan—its Texas Water System—is based on this imported water without there being any certainty at all that Texas can get hold of it. Assurance is given that no canal in the system will be built without that certainty, but it is hard to see how very much else could be justified if it failed to materialize. The Lower Mississippi River Commission, a Corps of Engineers agency operating out of Vicksburg, is making a study to see if the river can spare that kind of diversion, but does not expect to come up with answers before 1973. Large troublesome questions are nevertheless visible.

Economically, a diversion in north Louisiana and an import route across to northeast Texas would be best, but the objections of river towns downstream seem certain to force the takeout point below New Orleans, whence a canal would run across marshy south Louisiana to the Sabine. To avoid salt-water invasion up-river as a result of the diversions, they would have to be restricted to periods of heavy flow—perhaps, according to some federals, as little as two months out of the year (a restriction, incidentally, which might vastly escalate Plan costs for conveyance and storage facilities and peak pumping requirements within Texas).

No riverside storage for such quantities of water is likely to be feasible in flat Louisiana, so that the water would have to be taken on into Texas and most of it stored there for the rest of the year against the short heavy regional demand for it in West Texas and down along the coast during the growing season. To transport 13 million acre-feet of water across Louisiana and to various points in Texas in two months' time would require some whalish canals. A little bungling amateurish calculation on the size of the Louisiana segment might be worthwhile, there having been no official figures furnished. During each day of diversion, some 216,667 acre-feet would have to flow through this ditch. Flow in terms of cubic feet per second, the usual yardstick, would have to be about 108,000 c.f.s. (For comparison, the mammoth California Aqueduct carries only 24,000 c.f.s.) Assuming a water velocity of around two miles an hour and a canal depth of forty feet, and omitting the rest of a tedious computation, the Louisiana-Texas import ditch would have to be something over 900 feet wide. Even if the import period were somewhat longer, the thing would still be Brobdingnagian. Such dimensions as these make it clear that the idea of substituting tunnels for canals, advanced by certain Plan partisans to sooth environmentalists, is a wispy sort of dream.

The marsh-bayou-estuary complex of environments in southern Louisiana has huge economic and ecological value, and the disruptive implications of a canal of this size, cutting through the drainage patterns, cannot be doubted. One much smaller canal's construction across Florida was recently stopped by President Nixon himself because of the protests of conservationists and others, and the uproar the Texas import facility would detonate would without the slightest doubt be louder and angrier by far. It has already started, and since the subtraction of Mississippi water is involved, it does not all have a strictly conservationist tone. Senator Russell Long, chairman of the Senate Finance

Committee, lately told Louisianans: "Texas will get our water over my dead body." Senator Allen Ellender and Representative Hale Boggs and others have said more or less the same thing, and Louisiana newspapers have been whipping up the flames. Noise all the way to the Canadian border from upstream states that have a riparian interest in what is done with the great river's flow has begun to be heard, and a great deal more will be. So that even should the Lower Mississippi River Commission enthusiastically approve the diversion, the water's availability to Texas is extremely doubtful.

Its suitability for all the uses projected for it has been questioned too. The Mississippi is the main cloaca of a not very tidy continent and despite the huge and cleansing volume of its flow, the quality of its water reflects that fact. It carries objectionable quantities of bacteria, chlorinated hydrocarbons (does anyone of conservationist bent not remember the great endrin fish kill of 1963 along the lower river?), mercury, lead, arsenic, and other exotica, and there is no possibility that a flow on the order of 100,000 c.f.s. or even much less could be subjected to treatment adequate to remove the worst of these substances. Mixed in the system with native Texas waters, these blessings would be distributed across the state.

As for the use to which the biggest single gout of the importation would be put—irrigation on the High Plains—Reclamation officials claim they can see no probable chemical conflict between acid Mississippi water and alkaline Plains soils. But they are vehement against the idea that is being talked up on the Plains (evidently with Texas Water Development Board acquiescence) of deliberately recharging the Ogallala formation with such imported water. One federal engineer told me he could think of at least ten good reasons for being opposed to it—among them the assured biological impurity of Mississippi water, the impossibility under Texas law of collecting its delivery cost from users once it had been injected underground, a double set of costs deriving from transporting it out there and then having to pump it again to the surface, *and* an indicated chemical incompatibility that could lead to gummy precipitation underground and clogging of the aquifer's indispensable porous structure, hence to its permanent ruin.

This probable chemical antipathy between Mississippi water and the rocks and clays of the Ogallala is an interesting matter which has not been aired very widely. The fact is that if such imported water were used extensively on the *surface* of the High Plains for growing crops, a large amount of it would seep down to the aquifer whether or not anyone intended for it to do so. Soils on that tableland vary widely, a fact which influences the choice of crops and the possible profits in different sections. Where the soil is heavy, tending toward clay, less irrigation water is needed and not much of it escapes downward from the upper soil horizons. Where sandy permeable land predominates, however, farmers may need to dose it with three feet or more of water a year for prime results on some crops, and as much as half the water applied, according to a ground-water hydrologist I talked to, may find its way down to the Ogallala. In overall terms, engineer Robert Hendrick estimated in 1958 that about a quarter of all the irrigation water applied to the South High Plains got back to the formation, and I have seen more recent estimates that run as high as 39 percent for this "return flow" recharge. If that down-filtering water were chemically antagonistic to the aquifer's materials, large lasting trouble would obviously ensue.

Big dry-country irrigation is the Texas Water Plan's main curse, the albatross dangling rottenly from its neck. It is the thing that drove the planners to the Mississippi, the cause for which they jarred the East Texas hornets' nest with their proposals for huge interbasin transfers, the reason they would not stand up for ground water law reform or leave space in their Plan for conceivable new forms of water technology. It is itself a form of currently available technology, this time for the mass growing of foods and fibers, to which the Plan would tie the state for fifty years and more as tightly as to the currently feasible system of dams and ditches designed primarily to feed it water.

It is not hard to let yourself be awed by big irrigation's magnitude and fecundity as you drive up through the Llano Estacado in, say, September when the warm-season crops are coming on toward harvest and the winter grains are sowed and sprouting—particularly if you have farmed a little yourself under more hazardous conditions, and even more particularly if you are far enough along in years to remember the big dusty ranches and the occasional wide-rowed dry-land farms that used to be typical there. With that memory in your head, the succession now of unending green flat fields is a little unbelievable—cotton and grain sorghum mainly, with here and there patches of alfalfa or new wheat or any of a dozen other crops that do well in that climate, with water. If irrigation is in progress, the big motors that work the centrifugal well pumps hum or roar, according to whether they are electric or gas driven, and the clear cold Ogallala water flows in ditches alongside the fields, with arrays of curved siphons lifting it out and directing it down the rows.

Those rows are close together and so are the plants within them, for with heavy chemical fertilization and plenty of water the old open spaces are no longer needed. Light planes fly low, trailing long clouds of poison against the bugs and weeds such a concentration of greenery, moisture, and nutrients fosters. Big tractors and mammoth combines growl and clatter across the landscape. Dark squat cotton grows on toward its winter harvest, and the gold or russet heads of sorghum grain crowd one another, uniform short-stemmed hybrids tailored genetically for the machinery that will reap and thresh them.

Up toward Hereford and Friona the enormous feed lots that will use much of the grain spraddle across their own wide acres around big elevator bins, enveloped in a rich stink of dung. The checkering of steel pens around the larger ones holds 40,000 or more gorging, hormone-lulled steers at a time. Big feed trucks crawl along the aisles, spouting a milled mixture into fence-line

bunkers, and through the pens move endlessly the mounted doc-
toring crews, armed with bloat remedies and sprays and antibi-
otics and other weapons against the ills that assault those
jam-packed beeves. (Sad to say, such attention does not keep
them all happy; during the 1971 February blizzard there, steers
walked out of some feed lots by the hundreds on snowdrifts that
ramped the fences, and were found if at all up to twenty or thirty
miles away. . . .)

America, perhaps you think, and swell a bit inside with the
pride of bigness to which even unbusinesslike natives of the
United States are likely to be susceptible, occasionally and despite
themselves. . . .

The bigness of High Plains farming is real and proud enough.
The trouble with it is that like most such bigness it is built on
eating up the world, spending real capital in the form of a resource, cashing in today and the hell with tomorrow. It is built
mainly on mining the Ogallala, and when the Ogallala is gone, or
so far reduced that it is no longer available for farming water,
the bigness will be gone too, along with the potential for other
more lasting kinds of bigness, unless somebody bails the Plainsmen out. And the bailing out, if it takes any such form as that
prescribed in the Texas Water Plan, would have additional great
costs in terms of natural resources.

The situation—on the High Plains anyhow, and to a lesser
degree in other places where ground water is being overdrawn—
is analogous to the exploitation of a vein of copper or a deposit of
petroleum. The substance is taken out and used for making
money, and when it is gone it is gone. In recognition of the
analogy, Plains farmers some time ago sued the Internal Revenue
Service to force it to grant them a cost depletion allowance on
consumed ground water, won their case, and since that time have
been enjoying a tax privilege rather similar to that which everyone begrudges oilmen.

This being so, an old and respected Texas water engineer not
friendly to the Plan pointed out to me, other possible parallels

suggest themselves. "They opened up a barrel of snakes when they filed that suit," he said. "It's just as if you had yourself a little old oil field and you pumped away on it for twenty or thirty years and took your depletion every year at income tax time. Then when it's all sucked out, you go to the government and you say, 'Look, they've got a slew of oil up there in Alaska. Why don't you build a pipeline and shoot some of it down here to me so I can keep on being an oilman?' "

The only figure available just now regarding the possible cost of outside water delivered on the High Plains is the $168 per acre-foot (of East Texas water) given as a rough estimate in the 1966 preliminary report. The figure was not repeated in the 1968 Texas Water Plan, nor was another relating to Mississippi water substituted for it, though outsiders playing with the Plan's own figures have computed that electric pumping costs alone would run at least $30 an acre-foot. Currently the Bureau of Reclamation is working up some tentative estimates of what imported water would cost on the Llano Estacado, and no one expects them to be nearly low enough for Plains farmers to pay and still make a living, even under the interest-free Reclamation system. The Bureau itself has said they definitely will *not* be. Not many people expect them to be even low enough that Plains farmers with special-tax help from all their Plains neighbors could pay them, in a conservancy-district taxing arrangement of a type that the Bureau has operating in a couple of regions of New Mexico, or under some similar system.

In a 1970 report from the Texas Agricultural Experiment Station, a team of experts reached the conclusion that if living standards of farmers and land values are to be kept up, current costs for water pumped from the Ogallala—near or exceeding $25 an acre-foot—are too high for any Plains farmer to pay unless he has a farm of at least 480 acres raising mainly cotton, and unless also under the mandarin complexities of the cotton-marketing system he gets twenty-eight cents a pound for his lint. If his cotton brings twenty cents, he will have to work at least 960 acres, still mainly in cotton, and will not be able to afford to pay more than $10 or $15 per acre-foot for his water. Where cotton is not the main crop, in general $15 is the top permissible water cost. Furthermore, Bureau of Reclamation officials have flatly stated that if federally financed water goes to the High Plains, policy will require that it not be used to irrigate commodity crops declared surplus to national needs, and cotton is one of the main such surplus crops.

It does not take a very keenly honed set of economic perceptions to see what water at $168 an acre-foot, or a half or a quarter or even an eighth of that price, would mean to High Plains farmers able to pay only $15. It would not mean anything at all. The Texas Water Planners or someone would have to identify a very large number of nonagricultural beneficiaries of Plan-sponsored High Plains irrigation, and find a way of making them chip in heavily on that cost, before a drop of farming water could be delivered there. This appears to be the basis for the Plan's repeated emphasis on the indispensability of irrigated farming to both the state and national economies. Regarding the evidence, one is practically forced to the conclusion that this emphasis is aimed at softening up the public for some ultimate bureaucratic legerdemain that will effect a large, nonreimbursable diversion of tax or other public money to Texas irrigation water costs, over and above bond issues and established federal subsidies. If the Plan report had been written more for the presentation of facts and less for salesmanship, such things might be clearer. But to get at many matters, it is necessary to delve behind or beyond the report and to conjecture.

Another subject that has inspired delving and conjecture is the possible extent to which the Texas Water Plan is designed to evade present acreage limitations on land irrigated out of federal projects, and therefore to abet and subsidize corporate-scale farming while discouraging smaller family units. No mention of the acreage limitation or of farm sizes appears in the Plan report's main discussion of irrigated farming, "Water Requirements for

Agriculture," but unsupported, brief, stout statements about it crop up in the opening chapter which details the Plan itself, as follows:

Under "Planning Concepts":

It will be important to assure economically effective farm units within irrigation areas to meet the costs of water supply.

Under "Conclusions":

The present acreage limitation provisions of Federal Reclamation Law will need to be revised if the State is to have an economically viable agriculture in Texas under Reclamation projects.

Under "Recommendations":

That the President and the Congress of the United States. . . . amend the provisions of Federal Reclamation Law relating to acreage limitations so that economically productive farming units can be developed or sustained under Reclamation projects.

It is curious that these bald assertions of the need to change a major federal law, which has already been the subject of hammer-and-tongs fights in Congress and the Supreme Court and so far has survived assaults against it, should be stuck into the Texas Water Plan without any supporting material. Curious enough to have aroused some sharp criticism and debate, notably during the period preceding the 1969 bond election. Professor Paul S. Taylor, a University of California economist with bitter experience of his state's catastrophic attempt to finance its own water system after failing to get the Reclamation limitation changed for the benefit of a few huge landowners, wrote an article for *The Texas Observer* warning Texans to look out for such shenanigans in the Plan. Subsequently Stuart Long, an Austin newspaperman and a member of the governor's Committee of 500 to promote the Plan, devoted a column to answering Dr. Taylor in which he claimed that no state money was destined for irrigation under the Plan, and that the concept of a 320-acre farm (irrigable by a man and wife under Reclamation law) belonged to "mule-power days." Ronnie Dugger, publisher of the *Observer,* pointed out the Plan's suspicious fuzzinesses on this subject, supported family farms as still a good idea, and said he believed there were indeed shenanigans somewhere behind the arras.

Almost certainly there are, though their exact nature is impossible to make out, the main evidence of their presence being merely a large empty space in the Plan's examinations. Whether or not there lurk around the outskirts of things any high-pressure speculative forces of the type and scale of those that infected the California water-planning effort, who would stand to profit fatly from the Plan's distribution of water to new irrigation areas and even more fatly from amendment or removal of the Reclamation restriction, I have heard no one say. But the possibilities are, given the flavor of Texas politics and the old patterns of Texas landholding and the humanness of human nature in the state, that there are more than a few. The Texas Water Plan issues a flat-out invitation to them.

There seem to be—the Plan is not very specific—somewhat more than two million acres of such new land proposed for expansion of the main irrigation areas—the High Plains, the Lower Coast, the Rio Grande, the Trans-Pecos—with a few additions and some shrinkages projected elsewhere. These new-land areas at present are often in grass or brush, owned in large chunks, and available until lately at low prices per acre. If some of the large chunks are not now being held by enthusiastic proponents of the Plan, and if other Plan advocates are not ready to pounce the instant the Plan seems to have a chance of going through, the whole grubby history of American land speculation is a lie.

Until recently large, corporate-style, irrigated farming has not been a dominant force in Texas agriculture except to a limited extent in the Rio Grande Valley with its heavy fruit and vegetable production tied in with processing interests. If big growers in that area, with large established rights to Rio Grande water under Texas law, were suddenly to become dependent on a supply from the coastal aqueduct subject to Reclamation restrictions, they would be much worse off than they are now with the river occasionally unable to furnish the water the law entitles them to. As for new lower-coast and "Valley" land to be irrigated out of the aqueduct, the planners would clearly like to get it exempted too from the old agrarian limitation, despite the fact that in that climate where crop after crop can be sowed and harvested all year long, small farms can be definitely profitable enterprises. Why the planners' preferences extend in that other direction has to be a matter for guessing.

On the High Plains as lately as 1958, an independent engineer named Hendrick, making a report on the Llano Estacado to The Travelers Insurance Companies for mortgage-evaluation purposes, found that the majority of farms were about 160 acres in size. (His conclusion, incidentally, was that the irrigation economy there was doomed, and that lending agencies should cease to support the rape of the Ogallala.) In "mule-power days," back in 1912 or so when some irrigation began around Plainview, land for farms was sold in 40-acre blocks, though some purchasers took three or four or more, wetting their crops with water that cost about $1.80 an acre-foot to pump, for the Ogallala then was nearly brimming over.

As the cited Texas Agricultural Experiment Station report has observed, however, pumping costs are getting rough, and the rougher they get the harder it is for a man with small acreage to make ends meet, particularly with the ever more complex and monstrous machinery he has to buy or rent, the fertilizers and pesticides, and the other accessories of chemicalized high-yield agriculture. The fact is that irrigated farming on the High Plains has come to be a marginal enterprise, and marginality favors bigness, as do American business and industry and, in most ways, government. Hence increasingly the smaller farms tend to flow together into larger blocks under individual or corporate ownership, and smaller owners either get big or leave the land in that cityward drift of population which philosophers and economists and presidents and others have deplored but no one yet has managed to stem in the slightest. Thus if you bring in expensive imported water to encourage a continuation of irrigated farming on the Plains, the only thing you will be encouraging is marginal big-scale operations. Which is clearly what the planners are willing to encourage.

Reclamation irrigation law and all the mighty apparatus that carries it out were designed mainly for a social and political purpose—to nurture family-scale farming on moderate tracts made productive with good cheap water. Whether or not irrigation is a lasting good and an apt use of precious water, that is their purpose, not maximum effective consumer-farmer ratios or any other such abstract notion of GNP perfection. In the right places the Reclamation program can still carry out this original purpose, as many of its projects prove. Half a square mile of decent soil provided with ample inexpensive water is not a hardship farm, nor ever was, nor ever will be, nor can you work it with a mule or two. Under intensive Old World management it could sustain 75 or 100 or more people with better food than many Americans get to eat, and in Stateside terms I know a coastal Texan, a good but not exceptional farmer in comparison with his neighbors, who cleared about $20,000 last year on just 190 irrigated acres, with living expenses a fraction of those a city man of equivalent income has to bear.

These things being so, why are Reclamation officials straining the circuits in their computers over a region like the Llano Estacado where, regardless of the rights and wrongs of the exploitation of the Ogallala, it has been clear for a good while that substitute water cannot be cheap and therefore that the scale of continued irrigated farming—if indeed any at all is feasible—cannot be moderate and familial?

Watching these men at meetings and hearings and such places, and maybe talking a little afterward with them, I have had the feeling that the best of them are asking themselves exactly that same thing, and wish someone would take the burden off. The burden being the Texas Water Plan.

IV. "Costs"

The manner in which economic analysis is commonly used to justify big public construction projects, whereby "benefits" are totted up against "costs" and found to outweigh them, is not a subject into which I am capable of wandering very deeply without getting up to my tail in alligators, nor do I intend to try. Economic analysis is a tool, and in good impartial hands it is an immensely valuable one. But when it is employed by people who yearn deeply to justify the project they are analyzing, it has a close kinship with medieval logic, which took joy in counting the numbers of hypothetical angels on the heads of pins, and is just about as rewarding to study. The byways into which it leads you are the abode of discount rates, and SC-RB's as versus AJE's, and the enormous variation in B-C ratios it is possible to obtain by using, on the same body of data, the differing methods favored by individual government agencies.

Here what matters most about this wishful approach to economic analysis is that it leads to big answers that don't have much relation to truth. Undoubtedly many of its practitioners have convinced themselves over the years that it has a law-like force. But the fact is that these are people with a stake in seeing public projects approved and carried through, and this standard approach is heavily loaded in favor of construction. Benefits of a number of different sorts are assigned cash values, are envisioned and touted as reaching down into the local shoeshine parlor and outward to Seattle and Chicago and Boston, and are supposed to echo through the halls of time enhancing man's welfare. Costs, however, are limited to the direct dollar expense of ramming the project through—site purchase, construction, maintenance, interest, etc.—and in the planning reports and proposals they usually involve nothing that would echo anywhere, either in time or outward from a specific construction site.

A given multipurpose federally-sponsored reservoir in the Texas Water Plan as proposed, for instance, might be assigned cash-valued, local and/or national benefits in several or all of the following categories:

(1) Municipal and industrial water supply.

(2) Hydroelectric power generation—direct, in terms of power sales, and indirect in terms of such things as consumer savings and the additional profits factories may make with this electricity.

(3) Agriculture—also direct and indirect, farm and nonfarm, local and national.

(4) Flood damage abatement—benefits exploding everywhere, all curiously considered to be national in scope for reservoirs. In spite of high federal uproar about the faults of flood control policy in recent years, one large item whose assigned cash value is added into these benefits is an "increase in net return from higher utilization of land," which accepts and celebrates the fact that flood protection stimulates building on flood plains downstream. As we have noted, though, this merely assures

that damages in the long run will be bigger than they have ever been before, and tends to head off more reasonable approaches.

(5) Recreation—computed engagingly by assigning a cash worth to each "user-day" of fun the reservoir is expected to provide.

(6) Fish and wildlife—often in terms of how much money hunters and fishermen are supposed to spend on their pursuits, though the different construction agencies' criteria vary.

(7) Pollution abatement through augmentation of the flow of dirty rivers—"the solution to pollution," etc. This "benefit" is hard to include with federal help these days, because before it really got ingrained in the system, Congress and other thoughtful federal elements began to see what a Pandora's box of expenditures it would open, just as all-out flood control had, while at the same time encouraging the dumping of filth and poisons into stream systems. Nevertheless, the Texas Water Plan includes low-flow augmentation as a quality-improvement tool and its effects presumably as a benefit.

Against all these direct and indirect benefits, "costs" are not allowed to include the long-term productive potential of inundated farm and timber lands, the enormous recreational and ecologic value of alluvial terrain and natural rivers, the reverberatory effects of water development on perhaps distant valuable resources such as the coastal estuaries, and a number of other rather tangible losses and damages, as well as some huge intangible ones. If truthfully and carefully inserted in truthful, careful benefit-cost computations, such negative forces would put most individual Texas Water Plan projects on the shelf without their ever being submitted to Congress and would knock the props out from under the Plan as a whole.

I have a chronic mild case of the rustic disease, and practice some forage agriculture on a little stock farm in North Central

Texas, a sort of peasant operation. At one point a few years ago, the farm was menaced with inundation by a big prospective reservoir, primarily for flood control, whose possibility the indefatigable Army Engineers were eyeing on the nearby Paluxy River, a small clear-water tributary of the Brazos. The Engineers seem subsequently to have shied away from the project, partly because of a state park established around some dinosaur tracks in the riverbed but mainly because the Soil Conservation Service, which considers little rivers its province, feinted in fast with a proposal for flood protection through a system of small headwater reservoirs, a lesser evil which local people preferred. But the experience started me to thinking about big reservoirs in terms of the economic loss of land, and the subject has bothered me ever since.

As earlier passages in this piece show, anyone who sets out to get horsy about a technical proposal is driven from time to time to mathematical exercises, for those he is opposing have not always put their computers at his service. The Texas Water Plan does not give area figures for its proposed reservoirs. During the early stages of controversy over the Plan, San Antonio biologist Delbert Weniger and a couple of fellow Sierra Club members made an area calculation of their own. Applying an area/capacity ratio derived from existing reservoirs, they deduced the proposed structures would inundate about 4,500 square miles of land, or 2,880,000 acres. As far as I can judge, recomputing from a different angle, this startling figure is only a little bit high. Making guessed interpolations on an incomplete recent list furnished by the Texas Water Development Board, I got a "maximum controlled pool" area of over 2 million acres, and inclusion of additional land subject to inundation by uncontrolled flood waters (and subject therefore also to acquisition) would raise that figure considerably.

Much of this potential lake-bed acreage is now level to gently sloping bottom and terrace terrain with good rainfall, traditionally the best farm and hardwood timber land in Texas, the al-

luvium where the richness of whole regions has been deposited
and concentrated over the millennia. In keeping with the old
American way of farming, some of it has been badly manhan-
dled, but it has eroded much less than steeper land and with
modern machinery and fertilizers and knowledge can usually be
brought back to full potential rather quickly.

To learn approximately how much of this specific sort of good
land there is in proposed Plan reservoir sites, I ran some meas-
urements of my own, choosing as an example the area that would
be flooded out by the big Cuero One reservoir slated for the
Guadalupe in DeWitt and Gonzales Counties, down toward the
middle coast. It is a region I know and care about. Some of my
people were ranching there along the river by the 1840s, and as
a boy I spent a part of most summers visiting relatives in the
town of Cuero. It was and still is a good place to be—the population a sort of rich and easygoing jumble of the basic Texas
ethnic groups, German and Negro and Anglo and Mexican and
Czech, the towns venerable and unafflicted with large boom
though prosperous enough, the rolling gravelly uplands dotted
with live oak and mesquite and good for ranching or hunting
quail and dove and deer or just for roaming on a pony or afoot,
and always the slow green Guadalupe in its alternately wooded
and open bottom, where we kids used to go for week-long fishing
trips, running our trotlines and smoking Bull Durham during the
night, swimming and sleeping and eating badly fried catfish by
day.

The climate is coastally mild and rather damp, and the crop-
lands—practically all of them in the bottoms along the river and
its tributary creeks—still support a good small-farm agriculture
after a century and a half of use, healthier and more diversified
now than in the days of cotton's reign. A friend of mine in the
Soil Conservation Service, who used to work there, says that
DeWitt County has a higher proportion of self-sustaining farmers, growing quite a lot of what they need and obliged to no one
for much of anything, than any place he has ever been. It is thus

something of an anomaly in a mega-technological age, but no one yet has managed to sell rural DeWittians on the idea that mega-technology is better than what they already have.

Mega-technology, however, is scheming to get a large hunk of what they have. The Cuero One reservoir at flood level would occupy about 59,500 acres, stretching upstream from a dam on the river close to the mouth of Cuero Creek, where my bearded great-grandfather used to run longhorn cows, nearly to the mouth of the San Marcos River just west of Gonzales, sixty or seventy river miles long in all with large arms up all the creeks. A Cuero Two reservoir, scheduled by the Plan to be connected later to this first one, would smother a similar additional expanse of land up Sandies Creek, and the ultimate, forked, monster lake would be a key element in the Coastal Canal system of the Plan dedicated mainly to the furtherance and maintenance of irrigation on the dry lower coast, the Rio Grande, and indirectly the Winter Garden.

No soils map being available, I sketched out on 1:24,000 contour maps the extent of good bottom and terrace land that Cuero One would cover—all the alluvial soil level enough for sustained safe cultivation, whether or not it is being so used at the moment. No Old World country could afford *not* to use it so, but neither does any Old World country have the casual wealth of wildlife and timber found there along the Guadalupe. To make certain the delineation was fair, I showed it to an acquaintance versed in such things, who said he would have included a good deal more land than I had. The amount of this kind of prime land within the reservoir site as I sketched it, measured with a planimeter, came to more than 43,500 acres, or 73 percent of the total flood pool expanse.

Humid Texas east of the thirty-inch rainfall line, where most of the Plan's new reservoirs and all of the really big ones would be built, is level to rolling country with widish river valleys similar to that of the lower Guadalupe. If there is any notable variation in the ratio of farmable to rough land within the respective reservoir sites, it would probably lean toward a higher proportion eastward, where the country flattens more. Therefore an application of the Cuero One formula to the whole acreage threatened with inundation under the Plan would seem to be quite conservative.

Allowing for conservatism—both in this respect and in my soil sketch—and also for some possible excessiveness in the 4,500 square mile figure, two million acres is probably a good fair round figure for the prime bottom and terrace land that would be lost, amply provided with rain for a wide variety of crops and convenient to perennial streams for supplemental irrigation in dry seasons. It is in this kind of terrain, and in the upland soils of the Blackland Prairies in Central Texas, and on the level plain along the upper coast, that the main long-term future of Texas crop agriculture probably lies. They are the natural farming regions of the state, their original and continuing lushness fostered by pure water that falls from the sky in more or less dependable quantity, maintains itself in the soil where plant roots can tap it, and feeds out through the stream systems in a cycle that evolved as the basis for humid-zone natural processes but is easily adapted to human purposes. With wise handling the soils in such humid regions can be not only kept in production indefinitely but actually made as good as they ever were when virgin, as people like Edward Faulkner and Louis Bromfield, among others, have shown.

The "California word men," if such they were, who gave the Texas Water Plan its verbal form, went to quite a bit of trouble to play down the agricultural potential of the humid regions of the state. Witness these extracts:

> Small cash-crop farms common in East and Central Texas in the past have largely been replaced by the development of larger units engaged in livestock production. Cotton production has shifted to irrigated areas. Trends toward larger farming units and a greater dependence on livestock in dryland farming areas are likely to continue.

About 1.6 million acres of the potential 2020 irrigation development, if irrigation water were available at reasonable cost, is located in the Blackland and East Texas Timber land resource areas and along major streams of Central and East Texas. Most of these irrigable areas are not readily adaptable to large-scale project irrigation because they are relatively small and scattered. It would be physically difficult to provide some of the areas with irrigation water supply projects, and the economic feasibility would be questionable. The agricultural trend in these land resource areas, however, is toward livestock raising and development of lands for grazing, for which irrigation is not generally required.

These passages retail at least two or three half-truths and a couple of flat lies. Livestock farming in the humid regions of the United States, including humid Texas, with improved and fertilized fancy-grass pastures occupying many of the old corn and cotton fields, is very possibly only a temporary phenomenon, based on luxury tastes in which Americans can presently afford to indulge themselves. We get out of meat perhaps a tenth or so as much energy and protein as is contained in the forage the meat animal consumes in the process of growth. Thoughtful men know—and have been saying—that sooner or later all good crop land is going to have to be restored to good condition and put back into crops if we keep multiplying. Even livestock farming, though, can and does make highly effective use of supplemental irrigation. The certainty of a couple of inches of water now and then, on summer pastures or winter-grazed small grains and legumes, may double the number of animals a place can safely carry. Many such farms are irrigating now out of local streams or aquifers, and more will be.

The statement about irrigable acreage in East and Central Texas would be laughable if it were not so designedly false; 1.6 million acres is a small fraction of the decent arable land in these sections that is capable of being irrigated. The Plan's emphasis on "project irrigation" shows how the figure was arrived at, and shows too the planners' bias. What they mean by irrigable land is tabletop-flat fields, preferably contiguous over a great sprawling area so that they can be provided with a checkering of traditional gravity canals and watered by traditional basin, border, and furrow methods—i.e., the High Plains, the Valley, etcetera.

This deliberately ignores a big upsurge in the use of portable field sprinklers, which are adaptable to any land that can be tilled, since the water applied comes from overhead like rain and soaks into the soil. In 1964, two million acres in Texas were irrigated thus—14 percent of all irrigation at that time and nearly twice as much land as had been sprinkler-irrigated six years before. I have seen no more recent figures, but anyone who drives about the rolling parts of the state during a dry summer will observe for himself that the use of these devices is still growing fast. In view of this, and of the facts that perennial streams are found in almost every main valley of the humid sections and few aquifers there are subject to overdraft, it is very hard to believe that "physical difficulty" and "economic feasibility" would be a fraction as problematical as they clearly are with the mighty Texas Water System proposed in the Plan, especially when the vastly less hoggish quantities of water and transport energy needed per irrigated acre are taken into account. Application of subsidies much more modest than those available to Reclamation irrigators—for the construction of small headwater reservoirs, main-stem channel check dams, wells, and perhaps a few pipelines, plus low-interest or interest-free loans to farmers for buying pumping and sprinkling equipment—could make this kind of irrigation available to nearly the whole of humid Texas. And the whole of humid Texas includes millions on millions of arable acres.

The planners' treatment of the wide expanse of rich prairie along the humid upper Texas coast, flat as a griddle and amenable to any sort of irrigation if and when irrigation is needed, is just as shifty and distant as their treatment of the East and Central Texas farm regions, and for the same reason. Recognition of the farming potential of the humid regions would play hell with the idea of the indispensability of irrigated farming in dry regions. It would also be an admission that East and Central Texas reservoirs are costing the state some of its best land resources, more and more each year as the mighty dams go up, with or without a state plan. And it would lead to a second admission that the best use of "surplus" water in the East and Central Texas basins, a far less wasteful and disruptive use than the Plan's proposed big outward transfers, would be supplemental irrigation of local farms. And that in turn would raise the specter of the humid regions' probably having good use in the future for their water "surplus," which under Texas law would restrict its exportation. Thus clearly the planners' infatuation with big dry-country irrigation projects has driven them to a denial of farming potential in any region that would not require the Plan's huge artifices to keep on farming. It has driven them to a large and demonstrable lie.

Big standard dry-country irrigation (yes, we are back to it inevitably) does not have a uniformly happy history worldwide, except where water, soil, and climatic conditions have been ideal. It is a water hog, for not only does it demand incredible quantities of water but it uses most of that water consumptively, returning only a fraction to stream systems and aquifers. (In contrast town water-and-waste systems, for all their usual dirtiness, do give back most of what they take.) Impartial expert observers have been saying with more and more frequency that the future of dry-country irrigation is quite cloudy; it is "old technology." Its main traditional troubles have been functional, for it is a continuing fight against the way that nature has set things up, and it is terribly vulnerable to such things as the failure or siltation of a water supply system, bad drainage leading to waterlogged land, and the accumulation of waterborne minerals in the soil, most usually salt. The history of agriculture going back into dimly perceived ages—vanished aboriginal cultures of our Southwest, the people of the ancient Indus, the Mideast—is splotched with indications of the failure of such farming, and troubles of this functional sort are still cropping up all over the place—in Egypt below the Aswan, in Afghanistan, in California, in Texas, in Arizona, and through the dry regions of the world.

With enough knowledge and money and labor, such irrigation disaster areas can often be reclaimed and brought back to use till the troubles recur, but if any good alternative source of farm products exists within a country, as it does in this one, sooner or later the effort is not worthwhile and the irrigated acreage is let go back to what it was before, or to worse. This happened in Mesopotamia after that region came under Rome, when the availability of wheat and other foodstuffs from the new-land fringes of the Empire, the Balkans and such places, made the arduous yearly task of cleaning silt from supply canals uneconomic, and irrigation petered out. It is happening in parts of California where landowners sometimes find the large cost of installing drain tiles to carry off saline water from plant root zones too much to bear. It is happening on the High Plains of Texas where pumping costs are getting out of reason, and sooner or later it would probably happen there in a different, chemical way even with imported Mississippi River water.

Other, specifically economic criticisms of such farming are accumulating. In this country, western irrigation is monstrously propped up—by such things as the Texas ground water laws which allow exploitation of a public resource, and more generally by the Reclamation program which furnishes water at well below its cost and by federal agricultural subsidies which insulate the farmer from the marketplace and make it profitable for him to keep on producing unneeded commodities—and a lot more of them with cheap-water irrigation than without. A subcommittee on agriculture of the National Planning Association, consisting of some of the best agricultural economists in the nation, recently did some irrigation benefit-cost calculations of their own, in terms of actual national values, relating specifically to proposed Reclamation "rescue operations" to help irrigation continue along the lower Colorado in California and Arizona, in central Arizona, and on the Texas High Plains (the importation scheme).

Tangible costs included are true total water costs (figured in at fifty dollars an acre-foot, but for the High Plains estimated to be actually much higher), additional U.S.D.A. price-support and other program payments directly connected with subsidized irrigation production, and the general marketwide lowering of farm income brought about by new, competitive, irrigated production of unsubsidized specialty crops. Benefits are the hypothetical, unsupported, free market value of farmers' enhanced production through irrigation, plus what would be saved in terms of immobile capital resources by rescuing irrigation in these areas. (It may be noted that all this differs hugely from the system used in the Texas Water Plan, but that it makes far more sense.) On this "tangible" basis the economists conclude that an acre-foot of water delivered to one of these proposed projects would cost at least seventy dollars in all, and bring in maximum benefits of about thirty dollars or possibly much less—i.e., the result would be a loss of at least forty dollars for each acre-foot. I will leave it to the reader to compute what the overall loss per year would be on 6.5 million acre-feet delivered from the Mississippi to the Llano Estacado. . . .

If this irrigated production were really indispensable to the state and to the nation, one might be able to grin and bear that sort of mathematics. But there is nothing indispensable about it. Since just after World War I, a half-century ago now, the main problem of American agriculture has been production that is surplus to national and export needs. The farming boom in places like the Texas High Plains has been built largely on planting and reaping unneeded crops and collecting an artificially high price for them under government support programs. Most economists, including those cited above, believe surplus production will keep on being the main problem for at least another couple of decades and possibly much longer. Ever more extractive farm technology, the "Green Revolution" that has so rapidly brought formerly destitute nations toward self-sufficiency in food production and lessened their need for our output, and the increasing possibility of a slowdown in population growth all favor that view.

More and more, informed observers are noting that careful re-employment of the immense areas of good or restorable farmland in the nation's humid regions, now often fallow or planted to pasture partly because of the national market effects of subsidized western irrigated farming, could probably feed the whole country in the future, and that when real national economic principles begin to rule, the trend toward renewed farming in the humid lands will accelerate. A Committee on Technologics and Water of the august National Academy of Sciences, in a forthcoming report, takes note of this and of probabilities like aquaculture and mariculture. Ultimately, the report says, basic food production is going to have to come from areas which can accomplish it most cheaply, and it observes specifically, in a look at the "least surprising situation—year 2000":

> Future expansion of [western] irrigation will face critical scrutiny because the food materials can be produced less expensively elsewhere and the motivation to subsidize projects when irrigation is a primary use will be reduced. . . .
>
> Irrigation, [i.e., supplemental] will expand in the central and southeastern U. S. where adequate supplies are available. This expansion will be on a localized basis rather than project type developments, but many producers will have eliminated water as a potential production controlling factor, particularly for food crops.

And it is worth noting that the southeastern U. S. is the resource region of which East and Central Texas are generally considered to be a part.

This idea comes as something of a jolt to those of us who grew up with the textbook notion that the older parts of the country had been "cottoned out" and "corned out" and that the dynamic center of American agriculture had shifted permanently to the irrigated West. The truth is that huge areas of humid North America can be relatively easily restored to high production of crops through well-known soil conservation and fertilization practices, and perhaps the main obstacle to such restoration has been market competition from the western irrigation areas, whose heavy subsidization has given them an edge. Nor is it far-fetched to note that much of the vast social dislocation of recent years, principally in the South but also in the Midwest and elsewhere, is traceable to that same fact. The Texas High Plains and the Imperial Valley of California have an improbable but direct relationship to the sociological complexities of Harlem and Watts.

For further observations on irrigated farming's indispensable value to the society that supports it, let us glance at a New Mexico report, *The Value of Water in Alternative Uses,* also by economists and edited by Nathaniel Wollman. In relation to the San Juan and Rio Grande basins of that state, they estimate that the "value added" worth of an acre-foot of water to the economy is as follows in the listed uses: agriculture, $50; recreation, $200 to $300; industry, $3,000 to $4,000. In terms of jobs, they estimate that 1,000 acre-feet in varying uses will ensure direct or indirect employment for the following numbers of workers: agriculture, 8 to 10; recreation, 33 to 47; municipal and industrial supply, 240 to 773. Similar emphases have been delineated in a National Academy of Sciences report on the Colorado River, which shows that water for irrigation is not necessarily an optimum route to wholesome regional development.

In short, except in places where the local sustained water supply is far in excess of what is needed for all other purposes, or in a country that has no alternative means of feeding itself, big dry-country irrigation is one of the lousiest buys around. This goes not only for the High Plains and the Trans-Pecos but for the lower Rio Grande and the Winter Garden and all those other subhumid and semiarid places for which the Texas Water Planners have such fondness that they would expend on them not only vast unwarranted sums of money but two million acres of the best land in the humid parts of the state.

There exists a view among some good, thoughtful, socially concerned people that the open flat places of the West, furnished with big government irrigation water and speckled with planned and subsidized "new towns," would be an ideal realm for a "return to the land," a means both of dispersing the packed populations of our impossible great cities and of shaping for them a chance at a green and sturdy and wholesome life, based on irrigated farming. It is a pleasant idea, but it needs examination. For one thing it would cost horrific sums of money, as is specifically noted by the authors of the National Planning Association report mentioned above:

> . . . The large scale, high technology operations characteristic of irrigated agriculture today create relatively little primary employment for the size of the investment. For example, data from Arizona and Texas suggest that 400 to 600 acre feet of water per year are required to support one man-year of on-farm employment. [This "primary employment" yardstick is different from the one used by the New Mexico economists also cited.] Public investments in existing and proposed large scale water conveyance systems range from $400 to in excess of $1,000 per acre foot of annual capacity, or at least $160,000 per man year of primary agricultural employment created.

To this can be added the other even greater losses caused by water development that I am skimming through in this chapter— the loss of land and fisheries, the enormous ecological damage, and such things. Dry-country irrigation even for benevolent social purposes is not nearly worth it, besides being a precarious form of agriculture for other reasons already mentioned. I believe strongly in the desirability of a large-scale return to the land— indeed, without some form of it I suspect that we are all going to go paranoid rather soon. There is a yearning toward the earth among us, and the likelihood of such a return is encouraged by such things as the extension of urban amenities into rural life, mainly through electricity, and sporadic government emphasis on dispersal of industry, which would put good jobs within commuting reach of country populations.

But like farming itself, such a movement would make most sense in the humid regions, whose very lushness and variety make them better able to bear the brunt of human numbers and would allow city dwellers to become countrymen without having to turn into supertechnological agriculturalists overnight. For $160,000, the minimum needed public investment in just one year's subsidized employment for one man on irrigated land, you could buy a man a good small farm (maybe on some of those two million reservoir-site acres in East and Central Texas) and teach him to run it and probably teach him also a skill that would let him hold down an industrial job nearby. For no American return to the land at this late date is going to take the form of the sudden conversion of millions of urbanites into full-time farmers.

Under-watered regions may find some agricultural hope in the long run through new technology currently under investigation and perhaps still to emerge—things like micro-spray systems, plastic greenhouse devices, and other minimal-water-use approaches to farming. Desalted sea water may eventually help, as may rainmaking, and better dry-farming techniques and crops. But the chances appear to be that those two million reservoir-site acres of prime bottom land scheduled by the Plan for obliteration have a potential economic value in terms of direct production of food, fibers, and timber on into the far future that outweighs the value of all the dry-country irrigation the Plan is shaped to rescue and subsidize. And the certainty is that the potential of all of humid Texas, east of thirty inches, makes a bad joke out of big irrigation's indispensability to the state.

Where in the planners' benefit-cost ratios do these considerations emerge?

* * *

Still with dour economic emphasis, at least to begin with, let us regard the Texas bays. Their productivity and the incredible potential volume of high-protein food they might be induced to yield under aquacultural management we noted earlier, as well as their role in the offshore commercial fishery. Would their ruin be a further cost of the Texas Water Plan?

It seems so. The planners' intentions toward the bays have been a matter of much argument—partly because they outfoxed themselves by scurrying past the subject in a "summary" version of the Plan issued at the same time as the main report and seen by many more people, including some conservationists and sportsmen who promptly blew fuses when they read it. As far as one can tell by perusing the shorter document, 2.45 million acre-feet allotted annually to the main bays and estuaries out of the coastal part of the Texas Water System is the sum total of fresh water inflow they would be receiving when the system and the Plan really got going. The average annual inflow to these same bays during the period 1941-1957, excluding rainfall directly on them, having been about 13.8 million acre-feet, reduction to the 2.45 million figure would clearly devastate them as estuaries in short order.

The proposal as detailed in the full report is less horrific. The 2.45 million acre-feet is supplementary water to be furnished the bays out of the Texas Water System in compensation for an expected dwindling of river inflows caused by further upstream development under the Plan. What the planners seem to intend to let the main bays have annually comes to about 10.1 million total acre-feet of water besides direct rainfall and some "return flow" water from town treatment plants, industry, and irrigation—i.e., a sort of stingy maintenance of the 1941-1957 "historical" status quo.

The trouble is that the 1941-1957 status quo was a poor status quo for the bays, since it was a period when river development was accelerating and the natural undepleted runoff that had always reached the bays was being curtailed year by year. Six or seven years of the period also represent the worst general drouth in Texas history. Furthermore big pollution, big dredging, and big bay damage of the other kinds we have observed really got into their stride during the era just after World War II. So from 1941 to 1957 the bays were already deteriorating, the process being most noticeable along the lower coast where fresh inflows had always been limited.

What real historical conditions consisted of along the coast is hard to learn at this point in time. For one thing, since they are subject to the influence of storms and tides and river floods and sediment deposition and other such dynamic changeful forces, the bays' shapes and connections and outlets to the Gulf and protective islands and relationships to the Texas rivers must always have been changing, and some such changes have been accelerated by human activity. Within recent times, for instance, Matagorda Bay has been divided into two separate segments by the advancing delta of the Colorado River, which used to feed that bay but now discharges directly into the Gulf. Most likely this process was accelerated by soil erosion from farming throughout the Colorado's basin, but the same thing or something similar must have happened long ago under natural conditions to the Brazos, which also runs straight to the Gulf. So does the Rio Grande, which conceivably might at one time have had influence on the nearby salty Laguna Madre, particularly when it had its full flow of 4.5 million acre-feet or so per year, reduced now to a trickle by upstream irrigation withdrawals. Passes through the islands to the Gulf, important in flushing and circulation patterns, also appear and disappear and shift locations capriciously. What does seem certain from available information, though, is that all the bays were once much richer and healthier places than they are today.

Not much real information about their functioning shows up in water planning reports, partly because little real information exists and partly because planners obviously do not like the bays. (I am not sure they all know they don't like them, but am sure

of the fact.) The fresh water they need in copious supply to remain proper estuaries is a contradiction of the pleasant engineering notion of bountiful "surplus" river flows, and it is clear
enough that if the bays' well-being is allowed truly to have weight
in the planning process, development of inland water resources is
going to have to be less colossal than superplanners want it to be.
Consequently the bays are usually passed by in such reports with
an appearance of concern and friendliness, thorough studies of
their problems are promised which never materialize, and the
superb natural recreation they furnish to people within driving
or vacation distance is assumed, in all those earnest planning
calculations, to remain at about the same level of use through
future years, while water recreation on built reservoirs burgeons
with the population, a "benefit" that computes nicely into reservoir justification.

Largely because of this distaste for estuaries on the part of
planners, I suppose, some fundamental things remain to be learned
about them. The exact effects of growing pollution, the salinity
balances and fluctuations and gradients needed and tolerable for
the many species of bay creatures, and the real possibilities of
preserving or even enhancing bay productivity are still rather
mysterious subjects even to experts. The Texas Water Planners
hired a competent firm of consultants, Bryant-Curington, Inc., to
assemble existing data on the bays into a report, with emphasis
on return-flow waste water as a factor in their functioning. This
report's recommendations were specifically for further research,
for learning what needs to be learned about how the bays do
work and what they could mean to Texas.

Made aware in 1966 that the bays had become a warm issue,
the planners in their own major 1968 report take note of this
want of data, and state their intention of backing intricate and
immediate studies to remedy it. Yet two years after issuance of
the Plan report, at a November 1970 session of an Environmental Advisory Panel (appointed belatedly by the Water Development Board after the polling disaster of August 5, 1969),

it emerged that the studies being carried on are small, badly financed, and unlikely to get at any of the important facts before a lot more river development takes place, whether or not the Plan as such is ever implemented. Successively an employee of the Lower Mississippi River Commission (concerned with Louisiana effects), a Corps of Engineers man from Galveston, and a federal Fish and Wildlife Service representative testified poignantly about the inadequacy of the time, money, and manpower allotted for such estuarial studies, and said that they knew of no one else who was getting much done in this field either. I have received emanations to the same effect from the Texas Parks and Wildlife Department.

On a basis of admittedly inadequate information, then, the planners seem to have set aside a minimal and very likely insufficient quantity of supplementary fresh water for the bays, committed the rest of the state's water to other uses including irrigation, and left the problem of estuarial data to remain a problem on into the future. Furthermore they did this while skirting widely around the other main threat to the bays—pollution. Nowhere in the Plan does the inadequacy of its concern with water quality meet the eye so clearly as here. The subject of quality is discussed here and there in the Plan, and in the section on the bays there is even a paragraph suggesting that pesticides and other wastes are possibly problematical in those waters. But in the action sections, concern with quality is usually in terms of milligrams per liter of dissolved solids—mainly salt and such things—without much mention of toxic and biological materials that are the guts of real pollution. And in the Plan's set of recommendations, which is where the meat of planners' intentions shows best through the skin of words, the only item I can find specifically concerned with water quality is one directed at the governor and the legislature, asking that a Clean Water Fund be set up for administration by the separate Texas Water Quality Board.

Quite separate. Logically this latter agency should have been plunk in the middle of the planning process all the time, but evidently it never was. It has had a hard row to hoe in the brief years of its existence and does not appear to be moving rapidly toward great accomplishments. Its handling of the system of issuing or withholding permits to discharge wastes, under which it operates, has led to charges by critics that it is a "licensing agency for polluters" and certainly some evidence suggests that this may be so. In terms of the Texas bays, it recently took a hassle and some name-calling to get the TWQB even to institute a study in the Corpus Christi Bay system (already dying as an estuary because of reservoirs on the Nueces) of damaging and noxious thermal, petroleum, brine, and other pollution some of which *had* been licensed by the board itself.

Most people who know and care about the bays have seen the Texas Water Plan as spelling out their doom. I believe they are right. If carried out, the Plan would most likely reinforce the bays' continued deterioration, and would offer no slight possibility of making them over again into what they used to be, much less of enhancing their old productivity still further, as could certainly be done if water and knowledge were freely available. In its enthusiasm for big irrigation and total water development, the Plan writes them off, together with those potential thousands of dollars' worth of shellfish per acre, per annum, and who knows what else?

Nor do the planners "cost" this loss. . . .

By steeling himself to a few hours of tough mathematics, I suppose a layman could assign some sort of dollar value to the long-run potential of a couple of million acres of humid arable bottom lands and a million or so acres of aquaculturable bays and thus, as economists say, "quantify" their loss. Procedures for this purpose exist, worked out by dedicated and impartial people in government and in such organizations as Resources for the Future, and I am certain that their application to even these partial costs of the Texas Water Plan would swamp its array of claimed benefits utterly and for good. Yet—quite obviously—I am no economist, and in honesty the main question for me is not a dollar question. I can see no real way to separate the productive potential, in terms of sweaty human economics, of those bottom lands and those bays from their much greater but incalculable worth in the whole scheme of things.

If the bays are starved and fouled into salty stinking pools of corruption, as they will be if what is going on now continues, who can imagine that the effect will be limited to the ruin of a vast commercial fishery and the finest open-water recreation in Texas? The aliveness of the Gulf of Mexico itself will be diminished hugely, and that of the seas beyond, and Texas will have done its part to make sure that the accelerating sickness of the oceans observed by people like J. Y. Cousteau (40 percent of marine life gone in a few brief years, for God's sweet sake; we *came* out of the sea) will move on faster still, toward a death that may mean our own death as a species too. Put a price on that.

Within the Texas regions, the streams and the stream bottom lands have a role in maintaining the wholeness of things that is not less central than that of the estuaries in relation to the sea. They are where the most richness is, inherited from the drainage basins over the millennia and processed into further richness still. From the bottoms it feeds out continually into the surrounding uplands as flesh and dung and moisture, chitin and dust and bone, and to and through the bottoms it is washed back downward and some escapes to feed the estuaries where the rivers end, but there is always more being created and circulated. Flooding, drouth-time low water, rotting, growth, trees, brush, grass, bugs, beasts, birds, fish, and bacteria are all part of it. You cannot vastly alter a river and its bottom or take them away without breaking that cycle of richness and fomenting vast disruptions in the way the river's country and its creatures and plants fit together and function. You can't do the same thing in a whole region without botching up what that region is. This is why wildlife people, for instance, tend to cringe and mutter when wildlife *benefits* are claimed for big reservoirs.

It has been said that if the Texas Water Plan were carried through, not a mile of wild stream or an acre of bottom land would survive in a natural state in the eastern two-thirds of Texas. The statement is probably not far from the truth. The danger is not just to those sections that would be inundated by reservoirs—though enormous hunks of some East Texas counties would be. Even where surviving river stretches downstream from reservoirs were not channelized for water conveyance, flood control, or other purposes, their rhythms of flow and even their chemistry and microbiology (through interbasin transfers and temperature changes and such things) would be greatly changed, and further change would snowball outward from that fact.

Do you need to have been a river addict to see that this would matter? Do you need to have known lightning bugs and owls and the purl of green water in lantern light, with the trotline surging in your hand as you pull the boat along it, or the exultation of a canoe in fast mean water, or river-bottom squirrel hunting at dawn with a good feist dog, or any of the thousand other pleasures that go with rivers, to have a sense of what such loss would mean? Human pleasure is the least part of its meaning.

Just as the rivers are not separable from the uplands or from the estuaries, and the estuaries are not separable from the sea, so neither is separable from the whole continent that stretches north and south and east and west of Texas, where big changes of this sort would reverberate also. Consider migratory birds in their billions that pass to and through Texas every year, the majority directly or indirectly dependent on rivers or bays and the lands that border them. Consider—for he is large, and has seemed to be a symbol that some men have a conscience—the precariously unextinct whooping crane, already menaced by changes at his Aransas wintering ground. And what of the wily pelican, whose beak holds more than his etcetera, but also more than fish these days? . . .

Ecologists—among them some as solidly respected as Dr. Frank Blair of the University of Texas—have said that the Water Plan, with its big new bodies of water laid out under the sun and wind, would very likely change the climate of the state and neighboring regions to some degree. No one knows how or how much, but neither does anyone with a sense of earth's intricacy think it does not matter. Nor is there universal ecstasy over the planners' hearty acceptance of the idea of salvaging water by the eradication of thirty or forty million acres of juniper, mesquite, cactus, elm, live oak, willow, salt cedar, cottonwood, and other brushy or phreatophytic plants, some of which don't naturally belong where they are but some of which do. Or over the prospect of drainage for farming of several million acres of sometimes ecologically valuable wetlands, mainly along the coast—which, like brush control, is a going federal program that was niched by the planners into their catchall structure without a question.

Another big going federal program tucked whole into the Plan has attracted less focused criticism—mainly, I suspect, because like me most conservation-minded people are reluctant to snarl at the Soil Conservation Service. Anyone even faintly familiar with the effect of this agency's programs on the ravaged American earth since it was organized out of the quasi-religious soil movement of the exhausted and desperate thirties, and familiar with the hard, good, continuing work of its field people in the counties and on the farms and ranches, respects the S.C.S. Terraces and stock ponds and contour tillage and good grass cover and rotated grazing and the rest—fly low over the rolling parts of West Texas with someone in a light plane if you want to see what they can mean to an abused region. With even a middle-aged memory you know the change they have wrought.

Yet in accordance with some fell principle, even this collection of heroes has been succumbing in recent years to the lure of big technology and construction. The systems of headwater reservoirs in small stream basins that they are authorized to build, for flood control and silt interception and sometimes other benefits, are usually unobtrusive compared to Reclamation and Corps of Engineers dams, less preemptive of good land, and generally more desirable if structural flood protection is really needed. But they can encourage a false sense of security about floods just as the big ones do, are justified by equally puzzling ratios, and are often hard on stream flows. Particularly in Central and West Texas where evaporation rates run high, the loss from the surface of one of these reservoirs may be enough to dry up a formerly perennial creek downstream during part of the year. A careful U. S. Geological Survey study and other research projects have shown that some reduction of a stream basin's yield of water, below a system of these reservoirs, will occur during the entire normal fifty-year period before sediment fills the scooped-out lower portions intended for such silt storage but serving in the meantime as lakes.

Mainly in flatter and wetter East Texas, the S.C.S. engages too in a great deal of stream straightening to carry high water off faster, a process known as "channel improvement." After one of these beneficial projects has been completed, where a wooded stream once meandered in a course it and the land had worked out intricately between them, rich with fish and dependent wildlife, an unshaded ditch slashes athwart a landscape of unobstructive, usually exotic grass, and a whole small natural complex of things is gone. It is like what the Army Engineers have done to rivers and creeks in most Texas cities and elsewhere, and it is just as barren and destructive. It also looks to be one hell of a long way from H. H. Bennett and those other vigorous earth-mystics who started the Service on its way.

Nearly 1,500 of the headwater reservoirs have been built in Texas already, out of a projected total of 4,000 or more. Ditched stream channels proposed by the S.C.S. alone, in addition to what the Engineers plan on larger streams, will total some 2,500.

On and on it could go, the list of damages the Texas Water Plan—and elements and programs within it that have a life of their own regardless of whether the Plan survives—would imply for the scheme of things. There is the question of all those new electrical generating plants, nuclear or East Texas strip-mined lignite or whatever, and the vast possibilities for new pollution of air and water inherent in them. There is Louisiana. There are plenty of things, for you do not propose a good many billions of dollars' worth of dams and ditches and accompanying facilities without creating sonic booms that bounce up and down the river valleys and far out on the Plains.

Costs . . .

V. Goals

I have a friend, a scholarly Iron Curtain exile with good personal reasons for viewing the world as a less than joyful place. Not long ago he told me he had worked out the basis for an optimistic philosophy. Earth, he said, is a dying and rotten planet. Man is the maggot sent by destiny to consume it and cleanse it out of the scheme of things. Thus man has a positive function.

If one believed that, one might find it easier to look at something like the Texas Water Plan calmly. One would just as soon not wax shrill and indignant and earnest, there being so much shrillness all around us as it is, and so much Christ-like earnestness. One knows that many of the people on the other side of the argument are very probably sincere about "growth" and "expansion" and "development" as the worthiest of goals, and believe that technology can lead men happily along to them. One knows and likes some fine stout High Plains farmers, who in self-defense have gone along with what was being done out there, and under existing circumstances one knows that the main possible comment on that is, Why not? One has a healthy sometimes wary respect for able engineers and knows that the Texas Water Development Board and the federal agencies have their share of them. One throws an eye down the list of the governor's Committee of 500 mustered to support the Plan and with ease discerns the names of eight or ten or a dozen people one has known, most of whom he likes well enough and some better than that.

Even disagreeing with these folks' thrust, one would be glad enough to let them all go their own way while he keeps going his, except for a certain largish difficulty. If they go their way, there will be no way left for him or any other Texan to go but theirs also. And one finds something wrong with that. By God, one does. . . .

Another friend of mine, no exile and no scholar but a countryman who lives now three or four miles from the farmhouse he was born in some fifty years ago, made what is perhaps the central comment that can be made about the Texas Water Plan and its principal promulgators. There is a Texas idiom that describes someone as being "all eat up" with one thing or another, usually syphilis or cancer or tuberculosis. "The trouble with them folks is," my country friend observed, "they're all eat up with the big ass."

It does seem that they are. Big ass, in the form of autocratic megalomania, is no new disease on the Texas scene, or on the general human scene for the matter of that. But I am not aware of any previous manifestation of it, in Texas anyhow, wherein the shape of the world that people are going to have to inhabit, the designation of those who are to prosper and those who are not, the kind of life they are going to lead, and a number of other important things connected with the public good, have been so arrogantly prescribed. The Texas Water Plan has far less to do with water than with a desired pattern of human existence. The pattern it desires and would enforce is a stark, unimaginative, magnified version of the pattern that has been evolving among us during the past few decades—perhaps in reality the past century or more—which increasing numbers of people, including our rebellious or disaffected young, have come to believe has little to do with real human needs but is opposed to them.

Have Americans in their millions been swarming uprooted to the cities where someone has convinced them the action is, there to teem and suffocate and rage if they are poor, or to half-escape outward if they can afford it to suburbs in search of a lost greenness and naturalness of existence that the suburbs themselves often destroy? Has the logistical technology required to maintain them in these impossible concentrations—the power and fuel, the mass-produced and processed food, the water, the systems for collection and disposal of wastes, the infinite array of gaudy undurable gadgets with which the more gullible of them are kept convinced that all this represents the good life—become a monster that is blighting and eating and poisoning the rivers and the sea and the air and the green green earth upon which men have always depended and always will? Is there an ache that seeks to dull itself through the fuddlement of drugs and alcohol, through destruction and dislike, through fat blindworm consumerism, through frantic sexuality and lurid canned entertainment? Are we drifting quickly closer to all that Orwell and Huxley, take your pick, foresaw for us long since, or to worse?

We wouldn't put it that way, say the planners frowning gently. We'd call it progress. Look at all that money everybody's making. And man, you ain't seen nothing yet. . . .

It has been often said—and repeated in relation to the Texas Water Plan—that engineers have no business formulating social goals. This is true, but the fact is that engineers really don't very often formulate such goals or even want to, though they may have a big effect on them through the techniques they prefer and through their very dynamic presence. What formulates social goals, in this day and place at least, is economic goals, and so steeped is American thought in economic expansionism—more, bigger, costlier, newer things and services for more and more people year by year, decade by decade, world without end—that only lately have a few doubts about its social effects begun to lodge themselves in the general consciousness. This being pre-eminently an age of technology, scientists and engineers as high priests of technology are pressed into the service of economic expansionism, and often these days they have to strain a gut to keep up with its pace. What engineers have no business doing is evaluating the benefits and costs of their own projects, but we looked into that at length. . . .

The people who voice goals are generally politicians, egged on by businessmen and industrialists who stand very close behind them in a place like Texas. Politics in Texas is not a very edifying exhibition, though I am told and can believe, looking around, that it is no worse than in many other states. It is ramified, peopled with dark emeritus presences who at times appear to war among themselves and at others are horribly one, and generative of cheesy odors that drift out at you unawares. I got my first full smell of it as a young instructor at the University in Austin not long after World War II, when a disgruntled friend from out of town, newly employed as a lawyer by one of the big oil companies, made me come down and keep him company in a hotel suite, where he was having to mix drinks for a crowd of swacked legislators while they guffawed at old-style pornographic Cuban movies and his boss circulated among them talking up some law the oil firm wanted passed. I believe that things have improved a little since, and that the state government harbored then and still does harbor a good many people of honor and intelligence. I know some of them.

Yet that old aroma lingers in my nose, kept fresh by unsavory uproars that rock the capital now and then, like the recent stock-and-banking scandal reaching up through controlling levels of the legislature apparently to the executive branch. Maybe, a waggish columnist wrote after the bond-issue flop of 1969, the people don't think there's $3.5 billion worth of honesty in Austin. . . .

Whether there is or not, and even if you are willing to grant that some of the people shoving at legislators behind the scenes are sincere enough in their belief that what is good for a given segment of business or industry or agriculture is good for Texas too, it is hard to believe that all the goals in something like the Texas Water Plan are sculptured with the guidance of sincerity and selflessness. Too many plums would hang on a tree like that. Big-construction firms, power companies, big farming, and a good many other enterprises would be standing just right to catch them as they ripened and fell. Nor would those who guided the Texas Water Development Board and the Plan's implementation, during those wheeler-dealer fifty years, be certain to remain immune to the intoxications of power and all those billions of bucks.

Reluctantly, one notes in himself a low suspicion that the plums had much to do with the way the goals came out. The suspicion is strengthened by the Plan's many evasions and half-disclosures, as well as by the unholy haste with which the open-ended water-bond proposal was rammed through the legislature and into the polls.

Plum picking may have been an honorable pursuit among us through most of history. The thrust it gave helped open up the continent for civilization, and that was what most men thought ought to be done. But it is less and less so now that the continent is fully open and pitifully vulnerable to our mechanized eatings and rippings. There is less to eat and rip now than there used to be, and what there is is all we have. Who eats on it eats on us all.

Among the various ingrained personal flaws of which the years have made me conscious, the big ass is not one. Perhaps its opposite is, thinking small. I lack desire to delineate new directions for mankind or to be an agent of great social and political change, nor am I certain that most such would-be agents are anything but puppets of illusion. More and more with time I find that the principal social and political thing I want is to be let the hell alone, and speckled through our frantic world I see a lot of others like me. The age and the place and the air somehow favor such withdrawal on the part of certain types, and favor too if you can manage it the study of solidities like rivers, beasts, woods, hills, stones, birds, bays, fields, crops, and how the wind brings rain, with room for books and music and family and friends. That is if you are built the way we withdrawers are, and I am not saying it is a good way to be built; very possibly it is not. . . . There have been other such times. Imperial Rome was one.

Mainly it is fairly easy to get yourself let alone; you find that after all no one much was chasing you. Yet through your Texas woods and hills and beasts and rivers and things, if you have let yourself care for them, the messy world of men comes at you anyhow. The wind smells not of rain but of sulphur compounds and half-burnt hydrocarbons. The old, good, fertile prairies go under subdivisions. The numbers of many wild things shrink year by year, and some species move toward extinction. Certain of the rivers you have known and cared about go stinking and dead, big dams flood others, and still others are channelized to nothingness. The sea itself is fouled and possibly dying. Grand Plans rumble like thunderheads along the horizon. Somebody bureaucratic eyes your creek, the one that is really yours and runs from cool pool to pool over ledge limestone. You have children, who will probably have children, and besides that, despite a tendency toward withdrawal, you do care about the race of upright animals to which you belong and, believing these things solid, you think the race should be allowed to keep on knowing them. Not that all are allowed to know them now. . . .

Therefore you stick your head out of your lair and open your big mouth and complain. What then do you propose instead?

I am not a planner, nor was meant to be. But it is not hard to see what a few concrete elements would be in a hypothetical sane water-management planning effort for Texas. They are nearly inescapable. They are implicit in the discussions of this treatise, and have been remarked on by numbers of people before me. The general principles behind most of them have been enunciated in scientific circles and even in government, through such agencies as the relatively new Federal Water Resources Council. They are unlikely to capture the enthusiasm of thinkers like those responsible for the 1968 Texas Water Plan, but that kind of enthusiasm may be something Texas and the rest of the nation are going to have to start learning to do without, for survival. Being unadept at programmatics, I freely admit that some of the following bits of wisdom may slightly overlap, and also that other items may exist that ought to have been included:

(1) *Flexibility*—avoidance of Grand Plans, which as we have noted necessarily make a heavy commitment over the long haul of years to presently feasible technology—hydraulic and agricultural and whatever—as well as to presently discernible goals. The best water scientists in this country are coming to believe that the day of Grand Plans may be drawing to an end, and that planning in the future will have to take into fundamental account a diversity of possible goals and means of reaching those goals, questioning itself at every step and backtracking whenever it finds that its assumptions were wrong. There is, of course, a vast gulf between that kind of planning and the tunnel-visioned, dinosaurish, forward surge proposed in the Texas Water Plan, which would play huge hob with the way the world works and never raise any real questions about the necessity.

(2) *Population projections*—a sane appraisal of the probabilities, based on expert opinions, with also, insofar as it lies within the realm of water planning, discouragement of any more population growth than is inevitably going to take place. In line with this, a recent wise public pronouncement by the governor of Oregon might be worthy of some contemplation; he announced to out-

of-staters, more or less: We're glad to have you for a visit, but for God's sake don't stick around.

(3) *Distribution of population*—economic and social planning that will persuade most people to want to live where the most water naturally is, thus minimizing the need for major water development. If dispersal of people from the congested cities ever gets moving, as it probably must in time, the part of Texas east of the thirty-inch rainfall line is where they ought to be encouraged to go.

(4) *Philosophy*—appointment of persons in charge of water planning who care about a decent world rather than about how much cash can be made out of impounding water and sluicing it here and there. This means ecologists and biologists and landscape and wildlife people and humanists, among others, and not in a polite advisory rank. Such a step would probably do more than anything else to rectify the present shameful practice of rigging project benefits and costs. Along with this emphasis on breadth of viewpoint, there should be a sharp-fanged provision that no one be allowed anywhere near the planning process who stands to make money out of the way it might go.

(5) *Legal changes*—overall and radical revision of Texas water laws and policies to align them with the scientific principle that water on the earth's surface and underground and in the sky is all part of one vulnerable dynamic hydrologic process which has to be protected for the future. Such protection would include a strong set of ground water regulations to enforce a "sustained yield" use of aquifers, and probably a harsh reappraisal of all surface water uses, and therefore would interfere with some practices now considered rights, but there is no way around that. "The public good," that much-flogged whipping boy, is much more at stake than it is in

reservoir-site and highway right-of-way condemnations, which clobber established rights also.

(6) *Agriculture*—a program designed to bring Texas farming into accord with hydrologic reality rather than to contort hydrologic reality to make it fit a destructive, uneconomic, and obsolescent pattern of farming. A good program of this sort would emphasize research into new crops and techniques for water-short regions, incentives for the revival and improvement of farming in the state's humid sections, and study of the possibility of making moderate amounts of supplemental irrigation water widely available there as crop insurance. Clearly this part of the planning process, like some others, would require a change in federal attitudes as well.

(7) *Thrift*—separation of water "needs" from "demands" with the aim of meeting the latter only within reason rather than encouraging extravagant use at the general public's expense. Man as an individual animal requires about five pints of water daily to keep his body going; the Texas Water Plan proposes providing about 342,000 gallons per year—close to 1,000 gallons daily—for each resident Texan, most of it for irrigation.

Supplies available now are not in the least inadequate, if "needs" are the standard of judgment. Texas Water Plan "existing and under construction" reservoirs as of 1968 can furnish a firm annual yield of about 9.1 million acre-feet, and safe withdrawals from Texas aquifers could add another 5 million acre-feet to this (Texas Water Development Board figures). This means that right now and with no further development Texas can count on a firm supply of at least 14.1 million acre-feet a year. If you exclude irrigation as a use (the economists having pretty well proven that in public terms at least it is a good deal more of a "demand" than a "need") and figure normal overall use to amount to about 250 gallons per day per capita, this quantity of water would sustain a population of around 50 million persons with standard industries. Obviously, God willing, there are not going to be that many Texans; just as obviously the water is not perfectly distributed around for present population patterns, and there is going to be some irrigation. But if irrigation's hoggish demands are not given priority and encouraged, there is no water crisis in Texas at all, and with minimal further development there is not going to be one for a great deal longer than fifty years, even if you accept the Plan's gargantuan population projection.

(8) *Floods*—action to stave off further vulnerable development of flood plains and to lay flood-protection costs on flood plain users. Large reservoirs and channelization ought to be at the bottom of the list of possible tools and even then on a "reimbursable" basis, with said flood plain users paying the tab. Yes, all this depends more on federal action than on anything else, but the state could dig in its heels against the seductive pull of Uncle's less felicitous present programs.

(9) *Bay and river preservation*—expenditure of large sums of money on concentrated research to get at the whole array of facts about Texas estuaries and rivers, with the object of maintaining the integrity of their functioning as one of the highest water uses.

(10) *Pollution*—write your own program. None of those around seem to be working very well, possibly because most are laced with polite reticence of the type displayed in the Texas Water Plan. A good program would be nasty and prying and carping and intolerant and full of teeth and superbly funded, and such a one had better show up in Texas soon. It had better be right in the middle of any water planning program too.

(11) *Relations with Washington*—reinforced wariness of the

big federal construction agencies, but from the standpoint of making sure that what they do is desirable
rather than that it is big and free of strings. From one
possible point of view, the 1968 Water Plan itself is a
catchall structure that represents several federal agencies' separate thinking about Texas water, and some of
its evils are federal evils, at work throughout the nation.
Not that the state's planners, apparently, needed to have
their arms twisted much to go along. . . . To be realistic,
there is probably more chance of policy changes for the
better in Washington than in Austin, and if and when
federal water policies start making overall good sense,
state planning undoubtedly ought to be subordinated to
them. But anyone who looks on the present federal
construction agencies as a uniform set of good guys full
of a desire to rescue us locals from inept state planning
is ignoring the evidence of his own eyes or hasn't used
them well. These federals are human, and consist of
mixed good guys and bad guys, often inside the same
suit of clothes. Their motives, like those of most of the
rest of us, are principally benevolent. But the main thing
they are presently full of a desire to do is to *construct,*
anywhere and any time and at any cost a nicely juggled
SC-RB will justify.

And "goals"? Shall we prescribe a way of life for 2020? It
seems unwise. We inhabit a time of rapid change, and change
toward what nobody really knows. Furthermore we have made
the largest environmental mess in the long span of man's racial
presence on this planet, or have allowed it to make itself, and
despite some emergent skimpy signs of hope there is no certainty
at all that we will be able to straighten the mess and ourselves
out, and as a species even arrive at 2020. This is not long-faced
doomsdayism but sober fact; there is doubt. Are we then a proper
fount of wisdom to issue judgments on the subject of what people

in that year, if there are any, should be like, and what they should want in the way of a world around them?

It would not be hard to weave one's own vision of an ideal future Texas (and nation, and world) of a sort, I truly believe, far more likely than the Texas Water Plan's expansionist dream to excite the gratitude of one's great-grandchildren if it were to materialize. Described Utopias come out looking pretty soupy most of the time, maybe always. But the people in mine would not be soupy, not if I could help it; no arrogant tampering with their genes or their humanness would have been allowed. In general they would not be ideal citizens or ideal consumers or ideal anything. They would be people—infinitely various, decent and cruel and troublesome and quiet and bright and stupid and passionate and phlegmatic and greedy and lecherous and ascetic in the ways that evolution and history have shaped—and it would not be dull to dwell among them.

But shared belief of some kind would keep them tolerably moral toward one another, as belief has most men through time. And the reasonable numbers of them (quite a few short of 30.5 million), together with their dispersion through a whole and functional land, would make them more bearable to the earth and to other people, giving their imperfections elbowroom. This Utopian Texas would have trees and rivers and wide grassy plains and woods and birds and beasts and hills and bays and all such wonders in good working order, allowed to shape themselves into varying regional wholenesses. And the unsoupy populace scattered through the regions who lived from and with this wholeness would be able to touch and know such things in daily life if they wanted, and those who preferred not to touch and know them could stay in towns and touch and know one another to their hearts' content. Texans would belong where they were, among sheep and goats and limestone on the Edwards Plateau, or beside a slow East Texas catfish river, or bilingual along the subtropical Rio Grande, or leathery below the breaks of the High

Plains, or whatever, wherever. Happily colonial, or getting them-selves let the hell alone. . . .

Technology would be man's genuine servant, not a predatory ravening thing, and would long since have flipped around and gobbled up its own earlier vomitings and excrements. Bread would be bread and not soft plastic foam; tomatoes would be tomatoes and not pink mush picked green five hundred or a thousand miles away. Poison would be poison and treated warily as such. Waste would be richness, not a problem, and would go back to the earth or into some new use by men.

Yes, one can weave, and his woven world seems good to him, far better than what the Water Planners want. Yet world weaving of whatever savor belongs really on the other side of the huge task of cleaning up and straightening out that faces us right now, if indeed we are slated to come out on the other side. Because only on the other side will anyone be able to see what sort of future world will even be possible, let alone ideal.

There is no room for doubt that strong, goodwilled planning is needed in Texas and everywhere else if there is to be any hope of balancing our demands with what the physical world around us can stand, for parts of it are beginning to make it known that they can't stand much more. In that balance—in a sort of "sustained yield" relationship of men to the planet—lies the only chance that those who come after us will have any dreaming choice at all in the manner of their existence, and in it too probably lies our only chance for survival. Therefore for now it seems that balance is a high enough goal for planning all by itself. Water planning or any other kind. . . .

The Texas Water Plan of 1968, which flatly rejected balance as an aim, has not been playing its tune very loudly of late. It is still official dogma in Austin, and water-scare articles in some of the state's main newspapers still occasionally pound the tom-toms for it, but on the whole the planners appear to be licking their wounds and biding their time. Besides the setback of the bond-issue defeat, there has been a large shrinkage of Texas influence in Washington since Lyndon Johnson returned to the limestone hills, things like ghettoes and war and space programs have been pulling hard on the Treasury teat, and there is also perhaps more general awareness than there was among Texas voters of what nearly got rammed down their throats, and awareness among Texas politicians of this fact. And the voice of the environmentalist is heard in the land, and the engineers who have for so long had a free hand to construct, huddle in groups and mutter about "tennis shoe ecologists." Even Governor Preston Smith, High Plainsman or no, has spoken of piecemeal water development as being perhaps better than overall action, at least for the time being.

It would be unwise, though, to construe these signs as meaning that the Plan is a dead duck, as some observers have tended to do. Possibly in its full 1968 form it is in trouble. Certainly the mounting arguments and obstacles in the path of Mississippi River water importation seem very strong, and in time that proposal may well be quietly dropped, though West Texas will probably not be very quiet about this if it happens. The only fundamental difference such a subtraction would make in the Plan's destructiveness within Texas, however, would be the elimination of the Trans-Texas Canal and certain structures associated with it. The rest would all still be there—the enormous preemptive gaggle of East and Central Texas reservoirs, the coastal ditch from the Sabine to the Rio Grande, the jugglings and sluicings here and there, the big new irrigation but with West Texas sliced out.

In May of 1971, a constitutional amendment providing more money for water resources program improvement and raising the allowable interest rate on water bonds from 4 percent to 6 percent was approved by Texas voters mainly because it had been cannily attached to a proposal for better funding of pollution control programs. For the moment the interest increase will apply only to long-authorized but unsold bonds in the amount of about $200 million. But it paves the way for other action. . . . On the drawing boards and in the halls of Congress and finally athwart the rivers the big dams do go forward, as we have seen, whether or not the Plan is mentioned in connection with them. Major prospective reservoirs on the Sabine, for instance, are presently being pushed hard by the federals, and in their specifications are great increments of storage for out-of-basin use, though the ultimate destination of such water is left hazy.

That destination is not hard to guess. Since at least as early as 1952, big proposals for transfer of East Texas water have had a common main destination in mind—new irrigation on the lower coast and the Rio Grande by way of a coastal aqueduct. It is hard to find any reason for believing that this has changed, particularly when one learns that H. P. Burleigh, for whom the original coastal aqueduct idea was popularly named, has lately retired from Reclamation and been appointed executive director of the Texas Water Development Board. He is an able and forceful man and he believes forcefully in irrigation, especially toward the lower end of Burleigh's Ditch.

Therefore the Plan is no dead duck, though it may be undergoing a period of molt. It waddles on toward its goals, and one of these days will show up in a bright new set of feathers, unless before that time good sense can seize control in the realm of Texas water.

The hope must be that good sense will.

Bibliography

Author's note: Though newspaper articles were important sources for this piece of writing, they were too numerous to be included here. Similarly, I have omitted some helpful unpublished items furnished me by Burgess Griesenbeck of Friends of the Earth, Austin, and by other people. This does not mean that I am not grateful both to the authors thereof and to those who brought these materials to my attention.

I. FEDERAL AND STATE GOVERNMENT PUBLICATIONS
  A. Texas
    1. Texas Water Development Board (and its predecessor agencies)

Bryant-Curington, Inc.: *Return Flows—Impact on the Texas Bay Systems.* (1966)

Carr, John T.: *The Climate and Physiography of Texas.* (1967)

Dowell, C. L., and Breeding, S. D.: *Dams and Reservoirs in Texas . . . December 31, 1966.* (1967)

Gillett, P. T., and Janca, I. G.: *Inventory of Texas Irrigation, 1958 and 1964.* (1965)

Grubb, H. W.: *The Importance of Irrigation Water to the Economy of the Texas High Plains.* (1966)

Kane, J. W.: *Monthly Reservoir Evaporation Rates for Texas, 1940 through 1965.* (1967)

Lockwood, Andrews, and Newman, Inc.: *A New Concept: Water for Preservation of Bays and Estuaries.* (1967)

McDaniels, L. L.: *Conservation Storage Reservoirs in Texas.* (1964)

A Plan for Meeting the 1980 Water Requirements of Texas. (Texas Board of Water Engineers, 1961)

The Texas Water Plan. (1968)

Water for Texas: a Plan for the Future. (the preliminary version, 1966)

Yarbrough, D. B.: *Laws and Programs Pertaining to Water and Related Land Resources.* (1968)

2. Texas Agricultural Experiment Station

Harman, W. L., Hughes, W. F., and Martin, J. Rod: *An Economic Analysis of Permissible Irrigation Water Costs in the Texas High Plains.* (1970)

Hughes, W. F., and others: *Use of Irrigation Water on the High Plains.* (1952)

Projected Life of Water Resources—Subdivision #1, the High Plains Underground Water Reservoir. (1969)

B. U. S. Geological Survey

Baldwin, H. L., and McGuinness, C. L.: *A Primer on Ground Water.* (1963)

Broadhurst, W. L.: *Ground Water in Texas for Irrigation.* (1951)

Cronin, J. G.: *Ground Water in the Ogallala Formation in the Southern High Plains of Texas and New Mexico.* (1969)

Gilbert, C. R., and Sauer, S. T.: *Hydrologic Effects of Floodwater Retarding Structures on Garza Little Elm Reservoir, Texas.* (1969)

Leopold, L. B., and Langbein, W. B.: *A Primer on Water.* (1960)

McDonald, M. R.: *The Irrigation Aspects of Ground Water Development.* (1954)

C. Other Governmental

Environmental Quality: the First Annual Report of the Council on Environmental Quality. (1970)

Progress Report on West Texas and Eastern New Mexico Import Project Investigations. (1968)

The Report of the U. S. Study Commission—Texas. 3 volumes. (1962)

"Water Conservation and Development in Texas." *Congressional Record—Senate.* (July 5, 1967)

Water Developments and Potentialities of the State of Texas.
(1958)

*Water Supply and the Texas Economy: an Appraisal of the Texas
Water Problem.* (1952)

Water: the Yearbook of Agriculture, 1955.

II. BOOKS, PERIODICAL ARTICLES, AND NONGOVERNMENTAL PUBLISHED
REPORTS

Addison, H.: *Land, Water, and Food.* (London, 1955)

Bell-Milam Land and Water Rights Association: *Development . . . or
Devastation?* (Buckholts, Tex., n. d.)

Brunson, B. R.: *The Texas Land and Development Company: a Panhandle Promotion, 1912-1956.* (Austin, 1970)

Dale, Tom, and Gill, Vernon: *Topsoil and Civilization.* (Norman,
1955)

Darling, F. F., and Milton, J. P. (eds.): *Future Environments of
North America.* (Garden City, N. Y., 1966)

Farvar, T., and Milton, J. P. (eds.): *The Unforeseen Ecologic
Boomerang.* (Warrenton, Va., 1968)

Hendrick, R. L.: *A Study of Ground Water Supplies and their Relation to Irrigated Farming on the South High Plains of Texas.*
(The Travelers Insurance Companies, 1958)

Holden, W. C.: *The Espuela Land and Cattle Company.* (Austin,
1970)

Kerr, A. M.: "Reef Shell—a Texas Raw Material." *Texas Business
Review.* (April 1968)

Leary, T. R., and Jurgens, C. J.: "The Fate of the Bay." *Texas Parks
and Wildlife Magazine.* (April 1969)

*Ogallala Aquifer Symposium, Texas Tech University, Lubbock, Texas,
1970.*

Ryan, R. H., and others: *An Economic Profile of Texas to 1990.*
(Austin, 1968)

Sauer, S. P., and Masch, S. P.: "Effects of Small Structures on Water
Yield in Texas." In *Effects of Watershed Changes on Streamflow,*
eds. Moore and Morgan. (Austin, 1969)

Stambaugh, J. L. and L. J.: *The Lower Rio Grande Valley of Texas.*
(San Antonio, 1954)

The Texas Almanac and State Industrial Guide, 1970-1971. (Dallas,
1970)

The Texas Observer. Articles on the Texas Water Plan by various
persons, including Ronnie Dugger, Delbert Weniger, Paul S.
Taylor, Stuart Long (a reprint), Terence O'Rourke, Greg Olds,
Kaye Northcott, and Mary Beth S. Rogers. (Issues of July 4, July
18, and August 1, 1969)

Tinney, E. R.: "Water for Western Federal Irrigation Projects." In *Water Resources Management and Public Policy,* edited by Campbell and Sylvester. (1968)

Webb, W. P.: *The Great Plains.* (New York, 1931)

———— (ed.): *The Handbook of Texas.* (Austin, 1952)

————: *More Water for Texas.* (Austin, 1954)

White, G. F.: *Strategies of American Water Management.* (Ann Arbor, 1969)

III. UNPUBLISHED MATERIALS OF PRIMARY IMPORTANCE

Dixon, R. M.: "The Southwest and the Drouth Problem." (1958) An early realistic look at High Plains agricultural economics by a member of the Texas Board of Water Engineers.

Hazleton, J. E.: "Statement to the Texas Water Development Board, November 24, 1970." An economist's critique of Sabine River proposals.

Lovejoy, W. F.: "Some Comments on the Texas Water Plan of 1968." (1969) Also economic in slant.

Shannon, R. A.: "Statement of Richard A. Shannon on Behalf of Sierra Club—Lone Star Chapter—and Texas Committee on Natural Resources to the Environmental Advisory Panel of the Texas Water Development Board, 14 November 1970."

"Statement of Region 5, U. S. Bureau of Reclamation, to the Environmental Advisory Panel of the Texas Water Development Board." (November 1970)

"A Statement to the Environmental Advisory Panel of the Texas Water Development Board by the Lone Star Chapter of the Sierra Club." (November 1970)

Twichell, T. (District Chief, U. S. Geological Survey): "Statement to the Environmental Advisory Panel, Texas Water Development Board." (November 1970)

Young, R. A., and Heady, E. O.: "Irrigation Development and Agricultural Abundance: Conflicting Elements in Public Policy Toward Agriculture." Report to Committee on Agriculture, National Planning Association. (April 1971)

Part II
California

The New
Romans

by T. H. Watkins

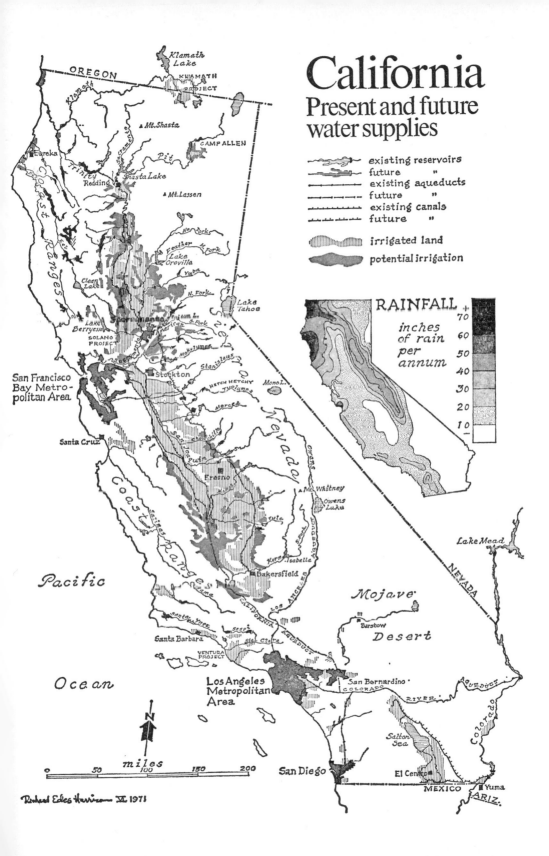

California
Present and future water supplies

existing reservoirs
future "
existing aqueducts
future "
existing canals
future "

irrigated land
potential irrigation

RAINFALL
inches of rain per annum

70 +
60
50
40
30
20
10
—

OREGON

Klamath Lake
KLAMATH PROJECT

Klamath

Mt. Shasta

CAMP ALLEN

Eureka

Pit

Trinity

Shasta Lake
Redding

Mt. Lassen

Coast Ranges

No. Forks

Feather
Lake Oroville
M. Fork

Clear Lake

Yuba

N. Fork

Lake Tahoe

Lake Berryessa

Sacramento

SOLANO PROJECT

American S. Fork

Nevada

Mokelumne

San Francisco Bay Metropolitan Area

Stockton

Stanislaus

Mono L.

HETCH HETCHY Tuolumne

Santa Cruz

Merced

San Joaquin

Chowchilla

Fresno

Coast Ranges

Diablo Ranges

Mt. Whitney

Owens Luke

Tule

Owens

Kern

Isabella

Lake Mead

Bakersfield

Mojave

NEVADA

Kern

Santa Ynez

Sespi

Sta. Clara

VENTURA PROJECT

Santa Barbara

CALIFORNIA AQUEDUCT

LOS ANGELES

Barstow

Desert

Pacific

Los Angeles Metropolitan Area

San Bernardino
COLORADO

RIVER

AQUEDUCT

Ocean

Colorado

N

miles
0   50   100   150   200

San Diego

Salton Sea

El Centro

MEXICO

Yuma

ARIZ.

Richard Edes Harrison XI 1971

I. Prologue

Logic, n.: The art of thinking and reasoning
in strict accordance with the limitations and
incapacities of the human misunderstanding.
The basic of logic is the syllogism,
consisting of a major and a minor premise and
a conclusion—thus:

Major premise: Sixty men can do a piece of work
sixty times as quickly as one man.

Minor premise: One man can dig a post-hole in
sixty seconds; therefore—

Conclusion: Sixty men can dig a post-hole
in one second.

—Ambrose Bierce

The history of California water is the story of superficial logic
wedded to need and carried to an extreme that threatens to bankrupt the state and warp its environment.

The need is the result of a peculiar California phenomenon, one common to the state since its beginnings as an American institution: its water is where its people aren't. Every major metropolitan and agricultural region in California is situated at some significant distance from the resource that makes life possible, but the most telling example of the syndrome is southern California, where more than 50 percent of the state's population now lives and which possesses only .06 percent of the state's natural stream flow. Most of the rest of the water is "locked up" in the Sierra Nevada and Cascade-Siskiyou ranges of the north.

The logic has the weight of all history behind it, dating from the time that Hezekiah "made a pool, and a conduit, and brought water into the city," as the Bible reports, and, following the logical thrust of the scriptures, for more than a century Californians have been making pools, and conduits, and bringing water someplace—frequently to former deserts. And it fully intends to continue making pools and conduits, pursuing its logic into all the water-rich nooks and crannies of the state, until one of the most remarkable engineering achievements in human history is complete: The State Water Project, designed to bring more than four million acre-feet * of water from the mountains and into the semi-arid lands of the San Joaquin Valley and the extruded megalopolis of southern California.

The Project, with its mighty dams, its complicated network of canals and pipelines, its power generators, and its enormous pumping plants, stands as a profound articulation of the logic that built hundreds of miles of flumes during California's Golden Era, that built the Owens River Aqueduct, the Colorado River Aqueduct, the All-American Canal, and which conceived and executed the Central Valley Project. It is the culmination of what one observer has called a century-long system of "bigger and bigger ditches" to bring water from where it was to where it was

---

* An acre-foot of water is enough to cover an acre of ground to a depth of one foot; it is 320,000 gallons—or, as historian W. H. Hutchinson has noted, enough water to flush approximately 60,000 suburban toilets simultaneously.

consumed. In a state whose society is so accelerated that ten years or less is long enough to establish a "tradition," then, the logic it has applied to the use and movement of water has all the hoary venerability of an Italian count's opinions on the function of royalty—and, some would say, about as much relevance to the world of today.

For a small army of critics has now risen to assault the tenets of that logic on a number of levels, questioning the value of tradition for its own sake and coldly scrutinizing elements of the California Water Project with a pitiless attention to detail. The Project, they say, was badly overplanned; the construction of its immense dams and hundreds of miles of tunnels, conduits, and canals was based on population projections that have since been subjected to a steady revision downward. They say the state has committed itself to the expenditure of a minimum of $2.5 billion for the completion of an enterprise that may be a financial disaster, that its interest and amortization rates alone almost certainly guarantee that it will be operating at a deficit of hundreds of millions of dollars over the next seven decades at least. They say that the water it was designed to deliver to farmlands in the San Joaquin Valley and to cities and real estate developments in southern California may not only be unneeded but that it will more than likely be infinitely more expensive than water from such alternative sources as waste-water reclamation, desalinization, and newly discovered geothermal deposits beneath the Imperial Valley. They say that it will be an ecological juggernaut, that its ultimate logic threatens the existence of the last of California's wild rivers on the north coast and that such elements of the Project as the Peripheral Canal and the San Joaquin Valley Master Drain spell almost certain destruction of one of the state's environmental treasures—the magnificent estuarine world of the San Francisco Bay-Sacramento River Delta region.

The critics say, in short, that the California Water Project, that triumphant climax to a century of engineering adventure, is a prime example of hydrological overkill.

These are not picayune and uninformed criticisms; they come from federal, state, and private engineers, university biologists, chemists, and economists—people with no axe to grind save that of common sense. Predictably, however, the bureaucratic response to this criticism has been an attempt to bury it under a cottony charge of "emotionalism" on the part of northern Californians determined to play dog-in-the-manger with California water. William R. Gianelli, director of the state's Department of Water Resources and an affable, energetic, and grimly sincere champion of traditional logic, articulated that response in an address before the League of Women Voters of Los Angeles County in September, 1970:

> The real facts in the matter are that some people in northern California do not want to share one drop of water with southern California, and they will use any excuse to prevent it. I'm a northern Californian myself, but I've never really seen any reason or logic in this verbal battle. I certainly don't see northern California protest when money from the Long Beach tideland oil resource is used to send northern California children to school. And I've never know a northern Californian to object to the fine fruits and vegetables which are produced in the south. We even think Disneyland is wonderful!

He can be granted his fondness for Disneyland, but such cute obfuscations go little toward meeting criticism on a rational level, nor do they help to illuminate the dimensions of a problem which the less visible members of the Department of Water Resources admit is very real. The California Water Project, conceived in tradition and executed in haste, may be one of the great white elephants in structural history. How it came to pass and what it may mean to California is a matter of no little significance to all of us, for California, "the most American of all the American states," is a bellwether for the rest of the nation in this as in many other matters. "To fully understand the water situation in California," Gianelli remarked in that same speech, "one needs to examine the past and take a realistic view of the present." Precisely—and while we are examining the past and viewing the present realistically, we might also speculate on the future, which may yet see us lugging around the sins of growth like a victim of elephantiasis hauling his privates about in a wheelbarrow.

II. The Water Imperialists

"The Yankees are a wonderful people," said *Californio* Mariano Vallejo. "If they emigrated to hell itself, they would somehow manage to change the climate." Like many of his people, Vallejo watched the American transformation of California with a mixture of dismay and admiration. The Yankees were giving them plenty to watch, as scores of thousands infested the foothills of the Sierra Nevada between 1848 and 1852, a race of demented Jasons scrabbling about after gold. To get it, they needed water. At first, the problem was simple enough; most of the early "diggins" were on the banks of streams and rivers, where the water needed to "wash" the gold through rockers and sluices was immediately available. As the early deposits were worked out, however, the gold-seekers moved into "dry diggins" well removed from the source of water, which then had to be transported to the mine workings through flumes.

The practice came into direct conflict with the age-old concept of "riparian rights" to water, which held that water diverted from a stream for nondomestic (i.e., urban or residential) use must be returned to that stream undiminished. For the purposes of mining, the law was inconvenient, so California proceeded to revise it along its own lines, coming up with the doctrine of "appropriation and beneficial use," which allowed the diversion of water for the benefit of enterprise without requiring its return to its source. The most dramatic exhibition of what the new concept made possible was hydraulic mining. Storage dams were developed high in the Sierra Nevada, and enormous flumes carried water at high speed down into the foothills, where it was channeled into nozzles and sent roaring against whole hillsides, washing away millions of cubic yards of gold-rich earth. It was industry on a huge scale; by the end of the 1870s, there were more than 400 hydraulic mining companies scattered through the Sierra Nevada foothills, and they consumed more than 72 million gallons of water every day. One company alone built more than 700 miles of flumes and ditches for the delivery and discharge of water.

It was also an enormously destructive industry. Not only did it create great, man-made canyons and badlands, in the process it dumped so much debris on the river plains of the Sacramento Valley that stream beds were raised as much as thirty feet in some places, greatly increasing the perennial danger of flood. The annual screams of the valley's farmers finally inspired the state legislature to take steps against hydraulic mining in 1884, requiring that the industry build holding basins for its muck, a ruinously expensive process that quickly killed the enterprise. The move was ironic because the concept of appropriation and beneficial use that had made the industry possible was the single most important contribution to the development of the irrigation projects that would ultimately make agriculture the largest industry in the state. In 1887, the legislature passed the Wright Act based on that concept, a law that permitted regions to form, and bond, irrigation districts.

In its most primitive form, irrigation had been practiced in California for more than a generation; it involved nothing more complicated than cutting a ditch in a stream bank, throwing a brush weir across the stream bed, and guiding the resulting flood waters through a series of ditches. But some of the most arable land in California existed in regions where the water supply was inconsistent at best and at worst almost nonexistent—the lower reaches of the San Joaquin Valley, for example, or the San Bernardino Valley of southern California. As agriculture expanded into these areas, it became necessary to store water during wet seasons for use during dry seasons, and throughout the 1880s ambitious private storage projects were erected in Merced, Riverside, San Bernardino, and San Diego Counties. Writing in *Scribner's* magazine in 1890, Walter Gillette Bates saw in all this the typically American attitude of applying enterprise and energy to the needs of progress. Irrigation, he said, was a problem "both for the present, and, still more, for the future of our country. . . . It is the problem of the reclamation of an empire. The people of the West, in their restless, American way, are attacking this problem from every side."

By the turn of the century, restless Californians had taken hold of water and put it to use on a score of fronts. They had tapped and diverted the waters of the Sacramento, San Joaquin, and Merced rivers in northern California; they had treated the comparatively anemic Santa Ana, San Gabriel, and Los Angeles rivers similarly in southern California and had dug nearly a thousand artesian wells to supplement that supply; and farmers in the Imperial Valley, deep in the southern desert foot of the state, were making plans to tap into the waters of the Colorado River and make the desert "blossom as the rose." Out of all this frenetic activity came the first half of that institution that would in time become known as California's "Water Establishment." The second half of that Establishment was also beginning to coalesce at that time, born of yet another California phenomenon: growth.

During the first fifty years after the California Gold Rush the state grew in population at a rate that even now startles the imagination. It is an axiom of California history that the state's population has doubled every twenty years since 1850, a rate of growth far ahead of that of the nation as a whole, and while that axiom is being revised by the current situation (more of this later), it was exhibited fiercely in those first fifty years, when the population increased from 92,597 to 1,485,053. Most of this growth took place in southern California, which one observer found growing "like an asparagus stalk after an April shower," at a rate of more than 80 percent every ten years, on the average. Most of this increase was the handiwork of railroad and real estate speculators, who touted the joys of the region in language that described it as being only a little to the west of Eden. "California is our own," one hack for the railroads wrote, "and it is the first tropical land which our race has thoroughly mastered and made itself at home in. There, and there only on this planet, the traveller and resident may enjoy the delights of the tropics without their penalties. . . ."

The city of Los Angeles, while relishing its sudden bloat and doing all it could to promote further growth, also began to wonder nervously if the Los Angeles River, its principal source of water, were going to be enough. The river contained enough water to support a population of more than 100,000—at that time a fairly astronomical figure—but as the rate of increase accelerated, the city fathers worried about the future. They were encouraged in this speculation by the members of a San Fernando Valley land syndicate, who suggested that the city anticipate its future needs by making immediate plans to tap the sources of the Owens Valley, 238 miles away.

The idea appealed to the visionary instincts of the Los Angeles Water Department, and thus was born one of California's unique institutions: water imperialism. Quite reasonably, the city expected outrage on the part of the farmers of the Owens Valley, who tended to look upon its water as their own, once the news of its plans got out. So to forestall any effective opposition, representatives of the department secretly managed to buy or obtain options to buy an immense amount of "riparian" land along both sides of existing irrigation ditches and the Owens River—in effect, giving itself the status of the largest single landowner in the valley.

That done, the water department announced its plans in 1905 and convinced the city council to authorize a bond issue of $25 million for the construction of an aqueduct and storage facilities. In the weeks before the vote on the bond issue, the citizens of Los Angeles were treated to an almost constant barrage of brochures, pamphlets, and newspaper stories—chiefly in the *Los Angeles Times* of Harrison Gray Otis—outlining the city's dire and immediate need for Owens Valley water. As a final persuasion, an artificial water famine was created—thousands of gallons of water were secretly dumped into the city's sewer system just before election time. It was enough; the bond issue was passed, and by 1907 construction of the aqueduct was under way, supervised by William Mulholland.

It was completed in 1913. The *Times* cheered with banner headlines, and thousands gathered on the banks of the canal to salute the first surge of water as it roared by—not on its way to Los Angeles, but to a reservoir in the northern end of the San Fernando Valley, where most of the 288 million gallons of water a day were funneled into the irrigation ditches of the valley. The land syndicate which had so vigorously pressed for the construction of the aqueduct just happened to own more than 100,000 acres of previously unimproved valley land, purchased years before at $5, 10, and 15 the acre. The existence of water for irrigation purposes enabled the syndicate to sell its holdings at prices as high as $1,000 an acre and an eventual profit of somewhere between 50 and 100 million dollars. It was, as one critic called it, no more nor less than a "colossal swindle" perpetrated on the citizens of Los Angeles, who were not to receive full benefit from Owens Valley water for many years—not until the city managed to annex most of the San Fernando Valley.

If the citizens of Los Angeles had been swindled, the farmers of the Owens Valley had been ruined. In the construction of the aqueduct, no provisions for storage in the valley were made; the water was simply siphoned off to the San Fernando Valley, and the Owens Valley land returned to a condition that approached aridity. The few farmers who managed to survive into the 1920s registered a blunt—if somewhat belated—protest when they dynamited the aqueduct in 1924. The break was repaired, and in November the farmers seized the main spillway of the aqueduct and opened it, diverting its entire flow back into the Owens River. Belated or not, the action had at least one major effect: it convinced the city of Los Angeles—by then genuinely desperate for whatever water it could get from any source—to buy up most of the remaining land in the Owens Valley, obtaining full and uncontested use of its water. In 1940, an eleven-mile tunnel was constructed through the mountains from Mono Lake to the Owens River, adding some water to the badly overcommitted stream, and a final imperialistic development was concluded in 1941 when the city constructed the Long Valley Dam and Crowley Lake. Owens Valley was now a suburb of Los Angeles.

The dismal chronicle of southern California's assault on the Owens Valley is by no means representative of the whole story of California's water use, but it is suggestive of the enormously powerful role water had begun to play in the state's life in the early years of the century, a role that crossed political, economic, and emotional lines with equal force. It was by no means a phenomenon exclusive to southern California. However much it might like to forget the fact, San Francisco perpetrated an exercise in water imperialism fully as ambitious—if considerably less sordid—as the Owens Valley adventures of Los Angeles when it went to the Hetch Hetchy Valley of the Sierra Nevada for the bulk of its own water supply. As early as 1901, San Francisco had investigated areas of the Sierra Nevada for potential water sources and had settled on Hetch Hetchy as the logical choice. Since the valley lay within the confines of Yosemite National Park, it was necessary to obtain permission for the construction of a dam and aqueduct from the Department of the Interior. Opposition of surprising force greeted the proposal, spearheaded by the Sierra Club under the direction of John Muir, who stubbornly maintained that the Hetch Hetchy Valley was quite simply too beautiful to be flooded by a reservoir, and supported by farmers in the San Joaquin Valley, who held that the waters that would be trapped behind a dam were necessary to their survival. Nevertheless, by ultimately taking its case to Congress, the city managed to obtain approval of the project in 1913. After the interruption of World War I, construction began in 1919, and by 1934 water stored behind O'Shaughnessy Dam was delivered 150 miles through a series of tunnels and pipes to reservoirs south of San Francisco. Since then, the city has kept up an almost continuous expansion of facilities, both in the Sierra Nevada and in its reservoir systems to the south.

The East Bay cities of Oakland, Berkeley, and Alameda applied similar muscle to the task of tapping the water sources of the Sierra Nevada as early as 1929, so it can hardly be maintained that northern California has exhibited a pristine respect for the ecological balance of an area when it is put up against what it considers its own needs. Still, the fullest and most telling examples of the growth of water imperialism continued—and continue—to be revealed in southern California, which was growing faster and which needed water most. It was not long after the completion of the Owens Valley aqueduct that the region began to cast an acquisitive eye toward its next most visible source: the Colorado River.

The Colorado was an attractive possibility. It coursed 1,750 miles from its source in the Rocky Mountains to its mouth in the

Gulf of California, discharging some 20 million acre-feet of water into the sea every year. It and its tributaries also drained a watershed of more than 245,000 square miles, comprising parts of Wyoming, Utah, Colorado, New Mexico, Nevada, Arizona, and California—not to mention Mexico—and since California's share of this watershed was only some 4,000 square miles, its use of the river was bound to be entangled with the needs, economies, and politics of six other states and one separate nation. This consideration would slow California down, but it would not stop it.

In 1901, the California Development Company, owners, operators, and chief promoters of agricultural land in the Imperial Valley in the southeast foot of the state, cut into the Colorado River near Pilot Knob Mesa, opposite Yuma, and diverted 400,-000 acre-feet of water into the valley via the Imperial Canal. The venture prospered, since the valley's soil was incredibly rich, but it was hampered by the river's intransigent inclination to flood occasionally. In 1905, one such flood smashed the inadequate restraints erected by the company and much of the river's flow drained to the northwest, creating the Salton Sea and destroying farm after farm. By 1911, it was painfully obvious to the Imperial Irrigation District, which had taken over control of the Imperial Canal and all its works from the California Development Company, that a major dam for both storage and flood control was going to be necessary; as well, a new canal would be an attractive addition—since the Imperial Canal was built for most of its length on Mexican soil and the district was committed to deliver up to half the river's diverted flow to rich delta lands below the border. The district not only wanted a new dam and canal—it also wanted the federal government to build them.

The idea was not completely outlandish. In 1902, the United States Reclamation Service (later the Bureau of Reclamation) had been created under the aegis of the Department of the Interior to construct major irrigation and flood-control projects throughout the West. Already, the service had constructed the

Yuma Project on the Colorado River, including Laguna Diversion Dam, and Theodore Roosevelt Dam and Granite Reef Diversion Dam on the Salt River of Arizona. Imperial Valley farmers (they are not to be confused with Jefferson's vision of the yeoman farmer; these were industrialists practicing agribusiness on a spectacular scale) considered their own needs at least equal to those of similar entrepreneurs in Arizona, and in 1917 the Imperial Irrigation District sent its lawyer to Arthur Powell Davis, Reclamation head, in Washington. Davis was persuaded to investigate the situation, and four years later the service recommended the construction of not only a new canal, but of a large water-storage, flood-control, and power-producing dam on the upper reaches of the Colorado. The site ultimately chosen was Boulder Canyon.

Recommendation was not creation. Before anything concrete could be settled, agreement between the states of the Colorado River Basin as to water allotment had to be reached. The attitude of the Upper Basin states (Wyoming, Colorado, and Utah) was articulated by Utah's governor, who proclaimed that "the water should first be captured and used while it is young, for then it can be recaptured as it returns from the performance of its duties and thus be used over and over again." The Lower Basin states, needless to say, disagreed vehemently, and in 1922 Secretary of Commerce Herbert Hoover met with seven state commissioners and after days of haggling managed to hammer out the seven-state Colorado River Compact. It provided that the river's annual average flow of 20.5 million acre-feet be divided as follows: 7.5 million would go to each basin; the Lower Basin was given the right to an additional 1 million acre-feet, if needed; and if any river water was allocated to Mexico through international treaty, it would first come from the surplus above the already apportioned 16.5 million acre-feet. The compact went to each of the state legislatures for ratification, and one by one they all signed it until only Arizona was left.

Arizona refused, convinced that construction of a major storage dam and an Imperial Valley canal would deprive it of its natural right to Colorado water. Moreover, Arizona wanted a dam at Bridge Canyon, some 100 miles upriver from Boulder Canyon, so that it could construct a gravity canal to carry water to the state's parched midsection. Pragmatically, the remaining states rewrote the agreement and passed it through again as a *six*-state Colorado River Compact. Arizona would not ratify the agreement until 1944, and carried on a running fight with California over its share of the Lower Basin allotment until 1964, when the United States Supreme Court ruled that California would have to give up as much as half its annual allotment once Arizona completed its long-dreamed-of gravity canal—the Central Arizona Project.

The farmers of the Imperial Valley acquired an ally in their campaign in 1923 when William Mulholland of the Los Angeles Water and Power District proposed that a second dam be included in the Bureau of Reclamation's plans for the Colorado— this one to store water for diversion to the cities of southern California through a 240-mile aqueduct. The proposal was predictable; the southland had long sinced taxed the capabilities of its ground waters, Owens Valley water was rapidly being exhausted, and the region had entered one more in a long series of population booms that by the end of the decade would see nearly two million people enter southern California and plant roots that had to be nourished with water. Mulholland immediately put in an early bid for more than 1 million acre-feet of water from the Colorado and began the task of organizing the Metropolitan Water District, a conglomeration of municipal water districts assembled from thirteen southern California cities and finally put together in 1927. With the district formed, Mulholland added urban southern California's weight to that of Imperial Valley farmers, and between them the two factions managed to pressure Congress into passage of the Swing-Johnson Bill in December of 1928. The bill authorized the construction of Boulder Dam, the major storage facility, Imperial Dam on the lower reaches of the river, and the All-American Canal, to deliver water to the Imperial Valley. It also provided that California's share of Colorado water be limited to 4.4 million acre-feet a year, plus a share in any surplus in any given year, and up to half the "extra" 1 million acre-feet given to the Lower Basin by the Colorado River Compact. Later, Parker Dam, to store water for use by the Metropolitan Water District, was added to what had become known as the Colorado River Project. And in September of 1931, the voters of the district went to the polls and passed a $220 million bond issue for the construction of the Colorado River Aqueduct.

Construction of Boulder Dam was begun in 1931 and completed in 1935. Parker Dam was completed in 1938, as was Imperial Dam. The Colorado River Aqueduct was finished in 1939 and the All-American Canal in 1940. The total cost of these projects was more than $400 million. It was the most ambitious and costly water development undertaking in the history of the United States up to that time, and the citizens of southern California—city dwellers and agri-industrialists alike—could congratulate themselves on having inspired one of the engineering triumphs of the century, one that would ensure them an adequate water supply for at least another forty years—and who could look beyond forty years?

While southern California was solving its water problem by reaching out to the Colorado River, the state's Central Valley was stumbling toward a confrontation with its own. This valley, one of the most productive agricultural regions in the world and today responsible for most of the state's annual crop production of more than $4 billion, reflects yet another peculiar California phenomenon: some of its richest land is removed from an adequate source of water. The upper portion of the valley, watered by the Sacramento River and its tributaries, contains about one-third of its arable land and two-thirds of its water; the southern portion, watered by the San Joaquin and a few anemic tributaries, contains about two-thirds of the arable land and only about one-third of the water. To juggle matters so that a more reasonable balance might be achieved was the purpose of the Central Valley Project of the 1930s, one of the largest irrigation enterprises in history and one helplessly bound up in a confusing welter of social, political, and economic considerations which even today almost pass comprehension.

The essential confusion in the story of the Central Valley was land monopoly on a phenomenal scale. During the years of its rule between 1822 and 1848, the Mexican government—with the largesse of a drunken shah—disposed of immense tracts of land to certain individuals, enabling such men as the Swiss emigre Johann Augustus Sutter to survey a domain larger than most American counties and some European countries. After American occupation of California, many of these would-be land barons (Sutter included) succumbed to the pressures of the industrial age, selling off their holdings to men with visions of empire, like Henry Miller, California's own cattle king, and to speculators of one ilk or another. The state of California continued in the profligate traditions of the Mexican government (there was so *much* land in California!), allowing great chunks of the public domain to be purchased incredibly cheaply under the provisions of the Swamp Land Act, and taking a somewhat cavalier attitude toward its definitions of exactly what constituted a swamp—a judgmental procedure frequently accelerated by carefully placed bribes. In addition, the state and the federal government both distributed railroad land grants generously, principally to the Southern Pacific Railroad as it built its way south to Los Angeles. As a result much of the best agricultural land in the Central Valley—as well as in many other parts of the state—was firmly locked up in the hands of relatively few owners by the turn of the century. (The tradition continues. Today, of the nearly 4 million acres of arable land on the west side of the San Joaquin Valley, more than 2.5 million are held by individuals or corporations—including the Southern Pacific Railroad and Standard Oil.)

A second source of confusion was in the monopoly of power—energy. As various land companies and corporations controlled much of the agricultural land of the valley, one power company, Pacific Gas and Electric (P. G. & E.), had managed to put together a power empire during the first thirty years of the twentieth century that thoroughly dominated central and northern California.

The land monopolists and the power monopolists were dead set against the Central Valley Project from the beginning, each for reasons of their own. Corporate landowners, having long since gained control of enough water to satisfy their own needs, were instinctively suspicious of a project that might promote competition from significant numbers of small farmers—and later were terrified that the 160-acre limitation provisions of the Reclamation Act of 1902 would be seriously enforced (a fragile possibility, as it turned out). P. G. & E., on the other hand, was unalterably opposed to the possibility that other and cheaper power sources might be generated by public projects. Between them, the two interests managed to entangle the Central Valley Project in a web of emotional, legal, and political issues for more than twenty-five years, a morass from which the project only recently has begun to extricate itself.

The project, which was largely a matter of bringing water from the Sacramento River watershed down to the San Joaquin River for distribution to irrigation districts in the southern end of the valley, was first articulated in the "Marshall Plan" of 1920, a rather simple, two-canal system promoted by a visionary by the name of Robert Bradford Marshall, a retired army engineer. In 1921, a bill (the Water and Power Act) was introduced into the state legislature to give the plan official approval. It was defeated, largely through the lobbying efforts of the P. G. & E. The issue was placed before the people in 1922, 1924, and 1926, but each time the initiative referendum was defeated—again, through the vigorous efforts of the power monopoly in conjunction with the land monopoly.

In 1930, the first California Water Plan was issued by the state. It was the first general inventory of the state's water resources, devoting itself to all phases of the problem, including flood control, saline intrusion from the sea, ground water sources, power, and irrigation. Among its many considerations was a plan for the development of the Central Valley, and this plan became the structural basis for the Central Valley Project Act of 1933. The act called for the construction of Shasta Dam on the far northern reaches of the Sacramento River, the Delta-Mendota Canal, Friant Dam on the San Joaquin River, the Madera Canal, the Friant-Kern Canal, the Contra Costa Canal, and a power transmission system to carry electricity generated at Shasta and Friant Dams. In passing the act, the legislature also called for the issuance of $130 million in revenue bonds to finance the grandiose scheme.

Opponents of Central Valley development set up an immediate howl, the pack led, as usual, by the P. G. & E., which viewed the project's proposed transmission lines as a personal threat. They forced a referendum against the act in December of the year, but in spite of a virulent campaign against it, the voters of the state approved the project by the thin margin of some 33,000 votes, and the state had committed itself to the construction of the most expansive reclamation project in any state's history.

Or had it? The revenue bonds it issued went begging. The depression years, when it sometimes seemed as if the whole world were going bankrupt, were not the best for speculating in bonds or much of anything else. Having conceived, planned, and authorized the project, the state then invited the participation of the Bureau of Reclamation in its completion—in fact, it simply asked the Bureau to take over, since it was obvious that the state could not afford to do it itself. Some observers have maintained that the state legislature never *intended* for California to finance the project, assuming that its approval would guarantee the extension of federal funds for its completion. These were the first generous years of the Rooseveltian revolution, and the government was displaying a ready eagerness to invest in such developments. However devious the legislature's reasoning may have been, the result was the same: the Bureau of Reclamation accepted the state's invitation, and in 1935 President Roosevelt authorized the expenditure of $12 million to begin the project.

The valley's agri-industrialists viewed this turn of events with alarm. They were willing enough to utilize the project's irrigation water, now that it seemed inevitable that it would be completed, but they feared the "catch" that went along with any water delivered from projects executed by the Bureau of Reclamation: the 160-acre limitation law. This law was quite deliberately designed to break up precisely the kind of land monopoly exhibited so dramatically in the Central Valley. It provided that landowners contracting for irrigation water from reclamation projects enter into an agreement to sell their holdings in excess of 160 acres (320 acres under California's community-property statutes) within ten years after the signing of water contracts. Taking little comfort from the fact that in the more than thirty years since its passage the acreage limitation law had not been enforced with any consistency or enthusiasm—certainly not in the Imperial Valley, whose farmers had been some of the earliest beneficiaries of reclamation water—the Kern County Land Company, Standard Oil, the Southern Pacific Railroad, and others of the valley's corporate owners set about attacking the whole business on a number of levels, concentrating on a campaign in California to persuade the state to "take back" ownership of the project and a lobbying effort in Washington to get the limitation provisions stricken from reclamation law. Neither effort succeeded (and has not to this day), but the corporations needn't have worried; the Department of the Interior accommodated them and landowners like them all over the West by either ignoring the law or allowing it to be controverted by any number of vaguely convenient loopholes.

P. G. & E., equally enthusiastic over the proposal that California regain control and ownership of the project, was no more successful in its efforts, and gradually came to an uneasy compromise with the bureau through a complicated agreement concerning distribution and transmission of public power through private facilities.

In the meantime, the Bureau of Reclamation, being a go-ahead organization, went ahead. By 1969, it had constructed not only the original elements of the project contained in the authorization act of 1933, but had added Keswick Dam, Folsom Dam and power plant, Nimbus Dam and power plant, Red Bluff Diversion Dam, San Luis Dam, the Corning Canal, and hundreds of miles of additional canal works. In 1969, the Central Valley Project delivered 4.9 million acre-feet of water into the lower half of the valley, most of it going to agricultural lands. Future elements include Auburn Dam and reservoir on the North Fork of the American River, Folsom South Canal—both under construction—and a number of similar projects, many of them designed to integrate with the State Water Project, among them the East Side Division of the Peripheral Canal (more of this later).

Broad in its scope and complex in its individual parts, the Central Valley Project is in many ways the vestigial expression of what might be called the last great age of American engineering —the reflection of an era when the hard-hat American engineer was viewed as an object of romance, not an agent of destruction. It was a time when such projects as Boulder Dam, Grand Coulee Dam, and the Tennessee Valley Authority were considered celebrations of man's ingenuity, of his ability to take hold of his environment and shape it to his needs. Unlike such other enterprises, however, the Central Valley Project seems destined to go on and on and on, as one element after another is added to the complicated concrete jigsaw—all of this in face of the fact that we have long since learned that engineering expertise is not itself justification enough to allow us to do everything that we *can* do, that we are capable of destroying far more than we create. There are those who maintain that the Central Valley Project, if allowed to continue unchecked, will be infinitely more damaging to the California environment than anything the state itself might consider; unfortunately, in spite of all the hoopla concerning California's so-called "ownership" of the Central Valley Project, the fact remains that it is in its entirety a federal enterprise, financed by federal money, controlled by federal officials, and built by federal engineers. If it is to be halted or revised in any way, the move must be made through the federal government, not the state—and it is axiomatic that the difficulties in implementing change increase geometrically from the state to the federal level.

The enforcement of Reclamation Law continues in a moribund condition. Large landowners still agitate for the removal of the limitation provisions, and the Department of the Interior still acts mostly as if they did not exist, allowing landowners, among other clever maneuvers, to pump water from ground basin storage enriched with project water—a clear evasion of the law. A rare example of implementation took place in 1964, when the Di Giorgio Corporation, which had signed its contract for water in 1952, finally got around to breaking up its $7-million farm and offering the "excess" acreage (i.e., land not entitled to project water) for sale at pre-water prices, as the law stipulates. In auctions held in 1964 and 1965 only three buyers made a bid for the land. Opponents of the 160-acre limitation, of course, have leaped upon this example as evidence that the law, designed to provide "land for the landless," as the U. S. Supreme Court once put it, is unworkable in modern society. At the same time, they shrewdly neglect to mention the fact that accommodating local appraisers so inflated even the pre-water price of the land that no one but a wealthy individual could *afford* to buy it. As it turned out, most of the land went to a San Francisco shipping magnate and his wife, and since neither is a resident of the valley (a condition required by the law) the legality of the sale itself is put in question.

For nearly seventy years, this is how Reclamation Law has been practiced (or not practiced) in California and many other parts of the West. A potential solution to this dismal state of affairs has been proposed in a bill (HR5236) recently introduced by Congressman Robert Kastenmeier, with the support of Congressmen Jerome Waldie and Ron Dellums, among others. Providing for the government purchase of excess lands, the bill would guarantee not only the enforcement of a law deeply founded in the American tradition, but for the first time in our history would implement the intelligent management of our agricultural lands —much as we long ago began to manage (though not always so intelligently) our forest and grazing lands. The essential provisions of the bill have been neatly outlined by Paul S. Taylor, its chief architect and a man who has waged a long and too often lonely crusade for the enforcement of Reclamation Law: "Present law requires sale of excess lands at the pre-water, pre-project price. Government authorization to purchase will provide a ready market, and in turn allow the government to sell or lease with appropriate land-use regulations that will preserve agricultural greenbelts and open spaces and check urban sprawl and slurb. Revenues from sale or lease can be assigned to public purposes including education, the land and water conservation fund, or used simply to replenish the hard-pressed National Treasury." The question is simple enough: the law is there to be used or not used. And if we choose not to use it, then we had better resign ourselves to the fact that reclamation projects costing billions of dollars—and paid for by all the people—will continue to subsidize the agricultural enterprises of a few.

Such are the brief outlines of California's water history between 1850 and 1935, when the Central Valley Project began. It has involved such abstractions as the specter of socialism and the shibboleth of free enterprise; and such realities as engineering skill and money. It has inspired violence and called poets to the defense of the wilderness. It has shaped the course of politics both inside and outside the boundaries of California. It has nurtured the growth of some regions and interrupted the existence of others. Crossing all lines and affecting all interests, it has been the single most important factor in the narrative of the state's history.

However complicated, the story does present two themes essential to an understanding of California's present and future water situation. The first of these is the gradual formation of what can quite legitimately be called a "Water Establishment," a recognizable group whose interests are inextricably bound up with water development and whose influence can and has been felt from the state capital in Sacramento to the national capital in Washington. Its strength and expertise were forged in the hard political, economic, and engineering realities involved in the transportation of water from one place to another. Water in California has created empires, and the Water Establishment is comprised of empire-builders. They know what they are doing.

The Establishment is an urban and agricultural partnership of wide scope. The urban faction is dominated by the Metropolitan Water District of Southern California. From its relatively modest beginnings in 1927 with 13 cities, it has since grown to include more than 100 cities, with a population of more than 10 million people—over 90 percent of the region's entire population and nearly half of California's population. The power it wields in the halls of state government is awesome. The agricultural faction is composed of large landowners in the Imperial Valley and those in the Central Valley—and for all their geographical distance they are powerfully united in one common goal: the privilege of using reclamation water without the inconvenience of reclamation law.

These elements have not always been so closely united as they are today. The Metropolitan Water District and the Imperial Irrigation District engaged in some not-so-gentle bickering over who was to get what during the years when the Colorado River Project was being put together, and when southern Californians voted nearly two-to-one to reject approval of the Central Valley Project Act in 1933, they did not do so out of any sympathy for the "plight" of Central Valley farmers; they simply did not want their tax money going toward the appropriation of water for anyone but themselves. Still, the urban and farming factions slowly grew through the years to a condition of interdependence and the certain knowledge that what was good for one was good for the other—that more water from northern California would enable the Metropolitan Water District to fulfill its obligations and possibly even expand its empire, that it would possibly free more water from the Colorado for use in the Imperial Valley to irrigate cabbages and flush alkaloids, pesticides, and salts from overloaded soils, and that it might enable the farmers of the Central Valley to escape the oppression of Reclamation Law by getting more of their irrigation water from state, rather than federal projects. These were compelling interests, and by the early 1950s they formed the basis of a coalition profoundly influential, hard-headed, and utterly determined to get its way.

The second eminently visible theme is the tyranny of precedent. Simply stated, the theory of water development as it has been revealed in this narrative is one of using as much as you want of what you have, and when that is exhausted, of going out and getting some more, from wherever you have to. If the statement seems harsh and simplistic, consider the fact that southern California cheerfully spent its ground water supply to the point of exhaustion in just forty years. As Carey McWilliams has written: "The artesian water supply was wasted, as a young spendthrift might dissipate a legacy, in a single generation." Consider further the fact that when it reached out to the Owens Valley for more water, southern California made no provisions for the future by the construction of storage dams. And finally, consider the fact that until very recent years, no water-hungry region of the state has seriously thought of investigating sources of water that do not involve the construction of dams somewhere else—even when an increasingly sophisticated technology was in a position to make such schemes practical. It is not an attitude unique to California; similar thinking has so thoroughly dammed up the flow of the Colorado River, diverting almost all of its water to one region or another, that Bureau of Reclamation people are soberly contemplating tapping the sources of the Columbia River in order to help the Colorado River meet its obligations.

Such is the stair-step technique of water development, and nowhere is it more thoroughly advanced than in California, where its implementation has achieved the level of an engineering art and the inviolability of tradition.

Out of these—the growth of a Water Establishment and the tyranny of precedent, themselves molded in the forge of history— have come the energies that produced the California State Water Project, which the Department of Water Resources has described as "an amazing venture." It is indeed, and it may also be the single most disastrous such venture in the history of a state never considered noteworthy for the farsighted use of its resources.

III. The Great Concrete Dream

During the post-depression and World War II years, southern California remained serenely confident that the Colorado River would fill its needs at least until 1980. But in 1946, it discovered it had a population of more than 4 million; in a little over five years, more than 500,000 people had been added to southern California while it wasn't looking. Moreover, the growth continued at an even more accelerated pace in the postwar years, and by the end of the decade Los Angeles alone had leaped from about 1.5 to 2.5 million. This was not supposed to happen, but it did, and southern California once again began to eye the waters of northern California, which had been left untouched since the completion of the last Owens Valley facility nearly ten years before.

Southern California was joined in this speculation by Central Valley landowners seeking an alternative to reclamation water, and the state itself, perhaps regretting the circumstances that had caused it to relinquish control of the Central Valley Project, began giving serious attention to future water development. As early as 1945 a State Water Resources Board was created to investigate present and future water needs. After issuing bulletins on the subject in 1951 and 1955, the board was supplanted by the Department of Water Resources in July of 1956. The following year, the department issued its first official communication, based on its own research and that of its predecessor. It was called "The California Water Plan," and was described as a "master plan for the control, conservation, protection, and distribution of the waters of California, to meet present and future needs for all beneficial uses and purposes in all areas of the state to the maximum feasible extent. It is a comprehensive plan which would reach from border to border both in its constructed works and in its effects. The Plan is a flexible pattern susceptible of orderly development by logical progressive stages, the choice of each successive incremental project to be made with due consideration to the economic and other pertinent factors governing at the particular time."

This remarkable document, comparable to the Book of Genesis in its scope (if not in the grace of its language), was a detailed elaboration upon proposals first suggested in the original Water Plan of 1930—and smacked eloquently of California's traditional patterns of water development. It discussed not only the present and future status of the Central Valley Project, but related it to an enterprise of its own making: the California Water Project, an effort that sought to meet the flood control needs of northern California, the future urban needs of the area south of San Francisco Bay, the irrigation needs of the Central Valley not satisfied by the Central Valley Project, the future urban needs of the central coastal region—which it reasonably predicted would become a metropolis second in size only to Greater Los Angeles and the San Francisco Bay Area—and, most cosmic of all, the future urban needs of southern California. Heavily based upon projections of population increase and agricultural expansion to the year 2020, the Project outline was a profound articulation of that venerable premise: get water from where it is and haul it to where it is needed—or is going to be needed.

Where it was, the report had decided, was on the Feather River watershed, some seventy miles north of Sacramento. As early as 1951, the Water Resources Board had recommended the diversion of four million acre-feet of water from the Feather River to the south, and the legislature had approved the idea in principle. Further study determined the proposal's broad outlines, and in 1955 it was submitted for independent review to the Bechtel Corporation, an engineering consulting firm. The firm's report was favorable enough for the Feather River Project to take its place as the central feature of the California Water Plan of 1957.

In 1959, after more studies, the Department of Water Resources issued its concluding report, which applied itself to the specifics of the whole business. The Project's essential components included a large storage, flood-control, and power-producing dam on the Feather River in the vicinity of Oroville, which would regulate the delivery of water into the Sacramento River and ultimately to the "pool" of the Sacramento-San Joaquin Delta. North of the Delta, an aqueduct would deliver water to a terminus in Marin County. South of the Delta, a similar aqueduct would deliver water to a terminus in Santa Clara County, and a major aqueduct would take water south along the west side of the San Joaquin Valley. Near the border between Kings and Kern Counties, a branch would deliver water to the central coastal region, and after crossing the Tehachapi Mountains the main aqueduct would branch again, a west section carrying water to a terminus south of the San Fernando Valley and an east section transporting it across the Antelope and Mojave plateaus, through the San Bernardino Mountains, and finally to a terminus near the city of Riverside. From this latter terminus, connections would be made to the Coachella Valley and the

Colorado River Aqueduct systems. When completed, the project would be capable of delivering up to eight million acre-feet of water annually.

Although some of the cost of the project would be absorbed by federal flood-control funds, the state's share in its construction was estimated to be about $2.5 billion, in itself an item that more than justified the department's later description of the plan as "an unprecedented water project." Financing would be through the issuance and sale of state bonds, which would then be repaid (including interest at 5 percent) from monies received from water districts utilizing project water and from the sale of electrical power.

Armed with this grand scheme and backed enthusiastically by the Water Establishment, the Department of Water Resources requested authorization from the state legislature. It was forthcoming in the last weeks of the 1959 session in the form of the California Water Resources Development Bond Act—more simply known as the Burns-Porter Act—which authorized the issuance of $1.75 billion in general-obligation bonds (not enough to complete the project, but all that the legislature felt it could reasonably get away with at the time and more than enough to begin it), gave the project official articulation, and placed the proposition on the ballot for the general election of November 8, 1960.

In keeping with the "flexible pattern susceptible of orderly development" proclaimed by the Water Plan, the language of the Burns-Porter Act was sufficiently general to give the new State Water Project an air of vagueness that would enable the Department of Water Resources to add, expand, or delete various elements of the project more or less as it saw fit, a consideration of no little significance, as later events were to prove. In the words of the act, the general-obligation bonds were to fund the construction of:

(1) A multiple purpose dam and reservoir on the Feather River in the vicinity of Oroville, Butte County. . . .

(2) An aqueduct system which will provide for the transportation of water from a point or points at or near the Sacramento-San Joaquin Delta to terminii in the Counties of Marin, Alameda, Santa Clara, Santa Barbara, Los Angeles and Riverside and for delivery of water both at such terminii and at canalside points en route. . . .

(3) Master levees, control structures, channel improvements, and appurtenant facilities in the Sacramento-San Joaquin Delta for water conservation, water supply in the Delta, transfer of water across the Delta, flood and salinity control, and related functions.

(4) Facilities for removal of drainage water from the San Joaquin Valley.

(5) Facilities for the generation and transmission of electrical energy.

(6) Provision for water development facilities for local areas. . . .

(7) Including for the foregoing . . . the relocation of utilities and highways and acquisitions of all lands, rights of way, easements, machinery, equipment, apparatus, and all appurtenances necessary or convenient therefor. . . .

In the months between the passage of the Burns-Porter Act in 1959 and the election of November, 1960, the voters of the state were assaulted by propaganda whose intensity was reminiscent of the 1907 election in southern California which had authorized construction of the Owens Valley Aqueduct. The emotional level was understandable; the $1.75 billion the voters were being asked to approve was the largest such bond issue yet considered by anybody, anywhere. For their part, the Department of Water Resources and its advocates (chief among them Governor Edmund G. Brown) thrust forward the population figure of more than 28 million people in southern California projected for the year 2020, a population whose needs could only be met if the citizens of the state took visionary action without delay and authorized the only feasible alternative to meeting that future demand: the California Water Project. Further, they maintained that their studies had shown that the bonds could be sold without difficulty, that there would be more than enough demand for project water and power to repay the bonds, and that the taxpayers were therefore not really committing themselves to anything since the state, in effect, was simply authorizing a self-paying proposition.

These arguments were assailed by critics of the measure, chiefly the *San Francisco Chronicle,* which unloosed a stream of editorials and articles ("The Water Hoax") and whose political cartoonist, the late Robert Bastian, enshrined the project forever in a series of drawings that depicted it as California's new "Octopus." For the state to indebt itself so profoundly in order to meet the presumed needs of a generation sixty years removed, the *Chronicle* stated, was an action that bordered on the insane; no one could be certain what those needs would be or how they might be met by an increasingly sophisticated technology. "If the voters go ahead," warned the *Chronicle,* "they are taking a desperate plunge into the unknown. The plan is a juggernaut. . . ." This view received some support shortly before the election from an unexpected quarter, when the majority report of a board of consultants retained by the Department of Water Resources issued a gentle disclaimer amid its generally favorable language: "Projections of growth of population and water demand contain elements of speculation and may prove erroneous for periods in the more distant future. . . . We question the wisdom of building at the outset in accordance with present anticipations of the total demands and technologies of the remote future."

The very fact that this report was issued long after the Department of Water Resources had managed to place the issue on the ballot seemed to strengthen another criticism: that the department had not fully and properly investigated the project's potentials and shortcomings before attempting to give it the force of law. Certainly, this was the argument of the board of consultants' minority report by Adolph J. Ackerman, who wrote: "Any inference at this stage that a proposed project has had the benefit of a complete engineering study and represents the best product of the engineering profession, in which the public can repose full confidence, is in my opinion wholly unwarranted."

The principal argument against the project, however, was one of economics. First, the opponents said, there was no guarantee that the bonds, once issued, would in fact be sold; if not, then the taxpayer would have to go directly to his pocket to keep the project going. Second, they maintained that the department had been superbly vague about the fact that the $1.75 billion was not going to be enough to complete the project; that being so, they asked, where was the additional money to come from? Thirdly, they pointed out that little attention had been paid to the inflationary increase likely in construction costs; the department's financial projections had been based on 1960 cost rates. And finally, they noted that the demand for water and power ultimately designed to pay off the state's indebtedness was based on those very projections termed ephemeral and unreliable by the department's own board of consultants. Under these conditions, the *Chronicle* stated, the proposition was little more than a "blank check to irresponsibility, a compound of unfulfillable promises."

For all its colorful rhetoric, the *Chronicle* was putting forth reasonable questions—questions made even more reasonable in the light of consequent developments. And it was not alone in asking them. Among other organizations and individuals stoutly opposing passage of the bond issue was the California Labor Federation of the AFL-CIO, which objected to what it called the water proponents' "panic-button" approach to the problem. The union also scotched the idea that opponents of the department's project were ipso facto opponents of water development of any kind:

We are told (said the union) that it is water that is important! We've got to get it to the people before it's too late! Don't rock the boat! And finally, look at all those jobs. . . . It must be stated emphatically that the question is not one of whether we favor moving ahead on water and power developments—everybody favors development. Everybody knows that the federal government can't and won't do the job alone. Everybody knows that the state must enter the water and power business along with the federal government, local districts and municipalities.

But under what policies? And at what price? Any price?

The opposition to the project's approval was an impressive performance, but not enough to overcome the logic of tradition and the tyranny of precedent. On November 8, 1960, the voters of California passed the measure by a vote of 3,008,328 to 2,814,384. It was not one of the largest margins of victory in the history of California bond issues, but it was sufficient. The State Water Project, the great concrete dream, was a reality— at least on paper.

The energies stored up in the Department of Water Resources through the years, nourished by all the reports and studies and grandiose imaginings, were turned loose on the California landscape with a kind of frantic fury, almost as if the department were proceeding on the theory (perhaps not unreasonable) that the more it finished as soon as it could, the less was likely to be taken away from it. A contract on Oroville Dam, the project's central storage facility on the Feather River, was let for $121 million in July of 1962. The dam was "topped out" in 1967 at 770 feet, which made it the tallest dam in the United States, and water began backing up behind it into the deep, tangled wilderness of the Feather River Canyon, eventually inundating the aging Gold Rush village of Whiskeytown. By July of 1969, Oroville Lake had reached its capacity of 3,537,577 acre-feet and was beginning its first summer release of water into the Sacramento River system through its Thermolito Diversion Dam, forebay, and afterbay systems.

Other essential, if less dramatic, components of the project were completed and functioning by the end of the decade, including the Delta Pumping Plant near Tracy, designed to pump water from the south end of the Delta into the California Aqueduct, the main conveyor of water to the south. Seven pumps were operational by 1969, and four more were planned for operation by 1983. The South Bay Aqueduct, too, was operational, including the South Bay Pumping Plant, Del Valle Pumping Plant, and Lake Del Valle. The San Luis Reservoir, a facility whose cost and water were shared equally with the Bureau of Reclamation's Central Valley Project, was completed in 1967 and by 1969 had achieved its capacity of two million acre-feet of storage. Fifteen miles of the Coastal Branch of the California Aqueduct had been completed and water was being delivered to Kern County land. The aqueduct itself was complete from the Delta to the massive pumping stations at the foot of the Tehachapi Mountains, and the department had every expectation that the facilities for conveying the water across the mountains to a terminus at Lake Castaic in northern Los Angeles County would be complete no later than the end of 1971.

By now, the California Water Project had grown to dimensions that must have surpassed the wildest imaginings of its founders, as the department took full advantage of the broad scope of the Burns-Porter Act. Its components—either constructed, under construction, or planned—included twenty-one dams and reservoirs with a total capacity of 6,825,957 acre-feet, a surface area of 57,900 acres, and 525 miles of shoreline; six major aqueducts with a combined length of nearly 685 miles, including 20 miles of tunnels; twenty-two pumping plants to lift and push water (whose energy requirements for the job were estimated at more than 13 billion kilowatt-hours); and six power plants capable of generating more than 5 billion kilowatt-hours of electricity.

Buried in all this triumphant statistical morass was the department's first major addition to the structural outlines of the California Water Project, one "authorized" by the Burns-Porter Act only if its language was bent to the breaking point and one that would later become a major point of controversy. By both the Department of Water Resources and the Bureau of Reclamation, whose pumps for delivery of water to the Delta-Mendota Canal were also situated near Tracy, the Sacramento-San Joaquin Delta was utilized as a "pool," a great natural reservoir for the storage of water delivered from northern watersheds through the Sacramento River system. Unfortunately, the Delta inevitably was contaminated with sewage and agricultural wastes and by the intrusion of salt water from San Francisco Bay. Fresh water delivered from the Shasta Reservoir of the Central Valley Project and the Oroville Reservoir of the California Water Project was too often "lost" into San Francisco Bay or severely subverted by wastes and salt.

To solve this dilemma, state and federal agencies put their heads together and considered the language of the Burns-Porter Act, which authorized the construction of facilities for the "transfer of water across the Delta." This seemed justification enough for them to come up with a "joint-use facility" called the Peripheral Canal—*around* the Delta. The canal would be a forty-three mile ditch more than 600 feet wide and 30 feet deep, beginning at Hood on the Sacramento River and ending near the Tracy pumping plants of the Bureau of Reclamation and the Department of Water Resources. Planned to handle a total of about 9 million acre-feet of water annually by the year 2020, the canal would have an actual capacity of more than 15 million acre-feet, a deliberate overcapacity designed to take care of seasonal inflows and to divert flood flows. Never a specific facility foreseen by the Burns-Porter Act, the Peripheral Canal by the end of the 1960s was an integral and "absolutely essential" ingredient of the State Water Project—although still on the drawing board. Complicating this affair was the Bureau of Reclamation's proposal that a branch, or division, of its own be tacked on to the Peripheral Canal; called the East Side Canal, this division would divert another 2,500,000 acre-feet annually from the fresh-water flow of the Delta.

While pushing facilities through to completion and expanding its plans to include items like the Peripheral Canal, the Department of Water Resources applied equal energy to another necessary task: the securing of water contracts from the municipalities, districts, and agencies whose projected needs were supposed to be satisfied by the State Water Project. On November 4, 1960— four days before the Burns-Porter Act was approved by the state's voters—the department negotiated a prototype contract with the Metropolitan Water District of Southern California, and when the legality of the contract was declared valid by the State Supreme Court in 1963, proceeded to negotiate additional contracts in regions scattered from the city of Yuba to the Ventura County Flood Control District. By the end of 1968, every bit of the project's 4,230,000 acre-feet of annual entitlement water had been contracted for by one agency or another.

The largest single user would be southern California, whose districts contracted for a total of 2,497,500 acre-feet a year; a little over 2 million acre-feet of this total, however, went to but one agency: the Metropolitan Water District. The San Joaquin Valley area, the second largest contractor, committed itself to 1,355,000 acre-feet, but again more than 1 million of this was contracted for by but one district: the Kern County Water Agency. The remainder of the total was distributed among districts in the upper Feather River area, the area north of San Francisco Bay, the area south of the Bay, and the central coastal area of Santa Barbara and San Luis Obispo Counties. By the end of 1969, these agencies had paid more than $97 million in principal and interest toward project construction.

Altogether, then, the department was justified in viewing this ten-year period as its "Action Decade." It had spent some $1.5 billion toward the construction of nearly 70 percent of the project's facilities, and the sheer bulk of its achievement was a matter of no little departmental pride. But something else was equally apparent by the end of the "Action Decade": the golden age of the water expropriator was nearing an end. Listing the department's accomplishments for 1969 in a special publication for March, 1970, Director William R. Gianelli included the following unremarkable statement: "We completed and reported on a special study of alternatives for Eel River development requested by Governor Reagan." Muted within those words is the story of the department's first major confrontation with project opponents since the election of 1960—a confrontation which resulted in its first unqualified defeat.

IV. Dams, Drains, and Canals

From the point of view of water developers, California's North Coast region is a great natural resource simply going to waste. Every year, nearly 30 million acre-feet of water in this area is washed into the sea, untapped, unutilized, free. Here are some of the last wild rivers left in California, chief among them the Trinity, the Eel, and the Klamath, and some of the largest sections of wilderness country not yet blessed with concrete. This lamentable state of affairs has been a source of no little frustration for the water engineers.

As early as 1951, the Bureau of Reclamation proposed that the Klamath River be dammed and that six million acre-feet of water be diverted "to irrigators, industries, and municipalities in the Central Valley of California, and central- and south-coastal areas of the State." This scheme was supplanted by the state's own Feather River Project, but federal interest in the region continued. After a period of particularly damaging floods in the mid-1950s, the U. S. Army Corps of Engineers began intensive studies of flood-control projects for the area in 1956. In 1964, it received the active support of the Department of Water Resources, for by then the Corps' plans had swollen to dimensions far beyond simple flood control.

In a December, 1967, *Interim Report* to the Army's Board of Engineers for Rivers and Harbors, the Corps called for the construction of a dam on the Middle Fork of the Eel River three miles upstream from the town of Dos Rios, an earth-fill dam 730 feet high and with a reservoir capacity of 7.6 million acre-feet. Its purposes were to "reduce substantially future flood damage in the Eel River Basin; provide additional water supply to meet the State of California Water Project requirements which are required by about 1985; provide a potential for hydroelectric power; and meet the expanding public need for water-oriented outdoor recreational opportunities." One of the project's most dramatic features was the Grindstone Diversion Tunnel, a twenty-one-mile hole through the Coast Range designed to carry water to Grindstone Creek in Glenn County, and from there through the Sacramento River system to the Delta pool. The Corps estimated that its total cost would be $398 million, of which the state of California was expected to contribute $153 million for the construction of the Grindstone Diversion Tunnel.

For years, the Corps had sulked in the shadow of the "glamour boys" of the dam-building business, the Bureau of Reclamation, whose immense projects all over the West diminished by comparison those of the Corps. Yet here was a dam of a size to challenge the best that the bureau had ever thrown together. The Department of Water Resources was delighted. For the relatively "minor" cost of the diversion tunnel, it would get the biggest dam in its entire system, one that would nourish the Delta's supply of water when it inevitably reached the point of depletion. It was stair-step water development at its finest, and the department threw its full weight behind the project. Particularly enthusiastic was William R. Gianelli, a Reagan appointee and a vigorous, articulate champion of colossal water development projects.

Almost immediately, the *Interim Report* encountered criticism by Professor Gardner B. Brown Jr., an economist at the University of Washington and one of the most respected analysts of water development projects in the United States. The report, he determined, was a statistical disaster and a prime example of optimistic bloat.

Utilizing the "benefit-cost ratio," the Corps had come up with a ratio of 1.9 to 1.0—$1.90 in benefits for every dollar in cost. The benefits were based on the sale of water ($26.1 million annually by the Corps' estimate), the savings in flood damage ($1.5 million), the sale of hydroelectric power ($210,000), and recreational uses of the reservoir ($1.21 million). But from the report's own facts and statistical methods, Brown calculated a .6 to 1.0 benefit-cost ratio—sixty cents in benefits for every dollar in cost. The actual cost of the Dos Rios Project, he said, was underestimated by at least 12 percent (adding $47 million to the total cost) and the benefits were variously *over*estimated: water-sale benefits by more than 60 percent (an annual revenue loss of about $18.5 million), flood control benefits by 17 percent (a $260,000 loss), hydropower benefits by 20 percent (a $40,000 loss), and recreation benefits by 10 percent (a $120,000 loss).

The discrepancy in cost figures, Brown said, was based on the fact that the Corps had allowed only a 20 percent contingency for price inflation between 1967, the year the project was proposed, and 1980, the year it was expected to be completed—but actual costs for similar projects had risen more than 30 percent in the same period of time. Moreover, he pointed out, the Corps' record in the construction of some 167 previous projects had shown that actual costs had been as much as *double* the original estimates. Said Brown: "No private construction company could have remained in business with such a performance record."

The benefit from the sale of water, according to the report, was predicated on the assumption that Dos Rios would deliver

700,000 acre-feet of water to the California Water Project every year—even though, as Brown noted, the Department of Water Resources itself maintained that except during exceptionally dry years no more than 250,000 acre-feet would be exported. Recreation benefits were based on the assumption that the reservoir would enjoy two million tourist visits a year. But what possible delights could be found in a lake whose surface level could fluctuate as much as 150 feet in either direction as Dos Rios water was stored, then flushed out during the summer months through the Grindstone Diversion Tunnel? The hydropower benefits were so minimal as to be ludicrous; the 4,800 kilowatt-hours predicted would have supplied only enough power to juice 263 homes. Finally, the flood-control benefit claimed by the Corps began to disintegrate when Brown pointed out that the report had claimed a flood-control benefit for Round Valley behind Dos Rios Dam—*a valley that would be inundated by 300 feet of water.*

The Corps replied to Brown's analysis of its report on October 17, 1968, when Colonel Frank C. Boerger presented a forty-one-page "Statement" before a joint public hearing of the California Senate and Assembly Committees on Water Resources. Critics of the *Interim Report* were disposed of quickly: "In some of the testimony presented on the Dos Rios Project we have found that some facts have been introduced in a negative context so that it is not always clear that they are facts. . . ." After issuing this masterpiece of obfuscation, Boerger dismissed the ability of anyone but a Corps specialist to comprehend the mysterious institutional expertise compiled in the report, then went on to reiterate all the good reasons why Dos Rios should be completed as soon as possible.

He was backed up by Gianelli, who insisted that Dos Rios was absolutely necessary if California's water needs were to be met by 1985. In taking this stand so vigorously and so vocally, Gianelli managed to cripple his own credibility, for it was in direct contradiction of the conclusions arrived at by his own engineers just two months earlier in a report entitled *Present and Future Water Supply and Demand in the South Coast Area:* "Contrary to general opinion that there would be a supplemental water demand by 1990, present and future supply is adequate to 2000. This ten-year difference has important economic consequences, since it means that investment in new importation facilities [including the Dos Rios Project] can be postponed ten years longer than was anticipated."

Economic objections were soon linked with environmental and social criticisms. If completed, the Dos Rios Dam would have flooded Round Valley, a prosperous farming region; destroyed the town of Covelo, forced the removal of 350 Indians from the Round Valley Indian Reservation, and inundated 400 ancient Indian burial sites, some perhaps 9,000 years old, a prospect loudly deplored by anthropologists and archeologists. Further, it would have reduced the flow of the Eel River to a miserable trickle and seriously threatened the annual chinook salmon and steelhead runs. The Corps had solutions to each of these problems, but conservationists considered them inadequate to replace what certainly would have been lost had the dam gone into construction.

Citing both the economic and environmental nightmares inherent in the Dos Rios Project, conservation organizations—chief among them the Round Valley Conservation League, the Save the Eel River Association, the Sierra Club, and California Tomorrow—began a vigorous campaign against the project in 1968, and by early 1969 had gathered support from such individuals and organizations as State Senator Randolph Collier, the Mendocino County Board of Supervisors, the Mendocino County Farm Bureau, the Mendocino County Flood Control and Water Conservation District, the state Department of Fish and Game, the state Department of Parks and Recreation, and many newspapers, among them the *San Francisco Chronicle* and the *Sacramento Bee*. The pressure exerted by this coalition was considerable. It was reflected in February, 1969, when the state Senate's prestigious nine-member Committee on Water Resources reversed its earlier recommendation of the project, further reflected when Norman B. Livermore Jr., Secretary of the California Resources Agency, recommended against it, and was finally and triumphantly reflected when Governor Reagan ordered the Department of Water Resources to abandon the Dos Rios Project and investigate other, less ruinous possibilities.

Without California's commitment to finance the Grindstone Diversion Tunnel, the Corps of Engineers could not build its lovely dam.

The Department of Water Resources, of course, could not be blamed for the peculiar idiocies of the Corps of Engineers' *Interim Report;* in fact, the department's own evaluation of the Dos Rios Project was consistently more subdued and reasonable. Nevertheless, by virtue of Gianelli's role as the John the Baptist of the project, the state agency was inextricably involved in it, a fact that strengthened the criticism of a growing body of skeptical economists and conservationists. These critics realized that the defeat of the Dos Rios Project did not by any means dissuade the department from considering the Eel River a major source of future water for the south. The department made no bones about that. Late in 1969 it stated that "the gentle, nearly sea-level terrain of the Delta forms a natural pool of fresh water through which all excess water in the Central Valley drains prior to wasting to the ocean. The State Water Project diverts a portion of this excess water. Eventually, increasing water use in the Sacramento Valley will so deplete the natural drainage to the Delta that the Middle Fork Eel River Development will have to be added to the Project. This development will supplement Delta flows with Eel River water which would otherwise waste to the ocean."

The course of water development, obviously, was going to continue in its old pattern, threatening the future with the tenets of the past. It was about time, critics said, that we took another and closer look at the whole concept of water engineering; and as criticism of the Project mounted it centered on two basic considerations: environment and economics.

So far, the Project had not been ruinously destructive to the California landscape. True, the Oroville Dam had destroyed one of the wildest canyons in the Sierra Nevada and crippled the flow of one of its major rivers, but the flood-control benefits it provided to the Sacramento River Plain were considerable; it could be lived with. Similarly, the Project's other facilities, while certainly damaging in one degree or another, had been short of disaster. But what would happen, the critics wanted to know, if the course of water development continued in its stair-step traditions? If the Eel River were dammed up to make up for deficiencies in the Sacramento, how long would it be before the Trinity River was dammed to make up for deficiencies in the Eel, the Klamath was dammed up to make up for deficiencies in the Trinity, the Rogue was dammed up to make up for deficiencies in the Klamath—and so on, until every free-running river on the Pacific Slope was part of an enormous pipeline? Was this not where current water development was taking us—and was the destruction worth it?

Critics were not impressed with the recreational benefits put forward by the department as one of the basic joys of the California Water Project, in spite of the shimmering promise in a handout prepared by the department for use in schools: "The State Water Project gives us new lakes where the youngsters can swim, father can fish, and mother can relax in the shade of a tree." Yet the great bulk of California's reservoir space for recreation before the Water Project—a total of 16,608,270 acre-feet—was located, like the water itself, in areas where it was least needed. Butte, Merced, and Trinity Counties, for example, while possessing only 1.07 percent of the state's population, were blessed with 51.36 percent of the state's reservoir space. The city of Los Angeles, on the other hand, with 35 percent of the state's population, had not one single reservoir for recreational use. The California Water Project was not likely to correct this imbalance. The Project's only major southern reservoirs, when complete, would provide only 529,000 acre-feet of recreation space between them—hardly enough to satisfy the needs of a population of more than 11 million.

Aside from such general observations, those concerned with the Project's impact on the environment have concentrated on two of its major proposed facilities: the San Joaquin Valley Master Drain (or the San Luis Drain) and the Peripheral Canal. The former project, unlike the Peripheral Canal, was specified in the terms of the Burns-Porter Act. Historically, the San Joaquin River acted as a natural "drain" for the waters of the San Joaquin Valley, transporting them into the Delta and ultimately San Francisco Bay. As agriculture expanded in the valley, the content of dissolved salts, pesticides, and other chemicals in the river's waters steadily increased; at the same time, irrigation demands on its water reduced its flow and subverted its ability to dilute its chemical load to levels capable of supporting life. Replenishment of fresh water from the Friant and Delta-Mendota Canals of the Central Valley Project, and later the California Aqueduct, was not enough, and the San Joaquin rapidly became an agricultural sewer whose water was unfit for irrigation—much less human consumption.

To solve this problem, the Department of Water Resources and the Bureau of Reclamation conceived of an artificial drain that would transport used water, with all its salts, nutrients, and pesticides intact, to the west end of the Delta—and dump it in. The ecological implications were profound: nutrients could contribute to the eutrophication of the Delta and even parts of San Francisco Bay, salts would only intensify the Delta's constant struggle to keep a proper balance between fresh and saline water, and the presence of massive amounts of pesticides would be lethal.

Writing in the Spring 1969 issue of *Cry California*, the journal of California Tomorrow, water specialist Frank M. Stead characterized the proposed drain as California's *Cloaca Maxima* and pointed out that creating a new drain in order to clean up an old drain was doing nothing to solve the *real* problem. This and other responses were so vigorous that the Department of Water Resources flinched from pursuing the project with much enthusiasm. Abandoned? Not at all—the department apparently never "abandons" any idea. In its *Bulletin* for March, 1970, the item "San Joaquin Drainage Facilities" was included as part of the whole Project; it sits there, like "Middle Fork Eel River," waiting for something good to happen. The Bureau of Reclamation, older and presumably less vulnerable to the wisp of public opinion, has revised the concept and commenced construction of what it calls the "San Luis Drain," a somewhat scaled-down but no less deadly proposal with precisely the same purpose.

Opposition to the joint-use facility of the Peripheral Canal has been even more intense, since it is potentially the single most devastating element in the entire California Water Project. Director Gianelli continues to insist in the face of a growing pile of contradictory evidence that the canal is good for the Delta, good for the California Water Project (not to mention the Central Valley Project), and good for us. Moreover, Gianelli blandly asserts that the canal is practically a *fait accompli,* from a legislative standpoint, basing that assertion on his own interpretation of the language of the Burns-Porter Act of 1959 (as noted earlier). "The Canal," he has said, "is an integral part of the Project, and, as such, has already been authorized by the State Legislature and approved by the voters." In the light of that statement, it should be emphasized once again that neither the state legislature nor the voters envisioned a canal *around* the Delta when they approved provisions for the "transfer of water *across* the Delta" (italics supplied).

Equally unanticipated by the voters was the Bureau of Reclamation's East Side Canal, a proposed tentacle of the Peripheral Canal that would siphon off another 2,500,000 acre-feet for diversion into the plumbing system of the Central Valley Project.

Since it is the larger and potentially more damaging of the two proposals, the Peripheral Canal has received the bulk of criticism; yet the East Side Canal is a genuine menace in its own right. In conjunction with the Peripheral Canal it would significantly deplete the Delta's fresh-water supply. What is more, the bureau's addition to the project is not dependent upon completion of the Peripheral Canal itself; the bureau would much prefer to have it hooked up to the primary canal, but if things don't work out, the agency fully intends to proceed on its own—much as it has proceeded with the San Luis Drain. This is a fact worth remembering as we consider the sundry pitfalls inherent in any kind of canal system for the Delta.

The 1,100-square-mile Delta is a delicate triangle of waters laced through rich peat-island farmlands, a transition area between the salt water of San Francisco Bay and the fresh water of the Sacramento-San Joaquin rivers and their tributaries. Such a blend has produced an enchanting estuarine web of life. The Delta is one of the few large estuaries left in the United States and the only one of its kind in California. But the fragile natural balance that has created it is uncommonly vulnerable to the works of man, particularly his waterworks, and it is already seriously damaged. The original fresh-water flow to the Delta of 30 million acre-feet a year has been reduced to about 18 million acre-feet by existing diversions from the Sacramento and San Joaquin rivers and by pumping operations in the South Delta region by the Bureau of Reclamation and the California Water Project. Municipal and agricultural wastes dumped into both the Delta and San Francisco Bay have significantly altered the quality of the region's water and already resulted in a number of major fish and bird kills. As conceived, the Peripheral Canal could be the *coup de grace* not only for the Delta but for San Francisco Bay itself.

That, at any rate, is the conclusion of conservationists—a conclusion supported by evidence from state and federal studies and by the opinions of a number of biologists and ecologists familiar with the natural requirements of the Bay and the Delta. Predictably, sober opposition to the canal has been met by Director Gianelli with accusations of "emotionalism" and princely unconcern for the facts of the matter. Consider as one example a speech given by Gianelli on September 25, 1970, to the League of Women Voters of Los Angeles County:

> Here are some of the accusations leveled at the Peripheral Canal:
>   1. "It will cause salt water intrusion in the Delta."
> FACT: The Peripheral Canal, when in operation, will actually release fresh water into the Delta from an easterly direction to (1) freshen up the dead-end sloughs that, for years, have not received an adequate amount of fresh water; and, (2) maintain the salinity intrusion line to a point *west* of the Delta.

True, the canal has been designed to release amounts of fresh water into the Delta as it carries water south to the pumping plants at Tracy. That amount is 1,500 to 1,800 cubic feet per second. But a report by the Kaiser Engineers prepared in 1969 for the San Francisco Bay-Delta Water Quality Control Program, a state agency, maintains that no less than 3,000 cubic feet per second is going to be necessary, and 5,000 would be preferable, both to hold back salt-water intrusion from San Francisco Bay and to dilute sufficiently the Delta's load of pollutants and nutrients—a factor Gianelli grandly ignored. He continued:

>   2. "The Canal will take 80 percent of the flow of the Sacramento River and deliver it to Los Angeles."
> FACT: At its maximum entitlement point—in 1990—the city of Los Angeles will receive only a small share of the approximately 2 million acre-feet of water per year delivered from the State Water Project to all of Southern California. This is hardly 80 percent of the flow of the Sacramento River.

This statement is almost admirable in its arrogance. First, it implies a kind of insane hatred of Los Angeles as the main point of canal critics, which simply is not true. Moreover, to this author's knowledge no critic has ever *made* such an accusation, and Gianelli does not document his "quotation." Second, southern California's annual entitlement is not "approximately 2 million acre-feet"; it is precisely 2,497,500 acre-feet, a considerable difference. Finally, it totally by-passes the meat of the objection, which is that the canal *will* divert up to 80 percent of the Sacramento's flow, and that fresh-water deliveries to the Delta and the Bay will be completely at the discretion of the bureau and the Department of Water Resources, as Contra Costa Congressman Jerome R. Waldie, one of the Project's most vigorous critics, has pointed out: "The menace of the Peripheral Canal lies with the fact that it gives virtual control of the entire Sacramento River and Delta to the U. S. Bureau of Reclamation and the State Department of Water Resources. . . . We fear that almost the entire flow of the Sacramento River will be diverted southward . . . with tragic consequences to the Bay-Delta area."

Gianelli wrapped up his "argument" with the following:

> 3. "It (the canal) will pollute San Francisco Bay."
> FACT: There is no way that a canal carrying surplus floodwater flow can pollute a salt-water bay. The accusation comes from those who contend that the canal would divert fresh-water flows that would normally have gone through the Bay system. The canal *would* divert some of the flood flows but then part of it would be returned to the Delta and to the Bay through the canal's release facilities. . . .

Again, one wonders where Gianelli got his "quotation," for this has *not* been the accusation of critics. As Kaiser engineers illustrated in 1969, reduced fresh-water inflows (and we have already seen how inadequate are the planned "releases") would subvert the ability of the Delta and the Bay to handle the pollution *that already exists.* A "wedge" of salt water creeping up into the Delta beneath a layer of fresh water would spread that fresh water westward toward the Bay, growing shallower and shallower as it went—and becoming so thick with its own pollutants that it would be incapable of diluting new ones. Such a condition would also create "nutrient traps," bodies of fresh water so shallow and so warmed by the sun that oxygen-consuming algae would proliferate, destroying the water's ability to support any other kind of life and producing what is known as eutrophication. Secondly, the "flushing" action which keeps San Francisco Bay clean—or relatively clean—is profoundly dependent upon large amounts of fresh water, together with tidal action from the sea. Testifying before a congressional committee in August of 1969, Gianelli dismissed this dependency: "Tidal action is the principal mechanism by which pollutants are alternately removed from the Bay. . . . The effects of tidal dispersion of wastes far overwhelm the effects of river outflows from the Delta." But a report by the U. S. Geological Survey in July, 1970, contradicted Gianelli's contention, maintaining that fresh-water inflows were at least as important to flushing action as tidal movement, and that the southern arm of the Bay was particularly dependent upon fresh water from the Delta region since it possessed no significant fresh water source of its own. The report said:

> Water-quality characteristics of south bay are influenced primarily by inflow of fresh water, man-made wastes, and tidal exchanges of water of varying salinity. Changes in any of these controls could have significant effects on the overall quality of the bay. This report qualitatively demonstrates that high and low seasonal inflows of fresh water to the bay's Sacramento River delta correlate inversely with salinity and phosphate concentration in the south bay. It suggests that net fresh water flow to the bay from this source is a major quality control under present conditions. Additional investigations are warranted to establish long-term significance of this suggested coupling.

Additional investigations are warranted. . . . One of the main objections of canal critics is that neither the Bureau of Reclamation nor the Department of Water Resources has made adequate studies of the potential effects of the Peripheral Canal. In traditional fashion, these agencies have simply plunged ahead on the strength of traditional logic—do it now, investigate later. Fortunately, the project has been attacked so enthusiastically from so many different quarters that on January 8, 1971, Director Gianelli—without once conceding that he might actually have been *wrong* about anything—admitted before a meeting of the State Water Commission that construction of the canal could be delayed for up to two years. This is not much, but in the lexicon of the Department of Water Resources it amounts to a major concession, and conservationists were quick to step into the narrow breach. On March 16, 1971, the Sierra Club, Friends of the Earth, and three individuals brought suit in Federal District Court in San Francisco to "force federal and state officials to give careful consideration to the environmental damage to the San Francisco Bay and the Delta caused by the State Water Project before proceeding further with the project." Specifically, the suit charged that the Peripheral Canal (joint use), the Delta Pumping Plant (Department of Water Resources), the San Luis Drain (Bureau of Reclamation), the East Side Canal (a branch of the Peripheral Canal and a Reclamation proposal), and the Tracy Pumping Plant (Reclamation) violate sundry provisions of the Rivers and Harbors Act of 1899, the Fish and Wildlife Coordination Act, the National Environmental Policy Act, the Estuarine Areas Act, and the Federal Water Pollution Control Act. On the basis of these alleged violations, the suit asked the court to decree "that existing and proposed diversions of water from the Sacramento and San Joaquin Rivers and their tributaries and the depositing of waste water therein by the State of California and United States Bureau of Reclamation . . . cannot proceed until the defendants have complied with the laws and statutes of the United States. . . ."

Gianelli's response to the action was predictable: "This is just more of the continual harassment to those state and federal projects—along the lines of the threats that have been made against them." The action was more than a "threat," and it is expected that it will be pursued vigorously (and opposed with equal energy). What effect it may have on the course of water development in the state remains to be seen, but it suggests that the day is long past when precedent and tradition will be given a free hand with the California landscape.

V. Bonded Insecurities

As predicted more than ten years ago, the State Water Project is in deep financial trouble. First, the general-obligation bonds of $1.75 billion authorized in 1960 did not sell as well or as quickly as the Department of Water Resources had promised. California's self-imposed 5 percent interest limit on such bonds made them uncompetitive with similar bonds by the end of the decade; and in 1969, the state was left with some $650 million in unsold bonds, and the Project was in danger of running out of construction money. The problem was solved—presumably—when in June, 1970, the voters approved a proposition raising the interest rate to 7 percent, thereby making the water bonds sufficiently competitive. This helped. So did the California Water Fund, a $200 million reserve created by transferring monies received from Long Beach oil revenues from the state Investment Fund. Another aid was the state's General Fund, out of which all costs for fish and wildlife enhancement on the Project are paid, and yet another source of construction revenue has been proposed by Gianelli, who plans to sell off some $150 million worth of the bonds authorized by the Central Valley Project Act of 1933—providing he can persuade the state legislature to raise their interest ceiling from 6.5 percent to 7.5 percent.

This patchwork system of fiduciary bandages may actually supply enough money to complete the present phase of the California Water Project (assuming that such items as the Peripheral Canal and the San Joaquin drainage facilities ever get off the drawing board). Still, one dismal fact remains: the $1.75 billion worth of bonds issued in 1960 and the proposed $150 million to be issued as leftovers from 1933 will have to be repaid sooner or later—at interest rates ranging from 5 percent all the way up to 7.5 percent. What this could mean to the future financial condition of the Project (not to mention the state) was suggested as early as 1966 by Joseph S. Bain, et al, in *Northern California's Water Industry*. The Project, the authors said, "promises approximately to pay for itself only if operated at least until about 2039 and only if capital investment is asked to bear an interest charge not appreciably in excess of 4 percent. With higher interest charges (or a shorter life) it would definitely be a loser; for example, with a time horizon of eighty years and interest charge of 5 percent the present value of its net deficit would be about $339 million." The life span of the Project is problematical, given the likelihood of other sources of water in the near future, and when this fact is added to the interest rates for some of the bonds at 7 and even 7.5 percent, one nervously wonders how much beyond $339 million the deficit will actually be.

The entire financial justification for the Project, of course, has been based on the assumption that there would be more than enough water users to repay the original $1.75 billion (presumably including interest charges). But an increasing stack of evidence suggests that even this is becoming a slimmer and slimmer hope as time goes on.

The agricultural use of water in the future is predicated on an increase of farming acreage on the west side of the San Joaquin Valley from about 900,000 acres at present to 1,156,000 in 1980 and 1,194,000 in 1990. This will probably occur if Project water is made available—but the question remains: is such expansion necessary; is it in fact even wise? About 30 percent of the land that will benefit from Project water in this region is owned by but six large corporations, including the Kern County Land Company and Standard Oil, as noted earlier, and much of the rest of it is held in parcels in excess of 1,000 acres. These agricultural factories indeed would like to expand operations with Project water. At least one critic, in fact, has maintained that they were the major force behind the Water Project in the first place. "The idea of moving the Feather River out of its own watershed," Erwin Cooper wrote in *Aqueduct Empire* (1968), "began as the brainchild of the big San Joaquin Valley landowners: the corporate farms, land management firms, railroads with huge acreages. . . . Their future lay in irrigated farming. The men who controlled them along with much else in California were unanimously dedicated to the proposition that the only way to beat the Bureau of Reclamation's 160-acre limitation on water for farmers was to have the state, rather than the federal government, operate a water distribution system." The author probably underestimated the influence of other sectors of the Water Establishment, but his basic premise is still correct: Project water will be, as economist Paul S. Taylor has said, "water for the landed, the more land the more water, opening the purses of taxpayers . . . to furnish it."

Aside from the ideological implications involved in a system that taxes all the people to the benefit of a few, the truly disheartening fact is that encouraging the expansion of agriculture with Project water may be an economic disaster. Project water is expensive; estimates as to its ultimate cost range between forty and sixty dollars an acre-foot. To afford it, farms will have to plant high-value specialty crops—such things as fruits, nuts, grapes, vegetables, cotton, alfalfa, and sugar beets. There is nothing new in this; specialty crops have been the mainstay of California agriculture for generations, and that is precisely the problem. The demand for such crops already is beginning to decline and prices are showing a downward trend. Many cotton farmers in California, for example, are already facing the thin edge of bankruptcy, and economists predict a significant decline in cotton acreage between now and 1980. Expansion will only aggravate the situation. California's agricultural industry could be crippled, and the demand for the 1,355,000 acre-feet of Project water in the San Joaquin Valley could evaporate like the wisps of a dream.

Similarly, the projected demand for urban water is beginning to show signs of a gap between dream and reality. The cosmic planning involved in the California Water Project is based on the assumption that the traditional patterns of growth in California are going to continue into the spectral future, unaffected by changing conditions. As Director Gianelli put it in 1969, "Population is expected to grow from a figure of some 19 million at present to about 54 million in the year 2020—an expansion of nearly two and a half times." Given that premise, the department's predicted population of 19 million in southern California by 1990—and the consequent demand for 3,601,000 acre-feet of water—is not only reasonable but unassailable. But the premise itself is being disintegrated by increasing evidence that California is *not* going to continue its patterns of growth—that, in fact, those patterns have already shown significant alterations downward. Sooner or later, it had to happen, as Daniel P. Luten wrote in *The California Revolution,* edited by Carey McWilliams in 1968:

> California cannot continue to grow forever, or even for a very long period, at a greater rate than the nation. Simple arithmetic shows that if California maintains its growth rate at the traditional 3.8 percent per year and the nation maintains its rate at the 1.6 percent of 1960, then in about 110 years, say 2070, the

populations of both the United States and California would be about a billion. That is, all Americans would live in California. This seems unlikely.

Unlikely, indeed, and becoming more unlikely all the time. In 1958, the growth rate was 4 percent; in 1961 it had dropped to 3.7 percent; in 1964 to 3.1 percent; and in 1967 to 2.1 percent. The growth rate has continued this decline, and while it is not likely that the population will ever level off, it is certain that the historic rituals of growth in California are being revised. And just as southern California had traditionally shown the most dramatic increases in the past, it is now displaying the most dramatic *decreases* in the growth rate—so much so that the Department of Water Resources was forced to revise its estimates once again in January, 1971, declaring this time that the projected population for southern California in 1990 would be 17 million, rather than the 19 million previously expected. There are those who will insist that even this is too high an estimate. Writing in the Fall 1970 issue of *Cry California,* environmentalist Mark Von Wodtke outlined a more likely possibility:

> There is enough evidence at hand today to conclude that the air resource of the Los Angeles Basin simply will not support a population of more than about 14 million, given both present petrochemical fuel-consumption trends and present and anticipated pollution-control programs, even assuming that the optimistic levels predicted by the various agencies responsible for health protection and pollution control can be achieved. . . . The limitations imposed by the air resource alone are so severe that any planning for the region which anticipates a population in excess of 14 million resource consumers—living as they do today—is gullible at best and criminal at worst.

This is an extreme opinion, perhaps, but it expresses a somber possibility and suggests that southern California's century-old love affair with growth for its own sake is in for some serious reconsideration, or else. Even assuming the possibility that Von Wodtke is dead wrong about southern California's ecological ability to support more than 14 million people, it is still likely that its population will be less than 17 million in 1990. For the past several generations, southern California has held two main attractions to the migrant American. The first was a combination of space and climate; but today, much of the region is a split-level celebration, a great blanket of Levittowns, and every day 375 acres of open space disappear beneath a smother of blacktop, concrete, and housing—all of this taking place beneath a pall of smog which is one of the great shames of technology. The second consideration has been jobs; yet today, southern California boasts one of the largest unemployment rates in the country, a situation which grows worse by the minute. Engineers with eight years of college and several more of experience stand in line for jobs as service station attendants. Altogether, it seems that southern California's lorelei call as a golden island of sun and opportunity has been cut to a whimper.

If southern California's growth rate over the next several years falls substantially below Department of Water Resource predictions, and if agricultural growth in the San Joaquin Valley produces more bankruptcies than salable crops—then who, one wonders, is going to pay for California's investment in its splendiferous Water Project? Certainly not the water users—there simply will not be enough of them.

But let us assume that the department can rest securely in its figures, that agriculture will enjoy a new boom, that southern California will continue to have one grand population explosion after another. Even then, the prospect in regard to the financial integrity of the California Water Project is not comforting. Water is not, in itself, a marketable commodity; like the air, it is considered a part of every man's natural inheritance. What the water consumer pays for, then, is not the water itself but the cost of delivering it to him. The cost of Project water delivery, as mentioned earlier, is expected to range between forty and sixty dollars an acre-foot by the time significant quantities are made available, a figure that does not take into account any increases that may be made necessary by the current inflationary spiral in all prices. This is a very expensive water-delivery system, more expensive than almost any other now in California. If it were the only system available, we could expect that the price would be paid without complaint. A man doesn't dicker when his survival is at stake. But what if there were alternative sources of water, water that could be delivered at prices substantially lower than those of the California Water Project?

It appears likely that such is going to be the case. As early as 1980—long before the farmers of the San Joaquin Valley and the citizens of southern California begin utilizing their full entitlements of Project water (assuming the department's figures are correct)—an increasingly sophisticated technology probably will bring the prices of other sources of water down to levels much below that of Project water.

One of these potential sources is waste-water reclamation. Within the next ten years, it is conceivable that major reclamation plants utilizing the processes of distillation, electrodialysis, and reverse osmosis could be constructed to treat the agricultural wastes of the San Joaquin Valley and the municipal and industrial wastes of southern California, discharging hundreds of thousands—perhaps millions—of acre-feet of treated water in ground basin storage for later pumping and re-use. Already, the technology of treating municipal wastes is far advanced; at Santee in San Diego County and at Whittier Narrows in Los Angeles County some 462,000 acre-feet of municipal sewage is being reclaimed every year, part of it being used to recharge ground water and part to create recreational lakes—at prices ranging from $19 an acre-foot up to $31 an acre-foot. Agricultural wastes are more complicated and expensive, since their treatment requires demineralization as well as the removal of organic materials, but methods of electrodialysis and reverse osmosis being tested at Coalinga, California, have already lowered treatment prices to about $144 an acre-foot, with the expectation of lower prices in the not distant future.

Another potential source is the obvious one: desalinization of ocean water. The hydrological cycle is itself a great desalinization plant, incorporating the methods of evaporation, condensation, and precipitation, and powered by solar energy and the driving force of winds. In desalting technology, man has simply attempted to reproduce mechanically the processes of nature. Sea water is introduced to an evaporator; heat vaporizes it, and the vapor is carried into a condenser, which cools it, leaving a distillate of almost pure water. The residue of salts and solids left in the evaporator is then flushed out with "feedwater." Simple as it is, the process is not without its problems, chief among them being the disposal of the waste salts—about 70 million tons for every million acre-feet of water treated. Proposed solutions to this problem have included the construction of conduits to carry the waste back to the sea, injection of it into otherwise useless surface basins or deep underground, or storage of it as solids. A more reasonable method would be to treat it for commercial sale, and the Office of Saline Water is currently conducting studies to that end.

Desalinization is expensive, but those who dismiss it as a viable possibility on the basis of cost alone tend to overlook the fact that between 1953 and the present, technology has lowered the price of desalinized water from about $1,600 per acre-foot to about $320, and it is expected that major technological breakthroughs by the middle or last half of the present decade will lower the price to competitive levels. The basis of this assumption is the growing use of nuclear energy in plants capable of producing not only desalinized water but electrical energy whose sale would help to offset the cost of water making. Optimists in this field, such as Glenn T. Seaborg, chairman of the Atomic Energy Commission, maintain that the employment of nuclear energy may yet be the single most important contribution to water technology in history. "If we develop breeder reactors to operate in the million-kilowatt range we may be able to produce enormous amounts of electricity very cheaply," Seaborg has said. "The use of very cheap large amounts of energy, in the forms of electricity and process heat . . . would allow us to economically desalt sea and brackish water, recycle water from sewage and industrial waste, and distribute all this as clean water for use by cities and agriculture." A breeder reactor, it should be pointed out, is nothing more or less than a nuclear machine that produces more energy than it consumes, a phenomenon capable of boggling the mind of anyone but a physicist. The problems involved with the disposal of nuclear wastes are profound, but they are at least a known quantity, and may be capable of solution.

However, a potentially even more significant source of both power and water has recently been discovered in the Imperial-Mexicali valleys of southern California and northern Mexico. Here, trapped between the floors of ancient seas and the sedimental layers deposited through the eons by the Colorado River, lies an immense body of water, heated to temperatures as high as 700 degrees and held in place under a pressure of 2,000 pounds per square inch. When tapped, it comes screaming to the surface of the earth at speeds that approach the speed of sound—20 percent of it steam, the remainder boiling water in a saline solution. The underground basin holding this superheated water is estimated to be 4 miles deep, 40 miles wide, and 100 miles long, and may hold up to *10 billion* acre-feet of water.

The implications of this find are tremendous, as noted by Robert W. Rex, a University of California at Riverside geologist who is heading up a research team in the Imperial Valley. First, steam-powered generating plants could produce up to 30,000 megawatts of electric power—a little more than the entire state is producing today—and produce it without pollution, nuclear or otherwise. Already, the Mexican government has drilled fifteen wells and begun construction of a seventy-five-megawatt plant at Cerro Prieto, some twenty-five miles south of Mexicali. Second, boiling water shot up from the innards of the earth would provide its *own heat* for the process of distillation needed to desalinize it—again a pollution-free situation—and cooling water for condensation could be pumped from the Gulf of California, then injected into the earth to replace the desalinized water. Under present technological capabilities, Rex says, anywhere from five to seven million acre-feet of desalinized water could be produced every year from this source, and the sale of electric power in combination with the lack of necessity for outside fuel could lower the cost to as little as thirty-two dollars an acre-foot.

Thirty-two dollars an acre-foot is infinitely cheaper than the delivery costs of water from the California Water Project, and while Rex himself is careful to point out that the geothermal sources of the Imperial Valley need further, more intense study before development, there seems every reason to believe that it may yet be one of the major sources of California's water and power—if not *the* major source.

Under the shadow of such potential developments, the economic future of the State Water Project appears pretty dim. For if cheaper water does in fact become available before the Project's full entitlement of 4,230,000 acre-feet is being used, it seems reasonable to expect that the citizens of water districts scattered from Kern County to San Diego County are going to want to use *it,* rather than expensive Project water, contractual agreement or no contractual agreement. When properly stimulated, the citizens are capable of being downright hard-nosed about it, a fact demonstrated recently when the voters of the Antelope Valley-East Kern Water District turned down a $49 million bond issue for the construction of facilities to carry Project water to district customers. This action, as Congressman Jerome R. Waldie has said, suggests "that the water engineers, corporate agricultural interests, and land speculators can no longer fool all of the people all of the time regarding water development." And if the 138,400 acre-feet contracted for by the district is minor when compared to the 2,011,500 of the Metropolitan Water District, its action is an augury of the potential future that must be giving officials of the Department of Water Resources the galloping fantods.

This, then, is California's State Water Project—the crippled and overgrown child of history, beset on all sides by miseries and with a future as vague as a statement of policy by William R. Gianelli. Now that we have this great concrete elephant, the question arises: what do we do with it—how do we revise it to save it from itself?

Some have suggested that a possible first move would be the repeal of the Burns-Porter Act of 1959. The proposal, oddly enough, was put forward by Norman Livermore, Jr., secretary of the California Resources Agency, in February of 1971. In defending an attack on the Peripheral Canal by the San Francisco *Chronicle* (*O tempora! O mores!* It was Livermore, it will be remembered, who persuaded Governor Reagan to abandon the Dos Rios Project), Livermore made the following challenge: "If the *Chronicle* and other opponents of the State Water Project expect to succeed in their endeavors to torpedo the State Water Project they would first have to go to all the voters in California and successfully repeal at least three actions passed by majority vote of the people of California. . . ."

Congressman Jerome Waldie, in a reply two days later, was quick to meet the proposal: "Mr. Livermore's challenge to the opponents of the California Water Project to go to the people of California . . . is most tempting. I believe that the people of California would indeed vote to scuttle the present Water Project and substitute in its stead a reasonable, scaled-down version which would provide for the export of excess northern water, only after the ecological and environmental needs of the areas of origin are met, and a full re-examination of need is completed and alternatives studied to meet the augmented demands of Southern California by methods such as recycling waste water, desalination, and geothermal deposits. . . ."

The idea has a degree of charm to it, right enough. But unfortunately, repeal of the Burns-Porter Act would be irrelevant. The act merely authorized the physical construction of the Project—and the Project is at this writing well over 90 percent complete or under construction. California has spent more than two billion dollars on it already, and the state is hardly in a financial position to spend more money in the process of tearing it up—or, as one critic has suggested ironically, planting it in watercress. Nevertheless, simply because the Project exists is no justification for using it to its full potential—and there are a number of things that can be done to keep us from sinking beneath the weight of our own miscalculations.

The first of these—and in many ways the most important—would be the creation of a new state water resources commission with its roots in twentieth century realities and not nineteenth century engineering romance; this commission should be given power enough to control the actions, proposals, and sundry excesses of the Department of Water Resources. That the DWR needs such control can hardly be argued against. Under the inflexible leadership of William R. Gianelli, it has displayed a resistance to change that suggests that it is either incapable of or unwilling to consider the implications of an accelerating technology and a society whose shifts in need and desire are as predictable as the fall of unloaded dice in a crap game. Gianelli's commitment to the tyranny of precedent is understandable, for he has been deeply involved with the State Water Project since its inception in the early 1950s. But, like any True Believer, the messianic zeal with which he has pursued the completion of his dream has led him into error more than once, as we have seen; he has contradicted his own agency, as in his advocacy of the Dos Rios Project, and has shown a convenient talent for molding the facts to fit his preconceptions, as in his "explanation" of the virtues of the Peripheral Canal. This kind of blind determinism must be excised from water planning in California—unless we are willing to compound the disaster we have on our hands.

Secondly, no further waterworks should be considered or constructed (including those of the Bureau of Reclamation) until the California Water Plan—the gospel by which the Project itself was inspired—is given a comprehensive re-examination to correct its errors of fact, interpretation, and goals. Like the Project, the Plan is hamstrung by traditional logic; it needs correction in the light of what we have learned since its conception. A revised water plan should reorganize state and federal systems in the state to supply legitimate water needs without further major construction, and should put much more emphasis on the development of alternative water sources—recycling waste, desalination, and, perhaps the most significant, geothermal deposits. In short, the amount of creative energy that has been released for the construction of dams and canals should be turned loose on the problem of determining a *reasonable* solution to California's water needs.

Beyond such general considerations, there are more specific actions that must be taken. Construction of the Peripheral Canal must be delayed until a thorough study of its environmental impact is completed, preferably by an agency outside the influence of the Department of Water Resources and accountable only to a joint legislative committee. Similarly, the Bureau of Reclamation must be enjoined from constructing its East Side Canal until every possible environmental impact has been investigated in detail. (Both of these proposals, of course, are emphasized in the current lawsuit against the Department of Water Resources and the Bureau of Reclamation.) Elements of the Project not yet constructed or now under construction, such as the North Bay Aqueduct or the remaining section of the Coastal Branch, should be delayed until such time as there is evidence to support their actual need. And finally, the remaining wild rivers of the North Coast should be arbitrarily declared off limits now and forevermore for water projects.

All of this requires a drastic revision of the concepts which have dictated water development in California for more than a century, but if the evidence of this report indicates anything, it indicates that something drastic must be done and done now to halt the ruinous course of our water policies. We must not be trapped in our history again, as we have been so many times in the past. The logic no longer works, and if we do not adjust to that fact, then we are in danger of providing one more in a long list of affirmative answers to a question economist Paul S. Taylor once asked: "Is it true that what we learn from history is that we learn nothing from history?"

A Note on Sources: The story of California's water development up through the Central Valley Project is told in a number of excellent books, among them *The Water Seekers* by Remi Nadeau (1950), *Southern California Country* (1946) and *California: The Great Exception* (1949), both by Carey McWilliams, and *Aqueduct Empire* by Erwin Cooper (1968). The best single source on the birth and development of the Central Valley Project remains Robert De Roos' *The Thirsty Land: The Story of the Central Valley Project* (1948). California's appropriation of the water of the Colorado River is told in some detail in *The Colorado* by Frank Waters (1946) and in *The Grand Colorado: The Story of a River and Its Canyons* by T. H. Watkins and contributors (1969); particularly noteworthy in the latter volume is Helen Hosmer's chapter on the development of the Imperial Valley and Paul S. Taylor's on the rise and fall of Reclamation Law as reflected in the use of Colorado water.

The structural growth of the California Water Project has been documented in a long series of bulletins from the Department of Water Resources, beginning in 1960 and continuing up to the present day. The curious story of the Dos Rios Project has been outlined by Lou Cannon's article in *Cry California* for Summer, 1968, "High Dam in the Valley of the Tall Grass," and by my own in the April 1969 issue of the *Sierra Club Bulletin,* "Crisis on the Eel." Notes on the growth of Project criticism were gleaned from a number of disparate sources, including the files of the Sierra Club and the *San Francisco Chronicle,* a series of articles by environmentalist Frank M. Stead in *Cry California,* and *Northern California's Water Industry: The Comparative Efficiency of Public Enterprise in Developing a Scarce Natural Resource* by Joe S. Bain, Richard E. Caves, and Julius Margolis (1966).

By far the single most useful source in determining the present and future prospects of the California Water Project was *California Water: A Study in Resource Management,* edited by David Seckler (1971). A massive and technically detailed study of every aspect of the Water Project, from finances to ecology, *California Water* is the most comprehensive study of the subject yet to appear. I am indebted to Professor Seckler and to the University of California Press for allowing me access to the manuscript before publication.

Finally, it should be pointed out that the opinions, fulminations, and whatever errata that may appear in "The New Romans" are the sole responsibility of the author, and none other.

Part III
New York

Down the Drain

by Robert H. Boyle

New York
Metropolitan Area
Water supply:
present and future

0		20		40		60		80		100

miles

~~~~~ major existing reservoirs
 " planned "
minor dam sites
existing aqueducts
planned "
canals
• pumping stations
▫ purification plants

*NOTE: in this area, the
mean annual rainfall is
not less than 30 inches
nor more than 50 inches.*

Richard Edes Harrison — VI 1971

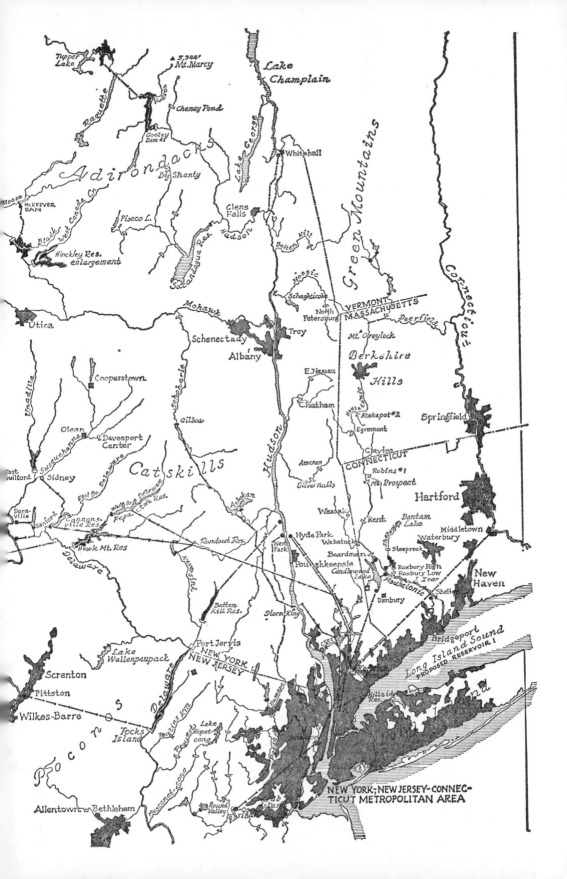

I. Waste

There is no shortage of water in the New York Urban Region, though it encompasses a three-state area with a population of 20 million. There is a shortage of *clean* water, a needless shortage of water for New Yorkers to drink in time of unpredictable drought, an unnecessary shortage of clean water at all times for man and for fish and for wildlife. The New York Region is a mess.

It is a mess in any number of ways. Most of the flowing water is poisoned. A number of New York and New Jersey beaches are closed because of pollution. Instead of yielding shrimps and other invertebrates, plankton hauls in the Atlantic off New York harbor fetch up cigarette filter tips and sanitary napkins. In the lower Hudson, and Raritan and Sandy Hook bays, bluefish, fluke, flounder and weakfish are afflicted with bloody stumps for tails, symptomatic of an often fatal fin-rot disease. Striped bass, the most esteemed gamefish on the northeast coast of the United

States, often taste of oil. Some species of fishes and birds are sodden with pesticides and other chemicals such as the PCBs or polychlorinated biphenyls, compounds used widely by industry and released into the environment by *accident*. At the north end of Constitution Marsh, a wildlife refuge across the Hudson from West Point, bottom samples tested near the outfall of a battery company showed not 16 parts per million of cadmium, not 16 parts per thousand, but 16 parts per hundred. In other words, the marsh bottom was *16 percent* cadmium—a potential mine. The documentation of carnage is endless. I recall the time Dr. Jack Pearce of the U. S. Marine Laboratory at Sandy Hook, New Jersey, spoke of these abuses before an annual gathering of the American Littoral Society. After he had finished speaking, a member of the audience asked, "Dr. Pearce, don't you think we need a disaster to wake people?" To which Pearce replied in a soft voice, "We have the disaster already."

The proportions of the disaster are not limited to pollution. As if the dirtying of the waters were not enough, planners now contemplate wholesale manipulation of major estuaries and river systems, the siphoning of lakes, the erection of enormous dams and the laying of mammoth conduits. Already reeling from past abuse, the New York Urban Region is about to suffer the same sort of ecological enema that is now being applied to Texas and California in full public view.

A scant 300 years ago, the lighting of a match in geologic time, the New York Region was not a mess but a paradise. The Dutch found it one of the most blessed places on the face of the earth. Everywhere there was lushness of life. Oak-chestnut-hickory forests extended for hundreds of miles, and along the rivers and coast the marshes were alive with ducks, geese, swans and shorebirds. In the woods were great quantities of game. Nicolaes van Wassenaer, a Dutch chronicler, wrote, "Birds fill also the woods so that men can scarcely go through them for the whistling, the noise and the chattering. Whoever is not lazy can catch them with little difficulty." There were ruffed grouse, heath hens (now extinct), turkeys "which weigh from thirty to forty pounds," and passenger pigeons (now extinct) "so numerous they shut out the sunshine." Deer were "incredibly numerous" and "as fat as any Holland cow can be."

The bays, rivers and streams of New Netherland enraptured the Dutch. The waters of the Mohawk, now a battered, turbid sewer, were described as being "as clear as crystal and as fresh as milk." The Hudson was "rich in fishes," with "a great plenty of sturgeon" and striped bass "of very good flavor." In the present New York harbor area were lobsters, mussels, scallops, clams and crabs. "In the summer-time crabs came on the flat shores, of very good taste," wrote settler David de Vries. "Their claws are of the color of the flag of our Prince, orange, white and blue, so that the crabs show sufficiently that we ought to people the country, and that it belongs to us." There were great stocks of oysters. Gowanus oysters from the East River grew up to a foot long and were deemed the "best in the country."

On Manhattan island, there were fresh-water brooks "pleasant and proper for man and beast to drink, as well as agreeable to behold, affording cool and pleasant resting places." Inland, Adriaen Van der Donck, author of the most detailed account of the colony, wrote, "there are also many fine springs and veins of pure water." In the hills and mountains "water flows out of fissures and pours down the cliffs and precipices, some of which are so remarkable that they are esteemed as great curiosities." Some streams possessed "the extraordinary quality of never freezing in the bitterest cold weather, when they smoke from their natural warmth, and any frozen article immersed in those waters thaws immediately. If the unclouded sun shone on those springs for whole days with summer heat, the water would still remain so cold that no person would bear to hold his hand in it for any length of time in the hottest weather. This peculiarity makes these waters agreeable to men and animals, as the water may be drunk without danger; for however fatigued or heated a person may be who drinks of these waters, they do no injury in the hottest weather. The Indians, gunners, and other persons use those waters freely at all seasons, and I have never heard that any *pleurisy* or other disease had been caused by their use."

In sum, Van der Donck confessed, "I am incompetent to describe the beauties, the grand and sublime works, wherewith Providence has diversified this land," and Jacob Steendam, an early settler on Manhattan, wrote:

> This is the land, with milk and honey flowing
> With healing herbs like thistles freely growing
> The place where buds of Aaron's rods are blowing
> O, this is Eden!

The first settlers of Manhattan drew their water from streams, ponds and wells on the island. Manhattan is the eroded root of a 400-million-year-old mountain, and except for a relatively shallow covering of topsoil and sand, it is solid rock, mostly mica schist. As the human population grew, the number of wells increased, and the quality of drinking water quickly deteriorated. Graveyards and privies drained into the same soil from which the wells drew water. A 1748 report said even horses refused to drink the water on Manhattan, and Collect Pond, the largest standing body of water on the island, became badly polluted because New Yorkers used it as a convenient dump for dead animals and other offal.*

In 1799 the state legislature granted a charter to the Manhattan Company to supply water to the city, but the company was little more than a device to allow Aaron Burr to get into the banking business. A small clause in the charter made it lawful for the company to use surplus capital "in the purchase of public or other stock, or in any other monied transactions." Apparently the deal was so potentially profitable that Alexander Hamilton was in on it with Burr; Hamilton's brother-in-law was named a

* For the history of New York City's water supply, see Nelson M. Blake, *Water for the Cities* (Syracuse, 1956), and Roscoe C. Martin, *Water for New York* (Syracuse, 1960).

director. The Manhattan Company (now part of the Chase Manhattan Bank) did supply water from a well to customers through pipes made of bored logs, but service was never satisfactory. Perhaps because the banking side of the business was so successful from the start, the Manhattan Company really did not care about water or how much it cost. Burr and his cohorts set a lunatic pattern of flat-rate pricing which is, in essence, still in effect in most of New York City today. It was based on the number of fireplaces in a house or building. The owner of a house with no more than four fireplaces paid a flat $5 a year. Any additional fireplace incurred a charge of $1.25 per year, up to a maximum of $20. Many customers left the water running all the time (some still do). Whenever there was a fire, the fire companies were allowed to drill holes in the log pipes. When the firemen were through, they drove wooden plugs into the holes, and this practice is supposed to account for the origin of the word "fireplug."

Soon, a shortage of water plagued New Yorkers. In 1828, fire ravaged Manhattan, and in 1832, 3,500 people died in a cholera epidemic. A committee of doctors and chemists pointed out that Manhattan residents were adding "about 100 tons of excrement every 24 hours" to the water-bearing sands of the island.

In 1833 and 1834 the state legislature gave the city the authority to establish a board of water commissioners, permission to raise money to pay for a water system, and power to condemn land and acquire water rights. The city's eyes fastened on the Croton River, a large tributary thirty miles up the Hudson. There was another disastrous fire, the worst in the city's history, in 1835. In 1836 work began on the Croton Dam and Aqueduct, to the anger and dismay of Westchester property owners. One owner, Joshua Purdy, presented the city with a bill of $3,012 for damages, declaring he had not "taken into consideration the inconvenience, trouble and anxiety of having between three and four hundred Irishmen upon my own farm and within a few rods of my dwelling house—for that no estimate could be formed nor any calculation made."

By 1842 both the dam and the aqueduct to carry water to the city were ready. The supply thus furnished by the Croton was supposed to be adequate for generations. It wasn't. The city fathers still gave no serious consideration to measuring water use. As Noel Perrin, a persistent critic of New York's water supply system, observed not long ago: "Not being students of Roman history, they didn't know about Frontinus, Water Commissioner of Rome from A.D. 97 to 100, who did use water meters, and with them saved a hundred million gallons of waste water a day, equal to nearly half of Rome's supply."

From the start, then, waste was built into the city's water supply system and by 1850 there was a clamor for more dams. Additional reservoirs were constructed on the Croton system, which drained a watershed of 375 square miles, extending into Putnam and Dutchess Counties and a sliver of western Connecticut. Water was also taken from the Bronx and Byram rivers in Westchester County in 1884 and 1897. After the turn of the century the Croton Reservoir itself was enlarged.

"Some of these reservoirs would have been required even to supply the growing city's just needs," Perrin wrote in a *Harper's* magazine article in 1963, "but most of them provided water to go directly from leaky faucets into waste pipes—or even from well-built faucets into waste pipes, since a good many New Yorkers left the water running all winter to make sure the pipes didn't freeze, and all summer to make sure it would be running cold when they wanted a drink. At New York City pressures a one-inch faucet left full-on will waste a thousand gallons an hour. There was no possible penalty for even the wildest waste. The owner of a New York house five stories high and from eighteen to twenty feet wide paid $10 a year for his water whether he used one pint or 900 gallons a day. Tenants, of course, paid nothing at all, and their landlords paid a dollar a year for them—per family, that is. Water use has naturally risen steadily ever since. At the moment [1963] it is 155 gallons per person per day, expected to reach 160 three years from now. In all, the city has dammed and flooded seventeen valleys, and spent about a billion dollars on dam construction, in the excitement of keeping up."

When the Croton River system was finally bottled up, the unmetered, leaky water supply system still was insufficient. There were suggestions to draw water from the Hudson River, but the river was already polluted, so much so that in 1888 the Congress of the United States passed the New York Harbor Act. This act is still valid. Had it been enforced by the U. S. Army Corps of Engineers, the waters of the harbor and its tributaries, such as the Hudson, would not be in the mess they are today. The relevant heart of the act reads as follows:

> Be it enacted by the Senate and House of Representatives of the United States of America in Congress assembled, That the placing, discharging, or depositing, by any process or in any manner, of refuse, dirt, ashes, cinders, mud, sand, dredgings, sludge, acid, or any other matter of any kind, other than that flowing from streets, sewers, and passing therefrom in a liquid state, in the tidal waters of the harbor of New York, or its adjacent or tributary waters, or in those of Long Island Sound, within the limits which shall be prescribed by the Supervisor of the Harbor, is hereby strictly forbidden, and every such act is made a misdemeanor, and every person engaged in or who shall aid, abet, authorize, or instigate a violation of this section, shall upon conviction be punishable by fine or imprisonment, or both, such fine to be not less than $250 nor more than $2,500, and the imprisonment to be not less than 30 days nor more than 1 year, either or both united, as the judge before whom conviction is obtained shall decide, one half of said fine to be paid to the person or persons giving information which shall lead to conviction of this misdemeanor.

Pollution of the Hudson didn't bother the city of Albany, which drew its drinking water from the same stretch of river into which the city of Troy poured its raw sewage. In 1872, O. F. Chandler, Ph.D., assured the Albany water commissioners that

he found nothing that could throw "the slightest suspicion upon the purity of the water of the Hudson or its fitness for supplying a perfectly wholesome beverage for the citizens of Albany." In 1885 Chandler was asked to make another study—he found "no evidence to lead me to change the opinion I expressed in 1872." *
He reported the volume of Troy sewage "so small in comparison with that of the river, that it does not make any impression on it," and he dismissed the research of Pasteur and Koch. "Nothing in the discoveries of these great investigators enables us to say that this water is unsafe. It is believed that typhoid fever and diarrhoeal diseases have often been disseminated by polluted wells, but no cases of these diseases have ever been traced to the waters of a large river." Similarly, Chandler did not fear that cholera could come from the Hudson. In the years that have followed, the polluted waters of the Hudson in the Albany area have become a source of wonder to modern sanitary engineers, who speak of the place with awe, if not reverence, as "the Albany Pool." During the summer months, the pool gives off a horrible stench, and the river water is essentially devoid of dissolved oxygen for a distance of perhaps twenty to thirty miles south of Troy Dam. The chief inhabitants of the river water are sludge worms, leeches and rat-tailed maggots.

In its quest for more water, New York City almost followed the recommendation of its commissioner of water supply who, in 1899, advised that the city sign a contract with the private Ramapo Water Company. This arrangement was attacked as a swindle; indeed, Governor Theodore Roosevelt damned the Ramapo contract as "grossly improper" and denounced city officials for verging on "actual criminality." There were studied pleas for metering, but these were ignored. The Board of Water Supply, created in 1902, bounded more than 100 miles northwest into the Catskill Mountains to dam streams draining into

* O. F. Chandler, *Report on the Waters of the Hudson River* (New York, 1885).

the Hudson system.* There in 1905 the city commenced, at enormous expense, the task of damming Esopus Creek to form the Ashokan Reservoir. An aqueduct, run on the gravity system, was bored through solid rock. Crossing the Hudson River at Storm King Mountain was a bit of a problem: the city engineers did not encounter solid rock below the riverbed until they were almost 800 feet down, and the aqueduct tunnel itself had to be bored through unstable granite rock 1,114 feet below sea level.† The city gloried in its triumph. A Board of Water Supply report issued in 1917 begins:

> A dream of many years ago has been realized in one of the greatest of civic achievements! Catskill Mountain water has been led to New York City. . . . Night and day the water now flows unceasingly from the mountains to Staten Island, 120 miles. Administrative, legal and physical obstacles have been surmounted. . . . New York City's Catskill Mountain water-supply system is the greatest of water-works, modern or ancient, and ranks

* In the Byzantine bureaucracy that is New York City government, the Board of Water Supply seeks out sources of water, builds the reservoir systems and then turns them over to the Department of Water Supply, Gas and Electricity. In the July 11, 1965, issue of *New York,* Noel Perrin, persistent critic of the water system, wrote: "If there were no new reservoirs and aqueducts, there would be no Board of Water Supply, a fact the Board is acutely aware of. Even without meters, the Board leads a cyclical life. Between spurts of reservoir building, it shrinks to almost nothing. Then comes a shortage, and authority to build a few more, and it swells like a balloon. This cycle is perfectly independent of the normal business cycle." In 1968, the water functions of the Department of Water Supply, Gas and Electricity were given to a new Department of Water Resources which was placed in a new superagency, the Environmental Protection Administration. The Board of Water Supply still continues as an independent entity.

† One never knows where allies will spring from in a conservation battle. In 1968, the city of New York formally joined the Scenic Hudson Preservation Conference, the Sierra Club, the National Audubon Society, the Hudson River Fishermen's Association and other groups in opposing Con Edison's plans to blow a hole in Storm King Mountain for a pumped storage hydroelectric plant. The city feared that drilling and blasting in unstable rock would imperil the nearby Catskill Aqueduct, which supplies New York with 40 percent of its water supply.

among the most notable enterprises ever carried out by any city, state or nation. For magnitude and cost and for the variety, complexity and difficulty of physical problems encountered it stands with the great canals, transcontinental railroad systems and New York's own wonderful rapid transit railways.

After all these huzzahs and more, the board report finally noted on page 25, "Conservation of the supplies through metering and other means for reducing waste and extravagant use may postpone the date when the city must once more undertake the extension of its water system."

Before the city was finished with its plans for the Catskills, it dammed the Schoharie Creek at Gilboa. The Schoharie normally flowed north to the Mohawk, the major tributary of the Hudson, but by damming the creek, the city could then drain it backwards through the eighteen-mile-long Shandaken Tunnel to the Ashokan Reservoir.

Next, the Board of Water Supply recommended three-stage construction of new reservoirs. The first stage called for a reservoir on Roundout Creek, a tributary of the Hudson, and a reservoir on the Neversink, a tributary of the Delaware. These are now the Roundout and Neversink reservoirs. The second stage called for a reservoir on the East Branch of the Delaware River. This is now the Pepacton Reservoir. The third stage called for more reservoirs in the Delaware system. This stage underwent some changes in the course of the years, and it eventually resulted in the construction of the Cannonsville Reservoir on the West Branch of the Delaware River. In addition to all this, the city constructed the Delaware Aqueduct, which runs for a distance of 85 miles and, at one point, tunnels 2,500 feet beneath a mountain.

The state of New Jersey took alarm at the city's plans for the Delaware, and in 1929 it filed suit against the city and the state of New York. The eventual decision by the Supreme Court, although denying New Jersey the injunction originally sought, ruled that New York could divert only 400 million gallons of Delaware system water a day, not the 600 million planned. The decision, written by Justice Oliver Wendell Holmes, began with the stirring words, "A river is more than an amenity, it is a treasure. It offers a necessity of life that must be rationed among those who have power over it." Besides reducing the amount of water New York wished to siphon off, the decision contained a couple of important provisos. For one, the court retained jurisdiction in the case, and for another the court set certain requirements for the release of water into the Delaware. Indeed, as a result of later court action, New York must release water to assure a flow of 1,750 cubic feet per second in the Delaware as measured by the gauging station at Montague, New Jersey.

As a result of the Depression and World War II, Roundout, Neversink and Pepacton reservoirs were not finished until 1951. Even then it took five more years to fill them with water. And still the city's unmetered water system leaked.

The whole question of metering and leakage was explored in a brilliant study, *Water Supply—Economics, Technology and Policy,* published by the University of Chicago Press in 1960 and written by a Rand Corporation study team of economists Jack Hirshleifer and Jerome W. Milliman, and James C. De-Haven, a physical chemist. They reported universal metering would save about 200 million gallons a day, and elimination of wastage from mains would save another 150 million gallons a day. Fixing the leaks in the mains would cost $750,000. Indeed, they added, "elimination of leakage in mains promised to make available an amount of perhaps 50 percent of the Cannonsville yield at a cost, per million gallons, of far under one one-hundredth of Cannonsville costs. As far as we have been able to determine, these conclusions have been nowhere challenged, and yet the recommended program of waste detection and elimination was never adopted by the city."

The Rand study appeared a year before the 1961 drought which hit 300,000 square miles of the Northeast and lasted five years. Abnormal wind patterns were responsible. Instead of coming from the west in the spring and early summer, the winds came from the northwest, bringing with them dry and sinking air masses which, according to a report prepared for the president by the Water Resources Council in July, 1965, "have weakened storm systems, and have suppressed the ascending air motions necessary to produce rain. The rain-producing storms have thus been occurring further downwind, off the Atlantic seaboard."

In New York City, officials wavered between issuing soothing words to the public or declaring an emergency. The commissioner of Water Supply, Gas and Electricity, Armand D'Angelo, hemmed and hawed. When reservoir levels dipped in 1963, he called for reduced water use. That winter, snow and rain prompted the commissioner to withdraw his appeal. As late as October, 1964, he told Mayor Robert Wagner, "I do not see at present any danger of a water shortage in New York City."

By the summer of 1965, the situation had become worse and the reservoirs had fallen to less than 40 percent of capacity. D'Angelo felt the heat from critics, and the discovery of a leak became front page news. Representative William F. Ryan found a gusher in Central Park. As photographers clicked away, he took off his shoes and sloshed around in the water like Harpo Marx frolicking in the lemonade vat in *Duck Soup*. Secretary of the Interior Stewart Udall charged that New York and other afflicted areas were "walking on the edge of disaster," and he accused the city of having "one of the leakiest and most loosely managed" water supply systems. He threatened to cut federal aid unless the city adopted water reforms. Even the president of the United States, Lyndon Johnson, took a knock at the city administration, although it was headed by a fellow Democrat. On August 11, 1965, in remarks made to the Water Emergency Conference in the Fish (sic) Room of the White House, Johnson said, "There is not much I can do about the third of Bob Wagner's water that we don't know where it is going." Commissioner D'Angelo seemed to be caught in a revolving door. On one occasion he announced that the city would never draw from the Hudson River because "the water is not very good water at all." Soon after that he reversed himself.

In September of 1965, the Senate Committee on Interior and Insular Affairs held a hearing on the "Northeast Water Crisis," and a number of witnesses came forward to flay New York City. Udall pointed out that, in a city such as New York, "without metering you cannot really account for your water. You do not know where it goes. You have no way of really knowing whether your system is operating efficiently or whether your costs are sound." He contrasted New York with Philadelphia which draws water from the Delaware and Schuylkill rivers. In 1959 Philadelphia had adopted universal metering. "The result is that Philadelphia, we found, uses 50 million gallons a day less today than they did in 1955."

Another witness, Elmer B. Staats, deputy director of the Bureau of the Budget, took dead aim at the New York water supply system. Said Staats:

> The first order of any business of water supplies and requirements should be to make a comprehensive assessment of what portion of projected requirements can be met through the conservation and more efficient use of existing water supplies. Leakage from urban water distribution systems in the Northeast is as much concern to the nation as the significant losses from the agricultural distribution systems supplying irrigation water in the arid West. As we approach the day when our water supplies can no longer be taken for granted, universal water metering will be needed as well as experiments to reduce wasteful water use through alternative pricing policies. These are not new ideas. Indeed, more than a century ago, one of New York City's leading newspapers concluded that: ["]The only reasonable method of preventing waste is to charge each house with the water that goes into that house, and the only possible method of ascertaining this quantity is to measure it.["] Then the amount of water that people are willing to pay for will be a very delicate test of

what they want to use. Sooner or later, then, the effect of metering and pricing policies on water requirements may have to be reevaluated.

Perhaps the fullest statement on the whole mess came from Dr. Donald F. Hornig, director of the Office of Science and Technology in the White House, who testified:

> Four years of subnormal precipitation have resulted in unusually low streamflow in the Northeastern United States. Despite the low precipitation and streamflow, it cannot be said that there is a gross shortage of water in the region. U. S. Geological Survey data show the normal runoff for the area to be about 20 inches over the 300,000 square miles of the drought area. This is equal to 300 billion gallons a day, enough to meet the needs of the entire country. Even in drought, that flow could serve many times the present population of the Northeast. The problems are localized and generally result from inadequate facilities to make use of the water which is available . . .
>
> Water development for New York City has followed a conventional pattern. A source of good water was located in the mountains, and surface reservoirs and aqueducts for interbasin transfers were constructed. Together with the water uses within the Delaware River Basin, the diversions to New York created a total draft on the resources of the basin which approaches the total yield during periods of low precipitation. The stage is thus set for a slowly increasing demand and a somewhat worse than usual drought to create a condition of shortage. This situation has occurred before in the United States and will occur more often in the future, unless we prepare ourselves.

Dr. Hornig suggested a number of alternatives to building more reservoirs and aqueducts:

> Many industries have found that they can effectively recycle their water so as to minimize the withdrawals from their source of supply. Other industries have safely and effectively used

treated sewage from municipalities to meet all or part of their needs. Air cooling instead of water cooling is possible in some situations. In the home we might reduce the amount of water used in toilet flush tanks, dishwashers, clothes washers and other appliances without harming the effectiveness of these appliances. Exploration would surely reveal other means of conservation in industrial and domestic use. We are just beginning to develop a research program aimed toward water saving ideas. Appliance and plumbing fixture manufacturers could quite readily modify their designs for water economy if encouraged to do so by pilot research efforts of the Government or if city ordinances required low-water-use devices for all new installations.

Technical means of water economy are not the only methods available. Economic incentives are possible. Metering of water deliveries so as to require the user to pay for water delivered is practiced in many but not all of our cities. To be effective, metering needs to be combined with a rate structure which encourages savings. Water rates are commonly lower the larger the quantity used. Yet the cost of a new increment of supply to a city is almost certainly much higher than the cost of the currently available supply. Thus one might well propose that water rates per unit of water use increase after the customer has used an amount which is reasonable for his needs. Such a rate structure combined with metering would encourage economy of use and the correction of leaks in the home or industrial establishment.

Full metering also permits a city to evaluate the leaks in its distribution system and to take measures to locate and correct these leaks. Conservation measures—both technical and economic—might well reduce municipal water use one-fourth to one-third without causing inconvenience.

Turning to a new approach, Dr. Hornig pointed out:

One of the largest sources of water available in any city is its waste water which is normally thrown away. Some 60 to 90 per cent of the water delivered to a city is returned to waste discharge. This waste usually contains less than 0.1 per cent of impurities and these impurities can be removed to make the water absolutely safe for human consumption. A closed recycling system such as will be needed on space ships for long journeys is not beyond the realm of the possible for cities and more limited recycling is currently practicable in many areas. At my request, the Department of Health, Education, and Welfare has just completed a feasibility analysis of 100 million gallons per day waste water purification plant which could be added to a secondary sewage treatment plant of the kind now used in New York City and northern New Jersey. Their report indicates that such a plant could be built for $33 million and would produce potable water at a cost of about 16 cents per 1,000 gallons. . . . Almost certainly these costs could be reduced still further through a research and development program. The suggested plant employs aeration chemical coagulation and sedimentation, carbon adsorption and chlorination to purify the effluent from a secondary sewage treatment plant. If the product water is mixed with water from other sources in a large system no other further treatment is necessary. For a completely closed system in which all water is recycled a buildup of salinity would occur and a desalting unit would be needed. Because of the very low salt content, electrodialysis could be used and the additional cost would only be a few cents per 1,000 gallons depending on the amount of salts to be removed. The costs quoted above include cost of land, treatment, and pumping costs to return the water to the distribution system.

Direct delivery of purified waste to the city distribution system is possible and can be completely safe. If it is too unattractive esthetically, the purified waste water can be used for recreational and decorative lakes, watering parks and golf courses, industrial processes, or can be recharged into the ground water. It must be noted, however, that there is very little practical difference between purification and direct reuse of waste water and the present widespread practice of discharging of wastes to a river from which a downstream city takes it water supply . . .

For cities such as New York, Los Angeles and San Francisco which draw large supplies from interior locations, use the water once and discharge it to the oceans, conservation and water reuse can be very important alternatives to the conventional approach. We would be conserving water that would otherwise be lost. We could be minimizing the need for vast and extra-ordinarily costly new water importation plans.

For all the ideas and suggestions prompted by the drought, little changed in New York City. When Robert Wagner left the mayor's office, Armand D'Angelo departed as water commissioner. The new mayor, John Lindsay, appointed James Marcus, a dapper name-dropper and son-in-law of John Davis Lodge, former Republican governor of Connecticut and ambassador to Spain. On the very day that Marcus was sworn into office as commissioner of Water Supply, Gas and Electricity, he announced, "I hope and urge that New Yorkers will conserve water to the best of their ability," and having said that arranged to attend a meeting to discuss how much of a kickback he would get for awarding a million-dollar "emergency contract" for the cleaning of Jerome Park Reservoir in the Bronx. Marcus has since pleaded guilty and been imprisoned.

It is to be devoutly hoped that New York City will change its profligate water policies. But even if the city were of a mind to change, the Corps of Engineers already has the whole region mapped out for more of the same. Waste.

II. Manipulation

One of the most important basic documents involving future water use in the New York Urban Region is not known to the public. Indeed, it is not known to some persons inside government who are deeply involved in water resources. The document is entitled *Feasibility Report on Alternative Regional Water Supply Plans for Northern New Jersey-New York City-Western Connecticut Metropolitan Area*. A joint venture of Metcalf & Eddy, Inc., and Hazen and Sawyer, the report submitted in August, 1969, to the Department of the Army, North Atlantic Division, Corps of Engineers, under contract number DACW 52-69-C-0001.

A notice labeled "important" serves as the Corps' foreword to the report, and it says in part:

Attention is invited to the preliminary nature of the study for which the draft report has been prepared. It was commissioned solely to formulate feasible engineering alternatives for a regional water supply for the area under consideration, without regard to the institutional restraints—legal, economic, or organizational—which might inhibit regionalization of water supply. Further, it does not attempt to quantify the effects that the proposed structures would have on the utilization of the water resources, modification of the water resources for purposes other than water supply, nor does it analyze the possible modification of the proposed structures to achieve other water resources purposes in addition to water supply.

This report, therefore, is intended only to demonstrate the physical possibilities of water supply regionalization. Another study is under way to analyze the institutional problems and to seek alternative solutions to those problems.

The two reports will then become working tools to assist the Federal, State, and local agencies and, ultimately, the general public to reach decisions as to the practicability and desirability of regionalization of water supply for the northern New Jersey-New York City-western Connecticut metropolitan area."

Despite these caveats by the Corps, several factors should be kept in mind. For one, the report was undertaken solely from a point of view not only of engineering feasibility but of a curious kind of engineering bias. Indeed the report states: "The investigation differed from conventional water supply studies in that instructions from the North Atlantic Division, Corps of Engineers, stressed engineering feasibility of the projects, and stated specifically that 'any jurisdictional authority, boundary limit, or details of project financing shall not limit or influence a selection.' Without this stipulation, many of the projects described might not have been investigated."

There is no new thinking in the report. There is no questioning of growth, no ecological considerations and, perhaps most importantly from a purely water resource point of view, no real examination of existing systems that may be highly deficient because of leakage or lack of metering. The basic bias in favor of the old let's-dam-this-river attitude, an attitude that has been very costly to the public good, comes through in a later chapter of the report called, in part, "The Long View," in which waste water reclamation and desalting are dismissed out of hand. For instance, the statement on page 65: "Improvements in treatment processes and techniques hopefully will cut costs and make reclamation desirable in many parts of the world. It should not be needed in the 'water-rich' study areas for some years to come."

So let us go now on a trip through this "water-rich" region, bearing in mind that a project, once proposed and tucked away in the Corps' files, has a way of enduring forever.

The Susquehanna

The Susquehanna River starts in New York, passes through Pennsylvania and Maryland, and eventually empties into Chesapeake Bay. The report deals with the East Branch of the Susquehanna which originates near Cooperstown, New York, flows past Binghamton and Wilkes-Barre and then joins the West Branch at Sunbury, Pennsylvania, to form the main stem of the river. The report notes that "regulation" of the East Branch of the Susquehanna and its tributaries has been considered in the past, and that "the Corps of Engineers has plans for reservoirs above Sidney at East Guilford on the Unadilla River, Davenport Center on Charlotte Creek, and at other sites." The report studies two new projects in detail. The first, labeled Susquehanna Project S-1, calls for "flood-skimming" the East Branch by construction of a pumping station at Sidney. The water would then be sent by tunnel to the New York City reservoir at Cannonsville, approximately twelve miles distant. Depending upon the amount of water diverted, a flood-skimming project would raise temperatures downstream—and temperature is a major factor governing aquatic life—and also reduce the flow needed to dilute pollutants.

As an alternate to S-1, Susquehanna Project S-2 would divert water from the East Branch at Doraville, New York, and tunnel it to a 50-billion-gallon reservoir planned on Oquaga Creek at Sanford, New York. Oquaga Creek is not in the Susquehanna Watershed; it is a tributary of the West Branch of the Delaware River. This apparently is all to the good as far as the engineers are concerned, for New York City could then "supplement" releases into the Delaware to meet the flow required by the Supreme Court.

The report cautions that diversions from the Susquehanna "would have to be arranged, however, so as not to interfere with downstream public water supplies from the East Branch, such as at Binghamton, New York; and at Sayre, Berwick, and Danville, Pennsylvania; and with industrial usage. Chesapeake Bay interests may be expected to resist any substantial diversion from the Susquehanna River Basin."

The Delaware

The Delaware is one of the major rivers on the Atlantic Coast. It has a watershed of 6,780 square miles and flows through three states—New York, New Jersey and Pennsylvania.

As far as the engineers are concerned, the key to the future of the Delaware is the Tocks Island Dam authorized by Congress in 1962. There is now growing public controversy over whether this dam should be built (about which more later), but in essence here is the plan. A dam 160 feet high and 3,200 feet long would be built at Tocks Island near the Delaware Water Gap, to impound a reservoir extending thirty-seven miles up the Delaware to Port Jervis, New York. This "multipurpose" reservoir is intended to provide flood control, low flow augmentation, 300 million gallons per day of water supply for northern New Jersey, power generation and ostensibly recreational opportunities. When Congress originally authorized the project, the cost was estimated at $90 million, but it has risen to $300 million.

Looking to the future, the report considers other Delaware projects. Delaware Project D-1 "would divert floodwaters from

96 square miles of the Beaverkill watershed." The water would be diverted into New York City's West Branch Aqueduct for probable storage in Cannonsville Reservoir, the capacity of which "would be increased 13 billion gallons by installing flashboards on the spillway."

Delaware Project D-2. The report, assuming that the Tocks Island Dam will be built, says water in the Tocks Island Reservoir "assigned to New Jersey would be released to provide some of the downstream flow regulation required of New York City. The water thus saved for the city's use would increase the yield of New York's Delaware River system and be taken to the study area through the Delaware Aqueduct." The report notes, "it is anticipated that some or all of the yield realized from this mode of using Tocks Island would be utilized in New Jersey. To deliver the water, a 25-mile pressure tunnel would be built from Kensico Reservoir in Westchester County to Secaucus in New Jersey. Connections with the principal northern New Jersey supplies could be made en route or at the terminus. The interconnection would permit seasonal balancing of load among the several systems."

Delaware Project D-3 considers "development" of some Delaware tributaries in northwestern New Jersey, such as Flat Brook, the Musconetcong, Pequest and Paulins Kill. Inasmuch as Flat Brook would be underwater as the result of building Tocks Island Dam, it would be "fully developed" anyway. Development of the other streams "would not warrant the investment needed."

Delaware Project D-4, the so-called Hawk Mountain Reservoir on the East Branch of the Delaware at Fishs Eddy, New York, would store 100 billion gallons of water and back up a considerable distance, not given in the report, but probably somewhere in the neighborhood of twenty-five miles, including about seven miles of the Beaverkill. There appears to be one major bureaucratic problem—the reservoir would flood out part of a brand-new superhighway, Route 17.

The Raritan

Aside from its South Branch, perhaps New Jersey's finest stream, the Raritan is an oft-tortured river which winds much of its way through the sprawl of industrial New Jersey and empties into the Atlantic Ocean south of Staten Island. The report examined eight Raritan River projects:

Raritan Project R-1, Main Stem Development. Under this project, the yield of the river could be increased 70 million gallons a day by full utilization of the present Round Valley and Spruce Run reservoirs, the Hamden pumping station and force main to Round Valley. In plans drawn for the North Jersey District Water Supply Commission in 1967, an intake and pumping station is to be built on the Raritan above Bound Brook. Also called for are the construction of a main to the region of Chimney Rock, a water treatment plant, a "balancing reservoir" (location not specified), and a twenty-eight-mile-long transmission main parallelling the Watchung Mountains to connect the commission's Wanaque Reservoir with Newark.

Raritan Project R-2. The state of New Jersey has proposed this project which calls for the construction of a dam near Somerville below the confluence of the South and North branches of the Raritan. The dam would contain a one-billion-gallon reservoir. According to a veteran observer of the Jersey scene, Fred Walczyk, editor of the *Angler's News,* "This dam is ridiculous. Round Valley Reservoir has been unused for five years, and it's more or less stagnant. This other dam will only compound the problem."

Raritan Projects R-3 and R-4. Under R-3, New Jersey water would be released from the Tocks Island Reservoir and be diverted at Frenchtown on the Delaware. There a 360-million-gallon-a-day pumping station would send the water to Hamden by aqueduct. From Hamden, the water would flow "in the Raritan River channel to an intake at confluence, where it would be pumped through a water treatment plant and aqueduct to Secaucus." Project R-4 is different from R-3 in that "Delaware River water would be diverted each year during six months of high runoff and stored in Round Valley instead of at Tocks Island."

Raritan Project R-5 is similar to R-4 except that "the capacity of Round Valley Reservoir would be increased from 55 to 75 billion gallons by raising the water level 25 feet." Of course, in order to do this, "two dams and a dike would be involved, with enlargement from bottom to top."

Raritan Project R-6 is somewhat complicated. To start, the Delaware-Raritan Canal, which runs 59 miles from the Delaware at Raven Rock to New Brunswick and which is grossly polluted, would be enlarged to increase capacity to 120 million gallons a day. The state of New Jersey has proposed the construction of a reservoir on Six Mile Run, and water from the canal would be pumped to it. According to the report, the Six Mile Run reservoir does not warrant construction because the land costs would be prohibitive.

Raritan Project R-7 has been proposed by the Corps of Engineers. It calls for a dam at Crab Island, five miles above the mouth of the Raritan. This would stop salt water from entering ten miles of the present estuary. Oddly, the report takes a dim view of the Crab Island dam. The water quality would be "poor," and the lake created by the dam "would be subject to warm temperatures, heavy algal growth, and accumulations of under-treated wastes. The water supply benefits of the Crab Island Dam would not warrant construction for this purpose alone. If the project were authorized for other reasons, the impounded waters might be developed for cooling and industrial purposes along the lower Raritan, but probably not for public water supply."

Raritan Project R-8. Under this proposal, a tidal barrier across South River (a Raritan tributary) would hold back the runoff from a 125-square-mile area. Increase in water supply is estimated at not more than 15 to 25 million gallons a day, and "While the project might provide substantial local benefits, it would not be suited for development as part of a regional supply for the study area. Since Crab Island Dam would accomplish the same benefits over a wider area, both projects would not be built."

The Passaic

The Passaic River system is wholly within New Jersey except for the Ramapo, a picturesque tributary which rises in the highlands of Orange County, New York. I did not have a chance to examine the report in full, but a map shows potential dam sites at a number of locations throughout the Passaic watershed: Darlington, Pompton Lakes, Point View Reservoir, Two Bridges, Washington Valley, Myers Road, Hardscrabble, Boonton Reservoir (raised), Tourne, Como, Longwood Valley and Dunkers Pond. Another map in the report illustrates diversion of Hudson River water at West Park, New York, south to the Passaic system through a pipeline and tunnel paralleling the New York State Thruway.

The Housatonic

The Housatonic River, which lies midway between the Hudson and the Connecticut, drains a slice of eastern New York, western Massachusetts and Connecticut, and empties into Long Island Sound. As far back as 1900, New York City officials looked into the possibility of damming the Housatonic for water supply, but they gave up the notion because of likely opposition by Connecticut residents. For the most part the report relies on previous Corps investigations of dam sites. Unfortunately, I was not able to examine the Housatonic system projects in full, but again, as with the Raritan, a map shows possible dam sites: in Massachusetts at Egremont, on the Green River; Clayton on the Konkapot River and Konkapot No. 2; in New York State, at Wassaic on the Webatuck Creek; in Connecticut, near Bulls Bridge where the Ten Mile River joins the Housatonic; Robbins No. 2 near Falls

Village; Mt. Prospect, on the Housatonic; Kent, on the Housatonic; and Steeprock, Roxbury High Dam and Roxbury Low Dam, on the Shepaug River. Some of these dams, which would destroy trout streams, are apparently considered for a scheme whereby water would be pumped from one reservoir to another, with the end result that a treatment plant and pumping station would take water from Candlewood Lake and send it through a twenty-five-mile long tunnel to Kensico Reservoir, one of New York City's impoundments in Westchester County. In line with this, the report also has a map showing a sixty-mile-long tunnel which would take water from the Connecticut River near Middletown and send it to the Kensico Reservoir. Another project would be to divert water from the lower Housatonic, above the existing Shelton Tidal Dam, to Trap Falls Reservoir, five miles west. The report notes, "The project would firm up the New Haven Water Company and the Bridgeport Hydraulic Company systems, thus enabling them to transfer water from existing sources to adjacent systems in western Connecticut."

Long Island Sound

The proposal to dam Long Island Sound and convert that salt-water ecosystem into a fresh-water lake was first advanced by Robert Gerard of the Lamont Geological Observatory in an article published in the August 19, 1966, issue of *Science*. Gerard's brainstorm was catalytic. From New York University, Alistair W. McCrone spoke up in a letter to *Science* to urge that a dam with locks be built across the Hudson just north of Manhattan as an "important adjunct" to Gerard's sound-reservoir proposal, while from the Hudson Laboratories of Columbia University, Robert U. Ayres suggested that one "obvious way" to increase the dilution of salt water in the sound without any dam at the seaward end would be to "divert the Hudson River through Hell's Gate by building two relatively cheap dikes across the Hudson River and the East River below the Harlem River."

From Battelle-Northwest in far-off Richland, Washington, W. I. Neef and E. T. Merrill wrote *Science:* "One possible benefit that Gerard does not mention is the creation of a fresh-water harbor by removal of material needed to build the dam. A dam 2 m high, 50 m wide at the top, 90 m wide at the bottom, and 12.8 km long would contain 18×10^6 m³ of material. This is sufficient to create a hole, which might be used as a harbor. Such a harbor near the mouth of the Connecticut River could provide sufficient capacity to relieve some of the congestion in New York Harbor."

Responding to these various proposals, the *New York Daily News* envisioned a New York City in 1996 "awash" with pure fresh water. "How did this miracle come about?" the *News* asked. "Who made the concrete desert bloom? It was accomplished by the forward-looking scientists and engineers who in the '70s and '80s planned and hammered through, over the opposition of professional scoffers, a billion dollar scheme to dam the Hudson River and Long Island Sound. The gigantic construction job transformed these bodies of water into two of the world's largest reservoirs which, of course, were renamed Lake Lindsay and Lake Rockefeller."

In May of 1967, Representative Hugh L. Carey, a New York City Democrat, took up the cry for damming Long Island Sound. According to Carey, construction of a barrier dam at the eastern end of the sound would not only convert the sound into a fresh-water reservoir but would serve as a causeway for Long Island and Connecticut traffic. He also suggested that a new jetport could be built on fill in a shallow area near Bridgeport, Connecticut, with runways extending out into the water on pillars sunk in concrete. "I think this is totally feasible," Carey said. "Even if we had to invest one billion dollars, the one project would solve the water, airport and transportation problem." He added, "That's how the West got developed. The East is provincial. We need to learn what to do. I'd like to put a Western solution to Long Island Sound. While we're talking here about the jet airport and water supply, the West goes ahead and puts up dam after dam and creates lakes that would make Long Island Sound look like a cup of water. They change the whole course of a river and take it as a matter of course."

Carey said he had asked Representative George Fallon of Maryland, chairman of the House Public Works Committee, to have the Corps of Engineers make a "feasibility study." Presumably, this is the reason why the Corps report looked into the sound. According to the report, conversion of Long Island Sound into a fresh-water reservoir would "take care of a population several times that estimated for the study area in the year 2020." Whether this aquatic overkill is good or bad, the report does not say. Dikes and navigation locks would have to be built at both ends of the sound. The eastern dike would be seven and a half miles long and built in water with a maximum depth of 150 feet, while the western dike would be only three-quarters of a mile long in water with a maximum depth of 50 feet. There would also have to be an emergency spillway (Hurricane Hazel in 1954 sent waves 25 feet high smashing into the eastern end of the sound), pumps, treatment plants and transmission lines to deliver the water to consumers.

Estimates are that it would take from eight to twenty years to reduce the salt content of the water in the sound to the chloride limit recommended by the U. S. Public Health Service, but the report says this length of time "might be shortened by pumping steadily from the reservoir into the sea."

The report notes that the Long Island Sound reservoir would have to be drawn down only six inches to supply two billion gallons of water a day. If the reservoir were drawn down eight feet, it could, in theory anyway, supply up to ten billion gallons of water a day. As a practical matter, however, this would be chancy since "substantial quantities of salt water would seep under the dikes or through the aquifers of Long Island."

The report cautions:

Connecticut rivers flowing into Long Island Sound carry the wastes from many communities. They disperse in the Sound rapidly [sic] and ultimately reach the Atlantic Ocean. If daily tidal flushing were eliminated, however, pollution would become intolerable unless sewage and waste treatment, much better than now available, were installed. The fresh-water lake would be relatively quiescent, if not stagnant, with only wind-induced currents to spread the waste throughout the basin. Pockets of concentrated waste would be almost certain to develop in some areas. Unless the treatment included the removal of nutrients, heavy algal blooms would be inevitable.

The Hudson

The Hudson River is 315 miles long. It rises in the Adirondacks and ends at the Battery, the south tip of Manhattan Island. After the spring runoff of fresh water, salt water often advances as far north as Poughkeepsie, a distance of 60 miles. This saltwater advance is essential to the estuarine ecosystem. An official of the Corps of Engineers has termed the lower Hudson "probably the most complicated estuary in the United States."

Despite befoulment of the Hudson in the Albany-Troy region, where sanitary engineers often go to gaze at the horror of it all, and in the vicinity of New York City, where the West Side of Manhattan alone empties 175 million gallons of absolutely raw sewage into the river, the tidal river remains a very productive spawning river for such fish species as the huge Atlantic sturgeon, the short-nosed sturgeon (one of the rarest fish in North America and officially classified as "endangered" by the U. S. Department of the Interior), shad and striped bass.

It is obvious from the report that the Hudson, "the largest single water resource within near reach of the study area," is about to be placed under siege. The same fate seems to await Lake Champlain and other bodies of water outside the Hudson drainage as well. Basically, the idea is to withdraw enormous volumes of fresh water from the Hudson at Hyde Park. But there is one major difficulty: the salt water that enters the tidal river from the Atlantic might move up, imperiling existing water withdrawal works. For instance, the city of Poughkeepsie, located below Hyde Park, uses the Hudson for its water supply at the rate of ten million gallons a day.

A rather remarkable map in the report pinpoints a number of sites where dams could be built to impound draw-down reservoirs for regulating fresh-water flow downstream. The prospective dam sites are as follows: Silvernails and Ancram on the Roeliff Jansen Kill; Chatham and East Nassau on the Kinderhook system; Schaghticoke and North Petersburg on the Hoosic River; Shushan on the Battenkill; Dead Creek; and Fort Hunter on the Schoharie. In the Adirondacks, prospective dam sites are at Wilcox Mountain; Big Shanty Mountain; Gooley No. 1 and Gooley No. 2 on the main stem of the truly wild upper Hudson; Cheney Pond; Chain Lakes; Piseco Lake; Shaker Mountain and Hinckley Reservoir expansion dam site. Without question, dams at many of these sites would ruin waters celebrated by campers, canoeists and anglers. Perhaps the greatest concern is over the upper Hudson at Gooley. Here the upper Hudson is at its wildest and most scenic. Here Winslow Homer painted some of his finest watercolors, such as *Leaping Trout, Casting in the Falls* and *Boy Fishing*. In an article in the March 1971 issue of *Audubon*, Laurence Pringle wrote of Gooley Dam: "Not only would 17 miles of the untamed upper Hudson be covered by the reservoir's backed-up waters, but parts of the Cedar, Indian, Goodnow, and Rock rivers would also disappear. So would Harris Lake, Catlin Lake, Rich Lake, and dozens of other lakes and ponds. The reservoir would stretch 26 miles north and west from the dam, at least when it was full. Like all reservoirs used for regulating stream flow, it would shrink in size during the summer. The water level would then drop about 60 feet, exposing vast areas of shoreline and mud flats."

The report examines a number of the "more favorable prospects" and also looks into the possibility of diversions to the Hudson from other water basins. All of these are based on the construction of intake, treatment and pumping facilities at Hyde Park, with the water to be dispatched to Kensico Reservoir in Westchester County via a fifty-mile-long tunnel. The amount of water to be withdrawn from the Hudson is enormous, 500 million gallons a day to start, with eventual withdrawal to reach 1,900 million gallons a day. Two tunnels, each sixteen feet in diameter, would be required to send the water to Kensico.

Under terms of what is known as Hudson Project HU-1, "In-Basin Storage for Flow Regulation with Water Supply Diversion at Hyde Park," three reservoirs would be needed. First Hinckley Reservoir would be enlarged, then Gooley No. 1 would be built on the Hudson, followed by the construction of Schaghticoke on the Hoosic.

Hudson Project HU-2 calls for the enlargement of Hinckley, construction of Schaghticoke and "ultimately a diversion from Lake Ontario to the Mohawk River." An intake on Mexico Bay would take in Lake Ontario water and pump it through a twenty-mile tunnel to the west end of Oneida Lake. "A second pumping station would lift the water from the east end of the lake through 15 miles of tunnel to the Mohawk River at Rome." (Earlier in the report, recognition was briefly made of the longstanding interstate and international disputes about water in the Great Lakes—after all, Canada is not just another state to be bulldozed willy-nilly by the Corps—and therefore "legal complications should be anticipated.")

Hudson Project HU-3, which has as part of its title the eye-catching phrase, "No Compensation for Diversions from Lake Champlain," calls for enlargement of Hinckley Reservoir followed by the construction of Schaghticoke on the Hoosic, followed by Dead Creek Reservoir which would be filled by "flood-skimming" the Hudson at Bakers Falls. But that is not all. Other facilities would include a pumping station at Whitehall, New York, near the Vermont line, for a twenty-two-mile force main to Dunham Basin at the high point of the Hudson-Champlain Canal, "whence the water would flow to the Hudson River at Fort Edward." The report adds, "To provide 700 mgd of the supply withdrawn at Hyde Park, drought-year diversion from Lake Champlain would not exceed 140 billion gallons, and would lower the lake level less than 1.6 feet."

The report takes frank note of the fact that "the lake is used widely for recreational purposes, and any change in the present regime might run into severe opposition." I guess it will. When I mentioned the proposed diversion from Lake Champlain to one Vermont official, there was a stunned silence. The Vermonter knew nothing about this scheme. As his voice came back, he said, in measured cadence like an angry Titus Moody: "They can start a war if they try this. Lake Champlain is sacred to Vermonters."

Hudson Project HU-4 is similar to the above except "the tunnel would be larger than the one from Bakers Falls to Dead Creek Reservoir in Project HU-3. These facilities would permit flood-skimming the Hudson River in the winter and spring to compensate for water drawn from Lake Champlain during the preceding summer and fall, and would also permit the refilling of Dead Creek Reservoir. The combined operation of using Dead Creek during the summer recreation season, and pumping from Lake Champlain thereafter, would yield 1,000 mgd as in Project HU-3. In Project HU-4, the construction of Schaghticoke Reservoir is scheduled last in order to bring the total yield up to 1,900 mgd." If Lake Champlain seems to get extra attention in the report it is because "diversions from Lake Ontario are considerably more expensive."

Hudson Project HU-5 "would draw from the New York City Delaware reservoirs on a seasonal basis, in combination with flood-skimming the Hudson River, for a total yield of 1,400 mgd before providing low-flow augmentation of the Hudson from in-basin reservoirs." By the last is meant enlargement of Hinckley and the construction of Gooley No. 1.

Just in case the salt-front should move up the Hudson, the report thoughtfully adds that "additional storage for salt-front control" could be provided perhaps by the construction of the Shaker Mountain reservoir upstream from the Sacandaga Reservoir and/or by raising the level of Piseco Lake. Besides helping keep the salt-front down the Hudson where it belongs, the Shaker Mountain project would "improve the power generation potential" at the Sacandaga Reservoir, which in 1930 drowned a beautiful valley with quiet villages like Batchellerville, where, as the local vernacular had it, "if you spit it sounds like thunder."

The Corps of Engineers (or New York City) is by no means confined to these horrendous Hudson projects described in the report. They are simply "the more favorable," but others are included to keep the options open, as certain phrasemakers are in the habit of saying these days.

Hudson Project HU-6 would divert the flow of the upper reaches of the Black River, which happens to be a tributary of Lake Ontario, and also the Moose River, which happens to be a tributary of the Mohawk, which happens to be the largest tributary of the Hudson. The "proposed McKeever diversion dam" would be built on the Moose, and a dam would be built at Forestport on the Black to impound a reservoir.

Hudson Project HU-7 would divert the flow from 507 square miles of the Raquette River watershed, north of Tupper Lake, to the headwaters of the Hudson.

Hudson Project HU-8 would divert the Deerfield River, a tributary of the Connecticut, into the Hudson via the Hoosic River.

Hudson projects rejected after preliminary analysis are use of the Wallkill River ("The valley is flat and offers no sites suitable for large capacity storage reservoirs"), an Adirondack Mountain Gravity Supply to New York City ("the cost of a 150-mile-long aqueduct to Kensico Reservoir overshadowed any potential benefits"), and impounding of eastern tributaries of the Hudson ("would require some 13 reservoirs . . . would be expensive").

The construction of a barrier dam across the tidal Hudson is not quite ruled out. True, substantial damages would have to be paid to the Penn Central inasmuch as the railroad tracks along the river would be flooded out; the barrier would "interfere" with navigation; elimination of tidal currents and mixing would "aggravate" sewage disposal; the "character of river water, spawning habits and ecology" * would change; and the actual engineering would pose problems, etc., but "ultimately, however, for demands of 1,500 mgd, or more, a barrier dam might prove more economical than going to more distant sources, and should be considered. The necessary investigations and engineering should be included in subsequent water supply studies of the region."

So there we have it—the Hudson, Housatonic, Raritan, Passaic, Long Island Sound, the Connecticut, the Adirondacks, Lake Champlain, Lake Ontario, the Delaware, the Susquehanna —all spread out like patients etherized upon a table—with water going from this lake to that river to this impoundment to that tunnel through this mountain into leaky main and dripping faucet.

* I believe this the only time the word ecology is used in the main body of the report.

III. Alternatives

For the better part of a year, I have been talking to ecologists, fishermen, water experts, pollution authorities and assorted public officials about the hydrological mess of the New York Urban Region. As a result of all that, I offer here some practical alternatives to the stale thinking of the past:

(1) First of all, metering, *universal* metering for New York City. It is insanity not to have it. Metering must replace the idiotic flat-rate fee now charged to individual water consumers on the basis of the width of their house. Metering will save the city at least 200 million gallons of water a day.

(2) Elimination of leaks in mains. In New York City this is another imperative. The 1951 Engineering Panel on Water Supply and the 1960 Rand Corporation study estimated 150 million gallons of water a day could be saved by fixing leaky mains. Later estimates have run as high as 400 million gallons a day.

(3) Study should be made of water rates, with a view toward establishing a realistic price that would make consumers think twice about lavish use even of metered water. "As an aside," the Rand experts noted, "it may be remarked that New York's present meter rate has remained unchanged since 1934, and the rate effective before that date had remained constant since 1870. Evidently, those concerned with New York's water problems had come to think of water rates as almost a constant of nature." The amount of water that would be conserved by a possible raise in price is unknown, but without doubt consumption would be prudent. It is time consumers (and engineers) lived within economic and environmental parameters.

(4) Other aspects of built-in waste of water should be ended. For instance, Dr. Merrill Eisenbud, former head of New York City's Environmental Protection Administration, has pointed out the waste caused by over-plumbing. Instead of using six gallons to flush a toilet, a person need use only two. (Putting some bricks in the tank can reduce the volume.) If every New York City toilet used two gallons instead of six when flushed, the city would conserve 100 million gallons of water each day. Add that to the figured volume saved by universal metering and elimination of leaks in mains, and there is a whole new reservoir system of possibly 700 million gallons a day, more than half of the city's present daily water consumption of 1,264,000,000 gallons.

(5) Instead of tapping the Hudson for enormous volumes of water, instead of robbing Peter to pay Paul by pumping water from Lake Champlain or Lake Ontario, or instead of building new dams across the landscape, all of which schemes pose ecological hazards not yet even glimpsed by the conduit-crazed, New York City and other communities should seriously explore reclaiming treated sewage water as potable water. Less costly than desalting, this may well be the ultimate solution. The idea that properly reclaimed sewage water is "unesthetic" flies in the face of ecological fact. The hydrologic cycle is never ending, and the water that any community drinks now has, at some time or

other, probably passed through the bladder of a Brahmin or been part of the blood supply of a gnat. Indeed, it is said that in order to get a drink of water in Cincinnati a toilet has to be flushed in Pittsburgh. If there are problems they should be explored. For now, it is certainly worth noting that a reclamation plant is operating in Windhoek, South Africa. After taking a drink of water from the plant, the South Africa prime minister pronounced it "delicious." But President Richard Nixon, adhering to a tradition of American squeamishness, said "No, thanks," when offered a similar glass at Hanover Park, Illinois.

At a reclamation plant at Fisheating Creek, Florida, radioactive cobalt is used to irradiate sewage without danger of contamination. After gamma rays kill coliform bacteria, the water is filtered and the particles removed. The end product is pure, clear, tasteless, drinkable water. A couple of civil engineers at New York University, Alan Molof and Matthew Zuckerman, used a different technique in a pilot project they ran for three months at New Rochelle, New York. Sewage was sent through an alkaline solution that broke down large organic molecules. Activated carbon was then used to adsorb all the small molecules. The Molof-Zuckerman technique is now being tested further by Envirotech Corporation in Palo Alto, California.

Molof is critical of current water treatment plants because they are "not responsive" to new problems. "They are designed on the old basis," he says. "These plants have no facilities for the removal of trace organics and inorganics which we are finding more and more, such as DDT. We can't grasp the idea that these insecticides that are getting into our water supplies could be removed in large part by putting something in our water plants, such as activated carbon, to at least give us some chance now of escaping some of these trace organic contaminants." Molof adds: "We have no special concern in our water quality picture for materials that can't be treated. And one material that we don't know how to treat is radioactivity. Why should we allow a material that can't be treated to be introduced into our environment in greater quantity?" *

Molof is also critical of standard sewage treatment methods. "The big process in sewage treatment, activated sludge, was developed in 1913, fifty-seven years ago," he says. "Yet the same old process is still being pushed by the government. How do you get new technology in this field? Engineers don't want it. They have been designing this type of plant for over fifty years. As a result, design costs go way down. You try to introduce new technology and the engineering costs go way up. We have no provision for compensating this additional cost. We have no method for encouraging an engineer to design a better plant which again leads us to the idea of government encouraging bad engineering." He suggests the federal government fund sewage plants on the basis of plant design and efficiency. In Sweden, he points out, sewage plants are funded on the basis of efficiency because "they reward good engineering and they reward you if you want cleaner water."

As a result of out-of-date engineering, Molof says, water-pollution bond issues actually solicit "a vote for less dirty water, not a vote for more clean water. Our whole concept, if you can imagine a thermometer with the top of it marked 'dirty,' is to go down the thermometer to 'less dirty.' . . . The design engineer tells you how less dirty you want your water. You have no choice. The bond issue meets the minimum standards set by the state and it is really less dirty water for which you are being allowed to vote. I believe that the engineer has no right to impose on us the water quality he thinks is best."

(6) Pollution abatement laws must be strictly enforced, especially the Federal Refuse Act of 1899, which is the best antipollution law on any books, anywhere. If the U. S. Army Corps of Engineers had only seen fit to enforce it over the years, Ameri-

---

* At this writing, twenty-six sites on the Hudson River alone are being considered for nuclear power plants that regularly emit radioactive wastes into water and the atmosphere.

cans would not have the polluted waters they have today. Here is the heart of the Refuse Act:

It shall not be lawful to throw, discharge, or deposit, or cause, suffer, or procure to be thrown, discharged, or deposited either from or out of any ship, barge, or other floating craft of any kind, or from the shore, wharf, manufacturing establishment, or mill of any kind, any refuse matter of any kind or description whatever other than that flowing from streets and sewers and passing therefrom in a liquid state, into any navigable water of the United States, or into any tributary of any navigable water from which the same float or be washed into such navigable water; and it shall not be lawful to deposit, or cause, suffer, or procure to be deposited material of any kind in any place on the bank of any navigable water, or on the bank of any tributary of any navigable water, where the same shall be liable to be washed into such navigable water, either by ordinary or high tides, or by storms or floods, or otherwise, whereby navigation shall or may be impeded or obstructed. Every person and every corporation that shall violate, or that shall knowingly aid, abet, authorize, or instigate a violation of the provisions of this section shall be guilty of a misdemeanor, and on conviction thereof shall be punished by a fine not exceeding $2,500 nor less than $500, or by imprisonment (in the case of a natural person) for not less than thirty days nor more than one year, or by both such fine and imprisonment, in the discretion of the court, *one-half of said fine to be paid to the person or persons giving information which shall lead to conviction.*" (Italics added.)

One organization that has done much to pioneer use of this law and bring it to public attention is the Hudson River Fishermen's Association, Inc. (HRFA). When the HRFA was founded in 1966, with the express purpose of conserving aquatic resources, it began to report violators—and there were many—of the Federal Refuse Act to the U. S. Army Corps of Engineers. From the start, the HRFA placed heavy emphasis on the oil discharges from the New York (now Penn) Central railroad yards on Croton

Point. The noxious and illegal discharges occurred almost daily, and at times were so extensive that ducks and other waterfowl drowned after the natural waterproofing in their feathers was destroyed by oil. On occasion, oil slicks from the Central pipe, which bore the date 1929, covered several square miles of the surface of the Hudson. Fishes and crabs that ventured into the area were deemed inedible. It took the HRFA a great deal of time and effort to bring the Central to account for its obviously gross pollution, but finally in 1970 the railroad pleaded guilty to four counts and was fined $1,000 on each for a total of $4,000. The HRFA then moved to collect half this amount as its reward as provided for by law. After some initial paper shuffling and throat clearing by government officials, the association finally managed to receive a U. S. Treasury check for $2,000. This money is being used to combat other polluters. The fine of $4,000 levied on the railroad was small potatoes compared to the amount of pollution the Central poured into the river, but this case was a first, and to the HRFA, the important thing was to establish the precedent.

(7) Marshes and wetlands should be made inviolate by law. These are among the most productive areas in the world (tidal marshland produces about ten tons of vegetation per acre compared to an inland crop of only one and a half tons), and converting them into garbage dumps, as New York City has with Great Kills on Staten Island or Westchester County has with Croton Point, or paving them over for highways, airports, factories, housing developments and the like is environmental suicide. Marshes are of critical importance for the propagation of numerous species of invertebrates, fishes, birds and mammals, and they are dependent on fresh-water inflows to keep down salinity. The building of dams or diversion of fresh water, dredging, filling and pollution take a deadly toll. Since 1938, for example, more than 15 percent of Barnegat Bay, New Jersey, has been filled in forever, and further defilement of the bay has also helped erode commercial fish catches.

Marshes are valuable to man in other ways. In times of storm or flood, they serve as great blotters to soak up water. In a 1970 report on Jamaica Bay, hard by Kennedy Airport, John Teal of Woods Hole Oceanographic Institution and William Niering of Connecticut College reported that the stands of *Spartina* grass act "as an efficient mechanism for converting some of the load of human sewage from waste products into usable material. In other words, the marsh functions as a free tertiary treatment plant." In line with this, biochemist Dr. Edward Buckley of the Boyce Thompson Institute suspects that the bacterial count has been rising in New York harbor waters because of damage wreaked on the once lush Hackensack Meadows nearby in New Jersey.

(8) There is an absolute need for ecologically oriented river basin commissions in the Greater New York region and elsewhere in the Northeast (and probably in the rest of the country as well). New York State did have a Hudson River Valley Commission, but many critics considered it ineffectual—and it is no longer functioning, a victim of cuts in the state budget. What is needed now is a strong commission, with carefully defined powers, involving the federal government and the states of New York and New Jersey. In 1966 Congress passed a bill introduced by former U. S. Representative Richard Ottinger calling for a federal-state Hudson River Valley compact. In approving the Ottinger bill, Congress gave its consent to the states of New York and New Jersey (and also to Vermont, Massachusetts and Connecticut, if they wished to participate) to negotiate with one another and with the federal government for purposes of entering into a compact on the Hudson River basin. According to the act, consideration should be specifically given to:

(a) the need to encourage all beneficial uses of the lands and waters of the Hudson Riverway including, but not limited to, commercial, industrial, and other economic development consistent with the preservation and rehabilitation of the natural, scenic, historical, and recreational resources of the Hudson Riverway;

(b) the need to encourage and support local and State autonomy and initiative in planning and action to develop, preserve, and restore the land and waters of the Hudson Riverway, insofar as such planning and action is consistent with comprehensive development, preservation, and restoration of the natural, scenic, historic, and recreation resources of the Hudson Riverway;

(c) the need to abate water pollution, protect clean water, and develop the water resources of the Hudson Riverway for beneficial use;

(d) the need to preserve, enhance, and rehabilitate the scenic beauty of the Hudson Riverway;

(e) the need to preserve, enhance, and develop archeological and historic sites, shrines, or structures along the Hudson Riverway; and

(f) the need to protect and enhance the fish and wildlife and other natural resources of the Hudson Riverway.

Negotiations on the compact have bogged down. However, a federal-state compact is a necessity; a number of federal agencies already have jurisdiction over much of the Hudson, and these agencies, which include the Federal Power Commission, the Atomic Energy Commission, and the Corps of Engineers, have been in the vanguard of the despoilers. A new and more powerful body is needed to subjugate them as well as such wayward state agencies as the Department of Transportation, the Public Service Commission, and the Atomic and Space Development Authority. It is imperative that the head of any federal-state Hudson Riverway commission be an environmentalist rather than an engineer. I have seen enough of engineers in such sensitive posts. We have been engineered to death.

(9) Nassau and Suffolk Counties should consider purchase of a 12,000-acre tract of land between Manorville and Riverhead which overlies the last untouched, underground source of drinking water on Long Island. According to Anthony Taormina, regional supervisor of fish and game for the state Department of Environmental Conservation, purchase is essential if Long Is-

landers are going to have uncontaminated fresh-water supplies in the future. Composed mainly of glacial sand and gravel, Long Island is a natural sponge for storing rainfall. As unchecked development has spread like cancer across the island, rain water carries into the ground water such harmful materials as nitrates and surfactants from detergents, and garden pesticides and fertilizers from lawns and golf courses. The construction of mammoth shopping centers and parking lots also poses problems to the underground supply. "There are 135 toxins in every automobile," Taormina says. "There is asbestos in the tires, hydrocarbon components in the fuel and lubricants, rust, flaking paint, to name just a few. Imagine a parking lot with 2,000 cars and no rain for two weeks. Suddenly there's a torrential downpour for twenty-five minutes. What drains away isn't water any more but a complex chemical solution." As illustrative of what already has happened to aquifers on the island, Taormina cites the ground water beneath Brooklyn and Queens which is contaminated from sewage. Curiously, the ground water beneath those two New York City boroughs has been rising in recent years because of leaks from both the sewage and water supply systems.

Taormina sees the 12,000-acre Riverhead-Manorville tract as Long Island's "ace in the hole." According to his figures, acquisition would cost only $48 million, and could be financed over three years with an annual surcharge of $18 on present water customers in Nassau and Suffolk.

Besides serving as an underground reservoir, the tract could become excellent fish and wildlife habitat and serve as a park and nature education center. Nassau and Suffolk Counties could both realize revenue and enhance the storage capacity of the aquifer by setting aside predetermined sites in the tract for sand and gravel mining. Sand and gravel operators have a horrible reputation among conservationists on the island, but Taormina, who in private life was one of the founders of the Environmental Defense Fund, points out, "The creative wealth of Long Island is sand and gravel, excellent fin fish and shellfish, some of the best farm soils in the country and fine ground water. If we destroy these resources, what do we contribute to the national wealth? Nothing! We become so many millions of parasites on the nation. If everyone acted the same way, we'd be a nation of paupers."

(10) Serious reevaluation should be made of the Tocks Island Dam and Reservoir project, with a view toward killing it. Loudly huzzahed by proponents as the recreation playground of the future for the megalopolis—10½ million annual visitors to the reservoir, which would be part of the National Park System—the whole scheme is beginning to loom, in the words of Fred S. Burroughs, president of the North Jersey chapter of Trout Unlimited, as "a monumental fraud upon the American taxpayer." Burroughs says that outdoor recreationists, who are supposed to be the main beneficiaries, "stand to be the unhappiest losers." He cites warnings by ecologists at Lehigh University indicating that there could be no productive trout fishery as a result of water fluctuations and surging and likely siltation from power generation. Indeed, the suspicion is growing among many that the Tocks Island plan is designed to make power companies rich at public expense. "Of course it's a big boondoggle," says Harry Darbee, the Catskill fly-tier and water expert. "Public money is going to build the dam, and private interests will benefit. The Army Corps of Engineers claims something like forty-five deaths resulted from the floods in 1955. None of these occurred in the Delaware Valley but on tributaries, and Tocks Island wouldn't have done a damn thing to stop this."

In a broadside Burroughs sent to me, he says Tocks Island "sounded like Utopia" when the Corps first unfolded its plans in 1962, in which the "recreational benefits—fishing, swimming, boating—in conjunction with the dedication of surrounding lands, in the vast new Delaware Water Gap National Recreation Area, would bring the joys of outdoor sport and reclaimed environmental sanctuary to millions annually from congested nearby urban and suburban regions."

To which Burroughs adds: "At first we believed them. For the

Army Corps of Engineers, in the business of 'selling' its projects to the public, is long skilled in the fine art of manipulative public relations and promotion. They sold the politicians. The Delaware River Basin Commission backed the scheme. And why not? Here were millions of funds in federal monies. Truly a band wagon to get aboard. And the private utilities—three New Jersey-based corporations—saw in the project a means of utilizing a high tax-payer investment as a beneficent windfall to permit development of a massive new pumped-storage hydroelectric facility at impressive cost economies. In the spell-binding euphoria of these assured rewards the public has been slow to awaken. . . ."

One of Burroughs's targets is the "benefit-cost ratio" of the Corps, which he terms an arcane formula "to justify the dividends from an array of benefits in relationship to the investment costs of a project of this nature. Significantly, as the estimated cost of the Tocks Island impoundment and surrounding recreational area rose from $90.3 million initially to $235 million presently, the benefit-cost ratios cited have fluctuated wildly. At the outset, this ratio was 1.6 to 1, indicating 'benefits' at the rate of $1.60 for each $1 of investment. In 1968, they became 1.4 to 1, but in 1969, they jumped to 2 to 1. Thus, while costs went through the roof, and despite serious and costly engineering errors by the Corps, we're now told we're going to get an even bigger return for our money than before. Most of this wizardry has been achieved by ascribing an ever-greater dividend to recreation."

As a result of persistent inquiry, Burroughs says, the Corps and the Delaware River Basin Commission have admitted that seasonal draw-downs will lower the level of the reservoir by eighteen feet which will expose 3,253 acres of mud flats to public view. In a year of extreme drought, the reservoir level will sink fifty-six feet, exposing 8,845 acres of mud-flat shore, and, Burroughs adds, "this does not include additional depletions from pump-off of a water supply of 300 million gallons daily, authorized to New Jersey. It does not include daily fluctuations of one to three feet additionally, to result from proposed pumped power generation. No angler need be told that such fluctuations deny the glittering promise of a viable and productive game fisheries resource. No swimmer needs a blueprint of the questionable joys in pursuing a fugitive water's edge to the shoreline. No canoeist, reveling in one of the last unobstructed, free-flowing river trips in the country, needs be warned of the magnitude of his forfeit."

On top of all this, Burroughs wonders about the massive impact of the 10½ million tourists who would come to play each year at the big mudhole. Consider, he says, "the problems of oceans of sewage disposal, in a region geologically unsuited to provide adequate soil percolation capacities; consider traffic and policing demands, in an area already choked with tourism and for which no sufficient new highway complex is in sight. Objectively and fairly, no one can deny the gift of the outdoors to the teeming public. But to put the picture in perspective, Yosemite Park, for example, comprising a facility approximately ten times larger in area than the proposed DWGNR preserve, has been incredibly taxed by the influx of only two and a half million visitors annually."

Then there is the problem posed by the dam to migrating fish. Proponents say installation of fish ladders will insure the perpetuation of upstream spawning runs, but to Burroughs that promise is "a lot of shad." He says no design technology can assure continuation of fish migration.

To stop Tocks Island, Burroughs plans to draw on the sanctions in Section 101 (Title I) of the Environmental Policy Act. "This legislation," he says, "enacted as Public Law 91-190, by the Ninety-first Congress (S. 1075) on January 1, 1970, provides, among other clear-cut prohibitions, that in any Federal proposal the responsible federal official shall study, develop and describe appropriate alternatives to recommend courses of action in any proposal which involves unresolved conflicts concerning alternative uses of available resources." God knows there exists, in the fervor of increasing thousands of opponents of this project, an unresolved conflict.

(11) Finally, New York City should see to it that the rivers and streams under its mercy have the right to live. The lower Croton River in northern Westchester County is a prime example of a stream in need of some mercy.

From personal experience, I do not know of any river in the metropolitan area that has the potential of the lower Croton. This river is one of the great natural treasures of the region, and it should be protected and respected. Starting in 1842, when New York City dammed the Croton six miles upstream from where it enters the Hudson, the river has been chopped into pieces as part of the reservoir system. The 1842 dam did not impound the entire river but merely checked part of the flow which was funneled to Manhattan via the Croton Aqueduct. In 1906 the huge New Croton Dam was completed. This dam, 3½ miles upstream from the Hudson, is more than 150 feet high, and instead of merely checking part of the flow, it shuts it off completely during the summer months. Water could flow from Croton Lake to the river below but New York City does not choose to make any release. As a result, part of the lower Croton dries up each summer, and life dies in these stretches.

Even so, the Croton comes to life in the spring. As the snow melts, Croton Lake begins to rise, and suddenly water begins to thunder over the dam into the river below. The Croton roars over small dams, churns through rapids and glides through deep pools down a magnificent granite gorge lined with hemlocks. It curves around several islands and then pours into the Hudson by the marshes on the south side of Croton Point. For more than a mile, the brackish tide from the Hudson reaches into the Croton, and striped bass, herring, smelt, blue crabs, shrimps and other marine animals throng into the river. In mid-May, when the runoff has slowed, the waters of the Croton are sparkling clear, and the careful observer can see the teeming life in the river. I know one skin-diver who has sat at the bottom of the "Rain Barrel," a twenty-five-foot-deep spring hole, to watch schools of striped bass and white perch.

In June or July, when the flow of water over the New Croton Dam ceases, parts of the Croton begin to dry up and die. Fish are trapped in isolated pools to die of disease or suffocation. The tides slosh back and forth near the mouth of the Croton, but the water soon becomes thick with dense mats of algae. The river is a wasteland, and despite requests for a "conservation release" of water, the city refuses to make it.

In sum, if the New York Urban Region is to offer a fruitful and productive life to residents, it is imperative that officials, both elected and appointed, learn to live within ecological limits and make proper use of what the region has to offer. As the three authors of the Rand Corporation study so eloquently put it in *Water Supply*:

> We should say at once, perhaps, that we do not believe that specialists in the field of water supply are any worse than the general run of mortals—but neither are they living saints, to be sheltered against all criticisms. There is a certain temptation for water-supply leaders to cast themselves in heroic mold as mighty battlers for the cause of pure and adequate water. To maintain the romance of this role, great projects are continually being conceived, planned and executed, some of these schemes being sound, others unsound, and some bordering on the manic. As compared with such dreams and schemes, the possibility of improving the efficiency of water use by such unromantic devices as elimination of waste or rationalization of pricing procedures may seem drab indeed—the more so as the large gains achievable by merely making better use of supplies in hand may indicate postponement indefinitely of vast new engineering wonders.

Of Sondry Folk

What Examples, Similitudes, Times, Places, and above all, Persons, with their speeches, and attributes, doe as in his *Canterbury*-tales (like these threds of gold, the rich *Arras*) beautifie his worke quite thorow.

HENRY PEACHAM, *The Compleat Gentleman*, 1622

Oure governour, And of our tales juge and reportour

Of Sondry Folk

*The Dramatic Principle in the
Canterbury Tales*

By R. M. LUMIANSKY
Illustrated by MALCOLM THURGOOD

AUSTIN : 1955
UNIVERSITY OF TEXAS PRESS

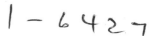

Library of Congress Catalog Card No. 54–10043
Copyright 1955 by R. M. Lumiansky
Printed in Austin, Texas, by the Printing Division
of the University of Texas

To my wife, Janet

Preface

Many scholars have written about the dramatic interplay present in various segments of the *Canterbury Tales*, but a detailed investigation from this point of view of the book as a whole has not been made available. This study offers analyses of the dramatic contexts within which each of the twenty-three performances by Chaucer's Canterbury Pilgrims is delivered; and from these analyses I have deduced a statement—more detailed and, I think, more illuminating than has hitherto appeared—concerning the operation of the dramatic principle which contributes so effectively to the lasting appeal of the *Canterbury Tales*. This statement, which forms a framework for the book, is developed at length in Part I and the Conclusion. The dramatic function of the General Prologue and the Links is treated in Part II. These framing statements and large elements in many of the twenty-three analyses (Part III) represent new ideas; in other instances I have attempted to select in sensible fashion from among numerous and often conflicting interpretations advanced by earlier commentators.

I am greatly indebted to many scholarly writers whose publications have treated matters of textual, literary, and cultural history. I also acknowledge gratefully a grant from the Tulane University Council on Research that allowed me time for work on this book.

Some material in this book first appeared in the *Explicator* (V [1946], item 20); Tulane *Studies in English* (I [1949], 1–29, and III [1952], 47–68); *PQ* (XXVI [1947], 313–20); *Journal of General Education* (III [1949], 309–12); *UTQ* (XX [1951], 344–56); and *PMLA* (LXVIII [1953], 896–906). This material is reprinted here in revised form with permission of the editors concerned.

R. M. Lumiansky

Tulane University
   September 15, 1954

Contents

[xi

CONTENTS

Illustrations

ILLUSTRATIONS

Of Sondry Folk

LIST OF ABBREVIATIONS

The following abbreviations are used in the notes and in the Selected Bibliography:

CT   *Canterbury Tales*
ELH   *English Literary History*
JEGP   *Journal of English and Germanic Philology*
MLN   *Modern Language Notes*
MP   *Modern Philology*
MLQ   *Modern Language Quarterly*
MLR   *Modern Language Review*
NED   *New English Dictionary*
PMLA *Publications of the Modern Language Association*
PQ   *Philological Quarterly*
RES   *Review of English Studies*
SP   *Studies in Philology*
TLS   London *Times Literary Supplement*
UTQ   *University of Toronto Quarterly*

The following shortened titles are used in the notes:

Robinson, *Works:* for F. N. Robinson (ed.), *The Complete Works of Geoffrey Chaucer* (1933). Line numbers, regularly inserted in the body of the present volume to facilitate reference to pertinent passages of the *Tales*, refer to Chaucer's text as it appears in Robinson, *Works*.

Sources and Analogues: for W. F. Bryan and Germaine Dempster (eds.), *Sources and Analogues of Chaucer's Canterbury Tales* (1941).

Bowden, *Commentary:* for Muriel A. Bowden, *A Commentary on the General Prologue to the Canterbury Tales* (1948).

Manly, *New Light:* for J. M. Manly, *Some New Light on Chaucer* (1926).

Curry, *Sciences:* for W. C. Curry, *Chaucer and the Mediaeval Sciences* (1926).

I : INTRODUCTION

The Point of View and the Assumptions

or centuries readers of Chaucer's *Canterbury Tales* have in various ways understood and commented upon its dramatic aspect. From twentieth-century critics who attempt to indicate this essential feature of Chaucer's literary genius, we have such remarks as the following: "The conception of the *Canterbury Tales* as drama is Chaucer's masterpiece"; ". . . the most astonishing characteristic of Chaucer's art is . . . what is commonly called the dramatic method"; ". . . the abundance of [Chaucer's] genius finds expression in terms of character, and, however much humour and pathos come into play, it is human character that starts him at his best."[1] And additional statements stressing the dramatic nature of the *Canterbury Tales* could be gathered by the score from the writings of other commentators.

The indisputable point here seems to be that Chaucer not only came in contact with human beings of all sorts in the course of his long public career as diplomat and civil servant, but that he took full advantage of the opportunity to observe closely the features, dress, habits, manners, quirks, affectations, and eccentricities of the people he met; and then, because of his interest in, and his keen observation of, mankind, he regularly conceived and developed his narratives as vehicles for character portrayal. Thus many of the individuals we meet in Chaucer's writings strike us as actors in a play, whom we come to know almost intimately from their performances. Upon this foundation—stated

[1] These passages, in the order quoted, are from J. L. Lowes, *Geoffrey Chaucer and the Development of His Genius*, 206; Manly, *New Light*, 294; and H. R. Patch, *On Rereading Chaucer*, 137.

here in its barest simplicity—Chaucer builds the intricate structure of his dramatic method.

Nowhere in Chaucer's work is this dramatic method so extensively employed as in the *Canterbury Tales*, for it was through the use of a pilgrimage as the framing device for a series of stories, and particularly through the creation of the Pilgrims as tellers of these stories, that Chaucer's dramatic genius found its fullest outlet late in his career. In fact, the *Canterbury Tales* seems to have originated and taken shape with the Pilgrims— the actors in the drama—as the steady center of focus. It will be my purpose in this book to analyze the performances given in the *Canterbury Tales* by Chaucer's actor-Pilgrims. Such analyses will serve a worth-while end in themselves if they in any way illuminate their various subjects; but these analyses taken together will also enable us to state, with a precision beyond that usually encountered, those specific techniques which make up Chaucer's dramatic method in the *Canterbury Tales*, and which constitute the dramatic principle for the book.

One conclusion which immediately emerges from this dramatic approach to Chaucer's book is that the stories, rather than being ends in themselves, are meant to be taken as complementary to the portraits and actions of their individual tellers. This does not imply that the tales are of little importance or that Chaucer was not greatly interested in good storytelling; it is to say, however, that the stories should be read in context. And the proper context for a given story consists primarily of the individual traits and the dramatic purposes of the Pilgrim telling that story. Accordingly, in attempting to interpret a particular Pilgrim's performance in the *Canterbury Tales*, a critic must first establish, to his own satisfaction at least, the traits that Chaucer intended us to associate with that Pilgrim, and the dramatic forces that govern not Chaucer as author but the Pilgrim as teller of the tale.

Although commentators are almost unanimously agreed upon the general view which I have been developing as a point of departure for this study of the *Canterbury Tales*, the possibility for considerable difference of opinion exists when we attempt a comprehensive statement treating the detailed workings of Chaucer's dramatic principle in the book. This difference of opinion seems to stem from three conflicting conceptions, which can perhaps be set forth most clearly by three representative quotations.[2] First, there is an almost complete negation of the dramatic approach:

Very few of the tales in the collection have much value for the characterization of their tellers. Chaucer shows, it is true, a due sense of propriety in assigning tales to pilgrims; thus, the gentry tell stories befitting their social respectability, and the smutty stories are put in the mouth of the common herd. But it would be a great mistake to interpret a given story as serving primarily to characterize its teller as an individual. Indeed, some of the tales seem quite unsuitable to their tellers as we find them described in the general prolog.

The second view is represented by the following comment on the Knight's Tale:

Chaucer always has two familiar rules or purposes in the *Canterbury Tales:* the more important is to tell a good story in accord with the literary climate of the day, and the other is to blend it with the temper and prejudices of the given pilgrim-narrator. The successful formula appears again and again; the "verray parfit gentil knyght, of his port as meeke as is a mayde," provides an illustration as authentic as those of the Wife of Bath or the Pardoner. It is therefore in keeping that, in its narrative essentials, the Knight's story shall cleave to the courtly line, the more so perhaps as this tradition is beginning to acquire a substantially antiquarian tinge by the time of Richard II.

According to this view, for Chaucer the quality and type of the tale were of first importance, and its suitability to its narrator secondary.

The third conception was set forth by Professor Kittredge, without doubt the leading exponent of a dramatic approach to the *Tales*. The often-quoted core of his argument follows:

The Canterbury Pilgrimage is . . . a Human Comedy, and the Knight and the Miller and the Pardoner and the Wife of Bath and the rest are the *dramatis personæ*. The Prologue itself is not merely a prologue:

<hr />

[2] The three quotations, in the order listed, are from Kemp Malone, *Chapters on Chaucer*, 211; E. B. Ham, *ELH*, XVII (1950), 256–57; and G. L. Kittredge, *Chaucer and His Poetry*, 154–56. Émile Legouis has an illuminating statement similar to Kittredge's; see his *Geoffrey Chaucer* (English trans.), 180–86.

it is the first act, which sets the personages in motion. Thereafter, they move by virtue of their inherent vitality, not as tale-telling puppets, but as men and women. From this point of view, which surely accords with Chaucer's intention, the Pilgrims do not exist for the sake of the stories, but *vice versa.* Structurally regarded, the stories are merely long speeches expressing, directly or indirectly, the characters of the several persons. . . . Thus the story of any pilgrim may be affected or determined,—in its contents, or in the manner of telling, or in both,— not only by his character in general, but also by the circumstances, by the situation, by his momentary relation to the others in the company, or even by something in a tale that has come before.

According to Kittredge, for Chaucer a tale exists primarily to characterize its narrator, and the quality of that tale—a question of secondary importance—cannot be considered apart from the presentation of its narrator.

The examination to be presented in this book is certainly more indebted to Kittredge's point of view than to either of the other conceptions. But throughout I shall use an approach which differs somewhat from his. In connection with the twofold problem of a tale by itself and the same tale in its dramatic context, I assume that both the stories and the storytellers in the *Canterbury Tales* have at least two purposes and that these two purposes regularly and intentionally mesh, so that the stories and the tellers, considered from the point of view of either purpose, gain vastly from their coexistence. On the simpler level, the story and the teller exist as separate entities—indeed, as types of medieval storytelling and of medieval society—but this existence then provides the firm foundation for the more complex level, on which the story and the teller serve a dramatic purpose and thereby add to, and gain from, each other. Which of these two purposes is more important is manifestly a question wide of the mark, since in terms of the book as a whole a given story or teller cannot be finally considered as existing solely for either purpose. Obviously, a tale's or a teller's separate existence contributes much to the dramatic existence of each; but there can be no final isolation of either tale or teller.

To be sure, there can be and there are, as we shall see, varying degrees of complexity among the various segments of the *Can-*

terbury Tales in the manner whereby one purpose meshes with the other; and there is also considerable variation in the success with which Chaucer employed this principle of double purposes for both his stories and his tellers—after all, his book was never completed, nor were the completed portions ever finally revised. But, in the light of his vivid introduction of the individual Pilgrims by means of the General Prologue, in the light of his setting up, by means of the Links and the Host, a movable stage from Southwark to Canterbury upon which the Pilgrims are to perform, and in the light of his assigning specific tales to individual tellers—however hazy this assignment may be in two instances—we are committed to the necessity of assessing a given tale or teller on the level of dramatic existence as well as on the level of existence as a separate entity. The "Pilgrims do not exist for the sake of the stories," nor do the tales exist for the sake of their tellers; rather, the crowning genius of Chaucer's enveloping plan for the *Canterbury Tales* derives from the fact that the Pilgrims and their stories exist for the sake of themselves and, at the same time, for the sake of each other.

Probably the most widely used generalization concerning this dramatic principle in the *Canterbury Tales* is that Chaucer gains dramatic effectiveness *by suiting the tale to the teller*. A generalization of this sort will be useful in the analyses which make up the body of this book so long as we understand, in accord with the preceding two paragraphs, that the statement must include its corollary that *the teller is suited to his tale*. In fact, the most pat generalization would be that Chaucer *suits the tale and the teller*. But, most importantly, we should observe that Chaucer suits the tales to the tellers—and the tellers to the tales—in a variety of ways.[3] The interpretations in Part III of this book of the performances by the Canterbury Pilgrims lead me to maintain that Chaucer employs three stages of dramatic development, or three techniques of dramatic presentation, in dealing with the Pilgrims and their performances in the *Canterbury Tales*. Let me define and illustrate each of them.

First of all, there is the simple suiting of tale and teller. We

[3] J. R. Hulbert has commented upon this variety from a point of view different from that used here; see *SP*, XLV (1948), 565–77.

are introduced to the teller by means of his portrait in the General Prologue; when his turn comes to perform, this teller recounts a story that fits what we earlier learned of his character. Such is the case with the Squire, a gay, lighthearted young man who tells, or begins to tell, the romantic tale of far-off Tartary, in which are evident certain attitudes that the Squire has acquired from his father, the Knight. There are no dramatic complications—no antagonisms pursued or axes ground—as contexts for the performances in this category.

Second, we find a large number of recitals for which there is motivation beyond the nature of the particular teller as revealed by means of his sketch in the General Prologue. For example, there is the Friar-Summoner controversy; these two worthies are professional enemies, whose enmity breaks into the open at the end of the Wife of Bath's Prologue. The tale each tells, as well as the prologue by which each introduces his tale—in other words, his whole performance—is aimed at discomfiting his adversary. It is important to note that this second technique of dramatic presentation includes the first. That is, the tales which the Friar and the Summoner tell are well suited to their characters as established in the General Prologue; but, in addition, their performances represent motivated drama, rather than the simple suiting of tale and teller. And the motivation for the performances in this category is essentially external, in that the drama here springs from outside circumstances, such as the professional enmity of the Friar and the Summoner.

Third and last, there is in several instances a complete dramatic revelation of a Pilgrim: first, by means of his portrait in the General Prologue; second, through his actions and words in his own prologue; and third, by means of his tale. Thus all the lines which Chaucer devotes to these particular Pilgrims combine to give us extended, well-rounded character studies. The Wife of Bath's performance illustrates this situation: we learn certain things about her from the General Prologue; her own prologue gives further details about her and sets up her antagonism to the antifeminists; then her tale, which certainly fits her character, serves as an *exemplum* illustrating her argument for female sovereignty. Thus this third technique of dramatic presentation includes not only the first (suiting of tale and teller) but also the second (external motivation of the drama); and then it goes beyond the second in the completeness and detail of character revelation. Present also is internal motivation for the performances in this third category. Not only do external circumstances come into play, but also the tensions within the individual Pilgrims dictate the performance. Important, too, in this technique is the fact that the teller is not fully aware of his detailed self-revelation.

These three techniques of dramatic presentation, the ranking of which obviously depends upon the complexity of dramatic interrelations surrounding the performances by the Canterbury Pilgrims, will be fully illustrated by the analyses which make up Part III and will be used for purposes of summary in the Conclusion. Since among Chaucerians "diverse men deem diversely" about these matters, it will perhaps be well to state here the five principal assumptions concerning the *Canterbury Tales* that will be used throughout this study.

First, in the interpretations I shall not be concerned with analyzing the action of the characters within the various stories except where such analysis contributes to establishing Chaucer's probable conception of a particular storyteller. Thus, in the Pardoner's performance, the presence of the *exemplum* involving the three rioters who seek and find Death is of importance to the analysis of the Pardoner's motives; but a detailed discussion of the old man who appears in that *exemplum* would be beside the point. Similarly, the Franklin's choice of a story stressing gentilesse and marital happiness is of importance here; but the literary function of the black rocks of Brittany within that story is not. On the other hand, the story told by the Wife of Bath bears detailed relation to the drama underlying her whole performance; consequently, specific analysis of many aspects of that story is quite in order. In short, this book is limited to the drama of the Canterbury Pilgrims, and does not pretend to consider the full drama within each of the narratives. The dramatic interplay within the stories is of great interest and importance to any student of the *Canterbury Tales*, but it is not always relevant to the aims of this study.

[9

A second assumption is called for because of the unfinished nature of the *Canterbury Tales*. In a number of places we think that we have evidence of Chaucer's earlier intentions in the assignment of tales. The Sergeant of the Law promises a tale in prose, but relates in verse the story of Constance; and the Shipman uses feminine pronouns in referring to himself. Probably we are to infer that at one stage in the composition of his book, Chaucer meant to assign the prose Tale of Melibeus to the Lawyer and the Shipman's Tale to the Wife of Bath. Now a question arises: To what extent do these traces of earlier assignment interfere with the working out of the dramatic patterns of which these tales are a part? It seems to me that whereas the traces of earlier assignment are immensely interesting, in that they furnish glimpses of Chaucer's working habits, they present no real barrier to interpretation of the drama; rather, they are an aid to such analysis. Presumably Chaucer had good reason for each of his changes in assignment of tales, and it is highly likely that these good reasons were chiefly a matter of dramatic suitability. Although the fabliau which the Shipman tells is adequately suited to the Wife of Bath, certainly the tale Chaucer finally gave her serves to a greater degree in making her performance an immortal creation; and, at the same time, the fabliau concerning the merchant of St. Denis is a fitting story for the Shipman to tell. Thus I am not bothered greatly by the faulty reference of pronouns, or by other minor evidences of earlier assignment of tales and lack of revision. Our main interest lies in the dramatic principle present in as final a version of the *Canterbury Tales* as is available. But it must be granted that because of the unfinished nature of the book, all the performances are not equally well worked out dramatically, and in several instances, as we shall see, the effect is not particularly successful.

The third assumption concerns the question of Chaucer's conscious artistry in the dramatic development of the Pilgrims. Although the view advanced by a number of critics in previous centuries of a naïve Chaucer, possessed of a fumbling native genius, has been thoroughly refuted by the writings of more recent Chaucerians, there are still many who hesitate to go very far in granting the subtleties of literary composition present in the *Canterbury Tales* except in specific matters concerning Chaucer's alteration of his sources for particular tales. Thus it is that we hear talk of this or that critic "reading meanings into" Chaucer's work, rather than illuminating the methods used in that work. In preparing this book I have assumed that in view of our limited knowledge of the fourteenth century, and in view of Chaucer's amazing understanding of human psychology and his equally amazing artistry in the techniques of utilizing that understanding in presenting his Pilgrims, it is unlikely in the extreme that a critic can illuminate to the full his portrayals; nor is the critic likely to "read into" these portrayals complexities of a degree not intended, so long as he bases his theories solidly on Chaucer's text itself and on the established findings of over one hundred years of steadily industrious and often brilliant scholarship. Look, for example, at the almost unbelievable "tightness of the weave" in the Merchant's story of January and May, where every sentence carries suggestions aimed at heightening the unlovely picture of an old man blinded by lust, a picture that reveals much of dramatic interest concerning the storyteller himself, the Merchant. In 1936, Professor Tatlock commented brilliantly upon Chaucer's skillful use of detail in this story, but there remained a number of aspects of Chaucer's possible dramatic purposes in this performance to which Professors Schlauch, Baugh, and Sedgewick, and Mrs. Dempster could call attention.[4] And doubtless future critics will have additional things to say about the Merchant's Tale. Of course, these interpretations differ at many points, and where they do, the intelligent reader will try to decide who presents the best case; he will not simply dismiss all the interpretations as "meanings read into" the Merchant's Tale.

My fourth assumption concerns what Professor Lawrence has called the combination of "artifice and realism" in the *Canterbury Tales*.[5] By "artifice" is meant those arbitrary characteristics of the book which are inherent in the conventions of late medieval storytelling and in Chaucer's framing plan; and liter-

[4] For these studies, in the order mentioned, see *MP*, XXXIII (1935–36), 367–81; *ELH*, IV (1937), 201–12; *MP*, XXXV (1937–38), 15–26; *UTQ*, XVII (1947–48), 337–45; *MP*, XXXVI (1938–39), 1–8.

[5] W. W. Lawrence, *Chaucer and The Canterbury Tales*, 24–63.

ary realism, we should remember, is not the same thing as full reality, but "a collective term for the devices that give the effect of reality." Thus, as artifice, we are asked to accept such facts as that most of the Pilgrims can speak in skillful verse, that thirty-odd people can all hear the storyteller despite the narrow, muddy road, that many of the Pilgrims know expert short stories and have considerable familiarity with learned material, that this whole company agrees to complete supervision by an innkeeper, that the omniscient Narrator remembers everything word-for-word, that no more than one person in the group from each class is the general rule, and that the telling of the tales would take neither more nor less time than seems available for them. These matters are far more bothersome to the critic who makes a list of them than to the reader who goes his way through the *Canterbury Tales* for the fun of it. For Chaucer, by his minute observations of dress and manners, by his frequent recording of personal likes and dislikes, and by numerous other devices which will be discussed in later sections, treats his company as a group of real people on a real pilgrimage, and it is as such that we shall examine them. Actually, the *Canterbury Tales* presents the effect of dramatic realism within a framework leading to the easy acceptance of certain artificialities.

The fifth and final assumption involves the frequently discussed question of the order that Chaucer intended for the stories in his unfinished book. All of the numerous manuscripts are dated later than Chaucer's death, and thus no one of them possesses any absolute authority. Further, these manuscripts show wide variation in the sequence of the stories, in the connections among stories, and in the presence and position of the Links. It was early seen, however, that the work falls into ten clearly defined groups or fragments, within each of which the order of the tales is relatively stable. Very careful examination of the manuscript evidence and of such internal evidence as references to time or place and cross references among groups has led to various theories as to the sequence of groups which Chaucer would have used had he completed the *Tales;* and, in addition, some scholars have argued that we cannot hope to determine Chaucer's intention in this matter.

The two theories that editors of the *Canterbury Tales* have followed are called the "Chaucer Society Order" and the "Ellesmere Order"; the former term results from the sequence employed for the editing of various manuscripts published by the Chaucer Society, the latter term from the sequence found in the Ellesmere manuscript. The following tables show the differences:

CHAUCER SOCIETY ORDER

Group A: General Prologue, Knight, Miller, Reeve, and Cook
Group B^1: Man of Law
Group B^2: Shipman, Prioress, "Sir Thopas," "Melibeus," Monk, and Nun's Priest
Group C: Physician, Pardoner
Group D: Wife of Bath, Friar, and Summoner
Group E: Clerk, Merchant
Group F: Squire, Franklin
Group G: Second Nun, Canon's Yeoman
Group H: Manciple
Group I: Parson, Retractions

ELLESMERE ORDER

Fragment I: General Prologue, Knight, Miller, Reeve, and Cook
Fragment II: Man of Law
Fragment III: Wife of Bath, Friar, and Summoner
Fragment IV: Clerk, Merchant
Fragment V: Squire, Franklin
Fragment VI: Physician, Pardoner
Fragment VII: Shipman, Prioress, "Sir Thopas," "Melibeus," Monk, and Nun's Priest
Fragment VIII: Second Nun, Canon's Yeoman
Fragment IX: Manciple
Fragment X: Parson, Retractions

It is immediately apparent that these two orders differ in the positions of VI (C) and VII (B^2); but neither order is without difficulties. According to the Ellesmere sequence, certain geo-

[13

graphical references do not make sense: Sittingbourne, forty miles from London, is mentioned much earlier than Rochester, thirty miles from London (III, 847, and VII, 3116); according to the Chaucer Society sequence, various artistic considerations are violated: for example, the Pardoner's interruption of the Wife of Bath (III, 163–92) meaninglessly follows his prologue and tale.

Recently, Professor Pratt[6] has convincingly defended a third order:

Fragment   I: General Prologue, Knight, Miller, Reeve, and Cook
Fragment   II: Man of Law
Fragment VII: Shipman, Prioress, "Sir Thopas," "Melibeus," Monk, and Nun's Priest
Fragment   III: Wife of Bath, Friar, and Summoner
Fragment   IV: Clerk, Merchant
Fragment   V: Squire, Franklin
Fragment   VI: Physician, Pardoner
Fragment VIII: Second Nun, Canon's Yeoman
Fragment   IX: Manciple
Fragment   X: Parson, Retractions

This sequence, which will be followed in Part III of this book, resolves the difficulties occasioned by the two orders set forth earlier. Further, it seems very likely from manuscript evidence that the whole problem of Chaucer's intended order for the *Tales* arose simply because at the time of his death the series which we call Fragment VII had been removed—perhaps to his work-table—from its proper place between Fragments II and III in his master set of manuscripts.

Here, then, are the point of view and the five fundamental assumptions which will be used for this study of the twenty-three performances by Chaucer's Canterbury Pilgrims. But before we begin to examine these performances discretely, it will be well to consider the function of the General Prologue and of the Links.

[6] R. A. Pratt, *PMLA*, LXVI (1951), 1141–67. This article includes a full discussion of earlier views.

II : THE MOVABLE STAGE

The General Prologue and the Links

*C*haucer's originality in selecting a pilgrimage as the framing device for the *Canterbury Tales* is often noted.[1] This framework he built by means of the General Prologue and the Links, i.e., the individual prologues and epilogues that occur between tales. It will not, however, be my purpose to remark further on his originality; nor is this the place to examine in detail many of the sketches of the various Pilgrims included in the General Prologue, or many of the individual Links; rather, I shall treat those aspects of the General Prologue which serve as preparation for the later dramatic performances by the Pilgrims, and shall emphasize the opportunity furnished by the Links for sustaining dramatic development. In other words, we are here concerned with Chaucer's use of the General Prologue and the Links to set up and to keep before us an adequate stage upon which to present his Pilgrims.

Look first at the opening sentence of the *Canterbury Tales:*

> Whan that Aprille with his shoures soote
> The droghte of March hath perced to the roote,
> And bathed every veyne in swich licour
> Of which vertu engendred is the flour;
> Whan Zephirus eek with his sweete breeth
> Inspired hath in every holt and heeth
> The tendre croppes, and the yonge sonne
> Hath in the Ram his halve cours yronne,

[1] See the chapter by R. A. Pratt and Karl Young in *Sources and Analogues*, 1–81. For a different view, see J. V. Cunningham, *MP*, XLIX (1951–52), 172–81.

And smale foweles maken melodye,
That slepen al the nyght with open ye
(So priketh hem nature in hir corages);
Thanne longen folk to goon on pilgrimages,
And palmeres for to seken straunge strondes,
To ferne halwes, kowthe in sondry londes;
And specially from every shires ende
Of Engelond to Caunterbury they wende,
The hooly blisful martir for to seke,
That hem hath holpen when that they were seeke.

I, 1–18

For our purposes, this passage deserves close attention because
of its appropriateness as an introductory statement to a narrative
in which we are to meet realistic human beings rather than stock
figures. Many critics have commented favorably upon this eight-
een-line sentence, most frequently because of its "poetic" nature.
It appears that they have generally used "poetic" to refer not to
the rhyme and meter but to the treatment of various aspects of
the arrival of spring: April showers, plants, Zephyrus, the new
shoots, the sun, the small birds. The truth is, however, that such
descriptions of the coming of spring are not at all unusual in the
literature of the Middle Ages; in fact, they are present even in
scientific writing. In other occurrences the critics have not
judged these descriptions of spring "poetic," and we are not often
told why Chaucer's lines deserve the term while similar passages
do not. Perhaps "poetic" needs further qualification before it fits
Chaucer's opening sentence. James Russell Lowell, in a well-
known comment, said that after repeating it to himself a thousand times, "still at the thousandth time a breath of uncontaminate springtide seems to lift the hair upon my forehead." But
Lowell did not state convincingly just why this is true of Chaucer's sentence and not true of other medieval descriptions of
spring.

The sentence is made up of two main parts: the description of
spring and the statement of the longing which people feel to go
on pilgrimages. The former idea is expressed in the two *when*-
clauses, the latter in the *then*-clause; thus the relationship of
these two parts of the sentence—and therefore of the two ideas

16]

they express—is causal rather than parallel. The truth of the second part results from the truth of the first part: because of certain characteristics of spring, people long in that season to go on pilgrimages. The sentence opens with the natural world and shifts, in its second part (the *then*-clause) to the world of human beings. Or, rather, the second part correctly places human beings in their relation to the natural world during a particular season of the year. And, within the world of human beings, the application is rapidly narrowed from pilgrimages in general to the specific English pilgrimage to Canterbury. "A breath of uncontaminate springtide" seemed to lift Lowell's hair when he read this passage chiefly because Chaucer specifically applied his description of the arrival of spring to the world of human beings.

Another important result of the combination of ideas which Chaucer included in this sentence is that therein the purposes and implications of a pilgrimage are examined in terms broader than the usual religious ones. In its simplest form the sentence says: "When spring comes, then folks long to go on pilgrimages." The fundamental spiritual nature of a pilgrimage is not thereby overshadowed or obscured, but the significance of a pilgrimage as a social event is also given emphasis. The long, hard English winter is just over; people are tired of living indoors, feeding fires, and bundling up in heavy clothes to go outside. Therefore, when April comes, they long to go on pilgrimages. And this statement of the social appeal of a pilgrimage—a vacation in the spring—strikes a familiar note in the experience of most human beings. Then, behind this broadened point of view from which Chaucer examines a pilgrimage, there lies the whole question of man's relationship to religion (the afterlife) and to nature (this life). The implication is that most people perhaps cannot successfully deal with religion, represented here by a pilgrimage, unless the spiritual aspects of religion are modified by natural, earthly considerations, represented here by the coming of spring. Chaucer's sentence surpasses similar medieval passages mainly because in it the often-used description of the arrival of spring serves to broaden and to make more humanly realistic the purposes of a pilgrimage.

It is immediately apparent that, when so understood, the opening sentence of the *Canterbury Tales* has an important introductory bearing on the rest of the General Prologue and on the *Tales* as a whole. As has been frequently said, the General Prologue is especially remarkable because the Pilgrims who are portrayed therein are realistic human beings. There are among these Pilgrims those who, like the Parson and the Plowman, are making the pilgrimage because of sincere devotion. There are others, like the Miller and the Shipman, who seem more concerned with the vacation in the spring. But the presence of most of the Pilgrims is the result of a combination of motives. For Chaucer, unlike most other medieval writers, knew enough about people to realize that unmixed black and white are colors which should seldom be used when painting living portraits. As we have seen, the first sentence of the General Prologue skillfully introduces the human element into the idea of a pilgrimage.

To say that Chaucer's choice of a pilgrimage as the framework for his collection of stories was a stroke of genius is to risk triteness. But it should be observed that the opening sentence, by placing the social appeal of a pilgrimage alongside its religious significance, serves an important function in adequately preparing for the use of this framework throughout the *Tales*. It not only prepares for our meeting realistic rather than one-sided people in the General Prologue, but it also makes us ready for Chaucer's keeping these people alive—that is, many-sided—during the pilgrimage itself by means of the three techniques of dramatic presentation defined in Part I.

Following this opening sentence, Chaucer begins his narrative:

> Bifil that in that seson on a day,
> In Southwerk at the Tabard as I lay
> Redy to wenden on my pilgrymage
> To Caunterbury with ful devout corage,
> At nyght was come into that hostelrye
> Wel nyne and twenty in a compaignye,
> Of sondry folk, by aventure yfalle
> In felaweshipe, and pilgrimes were they alle,
> That toward Caunterbury wolden ryde. I, 19–27

At once these lines introduce the story of the pilgrimage. With his usual expert economy in handling narrative openings, Chaucer rapidly gives here the answers to all the necessary questions: when?—one day in April; where?—in Southwark, at the Tabard Inn; why?—to go on the previously mentioned pilgrimage to Canterbury; and who?—"I" and a group of some twenty-nine other pilgrims. The second and perhaps less obvious purpose of the passage is to continue the combination, established by the opening sentence, of the two motivating aspects of a pilgrimage: religious devotion and a vacation in the spring. On the one hand, Chaucer here points out that he looks forward with "ful devout corage" to his pilgrimage; he will not slight the religious aspects of his trip. But on the other hand, he is well aware of the social possibilities and is quick to interest himself in the "sondry folk" who have already formed a "compaignye" that will make possible "felaweshipe" during the journey. And—most importantly, from his point of view as author—there can from such fellowship arise opportunities for the varied dramatic performances which the individual Pilgrims will give.

Fortunately, the atmosphere of the Tabard is conducive to fellowship, for no one could find fault with its accommodations (I, 28–29). Such an atmosphere is just what the sociable Chaucer, or our Narrator, as he might better be called, likes.[2] Everybody is in good spirits and busily goes about getting acquainted. The Narrator also moves easily about as he makes himself one of the group (I, 30–34). In these lines we quickly observe another introductory device for the drama that is to come later. For the Tabard possesses an air of pleasant, everyday informality in which the Pilgrims can relax and be themselves; furthermore, the reader can now guess that the Narrator is to be depended upon to get about and learn what is going on. He is a man who will miss none of the details in the gossip, the antagonisms, and the animosities that will inevitably spring up among the Pil-

---

[2] The idea of a sociable and gregarious Narrator in the *CT* is rejected—for no good reason, as I see it—in an article by Ben Kimpel in *ELH*, XX (1953), 77–86. See also the chapter on the *CT* in Henry Ludeke, *Die Funktionen der Erzählers in Chaucers epischer Dichtung.*

grims during the course of the pilgrimage. Also the narrative has progressed one step further, in that we have learned of the "forward" to get up early the next morning to start the journey, about which the Narrator promises to tell us.

Next comes the perfectly natural sentence to prepare us for meeting the Narrator's new companions (I, 35–42). By this time we realize sufficiently the probable keenness of the Narrator's powers of observation to feel that his descriptions of the other Pilgrims will be entertaining, and we begin to share his interest in these people as individuals to an extent that makes us willing for him to postpone his account of the trip in order to present the travelers. Moreover, his argument is a thoroughly sound one: if we are to understand and enjoy his account, we should first get to know the people who are taking the trip. The next 672 lines of the General Prologue present the portraits of the Pilgrims. In Part III, where we consider the individual performances, we shall examine carefully the particular traits set forth in many of these sketches. Here we are concerned with two technical devices which Chaucer uses in presenting the portraits, and which lead the reader to accept the Pilgrims as realistic persons. For in their form, as well as in their content, the portraits are a vital part of Chaucer's preparation for the dramatic events that will occur during the pilgrimage and the storytelling game.

First is the conversational ring of the style in which the individuals are described. This style continues the informal friendliness established by the Narrator's telling of his making himself a part of the group that entered this excellent inn, and it thus aids our acceptance of the Pilgrims' reality. One obvious means by which the conversational tone is conveyed to the reader is the Narrator's several references to the mechanics of what he is doing. He has taken this opportunity, while he has "tyme and space," to *tell*—not to write—about his companions; and he does not hesitate to remind us that this is an oral account, aimed at preparing us for understanding the coming narrative of the trip. Regularly a Pilgrim is introduced by the phrase "there was with us," or "there was," for we are dealing with the members of a particular group. After describing the Knight's character and travels, the Narrator will *tell* us of his array, but of the Lawyer's array he will *tell* no longer tale. Then, as he nears the end of the list, we are told "Ther was also a Reve, and a Millere,/A Somnour, and a Pardoner also,/A Maunciple, and myself—ther were namo." We are not allowed to forget that these sketches represent a rapid, oral interpolation which the Narrator kindly furnishes to help us understand the behavior of the Pilgrims after the journey begins.

Another means by which we are led to think of these sketches as parts of a natural, oral account is the Narrator's use of conversational exaggeration. The Friar is the best beggar in his order; no "vavasour" is so worthy as the Franklin, and no navigator so expert as the Shipman; the Physician is the world's best for talk of medicine and surgery; there could not be a better priest than the Parson; and so on. This sort of exaggeration is not unusual in everyday talk, and Chaucer had doubtless listened to enough stories around the Customs House to realize its value for producing conversational effects.

Chiefly, however, the conversational informality with which the sketches are delivered results from the Narrator's trick of halting momentarily his factual description of the clothes, appearance, or experience of a particular Pilgrim in order to insert a brief comment embodying his personal opinion. For example, in the sketch of the Sergeant of the Law, we are first told in a factual fashion:

> A Sergeant of the Lawe, war and wys,
> That often hadde been at the Parvys,
> Ther was also, ful riche of excellence.
> Discreet he was and of greet reverence—   I, 309–12

But in the next line the Narrator inserts his personal judgment: "He semed swich, his wordes weren so wise." Then the factual account is resumed for eight lines:

> Justice he was ful often in assise,
> By patente and by pleyn commissioun.
> For his science and for his heigh renoun,
> Of fees and robes hadde he many oon.
> So greet a purchasour was nowher noon:
> Al was fee symple to hym in effect;

> His purchasyng myghte nat been infect.
> Nowher so bisy a man as he ther nas.   I, 314–21

Then suddenly the Narrator puts in his evaluative remark: "And yet he semed bisier than he was." After that, the objective description is continued for the remaining eight lines of the sketch. Aside from the value of the Narrator's two brief personal comments in bringing alive his otherwise completely factual portrait of the Lawyer, these rapid expressions of opinion give this sketch the sound of everyday talk, in which a tinge of prejudice or gossip regularly turns up. Similar methods and results are present in the Narrator's pun on the philosophers' stone in the portrait of the Clerk; in the little joke he makes concerning "goldwasser" while describing the Physician; in the censure he passes on the Cook's "mormal"; in the mock innocence with which he suggests that the Shipman hails from "Dertemouthe"; in his sympathy with the Wife of Bath's deafness; in the bluntness with which he states a priest's responsibilities; and in his speculation concerning the Pardoner's physical defect. These instances, taken together, give to the sketches a ring of familiarity which inevitably leads the reader to think about the people described as living individuals who can play a part in the coming drama.

There is a second very effective device that Chaucer uses in the General Prologue to aid the reader in accepting the Pilgrims, from their portraits, as realistic people. Many critics have described this device as the combination of typical and individual traits; that is, a Pilgrim possesses certain characteristics which make him representative of a type, but, in addition, there is something about him which makes him stand out as an individual distinct from his type. Since the argument for the Pilgrims as representatives of types will not hold in some instances, a more exact way of describing this technique is to call it a combination of the expected and the unexpected. In any event, this latter terminology has the advantage of placing the emphasis upon the reader's reaction to the technique. Look, for example, at the Knight, with whose portrait the Narrator "first begins":

> A Knyght ther was, and that a worthy man,
> That fro the tyme that he first bigan

> To riden out, he loved chivalrie,
> Trouthe and honour, fredom and curteisie.   I, 43–46

So far, there is nothing surprising to a reader in these lines about the Knight. We expected to meet a brave and honorable representative of the age of chivalry. Neither are we surprised by the next twenty-one lines of the sketch, from which we learn of the Knight's wide travels and consistent success in campaigning. But then comes the unexpected shift:

> And though that he were worthy, he was wys,
> And of his port as meeke as is a mayde.
> He nevere yet no vileynye ne sayde
> In al his lyf unto no maner wight.
> He was a verray, parfit gentil knyght.
> But, for to tellen yow of his array,
> His hors were goode, but he was nat gay.
> Of fustian he wered a gypon
> Al bismotered with his habergeon,
> For he was late ycome from his viage,
> And wente for to doon his pilgrymage.   I, 68–78

From this latter part of the sketch we learn that the Knight is prudent, humble, circumspect in speech, modest in dress, and serious in religious devotion. And these are not traits we would expect to encounter in a professional military man. Thus, Chaucer's Knight is both courageous in battle and humble in manner, widely traveled and gently spoken, highly successful in war and truly devout. As a result of this combination of expected and unexpected traits, the Knight assumes memorable individuality in the mind of the reader.

It would seem, then, that in large part because of the conversational informality used in the portraits, and by the combining of expected and unexpected traits within a given portrait, we are led to accept the Pilgrims as convincing characters who can participate fully in the dramatic recital which we have been promised. But first the Narrator must pick up matters where he left them. The sketches completed, we therefore have a passage (I, 715–24) which serves as conclusion for the series of portraits and as reintroduction for the narrative of the pilgrimage. This passage refreshes our memory—possibly a bit hazy after the lengthy series of portraits—of the where, when, and why of this account, information that we had gained from the second sentence in the General Prologue. Now that we have met the people concerned, we can be sure that an account of their trip will be of interest. More specifically, this passage prepares for a report of the happenings in the Tabard Inn "that ilke nyght." But before giving this report, the Narrator wishes to make clear just where he stands with regard to certain dubious aspects of his responsibility. He accordingly launches at this point his mock apology (I, 725–46) : we should not consider him vulgar if he speaks plainly in reporting the words of his companions, for everyone knows that any reporter must either repeat matters as exactly as he can, no matter how crude they are, or else be guilty of lying. He also wishes forgiveness if he does not treat the Pilgrims according to rank. The effect of this mock apology is, of course, a whetting of the reader's appetite for what is to follow. The account will not be refined; if people act or speak improperly (as people sometimes do) we shall hear about it. And there will be no formalities about "degree"; these Pilgrims will be handled informally, not stiffly according to protocol. As preparation for convincing dramatic performances, this apology is a superb touch, suitably capped by the Narrator's "My wit is short, ye may wel understonde" ("After all, I'm just an ordinary sort of fellow, the same as you"). Now we are to get the report of the night's happenings, in which the Host, Harry Bailly, plays an important part.

The Host performs marvelously, making everyone "greet chiere," and we see why at the Tabard a guest was "esed atte beste." Soon a fine supper is served; "Strong was the wyn, and wel to drynke us leste." For the time being, the social aspects of the pilgrimage are uppermost. The Host is an impressive person, fit to be a major-domo of a palace:

> A large man he was with eyen stepe—
> A fairer burgeys is ther noon in Chepe—
> Boold of his speche, and wys, and wel ytaught,
> And of manhod hym lakkede right naught.   I, 753–56

He is also a merry man, but his love of mirth does not interfere with his business acumen:

> Eek therto he was right a myrie man,
> And after soper pleyen he bigan,
> And spak of myrthe amonges othere thynges,
> Whan that we hadde maad our rekenynges.   I, 757–60

And the Host's merry speeches include his proposals for the storytelling game.

Actually, the drama of the Canterbury pilgrimage can be said to commence right here in the Host's proposals (I, 761–821), if it did not start in the thirty-first line of the poem, with the Narrator's making himself one of the group. Certainly it is worthy of note that the Host's speech represents the first words spoken by anyone other than the Narrator. So far we have had expert preparation for dramatic effectiveness, but the drama has been static. Now the curtain rises, and the action begins. And this first action, in which the Host makes his proposals to the Pilgrims, is characterized by interesting dramatic overtones that include a rather subtle play of human relationships between the Host and the company of Pilgrims. In his first and very flattering speech, Harry tells the Pilgrims that he has just thought of a game which will entertain them while traveling and which will cost them nothing. He states, however, that before he will tell them his idea, they must all agree "For to stonden at my juggement,/And for to werken as I shall yow seye." At that, he orders the group to make evident by a show of hands whether or not they accept his stipulation, and he pauses for their decision.

The next four lines, in which the Narrator reports the group's acceptance of the Host's stipulations, show a bored and indifferent reaction on the part of the Pilgrims to Harry's first speech. At first glance, this reaction is a bit puzzling. The Narrator says, in effect: "We did not worry much about how we voted, for the matter seemed unimportant. The easiest thing to do was to let him tell his idea as he pleased." The indifferent attitude shown here by the Pilgrims is understandable when we realize that the easy assumption of authority and the concern for money apparent in the Host's speech might well have caused the Pilgrims to form an unfavorable first impression of him and to be somewhat suspicious of any idea to which he asked their blind agreement

That Harry felt this coolness and undercurrent of dislike is evidenced by the second line of his next speech: "But taak it nought, I prey yow, in desdeyn."

In his second speech the Host advances his suggestion of the storytelling game as a means of entertainment on the trip and offers his services—without charge—as guide. At the conclusion of this speech, he again asks for a vote from the Pilgrims. This time the agreement to his suggestion is enthusiastically unanimous. Oaths are sworn with "ful glad herte," and the Pilgrims voluntarily increase the Host's authority over them, making him their "governour," "juge," and "reportour," as well as "gyde." This warm reaction on the part of the Pilgrims to Harry's second speech, in striking contrast to the coolness they evidenced after his first, is an indication that they now feel somewhat relieved to find that his idea involves neither annoyance nor expense for them. Therefore, in an effort to offset their former indifference, they now bend over backwards in agreeing to Harry's proposal and to his leadership of the pilgrimage. On the basis of the friendly confidence thus established, the wine is fetched and drunk, and "to reste wente echon,/Withouten any lenger taryynge."

By means of this brief scene after supper in the Tabard, the Host is adequately introduced as the central unifying device for the *Tales*. He will control the company as best he can, and we shall often see the various Pilgrims through his eyes, as he appoints a new storyteller, comments upon a tale just finished, or attempts to bring forth private information from one or another of his company. But Harry is no mechanical master of ceremonies, to be used only as background against which the other Pilgrims are projected. By having the Host furnish many insights into his own character, Chaucer effects a complex dramatic development whereby we learn of such matters as Harry's married life, his taste in literature, and his political views. There can be no doubt that the drama of the Canterbury Pilgrims is made possible in large part by Chaucer's use of the Host as the unifying device.

From some points of view, the General Prologue should end at line 821, when the company goes "to reste"; the remaining lines

(I, 822–58) might better be considered the first link, a prologue to the Knight's Tale. As we have seen, the General Prologue, exclusive of this introduction to the Knight's Tale, is aimed primarily at preparing for the dramatic activities of the Pilgrims as they travel. It is now necessary to notice briefly the device Chaucer employs for retaining a movable stage throughout his book.

This device is the use of Links between the tales—short dramatic scenes in which various Pilgrims take part. The presence of these links allows for the appearance in action of the people whom we met at rest in the portraits that make up the bulk of the General Prologue. As an example, look at the introduction to the Knight's Tale which we just noticed. On the first morning of the pilgrimage, Harry gathers his "flok" together and leads them a short distance from Southwark. Then, with lordly authority, he reminds them of their agreement, the night before, to the storytelling game and to obeying his decisions. With that, he has them draw straws to see who shall tell the first tale. Whether by chance or through Harry's respect for "degree," the "cut fil to the Knyght," at which everyone is pleased. The Knight, behaving exactly in accord with what we learned about him from his portrait, says:

> Syn I shal bigynne the game,
> What, welcome be the cut, a Goddes name!
> Now lat us ryde, and herkneth what I seye.   I, 853–55

From this introduction we are in a position to look upon the story of Arcite and Palamon as a recital by the Knight, not just as one tale in a collection by Chaucer.

Immediately after the Knight's Tale we find another Link, the Prologue to the Miller's Tale, which offers even greater dramatic complication than the scene introducing the Knight's story. Not only is the Miller's Tale skillfully introduced by this link, but the Miller-Reeve antagonism is made evident and the way is thus also prepared for the Reeve's performance after the Miller's. By no means are all the Links in the *Canterbury Tales* so fully developed, and in some instances Chaucer provided no link to introduce a Pilgrim's tale. We can be almost certain, however, that had Chaucer finished his book, he would have given full attention to furnishing additional ones. And it is worth noting, I think, that the Links which come at the end of the *Tales*—Fragments VIII, IX, and X: Second Nun, Canon's Yeoman, Manciple, and Parson—represent as full and careful development as do those in Fragment I. Although Chaucer certainly did not start with the General Prologue and write straight through the Parson's Tale, there is every indication that throughout the composition of that portion of the *Tales* which he did complete, he realized fully the importance of the Links as a dramatic device.

At times we find within the *Tales* short scenes that are actually links even though they are not labeled as prologue to this tale, or epilogue to that. We have seen one example of this at the end of the General Prologue, in the lines introducing the Knight's Tale. Another occurs in the Friar-Summoner controversy near the end of the Wife of Bath's Prologue (III, 829–56). The Friar takes exception to the length of this prologue, and the Summoner attacks the Friar for meddling. Here, even before the current performance—that of the Wife—is completed, Chaucer has set up a motivated situation for the next two performances, those of the Friar and the Summoner. The opportunity for such flexibility in the use of links is one of the most prominent evidences of their value as a dramatic technique by means of which the Pilgrims are kept as the center of focus throughout the *Tales*. We turn now to the first of the performances by Chaucer's actor-Pilgrims.

III :

The Twenty-three Performances

1. THE KNIGHT

*I*n *the past*, the Knight and his recital in the *Canterbury Tales* have been favorite topics for critical comment, and, judging from the half-dozen or more studies which have recently appeared, this interest is in no danger of slackening.[1] Two aspects of the Knight's sketch in the General Prologue have received careful attention: his travels, and his possible connections with the Lollard movement. But his tale is a subject for investigators far more frequently than his sketch. Comparison of the tale with its chief source, the relation of the tale to the perhaps lost "Palamon and Arcite" mentioned in the Prologue to the *Legend of Good Women*, the significance of the astrological material in the tale, and analysis of the characters of Palamon and Arcite—these are topics which have interested most of those who have written about the Knight's Tale. Yet one fact emerges from a reading of all these studies: very seldom has this story been seriously considered in its dramatic context as a performance by the Knight, who is presented to us in the General Prologue and who also appears briefly elsewhere in the *Canterbury Tales*.[2]

[1] E. B. Ham surveyed many of these studies recently; see *ELH*, XVII (1950), 252–61.

[2] William Frost analyzed the tale from this point of view; see *RES*, XXV (1949), 289–304.

He loved chivalrie, Trouthe and honour, fredom and curteisie

Any discussion of the Knight and his tale from this point of view requires as preliminary the answering of three pertinent questions: (1) Are we justified in reading the story as a speech by the Knight? (2) In what ways have earlier commentators considered this story and its teller suited to each other? (3) How did Chaucer handle his source materials in forming this story?

The first of these questions can certainly be answered in the affirmative. The opening ten lines of the tale establish the narrative of Theseus' victory over the Amazons, his marriage to Hippolyta, and his journey homeward with his wife and her sister Emily. Then we have a series of direct comments from the Knight to his audience; for example:

> Lete I this noble duc to Atthenes ryde.   I, 873
>
> I wolde have toold yow fully....   I, 876
>
> But al that thyng I moot as now forbere.
> I have, God woot, a large feeld to ere,
> And wayke been the oxen in my plough.
> The remenant of the tale is long ynough.
> I wol nat letten eek noon of this route;
> Lat every felawe telle his tale aboute,
> And lat se now who shal the soper wynne;
> And ther I lefte, I wol ayeyn bigynne.   I, 885–92

Such comments leave no doubt about the dramatic situation: the Knight is talking directly to the Pilgrims. The end of the tale also makes this clear; the Knight says: "Thus endeth Palamon and Emelye;/And God save al this faire compaignye!" (I, 3107–3108). And the Miller's Prologue begins: "Whan that the Knyght had thus his tale ytoold" (I, 3109). The Knight is speaking to the company throughout his tale, and even though Chaucer should probably have revised line 1201,[3] critics err when they read passages in the tale as direct statements from "the author of the Wife of Bath," or state that in one instance "Chaucer himself steps outside the story [the Knight's Tale] long enough to remark that everything which may transpire in this world is precisely as God planned it."[4]

---

[3] "But of that storie list me nat to write."
[4] H. B. Hinckley, *Notes on Chaucer*, 113; Curry, *Sciences*, 161.

Consideration of the second question listed above indicates that though commentators generally find the Knight and his story well suited, there is a noticeable lack of detailed treatment of this subject. We encounter only such short remarks as that the tale "seems as if made for the Knight,"[5] that "a specimen of chivalric romance" is a proper story for a knight to tell,[6] that realistic military details in the story come naturally from the mouth of a fourteenth-century knight,[7] or that the tale is "perfectly suited" to its teller.[8] I find only one writer who feels that the tale is not well-suited to the Knight; he says: ". . . to this elderly, crusading Knight is assigned a tale of young love in a Grecian setting. Certainly this story would have suited the Esquire much better."[9] But the integrated Boethian elements of the Knight's Tale would indeed sound strange in the mouth of the youthful and inexperienced Squire.

As to the third question, concerning Chaucer's handling of his source materials, numerous scholars have compared this story with its primary source, Boccaccio's *Teseide*.[10] Chaucer increased the pace of the story by considerable cutting of his original and adapted the tale to the life of his own time. Most importantly, from our point of view, he made significant additions to his original.[11] Outstanding among these additions are passages from Boethius' *Consolation of Philosophy*. B. L. Jefferson indicated the extent of Chaucer's borrowing from Boethius[12] and stated, in connection with the *Troilus* and the Knight's Tale: "Chaucer did not use the Boethian material haphazardly for the interest that might be attached to the particular lines in themselves, but . . . he brings its consideration of the fundamental questions of human existence to bear in a large way on the lives of his characters."[13] However, Jefferson did not show in any detail just how

[5] Bernhard ten Brink, *History of English Literature*, II, 156.
[6] Robinson, *Works*, 4.   [7] Stuart Robertson, *JEGP*, XIV (1915), 226–55.
[8] Marchette Chute, *Geoffrey Chaucer of England*, 259.
[9] J. R. Hulbert, *SP*, XLV (1948), 575.
[10] See the chapter by R. A. Pratt in *Sources and Analogues*, 82–105.
[11] See Robinson, *Works*, 4–5.
[12] *Chaucer and the Consolation of Philosophy of Boethius*, cited hereafter as *Chaucer and the Consolation;* see also Curry, *Sciences*, 154–63.
[13] Jefferson, *Chaucer and the Consolation*, 120.

Chaucer brought the Boethian material to bear on the lives of the characters in the Knight's Tale.

Too often the Knight's Tale is considered only as an adaptation of the *Teseide*, as a romance of spectacle and movement, suited to the Knight merely by reason of his profession. Yet there is a clearly defined philosophical theme which dominates the Knight's Tale and which is not apparent to any large degree in the *Teseide*. This theme derives from the inclusion of terms and passages from the *Consolation* at crucial places in the chivalric narrative. And the resulting philosophical romance is thus skillfully suited to its teller, who is interested both in warfare and in man's relation to God. In order to see this suitability in full detail, let us first examine the Knight's character as it appears from the sketch in the General Prologue, enlarging upon an idea already presented in Part II, and then analyze the working out of the philosophical theme in his tale.

When, near the beginning of the General Prologue, Chaucer says that he will now describe the Pilgrims whom he met at the Tabard, we have just before the Knight's sketch the line, "And at a knyght than wol I first bigynne" (I, 42). From this line the reader naturally expects to meet a man who is courageous and who is both widely experienced and outstanding in warfare. Such expectations are fulfilled; the Knight is outstanding in his profession. But there is an unexpected element in his thirty-five-line portrait: this man is also notable for courteous conduct and piety, and these are not qualities regularly found in professional military men of any age. In the fourteenth century, "everyone knew how the true knight should conduct himself and everyone knew how seldom he was encountered in the world of actuality."[15] This statement gains support from consideration of Chaucer's comment about the Knight: "And though that he were worthy, he was wys,/And of his port as meeke as is a mayde" (I, 68–69). We can hardly fail to miss the force of the introductory "and though": even though the Knight was brave, he was pru-

---

[14] See H. S. Wilson, *UTQ*, XVIII (1948–49), 131–46, for a statement of the philosophical theme in the *Teseide* and in the Knight's Tale.

[15] Bowden, *Commentary*, 45.

dent and as modest as a maiden, contrary to the usual characteristics of "worthy" knights.

We now come to a consideration of the passages in the Knight's Tale which Chaucer took from Boethius' *Consolation of Philosophy*. This influential book Chaucer himself had earlier translated, and it seems to have been his favorite philosophical treatise. Three speeches in the tale contain the bulk of the borrowings: the speech of Arcite in *Prima Pars* (I, 1251–74), wherein he blames himself for seeking false felicity; the speech of Palamon in *Prima Pars* (I, 1303–33), wherein he finds the gods at fault; and the speech of Theseus in *Pars Quarta* (I, 2987–3040), wherein he discusses an established beneficent order in the universe. These three passages account for only about 100 lines among the more than 2,200 which make up the Knight's Tale.[16] Most of the 100 lines deal with one point, "the relation of Providence to man's happiness," and this point is, of course, at the very center of the *Consolation.*[17] Moreover, these three passages from the *Consolation* which Chaucer chose to add to his primary source represent the core of Boethius' argument and conclusion. It is also particularly noteworthy that Chaucer placed these passages at crucial positions in the Knight's Tale. The speeches of Arcite and Palamon come shortly after the two young knights are introduced, and furnish a key to the point of view held by each; Theseus' "bond-of-love" speech is placed near the end of the tale and sets forth the conclusion to which Lady Philosophy leads Boethius. Thus, as we shall later see in detail, the 100 philosophical lines in the Knight's Tale, coming from the *Consolation*, both motivate the characters and reflect upon the action occurring in the remaining 2,100 lines, which present the chivalric narrative of the *Teseide*.

But, in addition to the three speeches mentioned above, there are a number of shorter passages in the Knight's Tale either derived from, or reminiscent of, the *Consolation*. The very striking

[16] Jefferson, *Chaucer and the Consolation*, 130–31, 142–43.
[17] *Ibid.*, 118, 131.

34]

fact about these passages—so far unnoticed, I think—is that they regularly occur as explanation for the important events in the narrative. When Theseus decides to go hunting—a decision vital to the narrative, since it causes him to find Arcite and Palamon fighting in the wood, to learn of their love for Emily, and to arrange for the tournament—we have the following passage, based on Book IV, prosa 6, of the *Consolation:*

> The destinee, ministre general,
> That executeth in the world over al
> The purveiaunce that God hath seyn biforn,
> So strong it is that, though the world had sworn
> The contrarie of a thyng by ye or nay,
> Yet somtyme it shal fallen on a day
> That falleth nat eft withinne a thousand yeer.
> For certeinly, oure appetites heer,
> Be it of werre, or pees, or hate, or love,
> Al is this reuled by the sighte above.
> This mene I now by myghty Theseus,
> That for to hunten is so desirus.   I, 1663–74

It is the Boethian Destiny that causes Theseus to go hunting. Examination of the chain of important events, step by step through the Knight's Tale, shows that almost without exception the Knight accounts for each event by suggesting that it resulted from an influence outside the individual. This influence comes, in the majority of cases, from agents who hold established places in the hierarchy, set forth by Boethius in the *Consolation*, through which God deals with human beings. Providence, Destiny, Fortune, Nature, "cas," "aventure"—these are the Boethian terms that appear in the passages under discussion. A listing of the chain of important events in the Knight's Tale, together with the passages accounting for these events, shows this relationship:

1. The noble ladies persuade Theseus to fight against Creon; thus Arcite and Palamon come to be prisoners in Athens.

> Now be we caytyves, as it is wel seene,
> Thanked be Fortune and hire false wheel,
> That noon estaat assureth to be weel.   I, 924–26

2. Emily walks in the garden; thus Palamon and Arcite can see her.

> The sesoun priketh every gentil herte,
> And maketh hym out of his slep to sterte,
> And seith, "Arys, and do thyn observaunce."
> This maked Emelye have remembraunce
> To doon honour to May, and for to ryse.   I, 1043–47

3. Palamon looks out of the window; thus he falls in love with Emily.

> And so bifel, by aventure or cas,
> That thurgh a wyndow, thikke of many a barre
> Of iren greet and square as any sparre,
> He cast his eye upon Emelya.   I, 1074–77

4. Arcite, released through Perotheus' request, must return to Thebes to suffer the malady of love and leave Palamon near Emily in Athens.

> Wel hath Fortune yturned thee the dys,
> That hast the sighte of hire, and I th'absence.
> I, 1238–39
>
> For possible is . . .
> .   .   .   .
> That by som cas, syn Fortune is chaungeable,
> Thow maist to thy desir somtyme atteyne.   I, 1240–43

5. A vision of Mercury causes Arcite to return to Athens.

> . . . To Atthenes shaltou wende,
> Ther is thee shapen of thy wo an ende.   I, 1391–92

6. Palamon escapes from prison.

> Were it by aventure or destynee—
> As, whan a thyng is shapen, it shal be—
> That soone after the mydnyght Palamoun,
> By helpyng of a freend, brak his prisoun.   I, 1465–68

7. Arcite goes to the wood where Palamon is hiding.

> Now wol I turne to Arcite ageyn,
> That litel wiste how ny that was his care,
> Til that Fortune had broght him in the snare.
> I, 1488–90

8. Arcite selects a path near Palamon's bush; thus Palamon can overhear him.

> And in a path he rometh up and doun,
> Ther as by aventure this Palamoun
> Was in a bussh. . . . I, 1515–17

9. Theseus decides to go hunting, thereby finding Palamon and Arcite. Lines 1663–75, quoted and analyzed on page 35.

10. Theseus is moved to have mercy on the two knights.

> For pitee renneth soone in gentil herte. I, 1761

11. Theseus proposes the tournament to settle the love-debate.

> Thanne shal I yeve Emelya to wyve
> To whom that Fortune yeveth so fair a grace.
>   I, 1860–61

12. The gods arrange the defeat of Palamon in the tournament and the subsequent injury to Arcite.

> Now weep namoore, I shal doon diligence
> That Palamon, that is thyn owene knyght,
> Shal have his lady, as thou hast him hight.
> Though Mars shal helpe his knyght. . . . I, 2470–73

13. Arcite dies.

> Nature hath now no dominacioun.
> And certeinly, ther Nature wol nat wirche,
> Fare wel phisik! go ber the man to chirche! I, 2758–60

14. Palamon and Emily marry.

> Thanne is it wysdom, as it thynketh me,
> To maken vertu of necessitee. I, 3041–42

Of these fourteen events forming the narrative skeleton of the Knight's Tale, nine (Nos. 1, 3, 4, 6, 7, 8, 9, 11, and 13) are clearly explained as resulting from influences exerted by agents who appear in the Boethian hierarchy. For each of the remaining five events, a definite cause is assigned, and in three instances possible connection with the Boethian hierarchy is fairly obvious. The season (May) causes Emily to walk in the garden. "May" can here be understood as a representative of Nature.

"Pitee" causes Theseus to have mercy on Palamon and Arcite when he finds them fighting in the wood. Although this "pitee" is not an outside agent, it is often the equivalent, in Chaucer's usage, for the gentilesse, or noble conduct, which Lady Philosophy explained to Boethius.[18] The "necessitee" of which Theseus speaks in urging the marriage of Palamon and Emily is, of course, a result of the whole system set forth in the *Consolation*. The two remaining events involve the gods. A vision of Mercury sends Arcite back to Athens; and Saturn, Venus, Mars, and Pluto are involved in Arcite's mortal injury. Although these influences lie outside the Boethian system and are best regarded as a necessary part of the machinery of the story, they perform exactly the same function as do the agents from the *Consolation* in the motivation of the other events.

We are justified in concluding, then, that rather than being limited to the three speeches by Arcite, Palamon, and Theseus, the Boethian influence is so pervasive as virtually to control the action in the chivalric narrative which Chaucer took from the *Teseide*. This conclusion can be strengthened by careful examination, within the framework of the narrative, of the function and effect of the three speeches, and of the philosophical shifts which Palamon and Arcite experience.

Of the three Boethian speeches, the two by Arcite and Palamon (I, 1251–74, 1303–33) present an inescapable contrast. After his release from prison, Arcite says:

> Allas, why pleynen folk so in commune
> On purveiaunce of God, or of Fortune,
> That yeveth hem ful ofte in many a gyse
> Wel bettre than they kan hemself devyse?   I, 1251–54

And, he continues, "We seken faste after felicitee,/But we goon wrong ful often, trewely." Finally, he applies these views to his own situation and concludes that, since he cannot see Emily, he is as good as dead. Thus Arcite takes full blame for his miserable state and acknowledges the "purveiaunce of God." Meanwhile,

---

[18] Jefferson, *Chaucer and the Consolation*, 101–102.

Palamon entertains no such sweet reasoning. When he learns that Arcite is now at liberty "Swich sorwe he maketh that the grete tour/Resouneth of his youlyng and clamour." He thinks Arcite will be able to raise an army in Thebes and thereby win Emily, while he rots in prison. Then he cries out against the "crueel goddes," who, caring no more for mankind than for sheep, often permit the innocent to suffer. Consequently, he asks: "What governance is in this prescience,/That giltelees tormenteth innocence?" Palamon leaves the answer "to dyvynys," but he is convinced "that in this world greet pyne ys." His particular "pyne" is twofold: as a Theban he is kept in prison because of Saturn and Juno; and Venus torments him with jealousy and fear of Arcite. Thus Palamon finds no benevolent order or justice in the universe.

Although the two knights were indistinguishable when they were found in the pile of bodies after the battle, it is immediately apparent that at this point in the story, in their contrasting reactions to adversity, Arcite and Palamon represent to some degree the two states of mind that Boethius experiences in the *Consolation*. Arcite's view here is similar to that which Boethius has attained at the end of the book, after assimilating the teachings of Lady Philosophy; but Palamon here holds views similar to those of Boethius at the opening of it. The question at once arises as to just what shifts occur in the course of the Knight's Tale in the attitude held by each of the young men, as a result of the impact upon them of the series of incidents which they experience. Consideration of this question involves examining the characters of Palamon and Arcite in Boethian terms, and such an approach may well supplement the numerous studies, based almost exclusively on Chaucer's alterations of the *Teseide*, which treat the two heroes of the Knight's Tale.[19] The answer is relatively simple in the case of Palamon. With Arcite, however, we have an extremely complex problem.

Palamon's behavior preceding his Boethian speech is quite

---

[19] See, for example: H. N. Fairchild, *JEGP*, XXVI (1927), 285–93; J. R. Hulbert, *SP*, XXVI (1929), 375–85; P. F. Baum, *MLN*, XLVI (1931), 302–304; A. H. Marckwardt, University of Michigan *Contributions in Modern Philology*, No. 5 (1947); H. S. Wilson, *UTQ*, XVIII (1948–49), 131–46; W. H. French, *JEGP*, XLVIII (1949), 320–28.

consistent with the view expressed in that speech. In prison he impatiently roams back and forth (I, 1065, 1071) and steadily complains about his situation: " 'That he was born,' ful ofte he seyde, 'allas!' " (I, 1073). Then, at the sight of Emily, whom he mistakes for Venus, he prays for his and Arcite's release from prison (I, 1107). Finally, in the dispute as to who has pre-emption in loving Emily, Palamon addresses Arcite with the same injured air (I, 1129–51) that he later adopts in crying out against the cruel gods because Arcite is at liberty while he remains in prison. The point is that, throughout *Prima Pars*, Palamon has no conception of his place in a benevolently ordained universe and is intent only on attaining earthly happiness, or what Lady Philosophy calls "false felicity."

We see no change in his attitude until Arcite dies. Rather than accept his adverse situation with Boethian passivity, he manages, after seven years in prison, to drug his jailer and to escape with the help of a friend (I, 1467–75), and hides in the wood in great fear of death (I, 1518). His terrible anger (I, 1576–78) when he overhears Arcite's complaint causes him to force the duel in the wood (I, 1587). Similarly, in his prayer to Venus he says:

> Fynd thow the manere hou, and in what wyse:
> I recche nat but it may bettre be
> To have victorie of hem, or they of me,
> So that I have my lady in myne armes.   I, 2244–47

But with Arcite's death after the tournament, Palamon gives up his impatient complaining and his restless striving to fulfill his desires. He marches in the funeral procession "in clothes blake, ydropped al with teeres" (I, 2884), and after "certeyn yeres" (I, 2967) he is still in "blake clothes" and in haste comes sorrowfully in answer to Theseus' summons (I, 2975–80). Indeed, he is now called "gentil Palamon" (I, 2976), and is apparently most receptive to the Boethian philosophy that Theseus advances in his "bond-of-love" speech (I, 2987–3074). As "gentil Palamon" (I, 3077), who has now realized the folly of his blind pursuit of false felicity and has thus reached some understanding of an established benevolent order in the universe, he deserves Emily's hand and is a fit partner in a marriage which accomplishes wide political benefits (I, 2970–74): "And thus with alle blisse and melodye/Hath Palamon ywedded Emelye." The Knight takes his leave of this couple in words which suggest that Palamon's happy state results, in part at least, from his realization of his former misconceptions and his present acceptance of the Boethian view:

> And God, that al this wyde world hath wroght,
> Sende hym his love that hath it deere aboght;
> For now is Palamon in alle wele,
> Lyvynge in blisse, in richesse, and in heele,
> And Emelye hym loveth so tendrely,
> And he hire serveth al so gentilly,
> That nevere was ther no word hem bitwene
> Of jalousie or any oother teene.
> Thus endeth Palamon and Emelye.   I, 3099–3107

Palamon has bought God's love "deere," but he *has* "aboght" it. As suggested earlier, Arcite wrestles far more often than Palamon with the questions of man's relation to God and the individual's place in the universe. Arcite's first speech comes as advice to Palamon when the latter cries out at the sight of Emily:

> ... Cosyn myn, what eyleth thee,
> That art so pale and deedly on to see?
> Why cridestow? who hath thee doon offence?
> For Goddes love, taak al in pacience
> Oure prisoun, for it may noon oother be.
> Fortune hath yeven us this adversitee.
> Som wikke aspect or disposicioun
> Of Saturne, by som constellacioun,
> Hath yeven us this, although we hadde it sworn;
> So stood the hevene whan that we were born.
> We moste endure it; this is the short and playn.
> I, 1081–91

Here Arcite shows full awareness of, and compliance with, an established order, an order which "for Goddes love" should be accepted patiently. This Boethian view is, as we have seen, directly opposite to that held by the impatient Palamon in *Prima Pars* of the Knight's Tale. But almost immediately, when Palamon explains the cause of his outcry, Arcite looks at Emily and also falls in love with her. Falling in love brings an entirely new problem into his life, a problem of greater importance to him than imprisonment (I, 1118–22), and we soon see him giving up his former patient acceptance of his lot. He now argues bitterly with Palamon about pre-emption in loving Emily. When Palamon reminds him of their sworn brotherhood, Arcite quotes an "olde clerkes sawe": "Who shal yeve a lovere any lawe?" (I, 1164). Here is certainly a change from Arcite's former belief in immutable laws that produce situations which "may no other be." He continues:

> Love is a gretter lawe, by my pan,
> Than may be yeve to any erthely man;
> And therfore positif lawe and swich decree
> Is broken al day for love in ech degree.   I, 1165–68

Arcite now accepts love as a greater force than "positif" or man-made law,[20] and is eager to win Emily's "mercy and hir grace" (I, 1120).

It is of some importance to notice that the proverb which Arcite quotes here is from the *Consolation* and occurs in the course of the brief recital of Orpheus' loss of Eurydice, a story used as an *exemplum* pointing up the folly of seeking worldly happiness. In fact, the following moral is drawn from the story:

This fable apertenith to yow alle, whosoevere desireth or seketh to lede his thought into the sovereyn day *(that is to seyn, into cleernesse of sovereyn good).* For whoso that evere be so overcomen that he ficche his eien into the put of helle *(that is to seyn, whoso sette his thoughtes in erthly thinges),* al that evere he hath drawen of the noble good celestial he lesith it, whanne he looketh the helles *(that is to seyn, into lowe thinges of the erthe).*[21]

This context for Arcite's "sawe" indicates his possible knowledge of the risk he runs in shifting from his former patient acceptance of his lot, for "Orpheus lokede abakward on Erudyce his wif, *and lost hire, and was deed.*"[22] The point is, I think, that Ar-

---

[20] See G. C. Macauley, *MLR*, IV (1910), 17.
[21] *Boece*, Bk. III, m. 12, ll. 67–78, as presented in Robinson, *Works*, 418.
[22] *Ibid.*, ll. 65–67. (Italics mine.)

cite has now encountered an earthly end which he strongly desires to fulfill; in the face of this desire, his patient acceptance of prison, stated in his earlier speech, goes by the board.

Although as a result of falling in love he becomes, like Palamon, extremely impatient with his imprisonment, Arcite still maintains his former opinion that he and Palamon must spend their lives in the tower because of Fortune and the stars; he draws an analogy to the hounds, the bone, and the kite (I, 1177–80) and concludes his argument as follows:

> And, therfore, at the kynges court, my brother,
> Ech man for hymself, ther is noon oother.
> Love, if thee list, for I love and ay shal;
> And soothly, leeve brother, this is al.
> Heere in this prisoun moote we endure,
> And everich of us take his aventure.   I, 1181–86

It would seem that Arcite feels that he is controlled by two forces —Love and Fortune. He is determined to serve Love, but he realizes that his imprisonment is a part of an established plan.

Before long, however, it happens that Perotheus comes to visit Theseus and brings about Arcite's release. But Arcite is forbidden to remain in Athens and consequently can never see Emily again. His reaction to this event is stated in his Boethian speech, which shows him once more in the position of passive acceptance of his lot, for his experience has now taught him that it does no good to wish for changes.

Upon his return to Thebes he suffers the malady of love for "a yeer or two" (I, 1381). This alters his appearance beyond recognition; he becomes so feeble that there is every indication of approaching death. The two controlling forces, Fortune and Love, are leading him to destruction. At this point "hym thoughte how" the winged god Mercury appeared to him as he slept. Mercury says: "To Atthenes shaltou wende,/Ther is thee shapen of thy wo an ende" (I, 1391–92). Arcite awakens and decides to go to Athens to see Emily, no matter how much he suffers for it; he says, in fact: "In hire presence I recche nat to sterve" (I, 1398). This passage has been explained as an example of the deceitful oracle employed for dramatic irony.[23] Thus Mercury, possessing a supernatural foreknowledge, knows that the end "shapen" for Arcite's woe is death, while Arcite, a mere mortal, understands Mercury's ambiguous prophecy as a prediction of a happy reunion with Emily. In other words, we are told, the irony results from Mercury's foreknowledge and Arcite's misinterpretation through ignorance. To read the passage in this fashion is, I think, to disregard the preceding events and the consequent shifts in attitude experienced by Arcite earlier in the Knight's Tale. Actually, he seems well aware of the possibility of death as a result of his return to Athens; but he nevertheless chooses to follow Mercury's suggestion because of the misery of his present situation, which only the sight of Emily can alleviate.

Arcite has found in Thebes that Fortune and Love have placed him in a thoroughly unsatisfactory situation. The way in which the Knight states the appearance of Mercury suggests that the messenger of the gods is not a visitant sent to Arcite by a supernatural controlling agency to play the role of a deceitful oracle. Rather, Arcite, in his unsatisfactory situation and his preoccupation with the idea of returning to Athens and to Emily, seems to have conjured up Mercury to instruct him as he wants to be instructed—"Hym thoughte how that the wynged god Mercurie/ Biforn hym stood and bad hym to be murie" (I, 1385–86). Here is a situation strikingly similar to Africanus' appearance to the dreamer Chaucer in the *Parlement of Foules* (95–105), after Chaucer had read all day in Macrobius. And there are certain ominous circumstances about Mercury's visit of which Arcite seems well aware.

Arcite "took keep" that Mercury is dressed just as he was when "Argus took his sleep," that is, Mercury is dressed as a shepherd, and carries his "slepy yerde" (I, 1387–90). It is not absolutely clear that Arcite understood the danger foreshadowed for him when he quoted a part of the Orpheus legend as it appears in the *Consolation*; but here, in the reference to Argus, there can be no doubt as to Arcite's realizing that Mercury appears before him dressed exactly as he was when he visited Argus. The conclusion is inevitable that he must recall at this moment the story of Ar-

[23] David Worcester, *The Art of Satire*, 116.

gus' death: Jupiter, desiring Io, sent Mercury to kill Argus, whom Juno had set to watch Io.[24]

Further, Arcite's words after Mercury's statement indicate his awareness of the danger for him in returning to Athens (I, 1394–98); and his earlier experience has shown him the folly of striving against Fortune. Nevertheless, his alternatives at the moment are either to die of the malady of love in Thebes or to follow the dictates of Love and risk death by returning to Athens. Since Arcite is here a human being struggling for happiness under the control of Fortune and Love, he chooses the second alternative. But he is by no means the blind plaything of a deceitful oracle.

Having returned to Athens as Philostrate, Arcite serves "a yeer or two" (I, 1426) as page to Emily. Ennobled by love, he is "so gentil of condicioun" (I, 1431) that his reputation spreads through the court and Theseus makes him a squire. In this capacity Arcite prospers for three years (I, 1446). One day in May he gaily goes to a nearby wood to do honor to the season. But after his jollity he falls into sadness, for neither his being in Athens, where he can see Emily, nor his material prosperity has brought him happiness. In fact, as a servant of Love he is "Now up, now doun, as boket in a welle" (I, 1533). His melancholy calls forth an audible complaint (I, 1542–71) in which he states his great dissatisfaction with his present situation: the gods (i.e., Fortune) still oppress him bitterly by forcing him to maintain his disguise as a squire, and also Love leads him to his death, "That shapen was . . . erst than my sherte" (I, 1566). Arcite's decision, made four or five years earlier, to return to Athens has not brought him happiness. He still considers himself controlled by two governing plans, that of Fortune and that of Love. Within the two, the hardships brought on by Love seem to him far more grievous (I, 1569–71). He feels so little hope of solving his problems that he falls down in a trance (I, 1572–73).

Palamon has overheard this complaint and angrily challenges Arcite to a duel, again upbraiding him for breaking the oath of sworn brotherhood. Arcite once more states his defiance of positive law where love is concerned (I, 1604–1607), fetches the armor, and engages in the duel. When Theseus appears, halts the

[24] Ovid, *Metamorphoses*, i, 671–77.

duel, and asks who they are, it is Palamon rather than Arcite who answers. Arcite could, of course, have argued that he, as Theseus' faithful squire, was fighting in an effort to recapture Theseus' escaped prisoner. Such dishonesty would not have been surprising in a man who had lived as an impostor for many years. But when Palamon reveals the true situation to Theseus, Arcite remains silent. Death will not come to him unexpectedly: from the time of his imprisonment he has believed that Fortune was his foe, and he realized fully when he returned to Athens that Love might lead him to death. Moreover, once before, in desiring release from prison, he had seen the folly of striving against "purveiaunce of God." He is ready to consider himself as deserving death for not having passively accepted his destiny. But the ladies' pleading brings forth Theseus' sense of humor and his "pitee," and plans for the tournament are arranged. Arcite readily agrees to terms whereby Emily will be given "To whom that Fortune yeveth so fair a grace" (I, 1861). He perhaps sees in these arrangements the possibility of his attaining happiness within the spheres of both Fortune and Love, his controlling agents. If he should gain victory in the proposed tournament, he not only would win Emily and thus avoid death from Love (I, 1563–68) but also would escape the imprisonment and the exile brought upon him by Fortune (I, 1542–62).

This possibility seems uppermost in his mind when, shortly before the tournament, he prays to Mars for victory. Whereas Palamon in his prayer to Venus states that he does not care for military glory or victory in the tournament so long as he can have full possession of Emily (I, 2242–43), Arcite directs his prayer to the god of war, who, he thinks, can help him to win the tournament and thus to gain happiness within the two ordained plans which, in his opinion, govern his life. He consequently asks Mars to "have routhe upon my sorwes soore" (I, 2419)—all his "sorwes," not just those occasioned by Love—and to "Yif me the victorie, I aske thee namoore" (I, 2420). When, in answer to his prayer, the statue of Mars rings and murmurs "Victorie!" Arcite is "fayn as fowel is of the brighte sonne" (I, 2437).

In the tournament Arcite wins victory and expects an end to

the torments of both Fortune and Love; but the machinations of Saturn cause his horse to throw him, and he is mortally injured. When he knows that he must die, he sends for Emily and Palamon (I, 2762–63), in order to urge that, if Emily should ever "ben a wyf," she remember Palamon. In taking leave of Emily, Arcite speaks the well-known lines in which he not only attempts to summarize all his "sorwes smerte" (I, 2766), but also states his final bewilderment at the workings of a universe which, though ordained by "purveiaunce of God," has defeated him at every turn. He says:

> What is this world? what asketh men to have?
> Now with his love, now in his colde grave
> Allone, withouten any compaignye.
> Fare wel, my sweete foo, myn Emelye!
> And softe taak me in youre armes tweye,
> For love of God. . . .   I, 2777–82

Within the course of the Knight's Tale, Arcite begins with a patient acceptance of an established order whereby Fortune made his imprisonment inevitable; then, upon falling in love, he desires release from prison, but Perotheus' intervention and his own exile from Athens show him the folly of desiring things other than those which fall to his lot; next, at the point of death as a result of the workings of Love and Fortune, he chooses to return to Athens as Philostrate, but several years of prosperity within sight of Emily do not bring him happiness; finally, when he thinks the tournament furnishes him an opportunity of winning freedom from the adversities of both Love and Fortune, he prays to Mars for victory; but even victory leads only to death, and Arcite dies with no satisfactory solution to the problem of his relation to the governing forces of the universe. After all his wrestling with this problem, he can only make a final effort at a sensible reconciliation by urging Emily to remember Palamon if she ever decides to marry.

In conclusion, it is worthy of notice that Chaucer elected to alter his source in order to leave Arcite's philosophical questions unanswered. In the *Teseide*, Arcite goes up into the heavens and,

[47

A janglere and a goliardeys

realizing there the meaning of true felicity, laughs at those, including himself, who seek earthly happiness; but the Knight simply says:

> His spirit chaunged hous and wente ther,
> As I cam nevere, I kan nat tellen wher.
> Therfore I stynte, I nam no divinistre;
> Of soules fynde I nat in this registre,
> Ne me ne list thilke opinions to telle
> Of hem, though that they writen wher they dwelle.
> Arcite is coold, ther Mars his soule gye!   I, 2809–15

It remains only for Theseus in his "bond-of-love" speech to state the benevolence of God's ordained plan and to point out that there is no reason for lamenting Arcite's death at the height of his powers and reputation. Thus the way is prepared for the marriage of Palamon and Emily, which brings matters to a happy ending. The story is by no means a complete tragedy; as we learn later, the teller of this story does not like tragedy. In fact, the Knight says, when interrupting the Monk's recital, that it is much better to tell stories of a poor man who "clymbeth up and wexeth fortunat,/And there abideth in prosperitee" than to tell of prosperous ones who fall to low estate (VII, 2767–79).

2. THE MILLER

The Knight's recital, representing simple suiting of tale and teller, is followed by those of the Miller and the Reeve. These performances form a complementary pair within the structure of the *Canterbury Tales* and represent the second stage of dramatic development discussed in Part I. Not only do the fabliaux which these two Pilgrims relate fit with the coarse natures of their tellers, but, as we shall see, there is the added complication of an externally motivated antagonism, probably based on their personal experience as well as on traditional trade hostility.

From the Miller's sketch in the General Prologue (I, 545–66) our chief impression is of his strength and roughness. He is a "stout carl," muscular and of large stature, with broad shoulders and a thick chest. Expert in wrestling, he can heave a door from its hinges or butt it down with his head. Chaucer also gives a clear picture of his face: a broad red beard, a bristly wart on his nose, wide black nostrils, and an exceedingly large mouth. The Miller's behavior is in keeping with his appearance. He likes to gossip and tell dirty jokes, and he is not above stealing grain and overcharging for his work. He plays the bagpipe well and with this music leads the company from Southwark. We later learn that his name is Robin (I, 3129).

The pilgrimage is hardly under way before we get evidence of the Miller's disregard for good manners and of his liking for gossip and off-color stories. When the Knight completes his tale, the Host compliments him and then calls for a story from the Monk, next in rank to the Knight. But the Miller, who is drunk, has no respect for rank and loudly and profanely interrupts:

> . . . By armes, and by blood and bones,
> I kan a noble tale for the nones,
> With which I wol now quite the Knyghtes tale.
>
> I, 3125–27

Harry Bailly, who has noted the Miller's drunken state and has strong suspicions about the "nobility" of any tale he might tell, tries tactfully to silence him, but is unsuccessful and prudently withdraws from the argument. Now the Miller launches into his preamble. He knows from the noise he is making that he is drunk and asks that the company blame the ale of Southwark for any faults in his narration. For, he continues:

> . . . I wol telle a legende and a lyf
> Bothe of a carpenter and of his wyf,
> How that a clerk hath set the wrightes cappe.
>
> I, 3141–43

At once the Reeve breaks in:

> . . . Stynt thy clappe!
> Lat be thy lewed dronken harlotrye.

> It is a synne and eek a greet folye
> To apeyren any man, or hym defame,
> And eek to bryngen wyves in swich fame.
> Thou mayst ynogh of othere thynges seyn. I, 3144–49

It is here that the Miller-Reeve quarrel begins. The natural antagonism between a miller, who grinds grain, and a reeve, who, as overseer of a farm, has grain to be ground, has in the past been pointed to as the motivation for this quarrel, along with the fact that we are told in the General Prologue of the Reeve's being a carpenter in his youth (I, 613–14); and the Miller announces as his topic the cuckolding of a carpenter.[1] Recently, however, there appeared a better explanation of the basis for the quarrel.[2] It seems likely that the Miller-Reeve acquaintanceship must be of long standing, that the Miller worked years ago as servant boy in the Reeve's household at the time when the Reeve, then a carpenter, was made a cuckold by a cleric. This background makes the Reeve's violent interruption much easier to understand. If objection were being made to the Miller's topic simply on the ground that a carpenter is cuckolded, we would expect the Carpenter, one of the five Guildsmen present, to voice the complaint rather than the Reeve. But the Reeve probably knows the content of the coming story and is therefore able to tell the Miller that he will be both sinful and foolish to ridicule or insult any man and to circulate such a rumor about a wife. Naturally the Reeve wants the Miller to tell a story about "othere thynges."

We find further support for this explanation when we look at the story that the Miller relates. In the remaining lines of his prologue (I, 3151–66), he seems greatly to enjoy taunting the Reeve. Also, Robin the Miller knows the Reeve's name, Oswald, and knows that he is married. Further, he seems aware that Oswald is certainly not going to answer his question: "Why are you so angry about my tale now?" The force of the "now" apparently means: "You were cuckolded a long time ago; why worry about it now?" The Miller makes clear to Oswald in this speech

---

[1] Frederick Tupper, *JEGP*, XIV (1915), 265–70.

[2] R. A. Pratt, *MLN*, LIX (1944), 47–49. For different views, see W. C. Stokoe, Jr., *UTQ*, XXI (1951–52), 120–27; and C. A. Owen, Jr., *MLN*, LXVII (1952), 336–38.

that he is not suggesting that all wives are unfaithful; he is simply showing how one—namely, Oswald's wife—made her husband a cuckold. His point is, of course, that the Reeve just used bad judgment in selecting a wife. It may be that the Miller is considerably more sober than he pretends; under the guise of drunkenness he has enjoyed overriding the Host, and now he is having the fun of discomfiting the Reeve.

After this exchange, the Narrator enters his apology for having to repeat the Miller's low tale and advises anyone not interested to choose another story. In the narrative we meet an elderly and gullible carpenter named John, who has a young and skittish wife named Alice. Nicholas, a young cleric on the lookout for amorous adventure, has a room in their home. By convincing John of the imminence of a second flood, Nicholas manages to spend a night in John's bed with Alice, while John sleeps in a tub tied under the roof, which he is to cut loose when the floodwaters rise. But there is another young man, Absolon, also desirous of Alice's favors. When he asks for a kiss at her bedroom window, he suffers indignities which drive thoughts of love from his mind. Then he gets his revenge upon Nicholas by means of a red-hot iron. Nicholas screams for water to cool his scorched flesh; old John, hearing the one word "water," thinks the second flood has now come, cuts the ropes holding up his tub, crashes to the floor, breaks his arm, and becomes a laughingstock for all the neighbors, who believe Alice and Nicholas when they say the old man is mad.

Obviously the element in this tale which the Miller means to apply to the Reeve is the character of the carpenter. Old John, jealous of his young wife, is made a cuckold and an object of ridicule. Perhaps there is also another personal application to be made in the story: Robin the Miller may be Robin the servant boy in the carpenter's household. Two parallels in their descriptions support this identification: first, "The Millere was a stout carl for the nones" (I, 545), and "His knave was a strong carl for the nones" (I, 3469); second, in the Miller's sketch we learn "Ther was no dore that he nolde heve of harre" (I, 550), and, in the tale, Robin the servant boy "by the haspe he haaf it [the door] of atones" (I, 3470). Although it is true that Nicholas caused John to send Robin to London before the merry night described in the tale, we suspect strongly that upon his return Robin lost no time in finding out how John came to break his arm.

If our speculations adequately describe the basis for the Miller-Reeve quarrel, we see good reason for the distance separating these two Pilgrims as they travel: the Miller is at the head of the company leaving Southwark, while the Reeve rides always last.

3. THE REEVE

Most of the Pilgrims enjoyed the Miller's tale, and the Narrator tells us that only the Reeve seemed disturbed by it (I, 3859–63). We now know the probable reason for Oswald's anger; but the Narrator, as well as the other Pilgrims, does not know that the Miller's narrative probably resembled an actual incident, for Robin did not come right out with that fact. Thus the Narrator, a separate person from Chaucer the author of the *Tales*, can only conclude that the Reeve's displeasure stems from the fact that old John was a carpenter. We note, however, that Oswald's ire is now much less than when he interrupted the Miller *before* he had told his tale; the reason for this may well be that Oswald is considerably relieved to find that the Miller's account of John's cuckolding did not include a direct connection with him. At any rate, when he begins to talk now, he finds fault with the tale only a "lite."

The Reeve first says that he could easily tell a story about the cuckolding of a miller if he cared to stoop to ribaldry, but he is old and does not want to enter into such a game. The mention of his advanced years leads him to a lengthy personal statement concerning the loss of virility in old age.[1] No inconsistency exists

[1] For an analysis of this speech, see G. R. Coffman, *Speculum*, IX (1934), 272–77.

Noon auditour koude on him wynne

here with the picture of the Reeve gained from the General Prologue (I, 587–622). There he was an unattractive lean man of unpleasant disposition, skilled in farm management and very capable in detecting thievery in others, as well as in feathering his own nest dishonestly. Furthermore, his long calfless legs give evidence, according to medieval science, of his lustful, sensual desires, an interest fully apparent in his lecture on old age.[2] The General Prologue also suggests that the Reeve is no longer young: he has had charge of the accounting "Syn that his lord was twenty yeer of age"—presumably for considerable time, since his managing to become wealthy by secret dealings must have been done bit by bit over many years to escape detection.

The Host does not care much for the Reeve's remarks on old age and interrupts, speaking "as lordly as a kyng":

> ... What amounteth al this wit?
> What shul we speke alday of hooly writ?
> The devel made a reve for to preche,
> Or of a soutere a shipman or a leche.
> Sey forth thy tale, and tarie nat the tyme.
>
> I, 3901–3905

The Reeve, forgetting his earlier determination not to tell a bawdy tale, now asks the company's indulgence for a tale in which a miller is cuckolded. We find also that the Reeve tries here to cover up the real reason for his former anger by offering the lame excuse that he is a carpenter:

> This dronke Millere hath ytoold us heer
> How that bigyled was a carpenteer,
> Peraventure in scorn, for I am oon.
> And, by youre leve, I shal hym quite anoon;
> Right in his cherles termes wol I speke.
> I pray to God his nekke mote to-breke;
> He kan wel in myn eye seen a stalke,
> But in his owene he kan nat seen a balke.   I, 3913–20

The tale which follows, like that told by the Miller, is among the most brilliant in the whole collection. Two college boys from

---

[2] Curry, *Sciences*, 71–90. On the Reeve's position and duties, see H. Y. Moffett, *PQ*, IV (1925), 208–23.

Wel koude he knowe a draughte of Londoun ale

Cambridge University, John and Allan, set out to catch the arrogant Miller Simkin in the act of stealing their college's grain while he grinds it. Simkin, realizing their purpose, unties their horse, which runs away. Then he grinds the grain honestly, as the boys look on. But when they prepare to return to the college, they find their horse gone and must chase it; Simkin now steals half a bushel of their meal, which he has his wife bake into a loaf. Not until after nightfall do John and Allan get back with their horse. Because of the lateness of the hour, they ask Simkin to give them lodging for the night, and he agrees, celebrating his success at outsmarting these educated young men by drinking a great deal of ale. During the night the boys manage to take their revenge: Allan sleeps with Simkin's daughter, John with his wife. When Simkin discovers what is going on, the students beat him roundly, take their horse and meal, and go back to the college, picking up the stolen loaf, about which the daughter had told Allan, on the way out. "Lo, swich it is a millere to be fals!"

The application of this tale to its dramatic context is obvious. Simkin, in his rough, bullying ways, in his dishonesty, and in his drunkenness, bears close similarity to the loudmouthed Robin, whom Oswald seeks to spite. Thus the Reeve has settled his score with the Miller.

4. THE COOK

The Cook's performance presents difficulty to anyone analyzing the dramatic situation in which the tale is to be read; this difficulty stems primarily from the tale's being so brief a fragment that the reader has little indication of what its exact purpose would have been had the tale been completed. Nevertheless, from the fragment and the prologue which introduces it, we can see, first, positive evidence of its suitability to its teller as he is described in the General Prologue; and, second, some faint indication of its being used in a Cook-Host antagonism, though this dramatic antagonism is more hinted at than functional.

The fifty-eight-line fragment (I, 4365–4422) which the Cook relates does little more than introduce the chief character, Perkin Reveller. This gay young man well deserves his name, for he much prefers dancing, love-making, attending weddings, and drinking in taverns to remaining at work in the victualer's shop where he is an apprentice. He is always in attendance at parades and often plays dice in the street with companions of a similar stamp. With these companions Perkin is so generous that often his master finds the cashbox empty. Finally, Perkin is discharged and goes to live with an accomplice, whose wife keeps a shop for appearance' sake but practices prostitution for a living. At this point the tale breaks off, an unfortunate fact which those of us who find Chaucer's fabliaux to our taste will ever regret.

Considerable discussion has ensued as to why Chaucer left this tale unfinished. Although there may be some merit to the view that he abandoned the tale because he felt that three fabliaux in succession would be too much of a good thing,[1] or to the opinion that since he was in this instance not working from a direct source, as was often his custom, he therefore could not finish the story easily,[2] it seems to me a more likely explanation is simply that other duties or interests caused him to put aside the tale, which he never found opportunity to return to. Be that as it may, there is no denying the suitability of this fragmentary fabliau to the earthy Cook.

Three points stand out in the sketch of the Cook (I, 379–87): he is in the employ of the Guildsmen for the duration of the pilgrimage; he is very expert in his trade; and he unfortunately has a sore. Certain aspects of the first and third points are worthy of brief mention here. The main emphasis in the sketch of the Guildsmen (I, 361–78) is upon their *nouveau riche* characteristics.[3] Their equipment and clothing are ostentatiously new, and

[1] R. K. Root, *The Poetry of Chaucer* (rev. ed., 1922), 179–80.

[2] See the chapter by E. D. Lyon in *Sources and Analogues*, 148–54.

[3] E. P. Kuhl, *Transactions* of the Wisconsin Academy of Sciences, Arts, and Letters, XVIII (1916), 652–75.

their wives, who have no reason to complain about lack of money, are extremely appreciative of their place in society. We are not surprised, therefore, to find that these wealthy middle-class Londoners have brought along a cook for this pilgrimage, and the contention is not convincing that if the sketch of the Guildsmen were added to the General Prologue late—as is unlikely—we are to understand that the Cook was brought along by the Lawyer and the Franklin.[4]

More pertinent to our present interest are several comments that bear upon the Cook's "mormal." We cannot be absolutely sure whether this is a running or a dry sore,[5] or whether it is on the Cook's shin or chin.[6] It does seem clear, however, that this mormal indicates that the Cook is given to a disregard for sensible dietary habits and to lechery and love of licentious living.[7] The mormal, therefore, is not only a memorable individualizing trait in the picture of the Cook; it also helps explain the gusto with which he describes the gay doings of Perkin Reveller.

There is in the Prologue of the Cook's Tale (I, 4325–64) evidence of a Cook-Host antagonism. The "gentils" may not have liked the fabliau which the Reeve has just completed, but the Cook, Hodge [i.e., Roger] Ware, certainly enjoyed it. He expresses his approval by beating the Reeve on the back and exclaims at length on the fitting punishment the two college boys meted out to scornful Miller Simkin. Then he urges that the fun not be halted and volunteers to tell the company as best he can about a little "jape" that occurred in "oure citee." The Host agrees to this suggestion but feels called upon to warn the Cook that the tale must be good. Harry explains the need for this warning by pointing out that Hodge has sold many twice-cooked pies in his cookshop and has been bitterly cursed by many pilgrims who were sickened by the food he sold them, for there are numerous flies in his shop. After these thrusts, the Host attempts to placate the Cook by implying that he is only jesting:

[4] Carroll Camden, Jr., *PQ*, VII (1928), 314–17; Kemp Malone, *ELH*, XIII (1946), 41–42.
[5] Curry, *Sciences*, 48; Haldeen Braddy, *MLQ*, VII (1946), 265–67.
[6] See Manly and Rickert, *The Text of the Canterbury Tales*, V, 33. The better manuscripts have *shin*.
[7] Curry, *Sciences*, 50–52.

Now telle on, gentil Roger by thy name.
But yet I prey thee, be nat wroth for game;
A man may seye ful sooth in game and pley.

I, 4353–55

The statement that a man may speak the truth openly so long as he is jesting does not, of course, do much toward taking the sting from Harry's earlier remarks. But Roger Ware, like the Miller, is not the man to be intimidated by Harry Bailly. He comes back immediately with a Flemish proverb to the effect that a joke which is true is a poor joke, and then states his determination to even the score with the Host by telling a tale, presumably true, in which an innkeeper will play a part (I, 4358–64).

This lively scene not only gives us the names of both the Cook and the Host but also admits us as spectators to a brisk clash of tradesmen in late fourteenth-century London. There was at that time an actual innkeeper named Harry Bailly[8] and an actual proprietor of a cookshop named Roger Ware.[9] Further, for a contemporary reader the antagonism that we have just examined would have seemed perfectly natural in the light of legal restrictions at that time.[10] The laws governing victualers strictly prohibited cookshops from selling food not freshly prepared and for which reasonable rules of cleanliness were not observed; but the records show that many London cooks did not pay close attention to these laws. Thus the Host's thrusts at the Cook strike home. But, on the other hand, there were also laws to the effect that London innkeepers must not sell food or drink in competition with victualers, such as the Cook; consequently, many innkeepers moved outside the city limits to Southwark, where these laws could not be enforced. Accordingly, there is little reason for Roger Ware, a London cook, to love Harry Bailly, a Southwark innkeeper. And their antagonism in the Cook's Prologue is a natural development of their relationship as tradesmen.

Despite this expert dramatic framework which Chaucer has provided for a fully developed controversy, we cannot be sure just what Roger has in mind when he says that his tale of an inn-

8 Manly, *New Light*, 77–83.
9 Edith Rickert, *TLS* (1932), 761; E. D. Lyon, *MLN*, LII (1937), 491–94.
10 Frederick Tupper, *JEGP*, XIV (1915), 256–70.

keeper will not come now but will come before "we parte." It may be that at this stage in the writing of the *Canterbury Tales* Chaucer was still working according to the plan set forth in the General Prologue, whereby each Pilgrim would tell two tales going to, and two tales returning from, Canterbury, a plan he seems to have abandoned later. Or it may well be that the Cook's fragment treating Perkin, the idle apprentice, would have, if completed, constituted an indirect ridiculing of the Host, and that his saying that he will postpone his thrust at Harry is simply a device aimed at putting Harry off his guard. But such speculation is useless, for we have no shred of information about the matter. The Cook will reappear when in the Manciple's Prologue he is again involved in a controversy; but before then he must have opportunity to become "ful pale and no thyng reed" (IX, 20) as a result of too much strong drink.

5. THE SERGEANT OF THE LAW

Five sections in the *Canterbury Tales* concern the Lawyer: (1) the sketch in the General Prologue; (2) the Introduction to the Man of Law's Tale; (3) the Prologue of the Man of Law's Tale; (4) The Man of Law's Tale; (5) a part of the Epilogue to the Man of Law's Tale. The tale itself, in which we meet the steadfast Constance, has many similarities to a saint's life; however, the framework for the tale involves not only the Lawyer and the Host, but also Chaucer himself and possibly John Gower. As a result, this performance presents an even more difficult problem to a critic analyzing the dramatic relationships surrounding the tale than did that of the Cook. It will be well to grant at the outset that there are certain aspects of the problem which apparently cannot be explained completely.

First of all, there is the station of the teller of this tale: he is a

He semed bisier than he was

Sergeant of the Law in the General Prologue but simply a Man of Law in the remaining sections. As Professor Manly showed, a sergeant of the law in the fourteenth century was not just another attorney; rather, he was an extremely important and wealthy member of the legal profession.[1] One therefore wonders why in the performance by this Pilgrim the much less specific term "Man of Law" is used. The only workable hypothesis is that generally adopted: the Man of Law who tells the tale is the Sergeant of the Law in the General Prologue. It is the Host who, in calling for a tale from the Lawyer, originates this confusion of terms. Harry says: "Sire Man of Lawe, . . ./Telle us a tale anon, as forward is" (II, 33–34). One explanation, of course, for this shift in names is that the Host, though realizing that he is addressing a member of the legal profession, does not know that this Pilgrim has the high rank of Sergeant of the Law. Such a mistake might have arisen from the modesty of the Sergeant's clothing: "He rood but hoomly in a medlee cote" (I, 328). Sergeants seem generally to have dressed more richly. As an innkeeper the Host would have the habit of arriving at an estimate of a person's status by reference to his clothing—witness his comments about the Canon's shabby clothing (VIII, 629–39).

There can be little disagreement, I think, with Professor Manly's suggestion that Chaucer took a contemporary sergeant of the law, Thomas Pynchbek, as model for his Sergeant of the Law. This is not to say that the literary creation equals Pynchbek; it is to say, however, that there are humorous overtones in the literary sketch that would have been meaningful to anyone who knew much about Pynchbek—for example, the line "Ther koude no wight *pynche* at his writyng." A brief review of Manly's findings will perhaps be helpful here in making clear the outlines, at least, of the Pilgrim who is later to poke fun at Chaucer's literary efforts and then to tell the tale of Constance. Pynchbek was made a sergeant of the law not later than 1376, and he dealt extensively in land, his family thereby becoming extremely well to do. He belonged to the political faction opposite to that with which Chaucer seems to have been sympathetic, and the Pynchbek estates were near the estate of Chaucer's sister-in-

[1] Manly, *New Light*, 131–57.

law, Katherine Swynford, whom Chaucer's wife often visited. Furthermore, there is a story that Pynchbek had a quarrel with one of Chaucer's friends, William Beauchamp. Then, too, Chaucer most likely studied law at one of the Inns of Court, where he almost certainly would have known Pynchbek.

These facts seem to offer an acceptable explanation for the satiric tone which Chaucer uses when introducing his Sergeant of the Law (I, 309–30). These lines show that Chaucer does not wish us to take the Sergeant of the Law at the same high value which that worthy attaches to himself. Rather, we derive the picture of a high-ranking legal personage, who not only is markedly pompous in his words and actions but who also busies himself steadily in amassing money and land.

When we consider the Introduction to the Man of Law's Tale, we first find thirty-two lines of rather heavy admonition to the company by the Host. Although Harry is "nat depe ystert in loore" (II, 4), he computes from the sun that the time is ten o'clock, and he delivers to the Pilgrims a little lecture against wasting time in idleness. Then he calls on the Lawyer to tell a tale:

> Sire Man of Lawe, . . . so have ye blis,
> Telle us a tale anon, as forward is.
> Ye been submytted, thurgh youre free assent,
> To stonden in this cas at my juggement.
> Acquiteth yow now of youre biheeste;
> Thanne have ye do youre devoir atte leeste.   II, 33–38

Note the legal terminology in this speech: "forward," "submytted," "free assent," "cas," "juggement," "acquiteth," "biheeste," and "devoir." Harry intends to leave no doubt that he can address a professional man in the proper professional terms.

The Lawyer at once states his desire to keep his promise; there is, however, one trouble: he does not know any worth-while story which that writer Chaucer has not already told in such English as he could muster—though he was not very skillful with meters and rhymes. Indeed, the Lawyer continues, if Chaucer has not recounted these tales in one book, he has in another, "For he hath toold of loveris up and doun/Mo than Ovide made of mencioun" (II, 53–54). To prove this point the Lawyer refers to

Chaucer's early work *The Book of the Duchess,* and then to the later *Saint's Legend of Cupid (Legend of Good Women),* citing the individual stories in the *Legend* (II, 57–76).

It would seem from the bantering tone of the Lawyer's comments about Chaucer as a writer that the way is being prepared for some entertaining dramatic complexity. When we recall Chaucer's satiric treatment of the Sergeant of the Law in the General Prologue, we are not particularly surprised to find that this Pilgrim now pokes fun at Chaucer. A factor deserving consideration in this situation is that possibly we should understand that the Lawyer recognizes Chaucer, whereas the other members of the company do not. Certainly the contemporary London court-and-business circle was not so large but what a comptroller of the customs and a sergeant of the law would have met, and the close connection which Manly showed between Pynchbek and Chaucer certainly does not hinder such an assumption. Yet these two are the only Pilgrims drawn from that circle. That the Franklin accompanies the Lawyer (I, 331) does not indicate necessarily that the former knew the exact identity of his companion, though if the Franklin understands the banter here, the joke is the better. Clearly, the Host does not know the Sergeant of the Law, since he calls him Man of Law; and we see from the prologue to "Sir Thopas" that Harry certainly does not know Chaucer (VII, 695). The Lawyer's jests about Chaucer's clumsiness in poetic composition, about his writing in English rather than in Latin or French, and about his prolificness in telling love stories may result from his recognizing the poet as a member of the company. If so, we can see here the germ, at least, for a dramatic antagonism which might have been intended as a framework for the story the Lawyer is to tell. But this possibility is not developed.

Indeed, the Lawyer next shifts to a kind of defense of the moral content of Chaucer's stories. He says that Chaucer has never written about "Canacee,/That loved hir owene brother synfully" (II, 79), about Apollonius of Tyre, or about any other such abominable topics: "Of swiche cursed stories I sey fy!" (II, 80). This defense of Chaucer by the Lawyer has been interpreted as a thrust at John Gower, who in his *Confessio Amantis* did tell the two stories mentioned.[2] It is further argued that this jibe caused the two friends, Chaucer and Gower, to fall out. However that may be, the mention of these stories treating of incest seems to cause the Lawyer to abandon his jocular attitude toward Chaucer as poet; on the contrary, he goes on to pay Chaucer compliments:

> But of my tale how shal I doon this day?
> Me were looth be likned, doutelees,
> To Muses that men clepe Pierides—
> *Methamorphosios* woot what I mene;
> But nathelees, I recche noght a bene
> Though I come after hym with hawebake.
> I speke in prose, and lat him rymes make.   II, 90–96

The Pierides are, of course, the daughters of Pierus of Ema-thia, who, according to Ovid's *Metamorphoses*, vied with the Muses and were changed into magpies. Thus the Lawyer is saying that he is loath to vie with Chaucer as a storyteller. Yet he must tell a tale, and he does not really care if he comes after Chaucer "with hawebake," that is, with plain fare, a narrative which is not a brilliant literary production. Therefore, the Lawyer will tell a tale in prose and leave rhyming to Chaucer. This statement represents a complete reversal from the Lawyer's earlier jokes about Chaucer's lack of skill with meter and rhyme. It also seems to indicate that Chaucer at one time intended to have the Lawyer tell a prose tale rather than the rhymed story of Constance, and it is argued that the Tale of Melibeus was at that time assigned to him.[3] At any rate, despite these several seemingly impossible problems, we have seen that the possibility of an entertaining dramatic antagonism between the Lawyer and Chaucer, hinted at earlier, has been abandoned. From the last two lines of this introduction we learn that the Lawyer's earlier jocularity has now shifted to "a sobre cheere."

That the material we are now examining does not represent Chaucer's final revision for the Lawyer's performance is suggested by the fact that the last line of the Introduction would

---

[2] Margaret Schlauch, *Constance and the Accused Queens*, 132–34; this book includes references to earlier treatments of the question.

[3] J. S. P. Tatlock, *The Development and Chronology of Chaucer's Works*, 197.

lead us to expect the tale to begin immediately. Instead, we first
have the Prologue of the Man of Law's Tale; and this prologue,
which treats the evils of poverty and is practically a translation
of a section in Pope Innocent's *De Contemptu Mundi,* jars oddly
with the Introduction and with the story which follows. Of the
thirty-four lines that make up this prologue, the first twenty-two
set forth the dire results of lack of money. Of course, recollection
of certain lines from the Lawyer's sketch in the General Prologue
makes clear that this Pilgrim, to whom large fees and unentailed
land were so important, is completely in character when he holds
forth against the "condicion of poverte." However, such comments do not seem to fit with the preceding thrusts at Chaucer
and possibly at Gower, nor are they especially apposite as an
introduction to the tale of Constance, whose hardships do not
result primarily from poverty.

The last twelve lines of this prologue do represent a more
easily understandable transition from the stanzas on poverty to
the tale itself. Here the Lawyer praises "riche marchauntz" as
the ideal of happiness and prudence. Furthermore, since such
merchants travel to distant lands, they are bearers of news of all
sorts. Indeed, says the Lawyer:

> I were right now of tales desolaat,
> Nere that a marchant, goon is many a yeere,
> Me taughte a tale, which that ye shal heere.
>
> II, 131–33

For the second time, the way is cleared for the tale, and a further
connection with the prologue is established when we find that
the Sultan of Syria learns of Constance from the tidings brought
by "chapmen riche" (II, 135).

The story which the Lawyer tells permits far simpler and
clearer analysis from the dramatic point of view than do its introduction and prologue. Although this tale has been considered
inappropriate to its teller,[4] more recent critics have discovered an
increasing body of evidence for its dramatic suitability. Three
aspects of the tale, to be examined, are particularly pertinent in
this connection: the narrative method employed in the tale, the

---

[4] *Ibid.,* 172; T. R. Lounsbury, *Studies in Chaucer,* III, 436.

literary type to which the tale belongs, and the occurrence in the tale of terms from canon law. We should bear in mind that for Chaucer's tale of Constance the direct source is Nicholas Trivet's *Anglo-Norman Chronicle*, and that here, as elsewhere in the *Canterbury Tales*, Chaucer's alterations of his source constitute some of the surest evidence as to his efforts at suiting tale and teller.[5]

First, concerning the suitability to a lawyer of the narrative method used here, two quotations will perhaps suffice:

1. He [the Lawyer] tells his tale as if he were pleading before a jury, using every oratorical device, anticipating objections and answering them; quoting Scripture; at emotional points working on their feelings with bursts of horror or pity, praying, execrating, or breaking into passionate outcries.[6]

2. The narrative order is sound, the transitions are clear. The presentation is very sympathetic. The digressions from the narrative proper are comments pertinent to the course of action; the apostrophes arouse the emotion of the listener still further in behalf of the sufferer, or temporary client.[7]

Second, what seems to me a strong case has been made recently to the effect that the story told by the Lawyer should be classified as a sentimental tale rather than as a romance, and that as such it would have satisfied middle-class taste.[8] In the tale "blatant emotionalization, a show of verisimilitude, common piety, and broad, trite characterization are clothed incongruously in a semblance of the romantic manner." Such a sentimental tale is well suited to the Lawyer, a member of the middle class, who would not be disposed to tell the kind of romance most popular with the nobility.

Third, a more specific kind of evidence to show that Chaucer aimed at suiting this tale and its teller is to be found in the discussion by the Syrian privy council of the Sultan's marriage to Constance (II, 204–24); this section represents an addition by

[5] See the chapter by Margaret Schlauch in *Sources and Analogues*, 155–206. Recently an important study has appeared by E. A. Block in *PMLA*, LXVIII (1953), 572–616.

[6] W. H. Browne, *MLN*, XXIII (1908), 53.

[7] E. C. Knowlton, *JEGP*, XXIII (1924), 83–93.

[8] B. I. Duffey, *ELH*, XIV (1947), 181–93.

Chaucer to Trivet's version. "The Man of Law first thinks of the proposed marriage as a problem in canon law to be solved by the Sultan's advisers, presumably men of some legal background, and this reveals the interest of his own legal mind." The problem is *disparitas cultus*—the difference between the Sultan's Mohammedanism and Constance's Christianity—and canon law required that this difference be resolved by the Sultan's baptism.[9]

Another specific passage has point here. When Constance stands before King Alla to be tried for the murder of Hermengild, of which she is falsely accused, the Lawyer interrupts his narrative and uses one of the few realistic analogies to be found in the tale:

> Have ye nat seyn somtyme a pale face,
> Among a prees, of hym that hath be lad
> Toward his deeth, wher as hym gat no grace,
> And swich a colour in his face hath had,
> Men myghte knowe his face that was bistad,
> Amonges alle the faces in that route?
> So stant Custance, and looketh hire aboute.   II, 645–51

This offhand reference to a courtroom scene comes quite naturally from the lips of the Lawyer, who must have seen the pale faces of condemned criminals many times.

A further aspect of the tale deserves notice: throughout, despite her extreme hardships, Constance never seems to dispute the necessity for obedience to authority. When she is to leave for Syria, she unquestioningly obeys her parents, though to depart grieves her sorely:

> Allas! unto the Barbre nacioun
> I moste anoon, syn that it is youre wille.   II, 281–82

And she never for a moment attempts to act against the supposed command from her husband, King Alla, that she leave Northumbria within three days. Closely connected to this respect which Constance shows for authority is the possibility that the Lawyer's Tale should be regarded as, among other things, preparation for the discussion of "maistrye" in marriage, a topic which will assume great importance in a number of later performances by the

[9] P. E. Beichner, *Speculum*, XXIII (1948), 70–75.

[69

Pilgrims. The question at issue then will be whether or not women should have sovereignty over their husbands. In the Lawyer's Tale, at least four specific passages set up clearly the accepted antifeminist view, widely advocated by the contemporary clergy, who held that Eve first brought about man's fall, that women have duplicated her action ever since, and that a wife is a lesser being whose natural role is subordinate to that of her husband.[10] The Lawyer, as a conservative proponent of established authority and of law and order, might be expected to espouse these antifeminist arguments. In his tale we find the following pertinent comments:

> Housbondes been alle goode, and han ben yoore;
> That knowen wyves; I dar sey yow na moore.
>
> II, 272–73

> I, wrecche womman, no fors though I spille!
> Wommen are born to thraldom and penance,
> And to been under mannes governance.   II, 285–87

> For thogh that wyves be ful hooly thynges,
> They moste take in pacience at nyght
> Swiche manere necessaries as been plesynges
> To folk that han ywedded hem with rynges,
> And leye a lite hir hoolynesse aside,
> As for the tyme,—it may no bet bitide.   II, 709–14

> Sooth is that thurgh wommanes eggement
> Mankynde was lorn, and damned ay to dye.
>
> II, 842–43

The first and third of these comments are interpolated into the narrative by the Lawyer, while the second and fourth are spoken by Constance herself. Not only is the point of view which these passages set forth that to be expected from the Lawyer, but also this theme might well pave the way for the lively altercations to occur in future performances.

Perhaps the clearest indication of the suitability of the tale and the Lawyer comes in the opening lines of the Epilogue to the tale:

[10] See F. L. Utley, *The Crooked Rib,* for a survey of the argument about women in the Middle Ages.

> Owre Hoost upon his stiropes stood anon,
> And seyde, "Goode men, herkeneth everych on!
> This was a thrifty tale for the nones!"   II, 1163–65

The Host's "thrifty tale" takes us back to the Lawyer's opening protest: "I kan right now no thrifty tale seyn" (II, 46). Harry Bailly, at least, found the tale to his liking and, in calling upon the Parson for the next performance, shows that in his opinion the Lawyer has acquitted himself well, despite his learning:

> Sir Parisshe Prest, . . . for Goddes bones,
> Telle us a tale, as was thi forward yore.
> I se wel that ye lerned men in lore
> Can moche good, by Goddes dignitee!   II, 1166–69

6. THE SHIPMAN

As in the case of the Lawyer, the Shipman's performance shows vestiges of an earlier plan on Chaucer's part and a lack of final revision. The problems here, however, occasion a critic somewhat less discomfort than do those just considered in connection with the Introduction and Prologue to the Man of Law's Tale, for we can be fairly certain that the story known as the Shipman's Tale was previously assigned to the Wife of Bath. But before examining this situation in detail, we should look closely at the character of the Shipman, since, despite Chaucer's shift in assignment of the tale in question, one can maintain—successfully, I think—that the story and its teller are not completely unsuited and that there are also several hints of a dramatic antagonism to be observed.

In some ways the Shipman's presence is the hardest to account for among the Pilgrims who make up the Canterbury company. He is surely not going to the shrine of St. Thomas to ask forgive-

Of nyce conscience took he no keep

ness for his lack of scruples, his murdering of prisoners, or his thefts of wine—matters of which we learn from his sketch in the General Prologue (I, 388–410). His behavior on the pilgrimage, particularly his refusal to listen to a tale from the Parson (II, 1178–90),[1] is anything but devout. On the other hand, neither does a pilgrimage seem the kind of vacation the ship's captain would likely choose. Whatever the reason for his presence, the fact remains that the Shipman is a very likable person, who makes no bones about what he is. As with most sailors, his horsemanship leaves much to be desired, but he is ready for any emergency and seems to get a great deal of pleasure from life. Since this Shipman comes from Dartmouth and has a vessel named the *Madelaine*, it seems likely that he is modeled after Peter Risshenden, a shipmaster for the well-known contemporary freebooter John Hawley.[2] But, despite the Shipman's lack of scruples, he is a valuable and experienced man: "Hardy he was and wys to undertake;/With many a tempest hadde his berd been shake." And in his profession he is thoroughly competent.

Further, as we have noted, the Shipman has little sympathy with preaching and religious hairsplitting; rather, his is a comfortable acceptance of the fundamentals. He tells the Host, who after the Lawyer's Tale has called upon the Parson, that the clergyman shall not be allowed to preach:

> He schal no gospel glosen here ne teche.
> We leven alle in the grete God . . .
> He wolde sowen som difficulte,
> Or springen cokkel in our clene corn.   II, 1180–83

We gather also that the Shipman did not find much pleasure in the sober tale of Constance that the Lawyer has just finished; the master of the *Madelaine* greatly prefers stories of a gayer sort:

> And therfore, Hoost, I warne thee biforn,
> My joly body schal a tale telle,

[1] There is some difficulty with the manuscript situation of the Epilogue to the Man of Law's Tale. The lines in question, however, seem perfectly in keeping with the character of the Shipman as presented in the General Prologue. See R. A. Pratt, *PMLA*, LXVI (1951), 1148–57.

[2] Manly, *New Light*, 169–81; F. E. White, *MP*, XXVI (1928–29), 249–55, 379–84, and XXVII (1929–30), 123–28; Margaret Galway, *MLR*, XXXIV (1939), 497–514.

> And I schal clynken you so mery a belle,
> That I schal waken al this compaignie.
> But it schal not ben of philosophie,
> Ne phislyas, ne termes queinte of lawe.
> Ther is but litel Latyn in my mawe!   II, 1184–90

Such remarks are suitable to the sort of person we judged the Shipman to be from the sketch of him in the General Prologue.

The Shipman's story of the merchant of St. Denis satisfactorily fits the literary specifications that he set forth in the lines just quoted. It is an entertaining fabliau and belongs to a group of narratives that has been given the name "The Lover's Gift Regained." As in his other fabliaux, such as those told by the Miller and the Reeve, Chaucer seems here to have had no specific source;[3] but because of its narrative economy, its large proportion of natural dialogue, and its inevitable motivation of events by means of character, the Shipman's Tale is representative of Chaucer's mature work.[4]

That Chaucer at one time apparently intended to assign this tale to the Wife of Bath we surmise from the feminine pronouns in the opening lines of the story (VII, 1–19). Although it has been suggested that the Shipman is here reporting a view which he considers typical of wives, and that therefore lines 11–19 should be placed in quotation marks,[5] the text gives absolutely no support for this assumption. Consequently, our only alternative is to consider the speaker a woman. Three women are present in the company of Pilgrims—the Prioress, the Second Nun, and the Wife of Bath. Since this fabliau could by no stretch of the imagination be assigned to either of the first two, we conclude that the Wife of Bath was meant to be its original teller.[6] Even so, lines 5–10 still occasion some difficulty, for it is unlikely that the Wife would say that a woman's attracting attention at feasts and dances is not worth the money it costs. This statement, however, can best be considered as preparation for the emphasis which the

---

[3] See the chapter by J. W. Spargo in *Sources and Analogues*, 439–46; R. A. Pratt, *MLN*, LV (1940), 142–45.

[4] See Gardiner Stillwell, *RES*, XX (1944), 1–18.

[5] Frederick Tupper, *JEGP*, XXXIII (1934), 352–71.

[6] J. S. P. Tatlock, *The Development and Chronology of Chaucer's Works*, 205–19; R. F. Jones, *JEGP*, XXIV (1925), 512–47.

wife in the story places on the necessity for her having sufficient money to dress in such a manner as to do honor to her husband (VII, 179, 420–24). It is this argument, along with her readiness to afford her husband pleasure in bed, which the wife of the merchant of St. Denis uses to manage him as she wishes. And the Wife of Bath, as we know her from the General Prologue, seems also quite capable of using these devices for managing husbands. But her point here is that the merchant of St. Denis is to be the loser as a result of his accepting his wife's contention that she must have money for clothes in order to do him honor.

There is a more important aspect of the tale which clearly indicates its suitability to the Wife of Bath. The point of the story, I think, is that while the prosperous but boring merchant, completely wrapped up in his business, has little understanding of his wife and scant ability in managing her, the wife is expert in manipulating him and in conducting a secret affair. Although she tells the monk Don John that her husband is impotent and will not give her enough money (VII, 170–72), we have the merchant's own statement that she has enough for any thrifty housewife (VII, 245–48), and the reunion scene between the merchant and his wife at the end of the story shows that he is far from impotent. One suspects that the wife's statement to Don John of her pressing need for a hundred francs is simply a part of her attempt at rationalizing the night in bed which she hopes to spend with the attractive monk. From her point of view, her husband's most annoying trait is his absorption in making money (VII, 214–23), an absorption that occasions her considerable boredom, which she is eager to relieve by the closest means at hand—Don John, who she knows is not unmindful of her charms.

From the General Prologue we learn that Alice of Bath, who has had five husbands and who in her youth took lovers, is thoroughly familiar with all the intricacies of the art of love and therefore, like the merchant's wife in this story, is quite capable of having her cake and eating it too. In fact, in this tale the teller does not slight the merchant; almost as many lines are devoted to his wise comments upon, and successful conduct of, business affairs as are used for the account of his wife's success in the affair with Don John. And these two elements of the story are brilliantly, albeit somewhat frankly, brought together in the last two lines of the narrative:

> Thus endeth now my tale, and God us sende
> Taillynge ynough unto oure lyves ende.   VII, 433–34

The important word here is "taillynge," of course, upon which the teller puns. This word can refer to business dealings and to sexual intercourse: the merchant will be more than content with enough of the former, his wife with enough of the latter.[7]

There seems to me little support for the view that Chaucer, when he originally assigned this tale to the Wife of Bath, planned to work out "an exchange of hostilities, a polite quarrel between the Wife of Bath and the Merchant" on the pilgrimage.[8] For one thing, there is no motivation for such a quarrel in the sketches of either the Wife or the Merchant. Although it is true that in this tale a merchant is cuckolded and deprived of a hundred francs, his wife can hardly be regarded as the kind of protagonist the Wife would use if her chief purpose were to discomfit the Merchant. Neither in this tale nor in the sketch of the Wife of Bath do we find any emphasis on female sovereignty; in fact, the wife of the merchant of St. Denis, sincerely or not, ends by asking her husband's forgiveness (VII, 425). Moreover, the mention in the Merchant's Tale of the Wife of Bath (IV, 1685–87) seems clearly to stem from the Wife of Bath's Prologue, in which she describes her treatment of her husbands; since her prologue presumably was written after the Shipman's Tale, we are not justified in using passages from that prologue in an argument which assumes that she is the teller of the Shipman's Tale.

Our best conclusion, then, is that when Chaucer originally assigned the Shipman's Tale to the Wife of Bath, he considered the tale properly suited to her by virtue of its being a fabliau illustrating the kind of love-intrigue that the Wife herself had practiced in her youth. When, however, he worked out the far more dramatically complex performance which we know as the Wife

---

[7] Robinson, *Works*, 839, note to l. 434; Claude Jones, *MLN*, LII (1937), 570; R. A. Caldwell, *MLN*, LV (1940), 262–65; Albert H. Silverman, *PQ*, XXXII (1953), 329–36.

[8] Tatlock, *The Development and Chronology of Chaucer's Works*, 207.

of Bath's Prologue and Tale, he shifted the story of the merchant of St. Denis to the Shipman, presumably feeling that this fabliau would not sound strange in the mouth of the master of the *Madelaine*. To a considerable extent this view was justified.

The tale, as a story of cuckoldry, certainly falls in with the Shipman's dislike of highly moral and learned material, and fulfills his promise to "clynken" so merry a bell that he shall awaken all the company. There is also evidence in the narrative of the teller's rather specific knowledge of wine (VII, 70–73), which the Shipman could have gained in carrying cargo from Bordeaux (I, 396–97). Futhermore, the Shipman's telling a story of a merchant cuckolded is to a small degree motivated by the mention in the General Prologue of his regular success in outsmarting the "chapmen" for whom he works.[9] All in all, though it cannot be claimed that this performance is among the most effective examples of dramatic suitability in the *Canterbury Tales*, we are justified in finding it suitable to the character of its teller and in observing a trace, at least, of its suggesting a Shipman-Merchant antagonism.

So far as the Host is concerned, the Shipman has performed suitably and excellently:

> Wel seyd, by *corpus dominus*, . . .
> Now longe moote thou saille by the cost,
> Sire gentil maister, gentil maryneer!
> God yeve the monk a thousand last quade yeer!
> A ha! felawes! beth ware of swich a jape!
> The monk putte in the mannes hood an ape,
> And in his wyves eek, by Seint Austyn!
> Draweth no monkes moore unto youre in.
>
> VII, 435–42

Quite naturally, Harry interprets the tale in the light of his own circumstances. As an innkeeper he is concerned as to what sort of guests he harbors,[10] and he seems to miss the fact that the wife's boredom with her husband's constant concern for business brings about the cuckolding more than does the monk's perfidy.

[9] See M. R. Stobie, *PMLA*, LXIV (1949), 565–69.
[10] The meaning of Middle English "in" (VII, 442) is not equivalent to that of Modern English "inn"; it can also indicate a private home.

Al was conscience and tendre herte

7. THE PRIORESS

The character of Chaucer's Prioress has been most convincingly explained by Professor Lowes.[1] It appears that in the sketch of this lady (I, 118–62) Chaucer included many skillful touches which suggest the "delightfully imperfect submergence of the woman in the nun."[2] The result is a kind of gentle raillery, hardly sharp enough to be called satire but nevertheless indicative of certain limitations in the Prioress which result primarily from her concern with worldly matters.

In Chaucer's day the majority of nuns adopted their way of life for economic rather than for purely religious reasons, and they were most frequently from the upper classes.[3] Madame Eglentyne has risen to the office of prioress in her convent, and accordingly enjoys considerable prestige.[4] Professor Manly argued that she may be modeled to some extent after Madame Argentyn of St. Leonard's convent near Stratford-Bow.[5] However that may be, the Prioress is eager "to been estatlich of manere,/And to ben holden digne of reverence." She also makes great efforts to imitate "cheere of court": her table manners are above reproach, for her interest in etiquette is great. In this matter, as in the mention of her way of speaking French, her fine clothes, her ornaments, and her pets, Chaucer is laughing at this nun who interests herself in the behavior of fashionable people.

But an even more humorous touch is to be found in the description of the Prioress' physical appearance. Her smiling "ful

---

[1] J. L. Lowes, *Anglia*, XXXIII (1910), 440–51. See also E. P. Kuhl, *PQ*, II (1923), 302–309.

[2] See p. 442 of Lowes's article cited in n. 1 of this section, and his *Convention and Revolt in Poetry*, 60.

[3] Bowden, *Commentary*, 92.

[4] Eileen Power, *Medieval English Nunneries c. 1275 to 1535*, p. 69.

[5] Manly, *New Light*, 202–20. For different views, see Arthur Sherbo, *PMLA*, LXIV (1949), 236–46; and M. P. Hamilton's essay in *Philologica: The Malone Anniversary Studies*, 179–90.

symple and coy," her name itself, her nose "tretys," her eyes "greye," her mouth "ful smal" and soft and red, her broad forehead—each of these characteristics represents the ideal for the heroine of the contemporary romances.[6] Then there comes the line, "For, hardily, she was nat undergrowe," in which we can find further fun at the Prioress' expense. The size of this lady, who has numerous features similar to those of a romantic heroine and who tries so hard to copy the dainty manners of a fashionable lady, is sharply out of keeping with the rest of her appearance and with her would-be fascinating manners. For she is a large woman—"nat undergrowe," that is, not small—and this line, coming as it does after the humorous emphasis on her delicacy and daintiness, represents a brilliant use of understatement.[7]

In addition to the Prioress' various feminine affectations so far noticed, there is the similar matter of her exaggerated tender sensitivity. She weeps if she sees a dead or bleeding mouse caught in a trap, and especially if one of her "smale houndes" dies or is beaten. At least in insignificant matters, "al was conscience and tendre herte" with this prioress. The sketch of the Prioress ends with mention of her shining gold brooch, "On which ther was first write a crowned A,/And after *Amor vincit omnia.*" It is now generally agreed that the Love which here conquers all refers to divine love, rather than sensuous love. Chaucer makes considerable sport of Madame Eglentyne's fashionable affectations, but he does not accuse her of licentiousness.

After the Shipman has finished his tale, the Host speaks to the Prioress "As curteisly as it had been a mayde" (VII, 447–51). Harry Bailly's politeness here is doubtless understandable in view of her position and sex; but his excessive courtesy—"by your leave," "if I knew it would not annoy you," "if you so de-

---

[6] See the article by Lowes cited in n. 1 of this section and, for an opposing view, M. J. Brennan, *MLQ*, X (1949), 451–57.

[7] Miss Bowden (*Commentary*, 95), following Lowes, takes line 156 in the Prioress' sketch as a "quiet statement that she is well-proportioned ('nat undergrowe')." But the *NED* labels "undergrowe" an "obsolete variant of *undergrown*," which it defines as "imperfectly grown or developed," citing the line here in question; and Skeat (*Complete Works of Geoffrey Chaucer*, V, 18) explains "undergrowe" as "of short, stinted growth." Chaucer's "nat undergrowe" would therefore seem to mean, with reference to the Prioress, "markedly large." See also W. C. Curry, *The Middle English Ideal of Beauty*, 103; and G. H. Harper, *PQ*, XII (1933), 308–10.

sire," "if you would comply"—all within the space of five lines, suggests the possibility that Harry may be slyly poking fun at her extreme emphasis on "good manners," which was ironically stressed in her sketch in the General Prologue. In any event, the Prioress gladly complies with his request, and, after a prologue which is an invocation to Mary, she relates the story of the little schoolboy who, killed and hidden by the Jews, is later discovered through a miracle of the Virgin. Certain aspects of this story seem particularly suited to the combination of piety and affectation which we have observed in the Prioress.

First of all, the Prioress' Prologue and Tale show clearly, by means of their atmosphere of sincere religious devotion, that the bantering tone which Chaucer used in describing Madame Eglentyne in the General Prologue was not intended to indicate that she is open to adverse criticism on matters of fundamental faith. Although the material he assigned to her is taken from a large body of well-known miracles of the Virgin, which existed in the late Middle Ages, he has shaped this material in such a way as to have it convey to us a sense of her personal belief.[8] In the Prologue, made up in large part of borrowings from the services of the Church, Chaucer gave her what many critics consider some of the finest passages of lyric poetry in Middle English. Then, too, the Prioress takes occasion, when near the end of her story she speaks of the abbot who supervises the burial, to show her understanding of the proper behavior for a religious:

> This abbot, which that was an hooly man,
> As monkes been, or elles oghte be,
> This yonge child to conjure he bigan.   VII, 642-44

This comment, of course, seems to reflect particularly on the worldly monk, Don John, who makes a cuckold of the merchant in the immediately preceding Shipman's Tale. Perhaps it also reflects upon the luxury-loving Monk who is a member of the company of Pilgrims. Both her prologue and tale bear witness to the Prioress' earnest Christian humility. But what of the other aspect of her character, her feminine affectations?

We note at once that in her recital Madame Eglentyne keeps

---

[8] See the chapter by Carleton Brown in *Sources and Analogues*, 447-85.

[81

hidden most of her leanings toward "cheere of courte." Three points, however, seem to fit with her exaggerated tenderness and sensitivity. First, Chaucer changed the age of the little school-boy from ten to seven, thereby making him a more suitable recipient for the pathos of the Prioress' tale. Second, there seems to be a heightening of the mother's expression of grief when the little boy does not return home, and in this heightened grief we see some similarity with the Prioress' reaction to the loss of one of her pets. Third, there is the matter of the ending for the story. Chaucer apparently had the choice of a happy ending or the tragic ending that he selected, one that would seem to allow fuller revelation of the Prioress' character.

Miss Bowden finds a further matter which suits this tale and its teller.[9] For her, Chaucer implies in his sketch of the Prioress that Madame Eglentyne's charity and pity are aroused by such a matter as the suffering of a mouse, but that "she is not greatly concerned over the suffering of her fellow-man." In commenting on the passage in the Prioress' sketch which begins "But, for to speken of hire conscience" (I, 142–45), Miss Bowden continues:

This implication is later strengthened by her own *Tale* in which she tells with perfect blandness of the tortures visited upon the Jews [VII, 628–34]; and by the fact that when Chaucer writes of the charity of his Parson, he is explicit and clear in pointing out that here is a man who follows truly all the teachings of Christianity in loving his neighbour as himself. For Madame Eglentyne, then, the poet's *but* indicates a reservation. Despite her charm and dignity, she possesses a real imperfection not unmarked by the poet who has created her.

There are certainly those who will not be willing to agree with Miss Bowden on this last point. Personally, I think her interpretation defensible.[10] But, in any event, we have seen other details that indicate that Chaucer gave to the Prioress a story that mirrors the two facets of her personality. And, in conclusion, we should notice that the "quod she," inserted in line 581 of her tale, suggests strongly that this story was prepared with its teller well in mind.

[9] Bowden, *Commentary*, 99–100.
[10] A similar view is advanced by Sister Mary Hostia in *College English*, XIV (1953), 351–52.

8. THE PILGRIM CHAUCER

Following the Prioress' Tale, we have "Sir Thopas" and "Melibeus." These two recitals are set in a carefully developed dramatic framework provided by three exchanges between the Narrator and the Host. These exchanges are strategically placed before "Sir Thopas," between "Sir Thopas" and "Melibeus," and after "Melibeus," and are closely meshed with both the manner and the content of the two tales. To read these tales without careful regard for their dramatic framework would be almost certainly to neglect Chaucer's intentions. As we shall see, this whole performance by the Pilgrim Chaucer is aimed at exposing Harry Bailly to genial ridicule.

Until he is called on for a tale, our view of the Pilgrim Chaucer develops indirectly from his manner of telling us about the other people present and about the events on the pilgrimage. And, as we saw in Part II, our interest in, and enjoyment of, his book come to a considerable degree as a result of assumptions we are led to make about the character of the Narrator. From the General Prologue we conclude that here is a genial, sociable fellow who moves easily among any group of people and knows his way about in the world. Also, we recognize his acute powers of observation and effective reportorial ability. Then, when the storytelling game gets under way, we have reason to attribute to him a lively and delightful sense of humor. And we soon saw that the Narrator's sense of humor includes laughing at himself as well as at the other Pilgrims, for when the Lawyer poked fun at his clumsiness as a poet, the Pilgrim Chaucer let the joke stand unchallenged (II, 45–96). All in all, here is a man who well deserves attention and who can be counted on to entertain us. Consequently, we expect some fun when in the Prologue to "Sir Thopas" we see that the Host has called on the Pilgrim Chaucer to perform (VII, 691–711).

Now shul we heere Som deyntee thyng

Some critics have felt that in this passage the description of the Narrator as sober and retiring is inconsistent with the genial qualities attributed to him elsewhere.[1] Others maintain that his gravity here is to be explained by the moving effect of the immediately preceding Prioress' Tale.[2] It seems to me, however, not only that the Narrator is here consistent with his other appearances, but also that the scene is to be understood as his careful preparation—the present-day term"build-up" is apt here—for playing a joke on the Host. The core of the joke is to be that the Narrator, the literary sophisticate, will in his performance first make plentifully and entertainingly evident the fact that Harry Bailly lacks any real literary critical ability, despite the rapidity and certainty with which he criticizes the various tales; and, second, he will jockey the Host, a henpecked husband, into approving a tale in which a husband profits by accepting his wife's advice.

Since the glimpses of the Host are by design scattered through the *Canterbury Tales*, a reader may overlook the great care which Chaucer expended in portraying Harry's character. It must not be forgotten that the Host is Chaucer's chief unifying device for the group of stories and also for the group of Pilgrims. No other one of the Pilgrims is shown in so many situations which serve to delineate character, and Chaucer indicates a number of affectations and pretensions which Harry possesses. Most of these traits are those typical of an innkeeper, but we are here concerned with another sort of affectation which Chaucer has definitely stressed in his portrayal of the Host: Harry prides himself, without good reason for doing so, on his ability as a literary critic. In addition to his responsibility as guide and "governour" of the company, he is the self-appointed "juge and reportour" of the stories. Such a job demands literary critical ability, which Harry feels that he has; witness his statement "Fulfilled is my sentence and my decree" (X, 17).

As early in the *Canterbury Tales* as his second speech, the Host takes pains to exhibit with considerable pride his knowledge of the literary critical terms that qualify "best":

[1] T. A. Knott, *MP*, VIII (1910–11), 135–39.
[2] W. W. Lawrence, *PMLA*, L (1935), 90.

> And which of yow that bereth hym best of alle,
> That is to seyn, that telleth in this caas
> Tales of best sentence and moost solaas,
> Shal have a soper at oure aller cost
> Heere in this place, sittynge by this post. I, 796–800

There is notable similarity between Harry's pride here (and in the Clerk's Prologue) in his knowledge of literary critical terms and in the manner in which he recites medical terms after the Physician's Tale (VI, 304–17). The hearty approval which he accords the tale by the Knight (I, 3115, 3119) is delivered with the air of one fully able to recognize a good story when he hears one, as is his admonition to the Cook to make sure his story is "good" (I, 4345). This "ex-cathedra" attitude which Chaucer has given the Host is perhaps most clearly seen in his response to the Reeve's philosophical comments on old age:

> Whan that oure Hoost hadde herd this sermonyng,
> He gan to speke as lordly as a kyng.
> He seide, "What amounteth al this wit?"
>
> I, 3899–3901

There is little difference between the criterion for good literature which Harry implies here, as well as in his teasing rebuff of the Parson (II, 1174–77), and that which the Shipman later advances (II, 1185–90). But, unlike the Shipman, the Host does not openly admit his shortcomings; rather, he exaggerates his familiarity with literary material. Thus, in his remarks on the passing of time, just before he calls on the Lawyer for a story, Harry says:

> Wel kan Senec and many a philosophre
> Biwaillen tyme moore than gold in cofre,
> For "los of catel may recovered be,
> But los of time shendeth us," quod he. II, 25–28

It does not seem to me pure chance that Harry is probably wrong when he attributes this axiom to Seneca,[3] or that of the five instances in which Chaucer uses the familiar proverb "Everything has its appointed time," Harry alone cites Solomon as his source

---

[3] W. W. Skeat, *The Complete Works of Geoffrey Chaucer*, V, 134–35.

(IV, 6). Such errors as *"corpus dominus"* (VII, 435) and *"corpus Madrian"* (VII, 1892) also suggest his pretentiousness.

Closely related to Harry's ex-cathedra critical attitude is the fact that Chaucer seems to give us more than a hint that the Host feels a certain condescension of the sort typical of the practical man of affairs toward the supposedly impractical man of books. Professor Lowes described this one of Harry's characteristics as "courtesy . . . touched with that benignant affability with which the man of the world indulges the scholar. . . ."[4] This attitude is noticeable in the Host's comment to the Parson, after the Lawyer has finished the story of Constance: "I se wel that ye lerned men in lore/Can moche good, by Goddes dignitee!" (II, 1168–69). Again, in Harry's words to the Clerk, this same feeling is evident:

> Youre termes, youre colours, and youre figures,
> Keepe hem in stoor til so be that ye endite
> Heigh style, as whan that men to kynges write.   IV, 16–18

When one recalls the Clerk's poverty and his not being worldly enough to get a job, it seems likely that Harry's implication that the Clerk will someday write to kings is more indulgent than courteous.

One of the surest indications that Chaucer intended the reader to see the wide gap between the Host's fancied ability at literary criticism and his actual lack of perception is to be found in Harry's missing the fact that the merchant of St. Denis' absorption in business contributes importantly to his cuckolding (VII, 435–42). Similarly, in his critique of the Merchant's Tale, the Host, no doubt thinking of his own wife, blames May, failing to see that January's lust has blinded him (IV, 2419–25). Such performances do not justify the claim to sure critical ability which the Host states in reprimanding the Monk for telling tragedies: "And wel I woot the substance is in me/If any thyng shal wel reported be." (VII, 2803–2804).

If Chaucer the poet intended throughout the *Canterbury Tales* for the reader to be aware of Harry's unwarranted pride in his ability as a literary critic,[5] one may infer that this affectation

---

[4] J. L. Lowes, *Geoffrey Chaucer and the Development of His Genius*, 205.

[5] For a different opinion, see Émile Legouis, *Geoffrey Chaucer* (English trans., 1913), 179–80.

would have furnished particular enjoyment to the Pilgrim Chaucer, whose surer critical ability had been developed by many hours spent with his books. Thus it may be that an interpretation of the scene between Chaucer and the Host in the Prologue to "Sir Thopas," and of the immediate purpose for "Sir Thopas" itself, should take into consideration the possibility of a desire on the part of the Pilgrim Chaucer to make humorously apparent Harry's affectation of great critical ability. The lines of that scene bear out this supposition.

In the first two lines the Narrator reports the sobering effect of the Prioress' story upon the group. The solemn and moving effect of such stories for the mass of people in Chaucer's day cannot be denied; but that is not to say that the Pilgrim Chaucer, certainly no stranger to miracles of Our Lady or to saints' legends in general, meant to picture himself as deeply touched by her performance. This is the same Narrator who smiled understandingly at those traits universally feminine which the Prioress' withdrawal from worldly life had not obliterated in her personality; it is also the same Chaucer who saw fit to give humorous emphasis in the Introduction to the Man of Law's Tale to having sufficient acquaintance with saints' legends to produce a parody of them (II, 60–61). In short, the Narrator is here simply reporting the effect of the Prioress' story on the group at large, without necessarily indicating his own reaction to that story.

Furthermore, to connect the opening statement concerning the sobering effect of the Prioress' Tale with the Host's reference to the Pilgrim Chaucer's staring at the ground does injustice to the text, for Chaucer plainly states in the third line of this passage that the Host dispels the solemn atmosphere by joking. This joking is not reported in any detail and, presumably, was of a general nature. The effect of the Prioress' Tale has gone before the Host directs his attention and jests toward Chaucer. It seems to me that the fourth line of the passage is often similarly misread, and that it also indicates that the usual gaiety has been restored before the Host speaks to Chaucer. The line goes "And thanne at erst he looked upon me." Most critics have taken "thanne at erst" to mean "at first, for the first time"; but in every one of the seven other instances in which Chaucer used the phrase it means "not until then."[6] Thus the fourth line of the Prologue to "Sir Thopas" means "And not until then [that is, after he has dispelled the gravity by joking] did the Host look at me." There is no justification for the interpretation "And then he looked at me as the first butt for his jokes." *The Canterbury Tales* is, above all else, the record of a storytelling game in which, after one story ends, the Host usually selects the next teller. By means of the fourth line in this passage, Chaucer the poet intends simply to inform the reader that the Pilgrim Chaucer has been selected to tell the next tale.

In the succeeding twelve lines the Host addresses Chaucer with a jesting condescension reminiscent of his remarks to the Parson, but Chaucer's reply seems to indicate that he has already decided to tell the highly skillful and entertaining "Sir Thopas" for the purpose of showing up Harry's affectation of literary critical ability. Harry first asks: "What sort of man are you?" Then he states: "Thou lookest as thou woldest fynde an hare,/For evere upon the ground I se thee stare." Here "evere" means no more than "steadily, fixedly at this moment";[7] therefore, in these two lines the Host simply remarks that at this time Chaucer is staring at the ground as if in search of a rabbit. Perhaps that statement suggests that Chaucer, who has just learned that his turn as storyteller has arrived, is staring at the ground in an effort to prevent the Host's seeing the merry twinkle which has come into his eyes at the prospect of the joke he plans. It may be that Harry, certainly not always quick at perceiving the finer shades of human feeling, mistakes the staring at the ground for an indication of Chaucer's being of a particularly contemplative nature, for he next commands Chaucer to approach and to look up merrily. One assumes that he carried out both commands. Then the Host, in his usual manner, makes a joke about the size of Chaucer's waistline, ironically suggesting that a lovely woman would be delighted to embrace a man with such a figure. Chaucer, forced to look up from the ground and to give the Host a clear view of his face, is unable to conceal the twinkle of anticipation in his eyes. Therefore, Harry calls him "elvyssh," that is, mischievous,

---

[6] J. P. Roppolo, *MLN*, LXIII (1948), 365–71.
[7] See Knott's article cited in n. 1 of this section.

in that Chaucer is obviously enjoying a private joke rather than making that joke generally known by doing "daliaunce" with the other Pilgrims.[8] Following these thrusts, the Host reminds Chaucer that it is his turn to tell a story, and, as usual, demands a "tale of myrthe." Certainly this demand from the Host for a merry tale is too typical a remark to bring about any violent emotional reaction in Chaucer at this point, as some critics have claimed it does.

In his reply to the Host's speech, Chaucer assumes an ironic mock humility. He expects and hopes that the Host will be disgusted by "Sir Thopas," in which the kind of literature that Harry likes is burlesqued. Chaucer therefore enjoys issuing a warning to the Host not to be "yvele apayd" and claims to know no other tale than "Sir Thopas." He implies, however, that his tale has the authority of age, suspecting that Harry will express enthusiastic approval at the prospect of such a story. Chaucer is not mistaken, for Harry cries: "Ye, that is good," and proclaims to the company that the Pilgrim Chaucer, now that he has consented to do "daliaunce," seems to be the kind of man who can tell a rare story.

If we have guessed the immediate intention of "Sir Thopas," no one can deny that the joke was highly successful. In "Sir Thopas" Chaucer presents, as one critic said, "a good-humored rollicking burlesque, a 'tour-de-force' of high spirits, the brilliance of which has hardly yet been fully recognized. In no other poem can we so plainly and clearly see Chaucer at play, having no end of fun with the romances and his readers and himself."[9] In a similar vein, another commentator wrote: "Genius is airily at play in 'Sir Thopas,' and the original combinations of old motifs, the unexpected grace of such lines as those describing the Fairy Queen, are not to be demonstrated. They illustrate Chaucer's unimpeded originality in the very midst of closest imitation."[10] But the Host, with whom I think the Pilgrim Chaucer is also having a great deal of fun, misses the point completely. He does not see the poetic ingenuity illustrated by "Sir Thopas," nor

[8] Compare Lawrence's interpretation of "elvyssh"; *PMLA*, L (1935), 85, 90.
[9] J. M. Manly, *MP*, VIII (1910–11), 144.
[10] See pp. 486–87 of the chapter by L. H. Loomis in *Sources and Analogues*.

does he appreciate the delightful burlesquing of the metrical romances in such scenes as the arming of Sir Thopas or the fight with the giant. The broad humor of the hero's name, of his search for an elf queen, and of his swearing by homely fare is lost for Harry, who emphatically interrupts:

> Namoore of this, for Goddes dignitee,
> . . . for thou makest me
> So wery of thy verray lewednesse
> That, also wisly God my soule blesse,
> Myne eres aken of thy drasty speche.
> Now swich a rym the devel I biteche!
> This may wel be rym dogerel. . . .   VII, 919–25

The Host sees only ignorance of creditable poetic practice in this performance and manages to exhibit his knowledge of a critical term, "rym dogerel." The subtle joke on the Host planned by the Pilgrim Chaucer is working without a hitch, but the latter keeps a perfectly straight face, for his exposé of the Host is only half-finished. His next remarks are accompanied by an injured tone:

> Why so? . . . why wiltow lette me
> Moore of my tale than another man,
> Syn that it is the beste rym I kan?   VII, 926–28

Harry is not slow to answer this question with a vulgar comparison and to state that since Chaucer is only wasting time, he will not be allowed to recite further in this sort of verse. However, not wishing to be unfair to a Pilgrim who apparently is making a sincere effort to please, the Host decides to give Chaucer another chance. But this time he must tell something in alliterative verse or in prose, and his tale must contain "som murthe or som doctryne."

Chaucer agrees with alacrity, for Harry continues to play right into his hand:

> Gladly, . . . by Goddes sweete pyne!
> I wol yow telle a litel thyng in prose
> That oghte liken yow, as I suppose,
> Or elles, certes, ye been to daungerous.
> It is a moral tale vertuous.   VII, 936–40

Now the burden of responsibility is shifted to the Host, for he is going to hear a moral tale "vertuous" in prose—just what he has demanded; if he is not pleased by such a performance, then certainly the fault lies with him, not with the teller. But Chaucer goes on in greater detail to make sure that Harry will have no grounds for complaint; by citing the authoritative example of the four Gospels, he protects himself from the possible charge that his version of the story varies somewhat from other versions. The accounts of Matthew, Mark, Luke, and John all carry the same "sentence," and similarly, despite the great number of proverbs included, his tale will not vary in meaning from his source.

Chaucer now feels that he has the necessary groundwork laid for the completion of his joke at the Host's expense: he has left Harry no defensible reason for interrupting the coming tale. To make this point absolutely clear, he closes his introductory remarks with a firm statement: "And therfore herkneth what that I shal seye,/And lat me tellen al my tale, I preye" (VII, 965–66). Then he sets forth on the lengthy journey through his prose tale, "Melibeus." To suggest the nature of his second performance, a brief summary of this story will be useful.

Melibeus returns home one day, after roaming pleasantly in the fields, and finds that his enemies have broken into his house in his absence and have beaten and wounded his wife and daughter. Almost insane with anger, he vows to revenge this act, but Prudence, his wife, urges him to be patient, to call together all his friends, to ask them whether he should make war or remain at peace, and to be guided by their counsel. Melibeus calls the assembly but receives contradictory advice. He is still determined to make war. Prudence then marshals her authorities and manages to win Melibeus' consent to a plan whereby she will hold a secret conference with his enemies. When these enemies meet with her, she stresses the advantages of peace and the righteousness of Melibeus' anger. Convinced, the enemies put their fate into her hands. Upon Prudence's return home, Melibeus accepts the confession of guilt from his enemies in the spirit in which it is offered. Prudence at once summons all her relatives and old friends to hear the case. They decide for peace.

The enemies place themselves wholly at the mercy of Melibeus, who accepts his wife's advice and forgives them.

This tale is not, of course, original with Chaucer.[11] It was written by an Italian judge named Albertano of Brescia, who had the rather heavy-handed habit, as his three sons came of age, of presenting each with a moral treatise as a guide for his actions. This piece, entitled *Liber Consolationis et Consilii*, was given to the third son, Giovanni, in 1246. But Chaucer's "Melibeus" is a close translation of an Old French condensed paraphrase of Albertano's Latin, done by Renaud de Louens sometime after 1336. The tale is obviously an allegory: "Melibeus" means "honeydrinker," that is, a sensuous man; Prudence's name explains itself; and the daughter, given the name Sophie by Chaucer, represents wisdom or right-living. The three "olde foes" (VII, 970), who stand for the world, the flesh, and the devil (VII, 1421), wound Sophie in five places, her five senses. In other words, Melibeus' sensuousness damages his soul; he is saved only by taking his wife's advice, that is, by becoming prudent.

Such moralizing allegory was very common in Chaucer's day, and there can be no doubt, as various critics have maintained, that he and his audience looked upon the "Melibeus" with a great deal less disfavor than do most modern readers.[12] Several other points have been brought forward by these critics in answer to the modern reader, who, bewildered at finding such a long, dull piece, stuffed full of commonplace axioms, included in the *Canterbury* collection, asks: Did Chaucer really consider this a good story, comparable, say, to the Nun's Priest's Tale? Or is it that he was simply trying to represent by his collection every type of literature popular in his day? It is very doubtful that either of these possibilities leads to a satisfactory answer. More pertinent are the facts that the medieval audience "found mental stimulus in very obvious truths, and a perpetual relish in the gnomic style"; and that in this tale the themes of peace as pref-

---

[11] See the chapter by J. B. Severs in *Sources and Analogues*, 560–614.

[12] W. P. Ker, "Chaucer," *English Prose* (ed. Henry Craik), I, 40; J. S. P. Tatlock, *The Development and Chronology of Chaucer's Works*, 188–97; Leslie Hotson, *SP*, XVIII (1921), 429–52; the essay by W. W. Lawrence and that by R. S. Loomis in *Essays and Studies in Honor of Carleton Brown*, 100–10, 129–48; Gardiner Stillwell, *Speculum*, XIX (1944), 433–44.

erable to war, of the necessity for selection of wise counselors, and of the excellence of woman as counselor, would have had especial significance for Chaucer and his audience because of the contemporary political situation, in which the English people were tired of unnecessary war, very desirous of able advisers for the young and unstable King Richard, and well aware of such wise women in high place as Queen Anne, Queen Philippa, and Joan of Kent. Such facts make more understandable the presence in the *Canterbury Tales* of "Melibeus."

But we see a far more cogent reason for the Pilgrim Chaucer's relating the "Melibeus" after the Host has put an end to "Sir Thopas" when we read it in its dramatic context. Granted that Chaucer was of his time rather than of ours in regard to such extended moralizing, we still could not urge that he lacked the literary discrimination necessary to see the difference in kind and degree between the "Melibeus" and the Nun's Priest's Tale, or the contrast between the didactic story and its forerunner, "Sir Thopas." The "Melibeus," whatever else it is, certainly is the second half of the joke used by the Pilgrim Chaucer to make evident the Host's lack of literary taste.

Harry neither interrupts nor complains in the course of "Melibeus." In delivering this lengthy moralistic tale, with a proverb for every possible need, the Pilgrim Chaucer has presented the most routine sort of literary fare, in direct contrast to the highly original "Sir Thopas," which the Host rejected. Thereby, Harry's lack of any real qualifications for his job as literary critic on this pilgrimage has been revealed for anyone whose taste runs to material of a less strictly hortative nature than the "Melibeus." And this jest is all the better by virtue of the fact that "Juge" Bailly does not realize what has happened to him.

We have only to look again at the lines quoted from Chaucer's remarks introducing this tale to see the fun he rightly expected to derive from the Host's reaction. There he spoke of the story he would tell as "a little thing in prose" (VII, 937), "this little treatise" (VII, 957, 963), and "this pleasant [murye] tale" (VII, 964). We may argue that since "murye" usually means "pleasant" in Middle English rather than "gay" as now,[13] and since the

13 W. W. Lawrence, *Chaucer and the Canterbury Tales*, 153–54.

medieval audience did not find moralizing unpleasant, no irony is intended by the third of the phrases; but there is no escaping the humorous contrast between the first two of these phrases and the length of "Melibeus."

There is a second important aspect to this joke which the Pilgrim Chaucer is playing upon the Host. It almost seems that the Narrator took for granted that the Host would miss the allegorical meaning of "Melibeus" and would accept it as a straightforward story. For, somehow or other, our inquisitive Narrator had found out that Harry Bailly is a henpecked husband. Immediately following the "Melibeus," the Host launches a lengthy lament about his life at home (VII, 1889–1923). Here he regrets that his wife, Goodelief, was not present to hear this tale. Then he reveals her great impatience with him and concludes that someday she will make it necessary for him to leave home. Nor does he conceal his fear of her "byg armes."

We see that the Pilgrim Chaucer has maneuvered Harry into the position of finding a moral applicable to his own marital situation in a story preaching mastery for the wife, a state which the Host would hardly favor. Indeed, although Melibeus first refuses to give over sovereignty to his wife (VII, 1055–63), he later says to her: "Dame, . . . dooth youre wil and youre likynge;/For I putte me hoolly in youre disposicioun and ordinaunce" (VII, 1724–25); and all consequently turns out well. One suspects that if the formidable Goodelief had heard the "Melibeus," as her husband pathetically wishes, she would have led him a sadder life than that which he reports.

In many ways Harry deserves this double-edged joke at his expense, for by his pompous yet inadequate criticisms of the various tales, as well as by his ready use of his authority over the Pilgrims—a sharp contrast to his position at home—he has furnished more than enough motivation for the treatment he receives from the Pilgrim Chaucer.

A manly man, to been an abbot able

9. THE MONK

To banish his melancholy reflections about his wife, the Host briskly calls upon the Monk for merriment. He, however, is not eager to please Harry Bailly and purposely inflicts upon him a series of dull tragedies that do nothing to relieve the Host's gloom. Two questions in connection with this performance by Chaucer's Monk have given rise to sharp difference of opinion: Is the Monk a Benedictine or an Augustinian?[1] and: Is the Monk who now tells the tragedies consistent with the Monk of the General Prologue?[2] The first of these questions need not particularly concern us here, but arriving at a defensible answer to the second is, of course, vital to an analysis of the dramatic interplay involved. I hold, with Professor Tatlock and others, that the Monk is consistent throughout and that his recital is quite suitable, in the light of the antagonistic feeling which the Host arouses in him.

The most striking fact about the Monk as described in the General Prologue (I, 165–207) is his sensuous love of luxury and creature comforts. This monk has nothing to do with the asceticism usually associated with monastic life. He is an outdoor man, loves hunting, and spares no cost in providing himself with the finest horses and dogs for that sport: "He yaf nat of that text a pulled hen,/That seith that hunters ben nat hooly men."[3] To the ears of the Monk the bells which hang from his horse's bridle jingle much louder than does the bell of his chapel, for his interests do not center about the chapel. His sleeves are

[1] See Ramona Bressie, *MLN*, LIV (1939), 477–90, and LVI (1941), 161–62; J. S. P. Tatlock, *MLN*, LV (1940), 350–54, and LVI (1941), 80; E. P. Kuhl, *MLN*, LV (1940), 480.

[2] See Manly, *New Light*, 161, and *Canterbury Tales by Geoffrey Chaucer*, 572, 636; Ramona Bressie, *MLN*, LIV (1939), 489; J. S. P. Tatlock, *MLN*, LV (1940), 350–54.

[3] Concerning this "text," see O. F. Emerson, *MP*, I (1903–1904), 105–15; Rudolph Willard, University of Texas *Studies in English*, XXVI (1947), 209–51.

trimmed with the finest fur, he wears a valuable golden pin, his boots are of the best, and his brown horse is expensively equipped. Furtherfore, the Monk loves to eat, especially when the main dish is a roasted swan, and his appearance reflects this fondness: "He was not pale as a forpyned goost"; rather, "He was a lord ful fat and in good poynt," whose face and bald head shine as if he had been anointed. There is an unmistakable aptness in the Narrator's choice of a "pulled" hen—that is, a hen of little value as food—as the commodity which the Monk is unwilling to exchange for the religious rule against hunting.

The Monk is by no means hesitant to defend the way of life which he practices, and it appears that he expressed himself vigorously in this vein to our Narrator during the evening at the Tabard Inn before the pilgrimage starts (I, 173–76, 183–88). Such talk does not fit well with our ideas of what a monk should be. Yet we should not censure Chaucer's Monk too severely, for he is an "outridere"; that is, he has been appointed by his abbot to manage the estates and to conduct the outside business of the monastery. Some of the blame, at least, for the Monk's likes and dislikes must rest upon the institution, the Church, which allotted to an individual who presumably had decided to withdraw from the world work which necessitated his taking an active part in the business of that world. I am not saying, of course, that the Monk in any way objected to the job assigned him—far from it. But the great number of contemporary worldly monks,[4] in perfectly good professional standing, indicates that the Narrator's remarks about the Monk should not be read as direct satire and suggests that his statement "And I seyde his opinion was good" probably refers to his approval of the Monk's making his way in the world. In fact, the Monk seems well on his way to high place in monastic circles: he is already prior of a dependent monastery, and we are told that he is fit "to been an abbot."

A further point is to be noted from the sketch in the General Prologue. Although the Monk certainly does not respect his vow of poverty, no comment occurs here to indicate that he is licentious or otherwise guilty of sexual infractions of his rules. Granted that to suspect the worldly Monk of licentious conduct

[4] Bowden, *Commentary*, 109–15.

puts no great strain on credulity, nevertheless, this worthy "kepere of the celle" has, for all we know, good reason to take offense at such a charge.

The Monk, of course, along with the Prioress, is next in rank after the Knight among the members of the company. And the Host, ever mindful of "degree," calls upon the Monk to perform when the Knight has finished his tale: "Now telleth ye, sir Monk, if that ye konne,/Somwhat to quite with the Knyghtes tale" (I, 3118–19). We note here, beneath the surface of Harry Bailly's respectful "sir Monk" and his use of the formal pronoun "ye" rather than the familiar "thou," just a trace of belligerence towards the Monk in the phrase "if that ye konne." It would seem that Harry personally doubts the ability of this hunting Monk to tell a story equal to the Knight's. But this situation is not developed, since Robin the Miller, drunk on ale of Southwark, disregards rank and successfully demands the stage. After this setback, Harry is less punctilious in his effort to arrange the order of storytelling and does not do the Monk the courtesy of calling on him again until after the Pilgrim Chaucer has finished "Melibeus."

In the meanwhile, as we have seen, there are two reflections upon the worldly Monk. First, he is very like Don John in the Shipman's Tale, who is an outrider (VII, 65), loves food and good living generally (VII, 73–74), and apparently has sufficient connection with hunting to bring a present of wild fowl (VII, 72) and to use a simile based on a hare worn out and frightened by the pursuing dogs (VII, 104–105). Of course, Don John is not an exact replica of the Monk: for one thing, the former seems much younger (VII, 26); and, more importantly, he is eager for, and expert in, amorous intrigue. Nevertheless, sufficient similarity is suggested to give the Monk reason for some displeasure at the Shipman's Tale. Then, right after that story, the Prioress makes a remark (VII, 642–43) probably aimed at him; and there is perhaps a repetition of this thrust in her later comment: "This hooly monk, this abbot, hym meene I,/His tonge out caughte, and took awey the greyn" (VII, 670–71). But the greatest insult to the Monk's dignity comes in the Host's words when the latter for the second time calls upon him for a tale (VII, 1924–90).

After his lengthy description of the difficulties his wife causes at home, and with a possible reference to the Miller's having earlier prevented the Monk from performing, Harry says: "My lord, the Monk, be cheerful, for [this time] you shall actually tell a tale." Perhaps also from this statement we are to infer that the Monk's facial expression mirrors his justifiable displeasure at the treatment he has received so far on this pilgrimage; and, to make matters worse, instead of letting the Monk commence, the Host addresses him further, with very little show of respect:

> Ryde forth, myn owene lord, brek nat oure game.
> But, by my trouthe, I knowe nat youre name.
> Wher shal I calle yow my lord daun John,
> Or daun Thomas, or elles daun Albon?
> Of what hous be ye, by youre fader kyn?
> I vowe to God, thou hast a ful fair skyn;
> It is a gentil pasture ther thow goost.   VII, 1927–33

The tone of these lines is patronizing, and the fact that "Don John" is the first name suggested for the Monk calls forth unpleasant association with the sly monk in the Shipman's Tale. Also, the question as to the Monk's religious house implies that Harry's expectations of an untruthful reply lead him to require the Monk to swear "by youre fader kyn." The Host's overfamiliarity is particularly apparent in his shift from the formal to the familiar pronoun of address. But he is just beginning here his banter at the Monk's expense.

Without waiting for answers to his questions, the Host shifts to the Monk's physical appearance, commenting on his fair skin and obvious well-being, from which he concludes that the Monk is not a poor cloisterer but a "governour, wily and wys," with the stature befitting such office. Then with ironic sympathy[5] the Host laments the Church's rule of celibacy which prevents so able-bodied a man from begetting children:

> I pray to God, yeve hym confusioun
> That first thee broghte unto religioun!
> Thou woldest han been a tredefowel aright.
> Haddestow as greet a leeve, as thou hast myght,

[5] Robinson, *Works,* 852.

100]

> To parfourne al thy lust in engendrure,
> Thou haddest bigeten ful many a creature.
>
> VII, 1943–48

Needless to say, Harry's concern here with the desirability of increasing the population should not be taken seriously. He is manifestly making off-color jests because he takes for granted that a worldly monk, "in good poynt" and addicted to hunting and luxury, must inevitably be involved in frequent sexual activities. And we should note that Harry assumes sufficient familiarity with the Monk's supposed extramonastic exploits to continue his use of the intimate "thou," "thee," and "thy" with fluent ease.

Furthermore, the Host labors his point for eleven additional lines, in which he first proclaims that, if he were pope, the Monk and all professional religious men equally capable physically would have wives. This statement then leads him to the conclusion that "Religioun hath take up al the corn/Of tredyng, and we borel men been shrympes," in which there is the fairly obvious jocular and lewd comparison of the sexual organ of the secular male to a shrimp. This manner of satirizing the licentious practices of contemporary churchmen the Host carries to greater lengths by stating that "oure wyves" prefer sexual experience with churchmen, whose physical prowess makes them better able to meet "Venus' payment"; such, of course, was the case with Don John and the wife of the merchant of St. Denis. Then, to cap his attack, the Host repeats a device he had used earlier with the Cook: "But be nat wrooth, my lord, though that I pleye./Ful ofte in game a sooth I have herd seye!" Obviously, this is no apology at all; rather, it is a further attempt to arouse the Monk's wrath and to put him in the wrong for not being able to take a joke.

Surely the Monk had reason to be displeased at the Miller's rudeness, the Host's neglect, the Shipman's story, and the Prioress' passing comment. But the Host's lengthy and unveiled assumption that the Monk participates in sexual activities with willing wives might well have given rise to an explosion. Doubtless Harry is hoping for the entertainment that would be provided by just such an outburst. But the Monk was not born yesterday, and he has not made his way in the world without learning how to handle scoffers. He seems quickly to arrive at a shrewd estimate of the situation and realizes that his best move is to disregard completely the Host's provoking remarks, and to punish the Host for his vulgar familiarity by subjecting him to a dull, learned sermon. Therefore, we are told that "This worthy Monk took al in pacience"; and his first words are a refutation of Harry's suggestive implications: "I wol doon al my diligence,/ As fer as sowneth into honestee,/To telle yow a tale, or two, or three." Very likely the other members of the company are just as uneasy as the Host, who probably had expected a flustered defense from the Monk, at the prospect of his telling three "honest" tales.

The Monk does nothing to allay such uneasiness. On the contrary, he offers to tell the group the life of St. Edward the Confessor—a dreary suggestion, from the Host's point of view—or else first to relate some tragedies, of which he has a *hundred* in his cell. Here is indeed an alluring choice for entertainment while traveling—either the life of St. Edward, or a hundred tragedies plus the life of St. Edward! But the Monk seems determined on his revenge, and, giving the Pilgrims no time to choose, he starts right in with the latter alternative by defining tragedy in the medieval sense. This routine definition over, he apologizes beforehand for any error in chronology he might make. One surmises that this apology stems from the Monk's realization that time spent in hunting has made his learning a bit shaky.

There is no need here to examine in detail the material which makes up the Monk's Tale. Suffice it to recall that he delivers seventeen completely uninspired, brief narratives, in each of which a famous individual falls from high place to low. Seemingly in an antifeminist answer to the Host's implications that he has improper relations with women, the Monk commences his tragedies with Satan and moves next to Adam and Samson, who were betrayed by women, the agents of Satan.[6] The Monk's recital, in the true tradition of a medieval sermon,[7] serves to exemplify the moral that no man should trust in blind prosperity,

---

[6] D. W. Robertson, Jr., *ELH*, XIX (1952), 9–11.

[7] Claude Jones, *MLN*, LII (1937), 570–72.

for when Fortune decides to desert him he cannot halt her. Such material is thoroughly suited to a churchman, and we can see some point in a worldly monk's choosing to include the "Modern Instances" within his recital of standard tragedies. But here indeed is a performance in great contrast to the "myrie cheere" the Host requested earlier of the Monk; and we can easily imagine the agony Harry is experiencing at the thought of the Monk's continuing through his hundredth tragedy—and then telling the life of St. Edward. However, the Host, feeling that this is "proper" material, is unwilling to interrupt. Fortunately—for the reader as well as for the Host—the Knight halts the recital.

With the authority of the Knight to support him, the Host rushes in to attack by heaping scorn upon the Monk:

> Ye, . . . by seint Poules belle!
> Ye seye right sooth; this Monk he clappeth lowde.
> He spak how Fortune covered with a clowde
> I noot nevere what; and als of a tragedie
> Right now ye herde, and, pardee, no remedie
> It is for to biwaille ne compleyne
> That that is doon, and als it is a peyne,
> As ye han seyd, to heere of hevynesse.   VII, 2780 87

Whether or not Harry realizes that the Monk has repaid him for his earlier familiarity is not completely clear; but we do note that in this passage the Host mocks the Monk's style[8] (compare lines 2785 with 1991; and 2782 with 2766), and then goes on to say that the Monk's story is annoying everybody, for it is not worth a butterfly. This time, however, Harry is careful to use the formal "you" and "your," to return to his respectful "sire Monk," and to refrain from levity in connection with the Monk's name, Don Piers. Also, we find entertaining evidence of the success of the Monk's revenge in the sincerity with which the Host says that only the jingling of the bells on the bridle of the Monk's horse kept him from sleeping and falling off his horse during the recital. Then, regaining his usual largeness of manner, Harry uses a semiphilosophical tag about the waste of speech where there is no listener, again boasts about his ability to recognize a

[8] H. R. Patch, *MLR*, XXII (1927), 386–87.

good story when he hears one, and politely requests the Monk to relate a hunting story: "Sir, sey somwhat of huntyng, I yow preye." He feels that a request for such material cannot displease the Monk, and at the same time doctrinal matter will be avoided. The reference here to the bells and to hunting shows that we are dealing with the same Monk whom we met in the General Prologue.

But the Monk seems to have had his fill of Harry Bailly and feels that he has sufficiently repaid him for the former vulgar liberties. Don Piers therefore simply dismisses the Host with the statement: "Nay, . . . I have no lust to pleye./Now lat another telle, as I have toold." As effectively as did the drunken Miller, though in an entirely different fashion, the Monk has defied the Host's rule and yet run no risk of paying all the expenses for the trip. Here the Host seems to realize that he has been bested, for he turns quickly to the Nun's Priest, a Pilgrim whom he does not fear to browbeat, with "rude speche and boold."

In the controversy that we have been examining, it is the nature of the tale as a whole, rather than themes or characters or incidents within it, which bears the weight of the revenge. There can be no question here, I think, as to whether or not Chaucer and his contemporaries were fonder of brief tragedies used as *exempla* than is the modern reader. This recital serves a perfectly obvious dramatic function as a speech delivered by the Monk; as such it well deserves its place in the *Canterbury Tales*. We are fortunate, however, that Chaucer had the good sense to limit the use of similar literary-revenge pieces to two additional performances—the "Melibeus" and the Parson's Tale.

10. THE NUN'S PRIEST

To many readers, the Nun's Priest's tale of the regal Chanticleer and the lovely Dame Pertelote represents the high point of Chaucer's narrative art in the *Canterbury Tales*; and this delightful story gains much when it is considered within the carefully prepared dramatic interplay which surrounds it. As an *exemplum* and as a mock-heroic beast-fable making use of learned material, the tale is a suitable one for a cleric; and its subtle antifeminist theme makes it appropriate for a cleric under the "petticoat rule" of the Prioress. But, in addition, the tale almost certainly includes the thrusts by the Nun's Priest at the Host's two most recent attackers—the Pilgrim Chaucer and the Monk. In fact, Harry Bailly's reactions form the background against which the tale functions dramatically. First we shall consider the problem of the traits, both physical and intellectual, which Chaucer intended us to associate with the Nun's Priest.

Concerning the character of the Nun's Priest, the Narrator gives almost no explicit information. This Pilgrim appears in only one phrase of the General Prologue: "Another Nonne with hire hadde she [the Prioress]/That was hir chapeleyne, and preestes thre" (I, 163–64); many scholars feel that even this one phrase is not by Chaucer. Whatever characteristics we attribute to the Nun's Priest must therefore be derived from his part in the drama of the pilgrimage.

Recent criticism as to this cleric's physical make-up and manner holds that he is a vigorous, rosy-cheeked, fun-loving youngster, who serves as one of three brawny, two-fisted bodyguards for the Prioress.[1] Where so few facts are available, however, wide difference of opinion is permissible if it can be supported. The view to be advanced in detail here differs considerably from that

[1] Arthur Sherbo, *PMLA*, LXIV (1949), 236–46; M. P. Hamilton in *Philologica: The Malone Anniversary Studies*, 179–90.

This sweete preest, this goodly man sir John

stated above. I conceive of the Nun's Priest as a timid and frail person of indeterminate years, whom the Host is not afraid to address rudely and upon whom he vents the annoyance he feels primarily as a result of the Monk's behavior.

It will be useful to pause here for a review of the role which the Host has played in the sections of the *Canterbury Tales* preceding the Nun's Priest's performance. In the General Prologue, after a few moments of suspicion on the part of the company, he won the group's eager acceptance of his plan for the storytelling game and of his position of authority. But, after his pleasure arising from the Knight's Tale, he was successfully challenged by the Miller, somewhat annoyed by the Reeve's "sermonyng," and shortly thereafter threatened by the Cook. Then his satisfaction with the Lawyer's performance was quickly dampened by the Shipman's revolt against his authority. Although the Shipman's tale restored the Host's good spirits, he seemed not too pleased with the gravity resulting from the miracle related by the Prioress. Next, his patience was strained beyond its limits by the Pilgrim Chaucer's "Sir Thopas," and he was moved to a lengthy recollection of his domestic woes by the "Melibeus." In the succeeding instance, he was granted no relief by the Monk, whose tragedies he found exceedingly boring, and who calmly overthrew his authority by refusing to tell a tale of hunting.

Surely, up until the time he calls upon the Nun's Priest for a story, the Host has fared rather badly on the pilgrimage. Looked at in this fashion, the sequence and the nature of the performances in Fragments I, II, and VII seem to have been considerably influenced by Chaucer's desire to represent a regular rise and fall in the Host's spirits, with the humorous deflating of him as a steady aspect of the drama. So far, Harry has played an important role in connection with every Pilgrim's recital; we therefore may not be far wide of the mark if, in trying to derive an acceptable portrait of the Nun's Priest, we examine that Pilgrim and his tale as they reflect against, and fit with, the Host's recent behavior.

That, after the Monk's performance, Harry is in search of a Pilgrim upon whom he can relieve his pent-up irritation is borne out by the following lines:

> Thanne spak oure Hoost with rude speche and boold,
> And seyde unto the Nonnes Preest anon,
> "Com neer, thou preest, com hyder, thou sir John!
> Telle us swich thyng as may oure hertes glade.
> Be blithe, though thou ryde upon a jade.
> What thogh thyn hors be bothe foul and lene?
> If he wol serve thee, rekke nat a bene.
> Looke that thyn herte be murie everemo." VII, 2808–15

Though not bold enough to express his annoyance openly to the high-ranking Monk until after the Knight had interrupted the recital, Harry has picked out another churchman to whom he feels free to speak patronizingly and rudely. Especially noteworthy in this respect are his use in six instances of the familiar pronouns of address—"thou," "thyn," and "thee"—and his choice of "sir John," a familiar and even contemptuous appellation for a priest.

Apparently the Host is not wrong in his estimate of the Nun's Priest; the latter is unctuously humble and emphatic in his willingness to obey Harry's command:

> "Yis, sir," quod he, "yis, Hoost, so moot I go,
> But I be myrie, ywis I wol be blamed."
> And right anon his tale he hath attamed,
> And thus he seyde unto us everichon,
> This sweete preest, this goodly man sir John.
> VII, 2816–20

A considerable part of the unction in this speech rests in the echo in line 2817 of the Host's earlier unsuccessful command to the Monk to be merry (VII, 1924). The Nun's Priest says, in effect: "Even though the Monk would not do as you told him, *I will.*" One surmises that the impoverished Nun's Priest is far from sympathetic with his wealthy fellow churchman. In his answer here, the Nun's Priest is running no risk of incurring the Host's wrath; and the Narrator's calling him "sweete" and "goodly" serves to emphasize the accommodating haste with which he has just accepted Harry's orders.

In view of this interchange, I find it impossible to go along with those critics who visualize the Nun's Priest as brawny and

vigorous; logic as well as kindness demands that we think of anyone who lets the pompous Host "push him around" in this fashion as being possessed of timidity and meekness which result
from a lack of physical prowess. The phrase "this sweete preest"
in line 2820, with its suggestion of femininity, is also difficult to
align with a concept of a brawny, vigorous Nun's Priest. In addition, note the seemingly spineless agreement signified by the
repetition of the emphatic "yis," as well as the contrast between
the Nun's Priest's lean and foul nag and the Monk's brown-as-a-
berry palfrey (I, 207). From the two passages quoted above we
are surely safe in assuming that the Host looks upon the Nun's
Priest as one churchman to whom he can with impunity speak
"as lordly as a king." Further, from these passages can be observed the Nun's Priest's willingness to curry favor with the Host
by fulfilling the command for merriment which was refused by
the Monk, towards whom the Nun's Priest has no reason to be
favorably inclined. In no way do the lines examined so far suggest impressive physical stature for the Nun's Priest; rather, the
opposite is implied, for Harry Bailly would automatically extend
the same respect to a physically impressive Nun's Priest that he
proffered the Miller and the Shipman.

It is, however, in the much-discussed Epilogue to the Nun's
Priest's Tale that the Host finally purges his system of the an-
noyance which the Monk has most recently occasioned him.
There he speaks as follows:

> "Sire Nonnes Preest, . . .
> I blessed be thy breche, and every stoon!
> This was a murie tale of Chauntecleer.
> But by my trouthe, if thou were seculer,
> Thou woldest ben a trede-foul aright.
> For if thou have corage as thou hast myght,
> Thee were nede of hennes, as I wene,
> Ya, moo than seven tymes seventene.
> See, whiche braunes hath this gentil preest,
> So gret a nekke, and swich a large breest!
> He loketh as a sperhauk with his yen;
> Him nedeth nat his colour for to dyen
> With brasile, ne with greyn of Portyngale.

> Now, sire, faire falle yow for youre tale!"
> And after that he, with ful merie chere,
> Seide unto another, as ye shuln heere.   VII, 3447–62

It is immediately apparent that in these lines, present in only ten of the scribal copies that have come down to us, the Host reproduces the tone and a part of the contents of his earlier speech to the Monk (VII, 1932–61). For this reason, Professor Manly and some other editors of the *Canterbury Tales* have concluded that Chaucer probably canceled the passage quoted above when he later wrote the Host's speech to the Monk. However, other scholars have maintained that Chaucer meant this passage to stand as it is. The grounds for this latter view are simply that the manuscript situation is inconclusive, that the repetition here is not extensive, and that elsewhere, as in Harry Bailly's remarks about his wife, Chaucer did not cancel repetitive lines.[2] There is, it seems to me, an additional and equally cogent argument, based on internal evidence, against cancellation.

In this epilogue, Harry is in far better spirits than when he first called upon the Nun's Priest; consequently, he shows this Pilgrim the courtesy of twice calling him "sire," and finally even uses the respectful "yow" and "youre." But the Host is not yet entirely satisfied that he has wiped away all trace of the Monk's intractability toward him. Therefore, using "thy" and "thou," he repeats, in his remarks to the Nun's Priest, a part of the identical vulgar routine joke at which the Monk had earlier taken offense; the core of this joke is, of course, the suggestion that a churchman has great sexual powers. But this time we should not take the routine jest at face value, as have those critics who base their claim for the Nun's Priest's brawn on these lines. Harry is speaking ironically here, and the intent of the passage is the opposite of its literal meaning. The Host is contemptuous towards the Nun's Priest because this churchman is under the supervision of a woman, the Prioress; note the emphasis in line 3447 which Harry places on the cleric's position by his use of the title "Sire *Nonnes* Preest." That we know the Host to be a henpecked husband makes his contempt for the Nun's Priest's situation the

---

[2] Manly and Rickert, *The Text of the Canterbury Tales*, II, 422–23, and IV, 517; J. S. P. Tatlock, *PMLA*, L (1935), 100–39.

more readily understandable. Furthermore, Harry feels that, by virtue of his unimposing physical stature, the Nun's Priest is well suited for supervision by a female and for a job that keeps him in a nunnery.[3] These are the two aspects of the Nun's Priest which led the Host earlier to select him as the churchman upon whom his irritation at the imposing and powerful Monk could be vented safely. Now, the tale over, Harry wishes to demonstrate to the company that he can successfully apply to another churchman the vulgar joke which the Monk earlier caused to fall flat.

A careful look at the Epilogue reveals three additional details to support a reading of this passage as irony. The Host here omits completely the remarks, present in his similar speech to the Monk, on the Church's folly in not permitting the clergy to marry in order to beget healthy children to populate the world; the physique of the Nun's Priest receives the entire emphasis here. I take it that this churchman's pallor, extreme slenderness, skinny neck, narrow breast, and dull eyes would make too far-fetched even an ironic argument from Harry that such men were needed to populate the earth. Also, there is the ring of irony about lines 3450–54, where the Host says that if the Nun's Priest were secular he would be a "trede-foul aright" and have need of many "hennes." His position does cause him to be surrounded by many women—the nuns—and it was generally taken for granted that a churchman stationed in a nunnery indulged in sexual license.[4] But the Nun's Priest's physical appearance is not such as to suggest that he is a source of temptation to the nuns. Finally, there is the appearance of ironic exaggeration in the line "Ya, moo than seven tymes seventene." When so industrious a servant of Venus as Chanticleer seems content with only 7 "hennes," and when more than 119 seems beyond the desires of even the mightiest Eastern potentate, we can suspect at least that Harry's statement means that the Nun's Priest appears too weakly to have any need at all for "hennes."

Having delivered this ironic speech on the Nun's Priest's physique, the Host is thoroughly satisfied with himself and returns to his usual jovial frame of mind, gone all thoughts of his diffi-

---

[3] Eileen Power, *Medieval English Nunneries c. 1275 to 1535*, p. 144–45.
[4] *Ibid.*, chap. xi.

culties with the Monk. The Narrator tells us that Harry turns to the next storyteller "with ful merie chere," an attitude in striking contrast to the "rude speche and boold" with which he called upon the Nun's Priest after the Monk's rebuff (VII, 2808). Rather than concluding that Chaucer canceled the Epilogue to the Nun's Priest's Tale when he wrote, perhaps later, the Prologue to the Monk's Tale, I find in the Host's remarks every indication of Chaucer's skillful use of a repetitive tone and partially repetitive lines to convey the dramatic situation surrounding the Host's dealings with the Monk and the Nun's Priest. For an editor to cancel this epilogue is to ruin one of the most carefully developed scenes in the whole pilgrimage. The high comedy of this scene, for the reader and for Chaucer the poet, lies in the Host's missing the subtler points of the tale and holding up to ridicule the meek little priest who superbly defends him.

For if we have found that the Nun's Priest's physical stature leaves much to be desired, there is nothing at all wrong with his intellectual powers. The tale that Chaucer assigned him is the most charming and one of the most expert in the *Canterbury* collection. Also, in this story the frail Nun's Priest manages to please the Host, to offer rebuttal for the theme of "Melibeus," to laugh at the Monk, and to express his dissatisfaction at working under the Prioress' direction. In order to comprehend these matters fully, we need a brief summary of the tale.

A poor widow has in her barnyard a gallant and imposing rooster, Chanticleer, and his favorite hen, Pertelote. One night in the chicken house Chanticleer dreams that he will meet with disaster from a yellowish-red beast if he flies down into the yard the next morning. He believes that this dream is an omen, but Pertelote maintains that it results from indigestion. Chanticleer wins the ensuing argument on the cause of dreams, but the depth of his amorous feeling for Pertelote leads him to disregard his conclusion by going down into the barnyard. Nearby lurks Don Russell, the evil fox; with elaborate flattery he maneuvers Chanticleer into a vulnerable position, snatches him up, and starts for home. The screams of Pertelote and Chanticleer's six other wives bring the entire household, human and animal, to give chase.

But Chanticleer can take care of himself: he tricks the fox into opening his mouth and then flies to safety in a tree. The fox tries to lure him down, but Chanticleer has learned a lesson from his experience.

Such a bare outline does far less than justice to the humor, the charm, and the skill of this tale. No critical exposition can hope to indicate the first two of these characteristics half so convincingly as will a reading of the story itself; but several critics have turned the full light of scholarship on the expertness with which Chaucer handled his materials in this instance. And, as we would expect, his manipulation of these materials appears to have been dictated by his concern for the dramatic function which the tale, as spoken by the frail and impoverished but witty Nun's Priest, fulfills.

The exact source which Chaucer used for this tale, if any, is not known, but there are two closely analogous stories that can be taken as representative of the materials he had at his disposal; one is the French *Roman de Renart*, the other is the German *Reinhart Fuchs*.[5] There is no need here to examine these pieces in detail, but we can profit from a brief statement of the major alterations Chaucer made in the narrative elements of the story, for these alterations play a crucial part in effecting the theme of Chaucer's version. Most importantly, whereas the two analogues are stories in which the cock is an egotistical fool, "who, repeatedly warned, refuses to heed and suffers in consequence," in the Nun's Priest's recital Chanticleer comes to grief because his amorous interest in Pertelote leads him to put aside his correct interpretation of his dream. Chaucer establishes this difference by shifting the reactions of the two main characters to the dream. In the analogues, the hen considers it an omen, and the proud cock disregards her warnings; in the Nun's Priest's version, it is Pertelote who scoffs at the dream's significance, and the theme of the story thus becomes "the baleful influence of woman's counsel."

Another change Chaucer makes in this narrative is to diminish the role of the fox. Whereas the fox is the one character whose

[5] J. B. Severs, *SP*, XLIII (1946), 22–41.

name appears in the titles of the two analogues, the manuscripts of the *Canterbury Tales* have for this performance the rubric "The Nonnes Preestes Tale of the Cok and the Hen." This alteration serves, of course, to place emphasis on the husband-wife relationship, the core of Chaucer's story, and helps clear the way for the theme, the ill effects of accepting a wife's advice.

This theme places the Nun's Priest's Tale in the large body of antifeminist literature of the late Middle Ages and thus puts it in exact contrast with the preceding "Melibeus," related by the Pilgrim Chaucer, in which all turns out well because of the acceptance of the wise counsel that Prudence gives her husband. Harry may not have realized that the Pilgrim Chaucer maneuvered him into approving the "Melibeus," the theme of which is in entertaining contrast with Harry's immediately succeeding revelations about his own wife. But the shrewd Nun's Priest saw this point at once, and now in his tale defends the Host by showing that a husband is not always wise in following his wife's counsel. There is, of course, perfect appropriateness in the assignment of an antifeminist piece to the Nun's Priest, since the clergy was especially prolific in producing treatments of this theme. But this particular story is further suited to its teller because he is under "petticoat rule" from the Prioress.[6] Yet his position prevents his risking a head-on attack similar to those used by the Friar, the Summoner, the Miller, and the Reeve; besides, what we have already seen of his nature shows that he is not the sort of man to become involved in a straightforward controversy. Rather, he will employ subtlety in making his point.

Thus it is that we find in the concluding lines of his tale a statement of what at first glance seems to be his "moralite": "Lo, swich it is for to be recchelees/And necligent, and truste on flaterye" (VII, 3436–37). But the primary point which he wants to illustrate has been plainly stated earlier:

> My tale is of a cok, as ye may heere,
> That tok his conseil of his wyf, with sorwe,
> To walken in the yerd upon that morwe
> That he hadde met that dreem that I yow tolde.
> Wommennes conseils been ful ofte colde;

---

[6] W. W. Lawrence, *Chaucer and the Canterbury Tales*, 134–36.

> Wommannes conseil broghte us first to wo,
> And made Adam fro Paradys to go,
> Ther as he was ful myrie and wel at ese. VII, 3252–59

We can be sure that if we had the Nun's Priest to explicate his line "Taketh the fruyt, and lat the chaf be stille" (VII, 3443), somewhere beyond the Prioress' overhearing, he would classify the first of the passages quoted above as bordering on the "chaf," and point to the second as the "fruyt." But in his tale he is not out of earshot of the Prioress, and he does not want to offend her. Therefore he hastens to add the following lines:

> But for I noot to whom it myght displese,
> If I conseil of wommen wolde blame,
> Passe over, for I seyde it in my game.
> Rede auctours, where they trete of swich mateere,
> And what they seyn of wommen ye may heere.
> Thise been the cokkes wordes, and nat myne;
> I kan noon harm of no womman divyne.
>
> VII, 3260–66

Even so, the Nun's Priest has not completely drawn the teeth from his attack, for the "auctours" to whom he refers his audience spoke with force and at length in an antifeminist vein.

In addition to answering the Pilgrim Chaucer and to implying his dissatisfaction with the Prioress' rule, the Nun's Priest manages to accomplish two other aims in his performance. The general merriment of his mock epic, the antifeminist theme itself, and the avoidance of a tragic ending similar to the *exempla* recounted by the Monk are aimed at pleasing the Host, whose good humor when the tale is finished we have already noted. Then, too, there is a possible application of several elements in the tale to the Monk.[7] That worthy's confidence and general affluence are in as great contrast to the Nun's Priest's timidity and poverty as is his fine palfrey to the latter's nag. It would not be unnatural for the Nun's Priest to feel a few twinges of antagonistic jealousy, and we saw that he did appear to say, in answering the Host: "The Monk wouldn't do as you wished, but *I will*." Then in his tale he puts into Chanticleer's mouth one of the tragedies which

---

[7] S. B. Hemingway, *MLN*, XXXI (1916), 479–83.

the Monk has just related, that of Croesus (VII, 3138–40) ; some readers have felt that the Nun's Priest is thereby ridiculing the Monk and is trying to call his audience's attention to the similar strutting manner of both the outrider and the cock.

But there is more certain ridicule in the following lines by the Nun's Priest:

> For evere the latter ende of joye is wo.
> God woot that worldly joye is soone ago;
> And if a rethor koude faire endite,
> He in a cronycle saufly myghte it write
> As for a sovereyn notabilitee.   VII, 3205–3209

The Monk's oft-repeated point in his performance is that worldly happiness soon passes away, as commonplace a remark at the time as one might hope to find. When the Nun's Priest applies this same routine point to Chanticleer's near disaster with the fox, and then calls it a "sovereyn notabilitee" which an expert rhetorician might well include in a chronicle, the satire on the Monk's dull sententiousness is easy to see. One other passage by the Nun's Priest seems also to apply unfavorably to the Monk. In his account of Samson, the Monk says:

> Beth war by this ensample oold and playn
> That no men telle hir conseil til hir wyves
> Of swich thyng as they wolde han secree fayn,   .
> If that it touche hir lymes or hir lyves.   VII, 2091–94

Here is, of course, a typical antifeminist statement, which a careful listener might happen to recall upon hearing the Nun's Priest's apology for speaking ill of women. And the Nun's Priest seems eager to help his audience arrive at such a recollection; he illogically shifts in his remarks from "reading" to "hearing" authors who have treated the woman question: "Read authors where they treat of such material, and you may *hear* what they say about women." Once again he equates the Monk with Chanticleer, this time pointing to their similar views about women.

There are aspects of this performance other than its antifeminist theme that make it apposite for the Nun's Priest. The rhetorical skill necessary for turning a beast-fable into a mock epic, as well as the learning that makes possible the inclusion of the debate on dreams, the many references to literary material, and the statement of the free will-foreordination problem, is not surprising in an individual who has the training given the clergy. Furthermore, the *exemplum* technique and other sermon devices in the performance come naturally from a priest. But our next actor-Pilgrim, the Wife of Bath, will submit views in sharp variance with those we have been considering. She is now introduced by means of six lines which have only recently[8] been accorded a place in the accepted text of the *Tales:*

> "Madame, and y durst, y wold you pray
> To telle us a tale y furtheryng of our way;
> Then myght ye do unto us gret ease."
> "Gladly," quod she, "so that y myght you please,
> You and this wurthy company."
> And began hir tale ryght thus full sobyrly.[9]

11. THE WIFE OF BATH

Many of the finest Chaucerian critics have commented at some length upon the sections of the *Canterbury Tales* devoted to the Wife of Bath.[1] Although most of these critics have been sympathetic towards the Wife, the analysis presented here will emphasize certain fundamental flaws in her character. In the section devoted to the Shipman, we considered the tale which Chaucer originally assigned to the Wife; her controversy with the Friar will receive attention in the section treating the worthy Hubert; and her interruption by the Pardoner will be analyzed when we come to his performance. Here we are concerned primarily with the Wife's character as it appears from the Narra-

[8] R. F. Gibbons, *SP*, LI (1954), 21–33.   [9] See Robinson, *Works*, 1013.

[1] See, for example, W. E. Mead, *PMLA*, XVI (1901), 388–404; G. L. Kittredge, *MP*, IX (1911–12), 435–67; Curry, *Sciences*, 91–118; H. R. Patch, *On Rereading Chaucer*, 161–65.

In felaweshipe wel koude she laughe and carpe

tor's sketch of her in the General Prologue (I, 445–76) and from her own autobiographical prologue (III, 1–856), and with the dramatic motivation and implications of the tale which she tells the company (III, 857–1264). From consideration of these parts of the *Canterbury Tales*, we shall find that the Wife's outstanding traits are aggressiveness and amorousness, and that the two combine to produce her militant feminism, which leads her to argue strongly for female sovereignty. Obviously, the tale she tells is aimed at illustrating this tenet; and her tale fits into the context of her antagonism towards antifeminist clerics, such as the Nun's Priest, who has just completed his tale, and towards recalcitrant husbands, such as Harry Bailly. But we shall also see that in the course of her performance Chaucer causes her to make clear certain unfavorable aspects of her character which she does not intend to reveal; she no doubt would look upon such revelation as a source of embarrassment.

At the opening of the portrait the Narrator states that there was in the company "A good Wyf . . . of biside Bathe." In Middle English, "wyf" had a more generalized meaning than it carries today in that it could apply to any woman, married or not. In Alice's case, however, the specialized meaning is also particularly apt, since she has had five husbands. This lady is immediately individualized for us by the Narrator's statement that she is partially deaf. The reason for this infirmity is later made vividly memorable when in her prologue she tells of her exchange of blows with her fifth husband (III, 788–96). The Wife does not live in Bath proper; she is from "biside Bathe." Apparently this means that she inhabited the parish of St. Michael-without-the-North-Gate, a small community just outside the town walls, in which weaving was the chief occupation.[2] It is fitting, therefore, that the Narrator should next point out that in clothmaking the Wife surpassed even the inhabitants of Ypres and Ghent, two cities in Flanders noted for the finest weaving. Some readers have seen irony in this statement, suspecting that Chaucer meant us to understand that the Wife thinks better of her own skill than it deserves; but such a view fails to take into account the Wife's highly developed competitive urge in any en-

[2] Manly, *New Light*, 231–32, and *Canterbury Tales by Geoffrey Chaucer*, 527.

deavor she might undertake. We can feel fairly confident that she successfully exerted every effort to produce weaving which would rank with the best. This aspect of her character is evident in her reaction to any other woman's preceding her to "the offrynge": if another woman does so, the Wife is so angry that she is "out of alle charitee." The size and quality of her Sunday "coverchiefs," the quality and arrangement of her red stockings, and her shoes "ful moyste and newe" also show her determination not to allow any other woman to outshine her. And her face—bold, fair, and "reed of hewe"—is that of an aggressive competitor.

But the Wife's care for her appearance doubtless also springs from another competitive motive: her desire to attract male attention. Here there can be no question of her standing, for she has had five husbands, not to mention "oother compaignye in youthe." Her account of these five husbands will form the main portion of her prologue, and "thereof nedeth nat to speke as nowthe." The Narrator feels it sufficient in the sketch to note that the Wife, as an expert in love, knows both its cures and its rules.

It is easily apparent that the Wife must have been a valuable member of the Canterbury company because of her wide experience with pilgrimages—three times to Jerusalem, to Rome, to Boulogne, to St. James's in Galicia, and to Cologne—and because of her gay sociability "in felaweshipe." The General Prologue presents no more striking picture than that of the Wife, laughing and talking as she rides along easily on her "amblere," on her head a hat as broad as a shield, on her heels a pair of sharp spurs, and about her "hipes large" a cloth to protect her skirt from dust and mud. But we hear nothing from her until she begins her prologue, though we can be sure that she has noted with interest both the pictures of married life and the implications concerning dominance in marriage which have appeared in the various preceding recitals.

The Wife of Bath's Prologue, whatever else it may be, is primarily a masterful piece of dialectic, a purposeful attempt at vigorous argumentation. The Wife, aggressive competitor that we have seen her to be, will discuss matrimony, the field of competition which to her is most important. And, chiefly in answer to the Nun's Priest, she is going to use the opportunity afforded by her turn in the center of the movable stage on the road to Canterbury for as strong a presentation of her central view as she can muster, namely, that unhappiness in marriage can be avoided only when the husband grants sovereignty to the wife. When this prologue is examined carefully as such a piece of dialectic, it is perfectly unified and extremely close-knit. We are misled when we maintain, as do some readers, that the Wife's Prologue is divided into two sharply distinct portions by the Pardoner's interruption (III, 163–87), and that the first part (III, 1–162) treats the question of chastity, while the second (III, 188–828) alone concerns sovereignty in marriage. Rather, the matter uppermost in the Wife's mind throughout is female sovereignty, and the lines preceding the Pardoner's interruption represent what she considers necessary and pertinent introductory argument.

The Wife wastes no time in preliminary amenities; she leaps at once into a statement of her topic and of her right to discuss such a topic authoritatively:

> Experience, though noon auctoritee
> Were in this world, is right ynogh for me
> To speke of wo that is in mariage;
> For, lordynges, sith I twelve yeer was of age,
> Thonked be God that is eterne on lyve,
> Housbondes at chirche dore I have had fyve—
> If I so ofte myghte have ywedded bee,—
> And alle were worthy men in hir degree.   III, 1–8

The Wife's topic, then, is "the wo that is in mariage," and it is very important to notice here that the woe of which she will speak is that experienced by husbands who fail to grant their wives mastery, rather than any unhappiness which she herself may have undergone. The lines in which she thanks God for her five husbands, as well as the long segment of her prologue following the Pardoner's interruption, show that she intends this interpretation of "wo." Thus her whole attitude towards marital happiness is in a sense negative: she will show how to avoid misery, not how to be happy.

In the first eight lines of her prologue the Wife also reveals clearly her understanding that points in argumentation derive support from two kinds of evidence—personal experience and authorities; she hastens to indicate the extent of her experience, and she will soon quote authorities in great plenty. But her first aim in this discussion of marriage is to contravert two preliminary arguments which she considers fallacious: first, the idea that an individual should be married only once (III, 13); and, second, the claim that God commanded virginity (III, 62). Citing the Bible with easy familiarity—doubtless the result of her fifth husband's constant reading to her—she maintains that God, rather than forbidding more than one marriage, instructed us to multiply. Since Solomon, Lamech, Abraham, and Jacob had more than one wife and were still holy men, she can see no reason why she cannot have had five husbands; in fact, she will welcome the sixth when her present husband dies. Moreover, she is certain that God did not intend for everyone to be chaste, for "if ther were no seed ysowe,/Virginitee, thanne whereof sholde it growe?" (III, 71–72). She will grant that chastity is a higher state, but as for herself, she will freely enjoy the physical acts of marriage. In fact, she says:

> An housbonde I wol have, I wol nat lette,
> Which shal be bothe my dettour and my thral,
> And have his tribulacion withal
> Upon his flessh, whil that I am his wyf.
> I have the power durynge al my lyf
> Upon his propre body, and noght he.
> Right thus the Apostel tolde it unto me;
> And bad oure housbondes for to love us weel.
> Al this sentence me liketh every deel— III, 154–62

The Wife here states her policy of completely subjugating her husband by exhausting his sexual potency, and, at this point, the Pardoner interrupts to say that though he is about to take a wife, if matters are as Alice of Bath describes them, he will not enter into marriage. But the Wife tells him to withhold his decision, for before she has finished her performance he will hear of more important troubles in marriage (III, 172–77). As in the opening lines of her prologue, the Wife here announces her main topic, "tribulacion in mariage"; and this time she makes fully clear that this tribulation has been felt not by her but by her husbands, since she has been the "whippe" or held the mastery. Having disposed of the two preliminary questions to her own satisfaction, now, to illustrate in detail her central theme that only unhappiness can result for husbands who refuse to give their wives mastery, she is ready to recount fully her five marital experiences. And she seems to feel confident that because of her preliminary discussion, no antifeminist cleric can halt her exposition to interpose arguments concerning either bigamy or chastity—matters which, in her opinion, she has shown to be irrelevant.

In her autobiographical account, the Wife of Bath groups together her first three husbands. All three were completely under her thumb, and she apparently can no longer remember their distinguishing traits. Each was aged and rich, and each, like old January in the Merchant's Tale, uxorious. With complete shamelessness the Wife tells the company just how she unscrupulously controlled these three old men (III, 197–451). As she says, "I hadde hem hoolly in myn hond" (III, 211), a situation which she preserved by withholding her body from them or by scolding them mercilessly. The result she desired—and obtained—was that they gave her all their many possessions and were happy only when they did not oppose her.

With her fourth husband the case was considerably different (III, 453–502), for "he hadde a paramour." But Alice claims that she brought him to heel by making him jealous. Yet she does not seem to have found much pleasure in this marriage; when he died she quickly buried him as cheaply as possible: "It nys but wast to burye hym preciously."

Although Jenkin, her fifth husband, was hardest of all to subjugate, of him the Wife seems most fond: "I trowe I loved hym best, for that he/Was of his love daungerous to me" (III, 513–14). Jenkin had been a student at Oxford, and came to board with the Wife's closest friend, Alisoun. One Lent, while her fourth husband was away in London, the Wife walked in the fields with Jenkin and told him that if she were a widow she would marry him. This situation soon developed, when her fourth husband died; within a month, forty-year-old Alice and twenty-year-old Jenkin were married. Before long, however, the Wife had reason to regret her action: Jenkin would do nothing to please her. He beat her and read aloud to her many clerical

stories from his antifeminist anthology about wives who were unfaithful and who brought their husbands to ruin. But the Wife of
Bath was not to be so easily outdone, and she continued to go
about visiting as she always had, even though Jenkin forbade it.
To her, Jenkin's antifeminist stories were far more infuriating
than instructive, for she has no high opinion of clerics who write
and tell such stories:

> Therfore no womman of no clerk is preysed.
> The clerk, whan he is oold, and may noght do
> Of Venus werkes worth his olde sho,
> Thanne sit he doun, and writ in his dotage
> That wommen kan nat kepe hir mariage!   III, 706–10

This state of open controversy reached a high point one night
when Jenkin read to her of Eve's bringing mankind to wretchedness, of Delilah's betrayal of Samson, of the trouble Deianira
caused Hercules, of Xanthippe's oppression of Socrates, of the
terrible lust of Pasiphaë, of Clytemnestra's infidelity to Aga-
memnon, of Eirphyle's treachery towards Amphiaraus, of the
poisoning of husbands by Livia and Lucilia, of how Arrius
wished to rid himself of his evil wife, and of many other treacherous wives who brought their husbands woe. When the Wife saw
that Jenkin intended to continue reading such material to her,
she tore three leaves from his book and knocked him into the fire.
Then he angrily hit her upon the head. At this, the Wife pretended to be unconscious for so long that he thought he had killed
her and started to flee. But the Wife spoke to him recriminat-
ingly, and he contritely leaned over her to be forgiven:

> And neer he cam, and kneled faire adoun,
> And seyde, "Deere suster Alisoun,
> As help me God! I shal thee nevere smyte.
> That I have doon, it is thyself to wyte.
> Foryeve it me, and that I thee biseke!"   III, 803–807

Taking advantage of his kneeling position, the Wife hit him
hard. But after long wrangling, the two patched up their differences, which is to say that Jenkin granted Alice complete
mastery:

> He yaf me al the bridel in myn hond,
> To han the governance of hous and lond,
> And of his tonge, and of his hond also;
> And made hym brenne his book anon right tho.
> And whan that I hadde geten unto me,
> By maistrie, al the soveraynetee,
> And that he seyde, "Myn owene trewe wyf,
> Do as thee lust the terme of al thy lyf;
> Keep thyn honour, and keep eek myn estaat"—
> After that day we hadden never debaat.   III, 813–22

Since that day, says the Wife, she has been wonderfully kind and absolutely faithful to her husband.

The Wife of Bath's lengthy account of her relationships with her five husbands has served to illustrate her principal theme— that if a husband does not grant his wife sovereignty, he will suffer great woe. This was the topic she introduced in her opening lines and restated in her answer to the Pardoner, after she had disposed of the preliminary matters of bigamy and chastity. Now she is ready to go on to her tale of the punished knight and the ugly hag, and her purpose in telling this tale is exactly the same as that which she has had throughout.

Her story takes place in the days of King Arthur. A young knight of Arthur's court rapes a girl whom he chances to meet. There is great protest from the populace to the King, and the knight is sentenced to die. But the Queen and other ladies of the court beg so hard that mercy be shown him that the King finally gives the knight to the Queen, to choose whether he should live or die. The Queen tells him that he can save his life if, within a year and a day, he can tell her what it is that women most desire; if he cannot answer the question correctly, he must die. For almost a year the knight searches unsuccessfully for the answer. As he is sadly returning to the court, he meets an old hag, who tells him that she will give him the correct answer if he will promise to grant the next request she makes of him. The knight agrees and goes to the court, where he supplies the correct answer: Women desire most to have sovereignty. The knight is, of course, very happy at escaping death, but when the old hag demands that he fulfill his promise to her by making her his wife, he feels that

[125

death might have been preferable. Nevertheless, the two are married. When they are alone in the marriage bed, the knight turns his back upon his wife. She asks why this is so, and he tells her it is because she is so ugly, so old, and of such low birth. She replies that she can change these matters if he will do as she says, and then she preaches him a fine sermon on gentilesse. At the end of her sermon, she tells him that she will fulfill his "worldly appetit," and offers him the choice of having her ugly and old but faithful, or beautiful and young but possibly unfaithful. Faced with such a difficult choice, the knight answers that he will leave the choice to her. Then come the crucial lines:

> "Thanne have I gete of yow maistrie," quod she,
> "Syn I may chese and governe as me lest?"
> "Ye, certes, wyf," quod he, "I holde it best."
> "Kys me," quod she, "we be no lenger wrothe;
> For, by my trouthe, I wol be to yow bothe,
> This is to seyn, ye, bothe fair and good."   III, 1236–41

By granting his wife mastery, the unhappy knight has escaped all woe; in fact, "his herte bathed in a bath of blisse."

Both the answer to the question and the happy ending make it obvious that the Wife of Bath tells the company this story to illustrate the same point which she has had in mind since she first began her performance. She has kept steady emphasis on the theme that a husband can avoid unhappiness only by giving his wife mastery, a theme that quite naturally results from her combination of aggressiveness and amorousness, her two chief characteristics, which she herself explains astrologically (III, 603–26). Moreover, her performance, as if an answer to the Nun's Priest's Tale, has been delivered in a context of antagonism against husbands "That wol not be governed by hir wyves" (III, 1262), and against the antifeminist clerics who write only evil of women (III, 706–10).

But Chaucer does not permit this actor-Pilgrim to leave the stage with her performance so complete a success as she believes. As we shall see in discussing the Friar, "this worthy lymytour" takes pains to deflate the Wife of Bath in the eyes of the company (III, 1265–77). And, what is more to our point here, Chaucer has so constructed the Wife's performance that for the careful reader there are a number of evidences and implications therein that reveal the Wife in a less favorable light than she intends. Three such matters deserve attention.

First of all, she does not realize that from her account of her marriages a member of her audience can very easily equate her present situation with that of her first three husbands, whom she held up to such ridicule. She states that of her five husbands, three were good and two were bad. "Good," applying to the first three, she defines as rich and old and easy to manage; "bad," designating the fourth and fifth, means to her poor and young and difficult to manage. In the case of her first three marriages, the Wife is young, very attractive physically, and without money; hence her elderly husbands are so influenced by lust that they are willing to sign their possessions over to her in exchange for her physical favors. But by the time of her fourth marriage, though she has become a wealthy widow, her physical charms are fading, and, as her vehement protests suggest, her sexual powers must be supported by recourse to wine (III, 455–68). In this instance, physical attraction does not bind her husband to her; on the contrary, he takes a mistress. Although the Wife boasts that she subjugated him by making him jealous, we have reason to be a trifle dubious, for she later reveals that he was sufficiently independent of her to make a lengthy visit to London and leave her at home (III, 550). In the case of her fifth husband, the situation is exactly the reverse of her first three marriages. As she is well aware (III, 469–80), she is now old, while Jenkin is a handsome youth; and she, captivated by his physical charms and sexual potency, signs over her possessions to him. Although she finally manages to gain mastery over Jenkin, doubtless by unceasing nagging, we suspect at least that in the event of Jenkin's death she will fall easy prey to the first impoverished but attractive young man whose eye for her money leads him into wooing her.

Second, an important theme, of which she seems completely unaware, can be derived from the Wife of Bath's Tale. Even though she thinks that her story merely illustrates her argument that a husband should give his wife mastery in order to avoid misery, we can see that the knight in the story grows by virtue of his experiences and is converted from a callous lawbreaker into a courteous gentleman.[3] When we first meet the knight, he is an arrogant and lustful rapist (III, 882–88). Later he appears as a snobbish aristocrat when he berates and neglects his wife, though she has saved him from death, because of her lack of beauty, her advanced age, and her low rank. However, as a result of her sermon on gentilesse, in which she shows him the error of his attitude, he alters his manner completely and addresses her as she deserves. And this alteration comes before the knight knows that it will bring about his happiness. The knight wins happiness, not primarily because he granted his wife sovereignty, as the Wife of Bath thinks she is showing, but because, as a converted sinner, he has earned it.

Third, and perhaps most striking, is the sharp contrast between the Wife of Bath's completely unethical conduct towards her husbands, as described in her prologue, and the admirable rules of behavior set forth by the old hag in her sermon on gentilesse near the end of the Wife's story. There are many indications that the Wife identifies herself with the old hag in her tale. As we have seen, it is the hag who provides the answer to the effect that women most desire mastery and who demands mastery of her husband; female sovereignty is, of course, the central point which the Wife intends her tale to illustrate. Also, the situation between the hag and the knight—old, ugly wife and young, vigorous husband—bears close similarity to that existing between Alice of Bath and Clerk Jenkin; and, in view of the Wife's touching lament for her lost youth and beauty (III, 469–79), we might argue that the hag's magic transformation represents pertinent wishful thinking on the Wife's part and furnishes her with particularly satisfying vicarious pleasure. Furthermore, the climactic position of the bed scene in the tale, a theater of operations with which the Wife has been much concerned during most of her life, comes very naturally from this particular storyteller. But by no stretch of the imagination can we find any similarity between the rules of conduct laid down by the hag in her sermon and the principles of behavior practiced by the Wife of Bath.

[3] J. P. Roppolo, *College English*, XII (1950–51), 263–69.

This sermon seems to be Chaucer's deliberate addition to the tale; although we have no actual source for the Wife's story, the closest analogues—Gower's "Tale of Florent," "The Marriage of Sir Gawaine," and "The Weddynge of Sir Gawen and Dame Ragnell"—do not include such a sermon.[4] The old hag tells her husband that true gentilesse comes from God and is not inherent in noble birth; that both low rank and lack of wealth, rather than being disgraceful, may motivate virtue; that the young should be respectful towards the aged; and that lack of beauty may ensure fidelity. To none of these tenets has Alice of Bath subscribed in her relationships with her five husbands. And, most surprisingly, the Wife of Bath, in concluding her tale, is led to say that the knight's wife obeyed him in everything that might give him pleasure (III, 1255–56); such mastery the Wife herself would be willing to bestow upon no husband. Thus we find in this section of the *Canterbury Tales* not only the suiting of tale and teller within a context of dramatic antagonism, but also full-scale character revelation that goes beyond the intention of the storyteller.

12. THE FRIAR

Although it has been suggested that the Friar and the Summoner are enemies of long standing, perhaps having come in conflict in a district of Yorkshire, we have no proof of this.[1] Nor is such an assumption necessary to explain the obvious dislike which each of these Pilgrims feels for the other. As is well known, the open antagonism between them is sufficiently motivated by the clash of their professional interests. No two professions of the time were

[4] See the chapters by B. J. Whiting in *Sources and Analogues*, 207–68.
[1] Manly, *New Light*, 102–22.

An esy man to yeve penaunce

more often at variance.[2] The friars, much to the annoyance of the secular clergy and its subordinates, claimed that only the pope had supervision over them. The two types also clashed in their attempts to fleece the same victims. We should not be surprised, therefore, when during the Wife of Bath's performance, a quarrel breaks out between these Pilgrims, or when each uses his tale to discomfit the other. It is also important to note that the tale each tells is particularly suited to his character as presented in the General Prologue—a point too frequently overlooked in the commentaries—and that there is sharp contrast between the two Pilgrims and between their tales. The likable Friar keeps his temper and tells a good-humored story, while the repulsive Summoner is consumed with anger and includes two vulgar jests in his recital.

This quarrel begins when the Wife reaches the end of her autobiographical prologue. The Friar laughs and says: "Now dame, . . . so have I joye or blis,/This is a long preamble of a tale!" (III, 829–31). There is nothing especially offensive about this remark, particularly in view of the Wife's preceding line, "Now wol I seye my tale, if ye wol heere," in which she seems to invite expressions of opinion from the group. True, we may be sure that the Friar does not look upon Alice of Bath as the sort of woman with whom he would seek an intimate relationship—she is far too strong-minded for him—and he is doubtless opposed to her arguments for sovereignty of women. But, in answer to her comment, he merely observes that her prologue has been lengthy, and thus perhaps hopes to keep her from telling an equally lengthy tale. Certainly his comment is far from belligerent. Yet the Summoner breaks in at once. It seems as if he has just been waiting for a chance to pick a fight with the Friar, and assuredly he, not the Friar, begins their quarrel. He insultingly compares friars to flies, in that they meddle with everything, and accuses the Friar of interrupting the Pilgrims' fun (III, 833–39).

The Friar does not lose his temper because of the Summoner's attack; however, he makes no effort to shrink from the quarrel and indicates the method he will use to ridicule his antagonist:

[2] Frederick Tupper, *Types of Society in Medieval Literature*, 56–57.

> Now, by my feith, I shal, er that I go,
> Telle of a somonour swich a tale or two,
> That alle the folk shall laughen in this place.
>
> III, 841–43

At this the wild Summoner erupts with a roar:

> Now elles, Frere, I bishrewe thy face,
> . . . and I bishrewe me,
> But if I telle tales two or thre
> Of freres, er I come to Sidyngborne,
> That I shal make thyn herte for to morne,
> For wel I woot thy pacience is gon. III, 844–49

Note the irony in the Summoner's statement that the Friar's patience is gone; it is, rather, the former who has completely lost control of himself.

But the Host puts a temporary halt to this quarrel and asks the Wife of Bath to tell her tale. She feels a bit annoyed at the Friar and replies, with heavy sarcasm: "Al redy, sire, . . . right as yow lest,/If I have licence of this worthy Frere" (III, 854–55). The Friar is perfectly polite in his answer: "Yis, dame, . . . tel forth, and I wol heere." After a passing jibe at the ubiquity and licentiousness of friars, the Wife tells her story, following which the Friar proceeds to fulfill his promise to tell a tale about a summoner.

In the sketch of the Friar in the General Prologue (I, 208–69), one of the longest in the series, we are told that the Friar is called Hubert, a name, whether or not Chaucer realized it, which suits him extremely well, since etymologically it means "bright, lively, gay."[3] He is attractive and pleasant, and much given to sprightly and agreeable conversation. His musical accomplishments are considerable: he sings, and plays the fiddle, and is familiar with a large stock of ballads. He frolics like a puppy, and after he has sung, his eyes twinkle like stars on a frosty night. Though appealing, these are hardly qualities of first importance in a professional religious; but the Friar has a number of far less admirable traits typical of his professional group at that time.[4] The four orders of friars had come to England in the thir-

---

[3] For a different view, see Bowden, *Commentary*, 119.

[4] G. G. Coulton, *Five Centuries of Religion*, presents much material concerning

teenth century, and in the beginning were made up of genuinely
holy men, who begged for the few material things they required,
tended the sick, helped the needy, and led generally exemplary
lives. But by the fourteenth century corruption had set in, and
the friars became the scourge of England. They were extremely
numerous, primarily interested in gaining wealth and position,
and much given to indulging in sins of the flesh, especially immoral relations with women. As a result, documents from the
fourteenth century present an astounding number of diatribes
against the friars; in fact, hardly a good word about them is to be
found.[5] The Wife of Bath's passing thrust is typical of contemporary opinion:

> But now kan no man se none elves mo,
> For now the grete charitee and prayeres
> Of lymytours and othere hooly freres,
> That serchen every lond and every streem,
> As thikke as motes in the sonne-beem,
> Blessynge halles, chambres, kichenes, boures,
> Citees, burghes, castels, hye toures,
> Thropes, bernes, shipnes, dayeryes—
> This maketh that ther been no fayeryes.
> For ther as wont to walken was an elf,
> Ther walketh now the lymytour hymself
> In undermeles and in morwenynges,
> And seyth his matyns and his hooly thynges
> As he gooth in his lymytacioun.
> Wommen may go now saufly up and doun
> In every busssh or under every tree;
> Ther is noon oother incubus but he,
> And he ne wol doon hem but dishonour.   III, 864–81

Friar Hubert seems to practice the usual abuses of his class. He
arranges marriages for young women with whom he has had
sexual relations; he curries favor with wealthy landowners and
their wives by hearing confession pleasantly and assigning easy
penance in exchange for gifts; he seeks to please attractive
women by presents of knives and pins, very valuable household

---

medieval friars; see especially II, 124, and chaps. viii and ix. See also Karl Young,
MLN, L (1935), 83–85.

[5] Bowden, *Commentary*, 122–39.

items in his day; he frequents the taverns and feels that he is above helping the sick and needy, while he is courteous and humble to the wealthy; he leaves no stone unturned in making his begging profitable; he takes part in scandalous legal proceedings; and, finally, he dresses in a most expensive manner. Truly, this long list of nefarious activities bears witness to the corruption that had grown up among the four orders of friars in the 150 years since they reached England.

However, granted that Friar Hubert in his professional activities is no better than his colleagues, Chaucer, as usual widely tolerant, still seems to feel that this businessman of religion is not completely reprehensible, for Hubert's saving grace is that he is a likable fellow. As we have seen, he has numerous pleasing accomplishments and he works hard at making people like him. There is little that is mean, harsh, or bitter about Friar Hubert, and, though we should by no means overlook his matching his professional dealings to the current evil mode, we would not call him devious or malicious. In this respect, he differs greatly from his antagonist, the Summoner, and their two tales reflect this difference.

When the Wife finishes her tale, Chaucer reopens the Friar-Summoner controversy (III, 1265–85). To be sure, there is irony in the Narrator's words here, when he speaks of Hubert as "worthy" and "noble." Yet, despite his frowning at the Summoner, the Friar has courteously maintained silence during the Wife's tale. But before taking up this quarrel, the Friar settles his score with the Wife, cleverly repaying her for the jibes she made at friars. His device in this is subtle: he pretends to have missed completely the amusement value of her performance and places her in the position of usurping the function of her enemies, the clergy, by preaching. In addition, though he compliments her for treating many things well, he suggests that the company has found her material exceedingly boring. To my mind, there can be no doubt that the Friar comes out ahead in his secondary tiff with the Wife.[6] But he passes on immediately to the primary

---

[6] This point is usually overlooked by commentators; for example, J. E. Wells says: "The Wife . . . has her gibe at the limitors and other holy friars (D 866 ff.). The matter comes to nothing, however, for, at the end of her tale, the Friar is too

matter—discomfiting the Summoner—and in so doing implies that his chief concern is to relate a joke that will help the company to recover from the boredom brought on by the Wife. Here again the Friar refrains from an uncontrolled attack, but he effectively makes his point by seeming to apologize for the fact that his topic—a summoner—is one which permits no good to be said, since summoners incur everyone's hatred.

The Host appears afraid that the quarrel will get out of hand, for he very judiciously points out to the Friar that a man of his high position should not demean himself by bickering; instead, he should tell his tale and "lat the Somonour be" (III, 1286–89). But the irate Summoner does not want matters halted and cries out:

> Nay, ... lat hym seye to me
> What so hym list; whan it comth to my lot,
> By God! I shal hym quiten every grot.
> I shal hym tellen which a greet honour
> It is to be a flaterynge lymytour;
> And eek of many another manere cryme
> Which nedeth nat rehercen at this tyme;
> And his office I shal hym telle, y wis.   III, 1290–97

Here again the Summoner's manner is vituperative, whereas the Friar is perfectly controlled. The Host seems to realize this difference, for he roughly silences the Summoner and courteously requests the Friar to continue (III, 1298–1300).

But order is not yet assured. The Friar opens his tale with what, so far as we know, is an accurate description of the abuses practiced in the ecclesiastical courts of the time.[7] He tells of an archdeacon "in my contree" who was excessively zealous in extracting fines from all sorts of sinners, but especially from lechers. This archdeacon employs a summoner as his spy—"a slyer boye nas noon in Engelond"—and this summoner's method is to let one or two lechers go free if they tell him where to find "foure and twenty mo." Then the Friar applies his introductory

---

preoccupied with the Summoner to follow up her challenge."—*A Manual of the Writings in Middle English 1050–1400*, p. 721.

[7] L. A. Haselmayer, *Speculum*, XII (1937), 43–57; J. A. Work, *PMLA*, XLVII (1932), 425.

comments directly to the Summoner on the pilgrimage, pointing out that summoners have no jurisdiction over friars (III, 1327–32). As usual, the Summoner's rebuttal is vulgar; he bluntly compares friars to licensed prostitutes. Again the Host calls for peace and again makes evident his disgust at the Summoner and his respect for the Friar. The latter now resumes his description of the summoner in his tale. That worthy employs bawds as his agents, extorts bribes from sinners, and does not hand over these bribes to his archdeacon; in short, his chief interest is to wring money from the people, whether they are guilty or not. This point established, the Friar commences his narrative proper.

The Friar's Tale, for which no definite source has been found,[8] represents Chaucer at his best as storyteller. Its expert economy, inevitable motivation, natural dialogue, climactic structure, and ironic characterization have frequently been commented upon. The Summoner, riding out to force a bribe from an old woman, meets a friend disguised as a yeoman. Because of the summoner's greed, the yeoman, at the end of the story, takes him off to hell, that place where summoners "han hir heritage."

The Friar then says that he could describe in detail the pains of hell, but ironically concludes his performance by urging his audience to pray that summoners will repent of their misdeeds and become good men before the devil takes them. At the same time he manages to equate the Summoner with Satan, who lies in wait like a lion to slay the innocent. He has indeed entertained the company with extreme skill. The chief fact to notice here, however, is that, though the Friar has in no way sought to avoid open controversy with the Summoner, he has made his point by means of an entertaining, highly appropriate fabliau; and throughout, by maintaining good-humored control of his temper, he has kept his performance free of bitter and ugly vituperation. In so doing, he has evidenced the agreeable merriment emphasized by his sketch in the General Prologue. How widely the Summoner's nature and actions differ from his, we shall now see.

[8] See the chapter by Archer Taylor in *Sources and Analogues*, 269–74.

13. THE SUMMONER

Of the entire group of Canterbury Pilgrims, the Summoner seems to me the least attractive, both physically and spiritually. As Professor Curry has demonstrated, he has a kind of leprosy called *alopicia*.[1] The sketch in the General Prologue (I, 623–68) shows that his face is fiery-red, his eyes narrowed to slits, his brows black and scabby, his beard thin; and his cheeks are covered with suppurating "whelkes" and "knobbes," which no medicinal agent can dry up. Certainly there is good reason for Chaucer to say that children are afraid of the Summoner's appearance. We are also told why he is thus diseased: he loves to eat garlic and onions, to drink strong red wine, and to indulge in sexual license—the causes to which medical authorities of the time attribute *alopicia*. His love of wine is symbolized by the wreath he wears upon his head, his gluttony by the loaf he carries under his arm.

The Summoner's behavior is of a sort with his appearance. When drunk, he shouts out Latin tags that he has learned around the ecclesiastical court, but his learning goes no deeper. For a quart of wine as a bribe he will withhold his report on a man who is keeping a mistress; in fact, he keeps a concubine himself. Furthermore, he makes no bones about telling a rogue that he need not fear excommunication from the archdeacon if he can pay a fine, for "Purs is the ercedekenes helle." In connection with this view, the Narrator inserts a personal comment:

> But wel I woot he lyed right in dede;
> Of cursyng oghte ech gilty man him drede,
> For curs wol slee right as assoillyng savith,
> And also war hym of a *Significavit*.   I, 659–62

This comment, however, is not the simple negation of the Summoner's statement that it seems at first glance. Chaucer is

[1] Curry, *Sciences*, 37–47; see also H. B. Woolf, *MLN*, LXVIII (1953), 118–21.

Of his visage children were aferd

shrewdly pointing to the complete corruption of the Summoner and the whole ecclesiastical legal system of which he is a part. Thus he implies that, though the archdeacon's writ of excommunication is of equal value with his absolution, in such a corrupt system neither can be particularly meaningful.[2] One of the most unfortunate aspects of the system is that the young people in the diocese, in fear of the Summoner's spying on them and reporting their activities, place themselves under his control and seek his guidance. The Summoner's loudmouthed offensiveness is to be seen early on the pilgrimage when he joins with "his freend and his compeer," the Pardoner, in singing a lewd song.

We have already seen something of the contemporary ecclesiastical legal system; a few more details will fill out the picture.[3] The bishop turned over to the archdeacon the administration of the diocesan court, in which persons were tried for any crimes coming under Church jurisdiction—and such crimes were manifold. The archdeacon seems to have employed summoners not only to serve the summons which hailed such people in to court, but also to spy out prospective victims. The court had, of course, the power of excommunication, but it seems that both summoners and archdeacons were quite willing "to settle out of court" in exchange for a bribe. As a consequence, not the rich but the impoverished suffered excommunication. One can hardly imagine a more despicable field of endeavor than the Summoner's, or a less attractive individual in appearance and behavior than he is.

The Summoner's starting a quarrel with the Friar and his several disorderly outbursts are just what we should expect, in view of the description of him which Chaucer gave in the General Prologue. When the Friar completes his tale, the Summoner is so enraged that he is shaking "lyk an aspen leef." He makes only one request: that the company allow him to tell his tale without interruption. Then he says that the Friar should be qualified to describe hell, since "Freres and feendes been but lyte asonder" (III, 1674), and goes on to relate an anecdote, the point of which is that friars have their final dwelling place in Satan's anal tract.

---

[2] J. S. P. Tatlock, *MP*, XIV (1916–17), 261–62.
[3] L. A. Haselmayer, *Speculum*, XII (1937), 43–57; J. A. Work, *PMLA*, XLVII (1932), 419–30.

With that he concludes his prologue by saying: "God save yow alle, save this cursed Frere!/My prologe wol I ende in this manere." Both the vulgarity of the anecdote and the free expression of animosity towards the Friar come naturally from the mouth of this diseased and embittered scoundrel, and they continue the same sort of behavior he has exhibited earlier.

The tale which the Summoner now relates, and for which there is no direct source,[4] is on a par with that told by the Friar, in so far as structure, characterization, and dialogue are concerned. In it is a most detailed account of the unholy methods of the begging friars in the fourteenth century, and we can surmise the pertinency of this attack by noticing that the Friar loses control of his temper for the only time when the Summoner says that the begging friar of whom he is telling irresponsibly erases the names of donors for whom he has promised to pray: " 'Nay, ther thou lixt, thou Somonour!' quod the Frere" (III, 1761). There is, however, about this tale, in which old Thomas bestows the unwelcome gift upon Friar John, the same ugly air that surrounds the Summoner himself. Even the humorous device suggested by the lord's squire at the end of the tale has its unattractive aspects. Moreover, a close parallel exists between the wrath which Thomas feels toward Friar John and that which the Summoner exhibits towards Friar Hubert.

An attempt to decide who won the Friar-Summoner controversy would be fruitless. Each has openly attacked the other with a skillful story suited to its teller's character and filled with detailed elements applicable to the profession which the other practices. In the exchange, however, the Friar proved far less harshly acrimonious than the Summoner, a difference stemming perhaps from the different demands of their professions.

[4] See the chapter by W. M. Hart in *Sources and Analogues*, 275–87.

14. THE CLERK

Following the Friar-Summoner controversy, the Clerk relates the admirably suited tale of patient Griselda, which illustrates the moral that every individual should be steadfast in adversity (IV, 1145–46). The dramatic technique in this performance combines the realization of subtle personal application present in the narrations by the Nun's Priest and the Pilgrim Chaucer with something of the open debate evidenced in the Miller-Reeve and Friar-Summoner antagonisms. The Clerk, in a disguised answer to Alice of Bath's contention that in any well-run marriage mastery must be in the hands of the wife, tells a tale in which the chief figure, Griselda, is a wife whose guiding tenet is obedience to her husband; then, when his tale is over, he makes the direct application of his story to the Wife of Bath's argument.

The Clerk of Oxford, in his disregard for material gain and in his devotion to learning and teaching, is one of the most inspiring members of the company; and the sincere praise evident in the last line of his sketch—"And gladly wolde he lerne and gladly teche"—bears witness to Chaucer's appreciation for, and understanding of, contemplative, humanistic, intellectual, and spiritual values, despite—or perhaps as a result of—his own lifetime of immersion in the active affairs of court and market place. Chaucer's attitude is the clearer when we note that the portrait of the Clerk in the General Prologue (I, 285–308) immediately follows that of the Merchant, in whom such values are manifestly lacking and who there receives brief and unsympathetic handling.

The Clerk, we are first told, is well advanced in his study of the medieval curriculum, having long ago progressed to logic. The less pleasant consequences from his choice of a scholarly career are at once apparent: his horse is lean as a rake; he himself is by no means fat but looks hollow; and his clothing is thread-

Of studie took he moost cure and moost heede

bare. Contrast the Clerk in these respects with the well-fed Monk, with his expensive clothes, sleek horse, and discriminating palate. Further, the Clerk's chances for adequate income are diminished by his not being worldly enough to get and hold a secular job while he waits for a benefice, for he prefers owning books of philosophy to enjoying the usual luxuries. But, says Chaucer with a good-natured pun involving alchemy, the Clerk cannot make even philosophy pay by discovering the philosophers' stone to turn baser metals to gold. Instead, he spends all the money he can obtain from his friends "on bookes and on lernynge," and dutifully prays for the souls of his benefactors. The Clerk's chief interest is clearly stated in the line "Of studie took he moost cure and moost heede"; his reticence and the moral content of his few remarks reflect this interest (I, 304–307). We conclude that the Clerk's presence on this pilgrimage is motivated by sincere devotion and that he is not the man to contribute a great deal to the merry dalliance with which the Host is eager to surround the trip. But, as we shall see, he is sufficiently experienced as a teacher to lighten his "hy sentence" with a flash of raillery, for his austere reserve is delightfully accompanied by a sense of humor. Moreover, we should note that in contrast to Chaucer's usual method of combining expected and unexpected traits in the sketches of his Pilgrims, his presentation of this man seems completely typical of the contemporary picture of a good clerk.[1]

The Host does not share the admiration for the Clerk's way of life which the Narrator expressed in the General Prologue. When Harry calls upon the Clerk to perform, he patronizingly twits him for his silence, comparing him to a newly married girl, tells him to give up his contemplative manner, and demands a cheerful tale. But the Host wants to make sure that the Clerk will not deliver a boring sermon (IV, 2–14). As in his remarks to other professional men, Harry takes pains in addressing the learned Clerk to show that he is able to use the proper professional vocabulary. He now produces a series of rhetorical terms: he thinks the Clerk is pondering over some subtle point in dialectic ("sophyme"), and the Clerk must not use his "termes," his "col-

---

[1] See A. W. Green, *ELH*, XVIII (1951), 1–6; H. S. V. Jones, *PMLA*, XXVII (1912), 106–15.

ours," and his "figures" until he has occasion to write in the "heigh style." Such an attitude on the Host's part does not disturb the Clerk, and he agreeably replies that he will do as the Host demands. He will tell a tale that he learned from Francis Petrarch, the worthy Italian poet, now deceased, God rest his soul! In keeping with Harry's instructions, the Clerk further states that, though Petrarch graced his version of the story with a lengthy geographical prologue done in the high style, he will avoid length and rhetorical intricacies by omitting this prologue.

In the tale which follows we find that Walter, the young Marquis of Saluzzo in Italy, arranges a series of tests to prove the obedience of his wife, Griselda. In no instance does she question her husband's authority; as a result, the story ends happily. His narrative over, the Clerk draws his moral (IV, 1142–62): he has told this story, not to encourage wives to attempt the impossible imitation of Griselda's humility, but to show that every individual should be, like Griselda, steadfast in adversity. For, if a woman exhibited such constancy when tested by a mortal man, then we all should receive even more steadfastly the difficulties which God sends us, since God does not, like Walter, test people unnecessarily; indeed, He places hardships in our paths in order to strengthen us, for all His plans work toward our own good. Consequently, we should live in "vertuous suffraunce."

This moral, coming at the end of the Clerk's story, is supported throughout his performance by the emphasis he places on the beneficent results from cheerful obedience to constituted authority, even when such obedience entails hardship. This theme is evident as early as the Clerk's own expression of agreement to tell a "murie thyng of aventures" (IV, 15). He says:

> Hooste, . . . I am under youre yerde;
> Ye han of us as now the governance,
> And therfore wol I do yow obeisance,
> As fer as resoun axeth, hardily.   IV, 22–25

The Clerk is under the Host's management and will therefore obey him in any reasonable request. When the tale opens, we learn that the people of Saluzzo are "obeisant" and ever ready to do their lord's bidding (IV, 66–67); consequently, life in this noble country is happy and prosperous. When Griselda is introduced, she is praised for according to her father "everich obeisaunce" (IV, 230), and Janicula himself, when Walter asks for Griselda's hand, expresses his absolute obedience to his lord's will (IV, 319–22). Later, the officer whom Walter sends to take away Griselda's daughter voices the need for obedience to a ruler's commands (IV, 528–32), and Griselda herself, accepting this opinion, asks that he bury the daughter's body carefully only if Walter does not forbid it (IV, 570–72).

The necessity for a wife's exhibiting unquestioning obedience to her husband is, of course, a major concept in the body of the Clerk's Tale. This view, an established part of Church doctrine, is not surprising on the part of the Clerk. Walter first states that he wishes to ask Griselda whether she will "be my wyf, and reule hire after me" (IV, 327), and then he emphatically sets absolute wifely obedience as the condition upon which he will marry her (IV, 351–57). She, with equal emphasis, accepts this condition: "In werk ne thoght, I nyl yow disobeye" (IV, 363).

In the course of the story, as Walter carries out his cruel tests, Griselda repeatedly restates her determination to obey his every wish. When he says that their daughter must be killed, she replies: "My child and I, with hertely obeisaunce,/Been youres al . . ." (IV, 502–503); when he repeats the same argument with reference to their son, she says: "Dooth youre pleasaunce, I wol youre lust obeye" (IV, 658); when news comes of Walter's plan to take another wife, she does not question his desires (IV, 757–59); when he tells her she must return to her former home, she simply says: ". . . I wol goon whan yow leste" (IV, 847); and when he asks her to take charge of the preparations in the palace for the new wife, she states: ". . . I am glad . . ./To doon youre lust . . ." (IV, 967–68).

Walter realizes how well Griselda has fulfilled the condition which he set for their marriage, and speaks of the pleasure he has had in her "obeisaunce" (IV, 794); particularly concerning this point, the Clerk himself, in giving his audience advance information as to the happy outcome of his narrative, observes that all will come out for the best because Griselda exhibited clearly that no wife should desire anything except what her husband wishes (IV, 718–21). It seems clear, then, that the Clerk's concluding moral of steadfastness in adversity is founded throughout on the concept of cheerful obedience to constituted authority, and that this concept is chiefly illustrated in his story by Griselda's unquestioning obedience to Walter's unnatural demands. In presenting an *exemplum* characterized by "hy sentence" and in illustrating the Church's teaching of wifely obedience, the Clerk is consistent with the impression we gained of him from the sketch in the General Prologue.

It is likely that the more attentive and intelligent Pilgrims realized long before the Clerk had finished his tale that the theme and action of the story are in direct contrast with the Wife of Bath's argument for supremacy of a wife over her husband.[2] Certainly the obedient steadfastness in adversity which brings happiness to the household of Walter and Griselda bears little similarity to the methods whereby the Wife claims to have established happy relationships with her five husbands. An observant member of the Clerk's audience would also recall that, since the Wife's view is opposed to the established teachings of the Church and since in answer to the Nun's Priest she went out of her way to satirize clerics for their licentiousness and antifeminism, the Clerk has more than enough motivation for using his performance to answer her. In fact, the Wife even maintained that it is impossible for any clerk to speak well of a woman, except in a saint's life (III, 688–91). But it is not until the last six stanzas of his performance that the Clerk indicates clearly that he has just such a purpose. Indeed, there is some evidence in his narrative that he is trying to keep this purpose subtly concealed until he is ready to attack the Wife straight on.

This evidence consists of the efforts the Clerk seems to make to keep his audience in some doubt as to just what is the chief lesson it should draw from his tale. Alongside the steady emphasis on Griselda's obedient constancy in adversity, he offers recurring jibes at Walter's unnatural cruelty. When Walter first plans to test his wife, the Clerk says:

Nedelees, God woot, he thoghte hire for t'affraye.

---

[2] This interplay was discussed by G. L. Kittredge, *MP*, IX (1911–12), 435–67.

> He hadde assayed hire ynogh bifore,
> And foond hire evere good; what neded it
> Hire for to tempte, and alwey moore and moore,
> Though som men preise it for a subtil wit?
> But as for me, I seye that yvele it sit
> To assaye a wyf whan that it is no nede,
> And putten hire in angwyssh and in drede. IV, 455–62

The last four lines here are Chaucer's original addition to his two
sources, Petrarch's Latin and a fairly literal French translation
of Petrarch's story.[3] Again, when Walter decides to take the son
from Griselda, the Clerk comments on the needlessness of the
test:

> O nedelees was she tempted in assay!
> But wedded men ne knowe no mesure,
> Whan that they fynde a pacient creature. IV, 621–23

And again the passage is original with Chaucer.

The Clerk's lengthiest remarks of this nature come when
Walter conceives the idea of announcing his intention of taking
a new wife:

> But now of wommen wolde I axen fayn
> If thise assayes myghte nat suffise?
> What koude a sturdy housbonde moore devyse
> To preeve hir wyfhod and hir stedefastnesse,
> And he continuynge evere in sturdinesse?
>
> But ther been folk of swich condicion
> That whan they have a certein purpos take,
> They kan nat stynte of hire entencion,
> But, right as they were bounden to a stake,
> They wol nat of that firste purpos slake.
> Right so this markys fulliche hath purposed
> To tempte his wyf as he was first disposed. IV, 696–707

A few lines later, in stating the reaction of the populace to Walter's behavior, the Clerk once more stresses his unnecessary
cruelty:

> The sclaundre of Walter ofte and wyde spradde,
> That of a crueel herte he wikkedly,

[3] For a comparison of this tale with its sources, see J. B. Severs, *The Literary Relationships of Chaucer's Clerkes Tale.*

> For he a povre womman wedded hadde,
> Hath mordred bothe his children prively.
> Swich murmur was among hem comunly.
> No wonder is, for to the peples ere
> Ther cam no word, but that they mordred were.
>
> For which, where as his peple therbifore
> Hadde loved hym wel, the sclaundre of his diffame
> Made hem that they hym hatede therfore.
> To been a mordrere is an hateful name;
> But nathelees, for ernest ne for game,
> He of his crueel purpos nolde stente;
> To tempte his wyf was set al his entente.   IV, 722–35

Although we know here that all will turn out happily for Griselda (IV, 718–21), the important point is that Griselda is not aware of this and has every reason to consider Walter's actions beyond what she should endure. The Clerk's final adverse comment about Walter is simply to mention his "wikke usage" (IV, 785).

These passages might easily lead one to conclude that the Clerk's story is aimed at attacking unnecessary cruelty in husbands rather than at showing the benefits of wifely obedience and patience; to such a theme the Wife of Bath would certainly not object. True, she would probably have noted some slight contradiction of her statement on the subject when the Clerk said:

> Men speke of Job, and moost for his humblesse,
> As clerkes, whan hem list, konne wel endite,
> Namely of men, but as in soothfastnesse,
> Though clerkes preise wommen but a lite,
> Ther kan no man in humblesse hym acquite
> As womman kan, ne kan been half so trewe
> As wommen been, but it be falle of newe.   IV, 932–38

But such a half-hearted and inoffensive rebuttal would certainly not disturb her.

As if he plans to continue the disguise of his real intention, which he has maintained throughout his tale, the Clerk, after delivering his three-stanza moral (IV, 1142–62), seems about to

148]

pay an agreeable compliment to Alice of Bath, whom he even
mentions by name, as a kind of postscript to his story:

> But o word, lordynges, herkneth er I go:
> It were ful hard to fynde now-a-dayes
> In al a toun Grisildis thre or two;
> For if that they were put to swiche assayes,
> The gold of hem hath now so badde alayes
> With bras, that thogh the coyne be fair at ye,
> It wolde rather breste a-two than plye.
>
> For which heere, for the Wyves love of Bathe—
> Whos lyf and al hire secte God mayntene
> In heigh maistrie, and elles were it scathe—
> I wol with lusty herte, fressh and grene,
> Seyn yow a song to glade yow, I wene;
> And lat us stynte of ernestful matere.
> Herkneth my song that seith in this manere.
>
> IV, 1163–76

This passage amplifies the Clerk's earlier remark in explaining
why Walter's son did not test his wife: "This world is nat so
strong, it is no nay,/As it hath been in olde tymes yoore" (IV,
1139–40), for which reason Petrarch said that it would be impossible for modern wives to imitate Griselda, even if they wished
to do so. Until he reaches his envoy, the Clerk gives the impression that he accepts philosophically this deterioration in wives
and that he bears no grudge against the Wife of Bath.

This envoy, with which the Clerk ends his performance and
which we shall examine shortly, is marked in the manuscripts
"Lenvoy de Chaucer," but the title does not mean that the stanzas are spoken by the Narrator rather than by the Clerk. It does
mean that the scribes copying the manuscripts recognized and
indicated that these stanzas are original with Chaucer and are
not to be found in his sources. The Clerk's continuity from his
narrative to the Envoy is perfectly effected.

Another point worth noticing here is that the word "secte" in
line 1171, quoted above, can apparently either mean "sex" or
refer to a heretical religious group.[4] Arguments have been ad-

---

[4] See Helge Kökeritz, *PQ*, XXVI (1947), 147–51, and *NED*, "secte," sense 1. **d.**
(initial entry "sect").

vanced for each of these readings; that is, the Clerk here prays either that God will preserve the Wife of Bath and *all other women* in high mastery, or that God will preserve in high mastery the Wife and *all heretics* who share her views. The point at issue is whether or not the Clerk is calling the Wife a heretic. It seems to me that the Clerk here intends both meanings for the attentive listener in his audience but feels sure that the Wife of Bath will choose to understand his words as a compliment to herself and all women. This interpretation is in accord with the view that the Clerk wants to keep his satiric intent more or less under cover until he reaches his envoy.

But if until his envoy the Clerk appears desirous of disguising his intention of settling a score with the Wife, his six final stanzas (IV, 1177–1212) constitute an extremely skillful burlesque attack which gives him a clear victory in this debate concerning the status of a wife in the home. The first of these stanzas is harmless enough; in fact, except for the last line, the Clerk here expresses once more the moral against cruelty in husbands which, as we have seen, he prepared for throughout the tale; and in that last line he merely restates his point about deterioration in wives. Then the blow falls—in his last five stanzas. Here, with broad exaggeration and unveiled irony, the Clerk advises wives not to follow Griselda's example in patient obedience; instead, they should emulate Echo, whose tongue is never still. Wives should not be so innocent as to accept their husbands' commands, but, for common profit, should take over complete mastery in the home. Strong wives can accomplish this by main strength; weak wives should bring it about by constant complaining. Husbands are not to be feared, for wives can put them in their places by "the arwes of thy crabbed eloquence" and by causing them to be jealous of their wives' "freendes." In sum, a wise wife will let her husband "care, and wepe, and wrynge, and waille."

By thus exaggerating the point of view advanced earlier by the Wife of Bath, the Clerk has made glaringly evident the ridiculousness of any possibility for a happy home in which her theories are practiced; and at the same time he has managed to avoid advocating the opposite extreme, as represented by Griselda's unbelievable patience in the face of Walter's cruelty.

Furthermore, the Clerk has accomplished these aims without involving himself in any unbecoming bickering. Truly, the long years of study have not been wasted on this clerk, and Harry Bailly was correct in thinking that he was pondering "som sophyme" as he rode along before his performance, for that "sophyme" was his brilliant refutation of the Wife's arguments.

The Host's comment upon the Clerk's Tale furnishes a concrete example of the validity of the Clerk's contention. Harry says that he wishes his wife at home could have heard this story of patient Griselda. He restrains himself here from giving the details of his home life, but we earlier learned that Goodelief, his wife, behaves in accord with the Wife of Bath's theories and with the Clerk's exaggerated advice to both "archewyves" and "sklendre wyves" in his envoy. Later Harry will disclose that he wishes he were not tied to her (IV, 1226). So much for the possibility of a happy home where the wife exercises the mastery!

In addition to being motivated by the Clerk's antagonism towards the Wife's views on marriage, this tale includes "hy sentence" and "moral vertu" which suit it and its teller, as he was described in the General Prologue. In fact, there may be a real possibility that the unusual typicality, noted earlier in the Clerk's portrait and continued in his conversation with the Host, is a part of Chaucer's intentional dramatic plan to keep the Clerk's unexpected, individualizing traits—his sense of humor and his ability at controversy—hidden until the end of his performance, and thus to heighten the effect of his burlesque refutation of the Wife's arguments.

15. THE MERCHANT

For some reason that will probably never be fully clear, Chaucer's sketch of the Merchant in the General Prologue (I, 270–84) is characterized by such cautious disinterestedness and evident lack of sympathy that it stands unique among the series of portraits. By remarking that this Pilgrim sits "hye on horse" and speaks his opinions "ful solempnely," Chaucer conveys the impression of a pompous individual who thinks very well of himself; and the Merchant's beard, forked in the prevailing fashion, as well as his expensive boots and beaver hat from Flanders, shows that he takes unusual care with his appearance. In his description of the Merchant's business dealings, Chaucer indicates clearly that this man practices illegal methods prevalent among merchants at the time.[1] He sells French gold coins in "eschaunge," despite the laws prohibiting traffic in foreign money; he engages in "chevyssaunce," or usury, and thereby breaks the laws of both Church and State; and he keeps his wits about him in order never to disclose his own indebtedness, thus misleading those with whom he deals. Also the Merchant is loud in his demand for governmental help in maintaining favorable business conditions: he wants the sea kept free from pirates between the Dutch and English trading ports, Middelburg and Orwell. But the Merchant's greatest sin, in a social sense at least, is that he is a terrible bore, "Sownynge alwey th' encrees of his wynnyng"; he subjects anyone who will listen to detailed accounts of his own business acumen. Evidently the Narrator prudently avoided such torture by staying out of the Merchant's way, for he says: "But, sooth to seyn, I noot how men hym calle"; despite the close sociability among this group of travelers, the Narrator did not even take the trouble to learn the Merchant's name.

Although the traits mentioned in the preceding paragraph

[1] Bowden, *Commentary*, 146–53; T. A. Knott, *PQ*, I (1922), 1–16.

Sownynge alwey th' encrees of his wynnyng

build up a far from attractive picture of the Merchant, both as a person and as a business man, the Narrator makes some small effort to cover up his own seemingly negative attitude. He says: "For sothe he was a worthy man with alle": in spite of being a pompous bore who breaks laws in an unprincipled fashion, he is a "worthy" man. The choice of such a noncommittal word as "worthy" is certainly meaningful, for it does little more than pay lip service to offsetting the Merchant's unattractiveness.

It has been suggested that the attempted restraint in expressing disapproval of the Merchant, and the decision not to give him a name, result from Chaucer's unwillingness to run the risk of having some powerful London merchant think himself the subject here for ridicule.[2] In fact, a particular merchant named Gilbert Maghfeld has been pointed out as a possible model for this sketch, and it seems that Chaucer actually had borrowed money from this man. But we can only speculate about such an identification and about Chaucer's personal reasons for seeming eager to cover up his real feelings. It takes no speculation, however, to conclude that the tone and manner in Chaucer's presentation of the Merchant differ markedly from those used with any other Pilgrim. Usually, whether the individual under discussion is the righteous Parson or the rascally Pardoner, the Narrator seems to say to us: "Here is a person whom I was glad to meet and whom I think you will like to know. We don't have to pass any judgment on this Pilgrim; we can simply enjoy the interesting aspects of his character." This attitude is present even in the section treating the evil Summoner; and there is good-natured joviality in the Narrator's ridiculing the Sergeant of the Law. But in the case of the Merchant, Chaucer shows his own lack of sympathy, makes no effort to interest us in him, and says, in effect: "I am sorry that this man was a member of our group." As we shall see, this uniqueness of tone in the Merchant's sketch is matched by the uniqueness in atmosphere of the tale he tells.

We hear nothing from the Merchant until the Clerk has finished his story of Griselda and the henpecked Host has made brief practical application of that tale to his own married life. Then, without being called on, the Merchant breaks in with a

[2] Manly, *New Light*, 181–200.

vigorously bitter statement of his own unhappy marital situation:

> Wepyng and waylyng, care and oother sorwe
> I knowe ynogh, on even and a-morwe,
> ... and so doon other mo
> That wedded been. I trowe that it be so,
> For wel I woot it fareth so with me.
> I have a wyf, the worste that may be;
> For thogh the feend to hire ycoupled were,
> She wolde hym overmacche, I dar wel swere.
> What sholde I yow reherce in special
> Hir hye malice? She is a shrewe at al.   IV, 1213–22

At first glance, it is surprising for a man so closemouthed about his financial difficulties as is the Merchant to deliver uninvited this frank disclosure of his marital troubles. But the answer is not far to seek: he has been angered by the Wife of Bath's account of her treatment of her husbands, and the effect upon him of the Clerk's narrative is such that he is moved to forget, for once, his customary restraint. His first words are more or less an echo of the Clerk's last line (IV, 1212), and in giving further details of his miserable state, the Merchant explicitly indicates the Clerk's story as the immediate occasion for his outburst (IV, 1223–39). Indeed, he gives a far from pretty picture of wedded bliss. Married but two months, he can only curse his state and that of most married men. Certainly his careful shrewdness in matters financial was not duplicated two months ago by an equally expert judgment of women. And it is hard to refrain from the suggestion that the Narrator, whose dislike of the Merchant was apparent in the General Prologue, enjoys greatly the latter's revelation of his unhappy choice of a wife. In any event, the Host is quick in his attempt to turn this outburst to the benefit of the storytelling game. Instead of asking the Merchant the question which must have been uppermost in everyone's mind—"Why did you marry such a woman?"—Harry says, with unusual brevity: "Now, ... Marchaunt, so God yow blesse,/Syn ye so muchel knowen of that art,/Ful hertely I pray yow telle us part" (IV, 1240–42).

The Host likes nothing better than to draw personal revelations from the Pilgrims, and in this case he is hopeful of hearing the confessions of a fellow sufferer in wedlock. But the Merchant seems to regain some of his usual cautious poise, and, in agreeing to Harry's request, states that he will talk no more of his own situation: "Gladly, . . . but of myn owene soore,/For soory herte, I telle may namoore" (IV, 1243–44). Such attempted restraint about personal matters is in keeping with what we know of the Merchant from the General Prologue, but, considering the bitterness of his preceding remarks about his wife, it is almost beyond belief that the Merchant could relate a story treating marital misfortunes without there being some connection between that story and the "cursednesse" of his own wife. The point is, I think, that by his disavowal he is simply trying to cover up his own stupidity in his selection of a wife. But, as we shall see, he thereby misleads only himself, for in his tale he inadvertently sheds a great deal of light as to the cause for his present "sorwe." I am not saying that the Merchant's Tale is pure autobiography, or that January in the tale is the Merchant. But I am saying that because of the wide discrepancy between what the Merchant thinks is the "moral" to be drawn from his tale, on the one hand, and the inevitable conclusion to which that tale leads, on the other, the Merchant unwittingly gives considerable grounds upon which to base speculations about the reason for his own marital situation.[3]

There is nothing at all appealing or cheerful about the Merchant's story. In its cold intellectualism, its lack of genial raillery or healthy animal enjoyment, and in its piling up of sharply satiric details, it conveys a bitter irony unique in Chaucer's writings. Neither of the chief characters arouses the least sympathy in the reader, and a dirtily obscene atmosphere is ever present. Why this is so, we cannot say. Perhaps Chaucer felt very strongly against the not infrequent marriages of old men to young girls, which probably occurred among his associates at court and in the city. Or maybe, as Professor Tatlock has suggested, he looked upon the Merchant's Tale as an exercise in a literary method other than that he regularly practiced.[4] Whatever the explanation, it is particularly striking that the uniquely unsympathetic

[3] G. G. Sedgewick, *UTQ*, XVII (1947-48), 337–45.
[4] J. S. P. Tatlock, *MP*, XXXIII (1935–36), 367–81.

portrait of the Merchant in the General Prologue is matched by this uniquely bitter irony in his tale. We thereby return to our original tantalizing conclusion: for some reason, Chaucer did not like his Merchant; an analysis of the dramatic implications of the tale as they reflect upon its teller will bear out this conclusion.

We saw that the Merchant, at the Host's request, sets out to tell a story that will illustrate the sorrow which most husbands experience as a result of their wives' "cursednesse," and which will thereby imply that marriage is inevitably a thoroughly miserable state for almost any husband. And, when this story is ended, the Host's sympathy is with January, and his interpretation centers on the perfidious wife; for him, May is the sole villain, and in his mind the tale shows only that wives are always trying to deceive their husbands, just as May by her treachery deceived January. Here is Harry's comment:

> Ey! Goddes mercy! . . .
> Now swich a wyf I pray God kepe me fro!
> Lo, whiche sleightes and subtilitees
> In wommen been! for ay as bisy as bees
> Been they, us sely men for to deceyve,
> And from the soothe evere wol they woyve;
> By this Marchauntes tale it preveth weel.
>
> IV, 2419–25

But we should observe, I think, that the Host's simple interpretation is considerably narrower than the Merchant's intention as to how his tale should be understood. For the Merchant, there must be two villains: May, automatically, but particularly January. The Merchant, like the Host, certainly considers May's treachery typical; yet he seems to attach greater blame to January on two accounts: for thinking that marriage could possibly be a happy state, and for accepting May's farfetched lie at the end of the story. In the mind of the Merchant, the probable two-fold moral of his tale is, first, that few marriages are likely to work because most women are faithless; and, second, that any husband is both stupid to feel certain that a marriage will turn out well and foolish to allow his wife to lie successfully about her perfidy. Only by assuming that the Merchant takes such a view of his story can we explain why he as teller expresses such angry disgust with January's words and actions; this disgust appears in a steady stream of bitter, caustic irony, woven into every section of this tale.

The Merchant uses only the opening four lines of his story to establish the narrative situation in which January is the central figure:

> Whilom ther was dwellynge in Lumbardye
> A worthy knyght, that born was of Pavye,
> In which he lyved in greet prosperitee;
> And sixty yeer a wyflees man was hee.   IV, 1245–48

Then immediately we begin to get indications of this knight's folly and of the Merchant's vitriolic attitude towards that folly (IV, 1249–66). January has in the past satisfied his lust with a variety of women, as do fools who are "seculeer," that is, laymen, who are not protected by religion from sin, as are the clergy.[5] But now in old age he decides to enter into the holy estate of matrimony, where he will be able to satisfy his lust regularly and will also have the protection of religion; and he hypocritically prays to God that he may enter into the "holy bond" of wedlock, in which the "blissful life" is a paradise on earth. This passage introduces one of the most important themes running through the story up to the scene of the wedding: January, wanting at sixty to make peace with the Church, figures out that he can by marriage accomplish this peace and still satisfy his lust. Thus all his talk about the holiness of marriage in this passage and in the following 130 lines represents his use of religion as protection for his doing just what he wants to do, namely, indulge in "bodily delyt." Two lines of the passage show clearly the Merchant's attitude toward January's rationalizing: first, by immediately stating "Were it for hoolynesse or for dotage,/I kan nat seye," the Merchant sets up a choice for us; then by the final ironic line, "Thus seyde this olde knyght, that was so wys," he indicates to us which alternative to choose: "dotage"—senile lechery—is January's motivation, not "hoolynesse." Consequently, we are sure from the very beginning of what is to come, for we know that, given his present motivation, January's marriage will not be either "esy" or "clene." The first twenty-two lines of the Mer-

[5] J. C. McGalliard, *PQ*, XXV (1946), 193–220.

chant's Tale, by their revelation of the rationalizing whereby January is using religion as an attempted disguise for his lecherous intent, inform us that the final cuckolding in the pear tree is already inevitable.

Perhaps the most skillful touch in these introductory lines comes in the clause "but swich a greet corage/Hadde this knyght to been a wedded man"—where the word "corage" can refer to both sides of January's double-talk. As in line 22 of the General Prologue, this word can indicate religious piety: the Narrator is there ready to go on the pilgrimage with "ful devout corage"; but, as in the Host's jesting words to the Nun's Priest—"For if thou have corage as thou hast myght,/Thee were nede of hennes" (VII, 3452–53)—the word can connote sexual potency.

The Merchant, in the second segment of his tale, devotes 130 lines (IV, 1267–1396) to presenting the reasoning—or better, false reasoning—whereby January arrives at his decision to take a wife. These lines come forth as musings which pass through January's mind, and in them the evidence that he convinces himself by a process of rationalization builds upon that apparent in the introductory section, but takes shape here in much bolder outlines. The Merchant now discloses January's folly with broad and unmistakable strokes. The core of January's argument here with himself is the ironic idea already introduced: marriage is pleasing to God. But, we are told, this fact is especially true when an old man takes a young wife with whom he can produce an heir. Bachelors, in their irregular licentiousness, are like beasts, while a wedded man experiences orderly happiness. His wife will faithfully obey and attend him, in sickness or in health, and writers like Theophrastus are completely wrong when they say that a wife is mercenary and easily unfaithful.

Theophrastus' comment foreshadows, of course, exactly the point of view and the conduct which May will illustrate. But January is sure that a wife is God's gift and that "Mariage is a ful greet sacrement." God intended a wife as man's helpmate and his terrestrial paradise; any man without a wife cannot hope for bliss. As January's thoughts about marriage progress, his conclusions are expressed with increasing certainty and vigor: "A wyf! a, Seinte Marie, *benedicite!*/How myghte a man han any adversitee/That hath a wyf? Certes, I kan nat seye." A married man will be so happy and his wife so thoroughly admirable that he can in no way be deceived; therefore, says January, "Do alwey so as wommen wol thee rede," if you wish to act wisely. To illustrate this point, he cites the examples of Rebecca, Judith, Abigail, and Esther; and we note that, ironically, the husband involved in each of these stories suffers. But old January is oblivious to such possibilities, for he has had no trouble in convincing himself that he should marry, and his musings conclude with a lyric statement of the ideal relationship experienced by husband and wife. The Merchant has now shown us conclusively that January's decision is the result not of "hoolynesse" but of "dotage." Yet the degree to which the Merchant hates this old knight's folly is even more fully illustrated in the coming section of the tale, where January acts upon his decision to take a wife (IV, 1397–1767).

January's first move is to send for his friends, to whom he delivers a long speech informing them of his purpose and asking that they find him a suitable wife. In this speech his argument is based on a paradox which plainly indicates his rationalizing. On the one hand, he says that he is old and near the grave and must marry in order to avoid punishment after death for his many years of lechery; on the other hand, he claims that despite his advanced years he is still possessed of sufficient virility to enter into the duties of marriage fully. He insists, therefore, that he will marry a young girl not over twenty, whom he can mold like wax, and we get an unpleasant glimpse into his filthy mind when he dwells expectantly on the prospect of his sexual relations with such a wife, while maintaining that his actions will honor God. January states emphatically: "I dote nat, I woot the cause why/ Men sholde wedde"; but the Merchant has made it abundantly clear that this old and lecherous knight knows nothing of the more admirable reasons for a marriage.

January's friends are divided in their reaction to his decisions, and two sharply differing opinions are presented by his two brothers, Placebo and Justinus. Placebo, a sycophantic courtier, says that January must have good judgment because he is a wealthy knight and should therefore carry out his plan. Justinus, a wise and experienced man with no illusions, urges January to exercise great caution in selecting a wife in order to avoid making a regrettable mistake. Obviously, the names of the brothers are allegorical for the purpose of irony: "Placebo" means "I shall please" and aptly describes a "yes man"; Justinus, whose name means "the just man," is the only clear-thinking individual in the whole story, thereby representing a sharp contrast with the Merchant himself, as well as with January.

But, as we expect, January rejects Justinus' wise warnings. He exclaims:

> Wel, . . . and hastow sayd?
> Straw for thy Senek, and for thy proverbes!
> I counte nat a panyer ful of herbes
> Of scole-termes. Wyser men than thow,
> As thou hast herd, assenteden right now
> To my purpos. Placebo, what sey ye?   IV, 1566–71

Notice that January addresses Placebo with the formal, polite "ye," while for Justinus he has only the familiar "thou." Placebo is ready with a pleasing answer: "I seye it is a cursed man . . ,/ That letteth matrimoigne, sikerly." And the Merchant thus shows that January's request for advice is merely a gesture, since he intends to take a young wife, whatever his advisers say. This situation is even more apparent in his next move: Although he has asked his friends to find him a wife, he makes the selection himself. Here again the Merchant gives us a whiff of the old knight's malodorous mind, for in reviewing the advantages and disadvantages of all the young girls he knows, January uses criteria that do not include the important aspects of disposition and character stressed earlier by Justinus; rather, his interest is primarily in matters physical, and, after making his selection, he lies in bed gloating over May's bodily charms. It is also a part of the Merchant's ironic treatment that January has selected a girl of no wealth and station, whose family will agree to an immediate marriage.

Now January calls his friends together to tell them that they need search on his behalf no longer. He is certain that he has made the wisest possible choice, and asks them not to argue against it, since his "purpos was plesant to God" (IV, 1621). Again, in what has become a regular habit for him, he uses religious talk as a cover for his lustful intent. This time his rationalizing is such that it would be laughable if it were not surrounded by lecherous implications. He tells his friends that he has only one worry: he has heard that an individual cannot have "parfite blisses two" (IV, 1638); a man cannot hope for heavenly bliss if he experiences such pleasure on earth "As alle wedded men doon with hire wyvys." The Merchant has Justinus give the fitting answer to this ridiculous problem. Using the religious contexts which January has hypocritically chosen, Justinus tells him not to worry too much over this question, for it may happen that January's wife will turn out to be his purgatory, and then his soul can skip up to heaven unimpeded. But for January such a possibility is beyond consideration, and the marriage preparations are quickly carried out.

The Merchant's description of the wedding contains numerous mordant touches which continue his ironic treatment of January's lustful stupidity. He says that he will not go into detail, for it would take too long to recount "every scrit and bond/By which that she was feffed in his lond" (IV, 1697–98), and we thereby see clearly May's mercenary intent, of which January pretends to be oblivious. As she stands before the priest, May is compared to Sarah and Rebecca for wisdom and fidelity—certainly an ironic comparison. The priest makes "al siker ynogh with hoolynesse" (IV, 1708), but we are forcibly reminded that there is nothing holy about January's desires. The wedding feast is a splendid affair, provided with the finest of everything that Italy can furnish; but Venus laughs at, not smiles with, every person present, "For Januarie was bicome hir knyght" (IV, 1724); and Martianus could not adequately describe this marriage, for "Whan tendre youthe hath wedded stoupying age,/ Ther is swich *myrthe* that it may nat be writen" (IV, 1738–39). It is not hard to believe that the Merchant means for "myrthe" in this sentence to signify more than just "pleasure." Then May's glances at January are likened to those Esther cast upon Ahasuerus, whom she hated; and we are told that January sits at the table thinking constantly of the physical pleasures of the wedding night, which he will enjoy after the feast; and he does all he can to hasten the guests away. He has but one regret: that so tender a creature as May must endure the fury of his sexual powers; and he vows to restrain himself out of consideration for her. This whole passage is characterized by the savage irony with which the Merchant regularly portrays January, but the old knight's lecherous rationalizing so well deserves such treatment that we feel no sympathy for him. The entire situation is inherent, of course, in the allegorical names of the two chief characters: January (old age) and May (youth).

The complication from which January's deserved cuckolding will come is not long in developing. Throughout the next section of the tale (IV, 1768–2155), the Merchant does not in the least diminish the ferocity or the frequency of his thrusts at January; if anything, the view of this aged lecher becomes increasingly repellent. During the dancing and drinking which follow the wedding feast, everyone is gay except the squire Damian, who, in true courtly-love fashion, falls in love with his lord's wife at first sight and retires to his bed, suffering severely from the malady of love. But there will be little else of a courtly nature about this affair as it progresses towards its consummation in the pear tree.[6] Meanwhile, the impatient January, naturally unaware of Damian's situation, manages to get rid of his wedding guests and prepares for bed. He now plies himself with many aphrodisiacs, such as are listed in the book *De Coitu* by the Arab Constantinus Afer; thus the Merchant exposes the emptiness of January's earlier boastful thoughts about his inexhaustible virility. May is led to the marriage bed "as stille as stoon" (IV, 1818), for she looks forward to the night's activities with far less enthusiasm than does her husband. The hypocrisy of this union is again underlined by the Merchant's mention at this point of the priest's blessing the marriage bed. But at last the newly wed couple are alone.

Nowhere in the tale is the atmosphere more nauseatingly unpleasant than in the account of January's love-making on his wedding night. He is now experiencing the situation for which he has longed and for which he has paid handsomely. He mouths a sophistical apology to May for the leisure with which he plans to enjoy this night, and he rejoices in his certainty that now "in trewe wedlock" his lechery is not sinful. But the Merchant pre-

[6] Margaret Schlauch, *ELH*, IV (1937) 201–12.

sents this ardent lover to us through the eyes of his young wife, and the picture is not appealing. May finds January's thick whiskers as sharp as the "skyn of houndfyssh," and she considers his antics when morning comes thoroughly ridiculous:

> Thus laboureth he til that the day gan dawe;
> And thanne he taketh a sop in fyn clarree,
> And upright in his bed thanne sitteth he,
> And after that he sang ful loude and cleere,
> And kiste his wyf, and made wantown cheere.
> He was al coltissh, ful of ragerye,
> And ful of jargon as a flekked pye.
> The slakke skyn aboute his nekke shaketh,
> Whil that he sang, so chaunteth he and craketh.
> But God woot what that May thoughte in hir herte,
> Whan she hym saugh up sittynge in his sherte,
> In his nyght-cappe, and with his nekke lene;
> She preyseth nat his pleyyng worth a bene.
>
> IV, 1842–54

The Merchant could hardly have devised a more devastating description of this ridiculous newlywed.

After resting from his amorous labors, January rises and goes happily about his palace, but custom demands that May remain in her room until the fourth day after the wedding. Meanwhile Damian, sick unto death with love for her, decides to write out his feelings in a letter, which he places over his heart. Three days later, when January and May sit eating in the main hall, January notices his squire's absence, and is told that Damian is ill. With pompous concern, seemingly motivated by a desire to appear magnanimous before his wife, he instructs May to pay Damian a comforting visit after the meal. Here the Merchant is showing us the old husband sending his young wife into the eager arms of his squire, and the expected result comes about. While January waits in bed for her return, May visits Damian; pleading for mercy, he slips her his letter, which she hides in her bosom until she can read and dispose of it in the privy. The locale in which this love missive is read by May sets the tone for her subsequent relationship with Damian. May returns to bed, and, when coughing brought on by old age and his years of licentious living arouses January from sleep, she submits to her husband's amorousness. But while January makes love to her, she is thinking hard about Damian, and the Merchant for a second time suggests her negative reaction to the old knight:

> And she obeyeth, be hire lief or looth.
> But lest that precious folk be with me wrooth,
> How that he wroghte, I dar nat to yow telle;
> Or wheither hire thoughte it paradys or helle.
> But heere I lete hem werken in hir wyse
> Til evensong rong, and that they moste aryse.
>
> IV, 1961–66

May's unpleasant afternoon with January is preparation for her decision concerning Damian. Although the Merchant says with heavy irony that the astrological situation at this time led May to accept Damian, we know very well that disgust with January as a lover is primarily responsible for the following conclusion on her part:

> Certeyn ... whom that this thyng displese,
> I rekke noght, for heere I hym assure
> To love hym best of any creature,
> Though he namoore hadde than his sherte.
>
> IV, 1982–85

Then in the very next line Chaucer gives his favorite remark to the Merchant for use in this ironic context: "Lo, pitee renneth soone in gentil herte!" May has been said to illustrate by her acceptance of Damian the courtly ideal of "pitee," but, without any trace of the usual courtly hesitation, she visits the sick Damian a second time and slips a note under his pillow, informing him that she will give herself to him as soon as possible. Damian at once recovers and pleases everyone with his charming behavior; but he is not here experiencing the ennobling effects of his lady's grace; he is simply looking forward gaily to the consummation of his desire for May. The Merchant is now beginning to make clear the results of January's folly.

Seeking to increase his sexual pleasures with May, January has had made a walled garden, the only key to which he keeps himself. That the beauty of this garden is to be put to unwholesome use is suggested when the Merchant remarks that Priapus, the phallic god, could not describe its beauty, and that Pluto and Proserpine, from the world of fairy, often frolicked there. We shall soon find these last two in January's garden, taking a hand in his marital affairs; there is, of course, an apt parallel in their presence there, for they are from the underworld, and Proserpine handles her husband with as great ease as that with which May will later control January.

For a time the garden is all that January had hoped it would be, "And thynges whiche that were nat doon abedde,/He in the gardyn parfourned hem and spedde" (IV, 2051–52); but, as every medieval person realized, "worldly joye may nat alwey dure." Fickle Fortune, like a scorpion, flatters him whom she will deceive; in short, she dampens January's lecherous joy by depriving him of his eyesight. And now he greatly fears that he will be cuckolded. For once, January has arrived at a sound conclusion, but the Merchant hastens to show that even this conclusion stems from the old knight's usual hypocrisy. January knows in his heart, of course, that his attractions for May, other than his wealth, are few; and he consequently expects, now that he cannot watch her closely, that she will be unfaithful to him. The thought of her loving or marrying another, even after his own death, fills him with burning jealousy, and, unwilling to admit his shortcomings in May's eyes, he evolves a protective system: he keeps his hand upon her at all times so that she cannot betray him.

This precaution drives both May and Damian to the depths of despair; she is consumed by a yearning for the squire, and he is "the sorwefulleste man" that ever was. But by writing to each other, they arrange to satisfy their desires. May makes an impression of the garden key in wax, and Damian prepares a copy from it. Unavoidably, as the Merchant intends, our thoughts here go back to January's statement to his friends that a young girl can be molded like wax by her husband; but now May makes wax literally the key to January's cuckolding.

With all her arrangements in readiness, May one day purposefully excites January's lust for her; he leads her to the garden, and she sends Damian in ahead, by means of the second key, to wait for her. The Merchant here points up the grossness of the May-Damian relationship by ironically comparing it to the sincere and tragic love affair of Pyramus and Thisbe, and by exhibiting Damian to us as he crouches in ignoble fashion under a bush, awaiting May's directions. But January is still the chief recipient of the Merchant's irony, and once again we find the old dotard expressing his lust in the terms of religion, when he paraphrases the Song of Solomon to invite May to the garden:

> Rys up, my wyf, my love, my lady free!
> The turtles voys is herd, my dowve sweete;
> The wynter is goon with alle his reynes weete.
> Com forth now, with thyne eyen columbyn!
> How fairer been thy brestes than is wyn!
> The gardyn is enclosed al aboute;
> Com forth, my white spouse! out of doute
> Thou hast me wounded in myn herte, O wyf!
> No spot of thee ne knew I al my lyf.
> Com forth, and lat us taken oure disport;
> I chees thee for my wyf and my confort.   IV, 2138–48

Of this speech the Merchant can only say: "Swiche olde lewed wordes used he."

As we have seen at considerable length, the Merchant has built up his narrative situation with detail after detail of savage irony. Now, in the last section of his tale (IV, 2156–2418), comes the inevitable conclusion, in which the lustful old knight gets his just deserts. But before presenting the conclusion to his story, the Merchant takes time to give a further example of January's complete hypocrisy. Having led May into the garden, January in his jealousy sanctimoniously says:

> For Goddes sake, thenk how I thee chees,
> Noght for no coveitise, doutelees,
> But oonly for the love I had to thee.
> And though that I be oold, and may nat see,
> Beth to me trewe, and I wol telle yow why.
>
> IV, 2165–69

We recall very well how January chose May for his wife, and there has been reason to suspect strongly throughout the story that he always realized clearly that her interest was primarily in his wealth; we are therefore not surprised at this point to find him advancing the fact that he will assign to her all his property as the chief reason why May should not make him a cuckold. But May is more than a match for him, and, by means of her first speech in the story, puts on a fine example of play acting. She weeps, claims to be "a gentil womman and no wenche," and forcefully declares her faithfulness to her husband. Then, at the finish of this fine speech, she signals Damian to climb the pear tree, where she will later join him and make January a cuckold. We should note in passing that the Merchant's not having May speak until so late in the story is a part of his effort to keep attention and interest focused upon the dotard January.

The climax of the Merchant's Tale is also accompanied by sharp thrusts at January. May claims that she has a great hunger for fruit, and January puffs with pride as he remembers that hunger for a specific thing indicates pregnancy; now, he thinks, his earlier boasts to his friends will be fulfilled and he will have an heir. May also plays upon his jealousy when she gets him to encircle the pear tree with his arms, as she goes to meet Damian in the tree by climbing up on her husband's back. As when he sent her to visit the sick Damian, January is once more helping his wife to reach the arms of her lover. And, most pointedly, the intervention of Pluto and Proserpine reduces January to a completely ridiculous position. When Pluto restores his eyesight, the old knight realizes fully what May is doing, but his lust—and perhaps his unwillingness to have Justinus say "I told you so"— cause him to accept the preposterous answer which Proserpine furnishes May, and to treat his wife as if nothing has happened.

Truly, the Merchant throughout his tale treats January with such frequent and concentrated bitterness that one wonders how the Host could have selected May as the sole bearer of guilt. In some ways the most effective device the Merchant employs in satirizing January is his extended use of physical blindness as a symbol for mental blindness. This idea is introduced when January selects May as the girl he wishes to marry. Using a proverb, the Merchant says at this point,

> But nathelees, bitwixe ernest and game,
> He atte laste apoynted hym on oon,
> And leet alle othere from his herte goon,
> And chees hire of his owene auctoritee;
> For love is blynd alday, and may not see.   IV, 1594–98

The reader, having seen at length the hypocritical bases for January's choice, is already fully able to guess that the Merchant's comment as to the blindness of January's love is prophetic. Then, as the plot unfolds, January's glaring lack of insight and the constant blearing of his judgment by rationalizing prepare us for the loss of his physical sight. The Merchant announces the blindness in the following words: "Allas! this noble Januarie free,/Amydde his lust and his prosperitee,/Is woxen blynd, and that al sodeynly" (IV, 2069–71). The words "noble," "free," and "lust" carry marked ironic implications; January is neither noble nor generous, and his "lust" is more a matter of lecherous pleasure than real happiness. Moreover, he has not gone blind "al sodeynly"; he has exhibited a startling lack of mental sight from the very beginning. Certainly January could never see the point of the Canon's Yeoman's wise remark: "If that youre eyen kan nat seen aright,/Looke that youre myndc lakke nought his sight" (VIII, 1418–19).

Some lines later the Merchant very clearly makes the point that January's vision was much impaired even before he lost the use of his eyes: "O Januarie, what myghto it thee availle,/Thogh thou myghte se as fer as shippes saille?/For as good is blynd deceyved be/As to be deceyved whan a man may se" (IV, 2107–10). The suggestion is that physical blindness for January is a fortunate thing, since he would have been just as easily cuckolded had he retained his eyesight. For, says the Merchant, Argus was deceived despite his hundred eyes, and so are many others who, like January, think deception cannot happen to them. Then the Merchant makes a subtle foreshadowing remark: "Passe over is an ese, I sey namoore" (IV, 2115). When mental insight is lacking, deception will come, whether or not an individual has physical sight; in such a situation the best "ese" (comfort) is simply to "passe over" (overlook) the deception. And that is exactly what

January will do at the end of the story when he accepts May's lame explanations.

Blindness figures largely in the section of the story involving Pluto and Proserpine. Pluto, in his jaundiced antifeminism, is as misguided as the Host later shows himself to be in his sympathy for January. Pluto says:

> Ne se ye nat this honurable knyght,
> By cause, allas! that he is blynd and old,
> His owene man shal make hym cokewold.
> Lo, where he sit, the lechour, in the tree!
> Now wol I graunten, of my magestee,
> Unto this olde, blynde, worthy knyght
> That he shal have ayeyn his eyen syght,
> Whan that his wyf wold doon hym vileynye.
> Thanne shal he knowen al hire harlotrye,
> Bothe in repreve of hire and othere mo.   IV, 2254–63

Pluto seems not to realize here that "lechour" better fits January than Damian, or that the restoration of his eyesight will not improve his judgment. Proserpine knows, however, that though a man sees a thing with both eyes, he can still remain "as lewed as gees" (IV, 2275). She therefore is determined to illustrate her point by giving May a successful lying answer. Pluto has long ago learned the folly of trying to outargue his wife, but to maintain his prestige he must carry out his promise to restore to January the use of his eyes. As soon as this happens, January jealously looks up into the tree to see what May is doing. And he undoubtedly sees.

In the remainder of the story—the debate between January and May—the Merchant very carefully shows us that regaining physical sight has done nothing to improve January's insight; for though Pluto gave him back the use of his eyes, he rejects what he sees and willfully remains blind. This process is presented in three stages, each more damaging than the preceding to our estimate of January. First, when May, in reply to his angry question as to what she is doing, says that she is struggling with a man in a tree because she was told that this act would cure January's blindness, the old knight bluntly and correctly states: "He swyved thee, I saugh it with myne yen" (IV, 2378). But, second, when May says that he is in error because his sight is not yet perfectly restored, January weakens his accusation: "And by my trouthe, me thoughte he dide thee so" (IV, 2386). Then, third, when she repeats that he is mistaken and upbraids him for not appreciating her kindness towards him, he gives up altogether and apologetically says:

> Now, dame, . . . lat al passe out of mynde.
> Com doun, my lief, and if I have myssayd,
> God helpe me so, as I am yvele apayd.
> But, by my fader soule, I wende han seyn
> How that this Damyan hadde by thee leyn,
> And that thy smok hadde leyn upon thy brest.
>
> IV, 2390–95

With full knowledge that January is still blinding himself as much as ever, May shamelessly and exultingly taunts him. "Ye, sire," she says, "ye may wene as yow lest." And knowing that she has January completely under her thumb, she concludes:

> Beth war, I prey yow; for, by hevene kyng,
> Ful many a man weneth to seen a thyng,
> And it is al another than it semeth.
> He that mysconceyveth, he mysdemeth.   IV, 2407–10

January first *saw* her unfaithful act, then *it seemed* to him that he had seen it, and finally he *thought* that he saw it. By these steps, the old man relinquishes the sight that Pluto has restored to him. Then he happily embraces and kisses his wife—"on hire wombe he stroketh hire ful softe"—and he leads her home. With ruthless bitterness the Merchant has shown that January cannot attain clear vision, no matter what he sees, for his lustful rationalization prevents his accepting reality.

The Merchant's purpose in the tale, then, is far wider than the Host realizes, for the Merchant's emphasis is steadily upon January's libidinous rationalizing and its inevitable results. But, as numerous critics have remarked, the dramatic texture of this performance is extremely tight, and there is a still wider third application of the story, which Chaucer as author seems to have intended and which we as readers can perceive. For us there should be three "villains" of the piece: May, incidentally; January; but especially the Merchant himself. Although the Merchant, unlike the Host, realizes that January is responsible for his own difficulties and heaps bitter satire on him for his folly, he unintentionally reveals in the telling of his story that he has not been willing or able to transfer his understanding of January's flaw to his own unhappy marital situation, which he described so vigorously in his prologue. The real moral of the Merchant's Tale is not that most wives deceive their husbands, or that most men are foolish even to consider marriage; it is, as the Merchant realizes, that this particular marriage between January and May is doomed from the start because of January's sinful false reasoning. The point to keep in mind is that Chaucer has the Merchant tell a tale with a moral applicable to his own situation, and then shows us that the Merchant lacks the wisdom and humility to make that application.

As a result of the performances by the Wife of Bath and the Clerk, marriage is the topic uppermost in the Merchant's mind as he addresses the Host in his prologue. He includes many general remarks on this topic as he angrily illustrates his point of view by a tale which bears similarity to his own two months of married life. But the Merchant apparently feels that there is one important difference between the two situations: his eyes have been opened to his wife, while January remains blind to May. Thus, in his tale, with a feeling of immeasurable superiority, he vents his anger on January with pitiless irony for swallowing May's lies. But the Merchant's foolish certainty in his prologue that most wives are bad and that any single man knows less of sorrow than a married man, shows that his own eyes have not really been fully opened, for he is not willing to admit that his particular marriage is unsuccessful for the same reason as January's; namely, his own lustful false reasoning led him to an unwise choice of a wife. In this way, the Merchant's Prologue and Tale, without his realizing it, reveal his pompous dishonesty as clearly as does his sketch in the General Prologue. He feels that he is to be praised for drawing from his marital experience the only feasible conclusion about marriage; but we suspect that from that experience he has not gained any insight into his own fallacious motivation.

That the Merchant approached his marriage two months ago with the same hypocritical line of reasoning that January uses is evident, I think, in the section of the tale in which January's musings are presented (IV, 1267–1396). There the personal pronoun "I" designates both January now and the Merchant two months ago; but the Merchant lets his present feeling of superiority over January seep through these musings by occasional negative remarks which would be otherwise inconsistent. Thus, as January reflects that a wife will outlast other transitory blessings, such as riches, the Merchant tartly observes that she may last "Wel lenger than thee list, paraventure" (IV, 1318). Again, when January reminds himself that a man and his wife are so closely united that no harm can come to either of them, the Merchant's dry comment is "And namely upon the wyves syde" (IV, 1392).

The Merchant's identifying the preliminaries to his own marriage with those which January goes through is nowhere clearer than in the otherwise puzzling reference by Justinus to the Wife of Bath:

> But lat us waden out of this mateere.
> The Wyf of Bathe, if ye han understonde,
> Of mariage, which ye have on honde,
> Declared hath ful wel in litel space.
> Fareth now wel, God have yow in his grace
>
> IV, 1684–88

It is the Merchant, of course, who has heard the Wife on the subject of marriage, and not Justinus, just a character in this story. But so exactly is Justinus at this moment the spokesman for the Merchant's point of view that the Merchant puts into his mouth the most telling satire he can recall against January's folly: the Wife of Bath's treatment of her husbands.

Yet there is a difference between Justinus' general point of view about marriage and the Merchant's; that the Merchant does not realize this difference contributes largely to his unwitting self-revelation in his tale. The Merchant does give Justinus his "own power of attorney," as one critic put it, to attack January's stupidity. But Justinus, though disillusioned in his own marriage, is a wise man who has attained inner peace and who is re-

As fressh as is the month of May

signed to his lot. His unhappy marriage does not lead him to condemn the whole system; he simply cautions January that the trick of a successful marriage lies in making a wise selection of a wife. The proud Merchant is as far from this sensible conclusion as his bitter anger is from Justinus' inner peace and resignation. Consequently, despite the distasteful atmosphere of this tale, the Merchant's amazingly tight-woven performance stands as an illustration of Chaucer's use of his dramatic principle with highly skillful complexity.

16. THE SQUIRE

We have had plentiful evidence that the unhappy marital situation of the Host is kept as a background against which are projected the views of marriage presented by the various Pilgrims. Now, following the Merchant's Tale, Harry again makes a comparison between the central female character and his wife (IV, 2419–40). This time the comparison begins favorably for Goodelief: unlike May, she is "trewe as any steel," though she is poor. However, the thought of his wife immediately leads the Host to recall her "heep of vices," such as her being a "labbyng shrewe," and he admits openly that he wishes he were not tied to her. Apparently, in Harry's opinion, a wife can have faults more annoying to her husband than infidelity; but, since making public his many complaints against Goodelief, he has heard Alice of Bath's views concerning a woman's right to deal dishonestly with a man, and he feels that he would now be foolish indeed to list his domestic grievances, for "it sholde reported be/And toold to hire [Goodelief] of somme of this meynee." The implication is here directed against the Wife of Bath. Therefore, he ends his personal reflections and calls upon the Squire for a tale of love (V, 1–8).

Numerous commentators have pointed out that in the succession of stories which make up the *Canterbury Tales* Chaucer followed a principle of contrast in the type and content of contiguous tales. What seems a more fundamental observation, however, is that this contrast derives from a principle of contrast in the personalities of the successive storytellers. Thus, the rough Shipman follows the proper Lawyer; the devout Second Nun appears after the impious Pardoner; the prosperous bourgeois Merchant, in what is an exact and perhaps purposeful reversal of the order of their sketches in the General Prologue, succeeds the impoverished and scholarly Clerk; and the witty Nun's Priest follows the sententious Monk. But nowhere in the book is the contrast between storytellers more immediately apparent than when the fresh young lover, the Squire, is called forward to banish the atmosphere which the bitter Merchant created by means of his unpleasant portrayal of old January. Harry Bailly is guilty of obtuse moments at times, but in this instance he certainly has his wits about him.

The most striking fact about the Squire as he appears in the General Prologue (I, 79–100) is his youthful happiness and zest for living: "Syngynge he was, or floytynge, al the day;/He was as fressh as is the month of May." He is a "lusty bacheler," who gives careful attention to his hair and to his clothing, and "So hoote he lovede that by nyghtertale/He sleep namoore than dooth a nyghtyngale." Not only is this squire the ideal of his type—well-developed physically, impressive "as of so litel space" in the 1383 campaign, properly educated in courtly love, horsemanship, musical composition, dancing, drawing, writing, jousting, carving, courtesy, and humility—but he also has an active interest in the world and the people who inhabit it. And although Miss Hadow thought the Squire notable for a kind of joyous naïveté, this young man has considerable learning and experience for his twenty years.[1]

[1] Grace Hadow, *Chaucer and His Times*, 81. Both Miss Hadow and Nevill Coghill (*The Poet Chaucer*, 167) state that the Franklin purposely interrupts and cuts off the Squire's story, because he realizes that the Squire is likely to run on at considerable length. I see no evidence for this view; certainly the Franklin's words to him (V, 673–94) suggest that the "worthy vavasour" would have listened happily until the Squire finished. See also E. P. Kuhl and H. J. Webb, *ELH*, VI (1939), 282–84.

The story that the Squire delivers, for which no source has been found,[2] presents a difficult problem as to why Chaucer left it "half-told,"[3] but there is considerable evidence for the dramatic suitability of the tale and its teller.[4] First of all, the Squire's Tale is a love story, and, as Harry Bailly said, certainly the Squire knows "theron as muche as any man" (V, 3); in fact, the first thing that we learned in the General Prologue about the Squire was that he is "a lovyere" (I, 80). Furthermore, it is perfectly in keeping with his station and interests for him to recite romance materials dealing with kings and court life. There are, however, two particular aspects of the Squire's Tale which make even clearer Chaucer's probable efforts to suit it and its teller: first, numerous expository comments in the course of the tale match surprisingly well with the qualities attributed to the Squire in the General Prologue; and, second, a number of passages in the tale echo materials to be found in the story told by the Squire's father, the Knight, with whom the Squire has been closely associated during a particularly impressionable period of his life.

When he introduces Canacee, shortly after the opening of his story, the Squire says:

> But for to telle yow al hir beautee,
> It lyth nat in my tonge, n'yn my konnyng;
> I dar nat undertake so heigh a thyng.
> Myn Englissh eek is insufficient.
> It moste been a rethor excellent,
> That koude his colours longynge for that art,
> If he sholde hire discryven every part.
> I am noon swich, I moot speke as I kan.   V, 34-41

Somewhat later, as he comments upon, and prepares to report,

---

[2] See the chapter by H. S. V. Jones in *Sources and Analogues*, 357–76.

[3] Gardiner Stillwell has set forth in detail the argument that Chaucer left the Squire's Tale incomplete because romance materials did not fit his realistic interests and abilities; see *RES*, XXIV (1948), 177–88. Stillwell regards the realistic passages in the Squire's Tale (e.g., V, 347–56) as comments by Chaucer, whereas I take them to be placed by Chaucer in the mouth of the Squire. As such, they do no great violence to dramatic suitability, for there is nothing in the sketch of the Squire which demands that he should show disregard for realistic people and human reactions. In fact, he has had opportunity to learn a great deal from his widely traveled, philosophical father, who, as Stillwell observes, "introduced humour and realism" into his tale.

[4] Marie Neville, *JEGP*, L (1951), 167–79.

the speech of the knight who rides into Cambuscan's court with gifts, the Squire says:

> And, for his tale sholde seme the bettre,
> Accordant to his wordes was his cheere,
> As techeth art of speche hem that it leere.
> Al be it that I kan nat sowne his stile,
> Ne kan nat clymben over so heigh a style,
> Yet seye I this, as to commune entente,
> Thus muche amounteth al that evere he mente,
> If it so be that I have it in mynde.   V, 102–109

In these remarks we see reflected several facets of the Squire's personality as it appeared in the General Prologue. His proper humility (I, 109) is apparent in his disclaimer of ability to describe Canacee's beauty or to equal the visiting knight's flights of oratory. Of course, he manages thereby to convey Canacee's excellent appearance far more forcibly than if he had tried to describe it. We also see in these passages his familiarity with formal rhetoric, which held a place in the training he had received (I, 96), and his general gaiety is probably to be observed in the pun on the word "stile."

The Squire's earlier reference to the "swerd of wynter, keene and coold" (V, 57) may well reflect his personal experience in the field, even though his "somtyme in chyvachie" seems to have covered warmer months.[5] But almost certainly his training in horsemanship (I, 94) lies behind his professional comment on the horse presented to Cambuscan by the visiting knight:

> For it so heigh was, and so brood and long,
> So wel proporcioned for to been strong,
> Right as it were a steede of Lumbardye;
> Therwith so horsly, and so quyk of ye,
> As it a gentil Poilleys courser were.   V, 191–95

The Squire's interest in courtesy makes thoroughly appropriate his comments on the visiting knight's manners, which could not have been improved by Gawain "Though he were comen ayeyn out of Fairye" (V, 96). And the respect which the Squire

---

[5] J. S. P. Tatlock, *The Development and Chronology of Chaucer's Works*, 148.

shows his superiors, the "knyghtes olde" (V, 69), in his reference
to the stories they have told him of the strange customs existing
in foreign lands, is to be expected from his respectful attitude toward his father (I, 101–102). Again, in the passage on sleep and
hang-overs (V, 347–67), matters in which a gay young man like
the Squire might be expected to have had some experience, we see
the same humorous turn which was probably apparent in the pun
on "stile." Then, in the description of the "lusty seson soote" on
which Canacee takes her morning walk (V, 388–400), can be
seen the Squire's zest for nature. Finally, when he speaks of the
revelry following the banquet in Cambuscan's court (V, 278–
90), we feel from knowledge gained in the General Prologue that
he is fully familiar with the "forme of daunces" and the "subtil
lookyng and dissymulynges/For drede of jalouse mennes aper-
ceyvynges," even though he says that "no man but Launcelot"
could describe them—for the Squire is not a "dul man." In short,
all these expository remarks are quite in keeping with such a person as was described in the Squire's sketch in the General Prologue.

The other pertinent point here is that a significant number of
passages in his story either echo or show connection with materials in the tale told by his father. The Knight is quite insistent
on narrative economy and wishes to "Lat every felawe telle his
tale aboute" (I, 890); the Squire seems to share this feeling and
says. "I wol nat taryen yow, for it is pryme,/And for it is no fruyt,
but los of tyme" (V, 73–74). Later on, he makes a similar point
against "prolixitee" (V, 401–408). Note, too, that his laudatory
description of Cambuscan (V, 9–27) gives to that worthy king
many of the virtues which characterized Theseus in the Knight's
Tale. Closer parallels, however, can be seen in the Squire's repetition of two of the Knight's central comments: "pitee renneth
soone in gentil herte" (I, 1761; V, 479), and make "vertu of
necessitee" (I, 3042; V, 593). There is also a familiar ring about
the Squire's "Though al the world the contrarie hadde yswore"
(V, 325), when we recall the Knight's "although we hadde it
sworn" (I, 1089). And it is perhaps noteworthy that the Squire's
passage concerning the desire that birds feel to escape from cages

[179

(V, 607–20) occurs in *Boece* almost immediately after the section from which the Knight takes Arcite's speech on the folly of desiring things we do not have.[6]

It is true that a number of the matters discussed in the last three paragraphs are often characteristic of Chaucer in his other writings. For example, many of his storytellers stress narrative economy, and "pitee renneth soone in gentil herte" occurs in the Merchant's Tale (IV, 1986) and in the Prologue to the *Legend of Good Women* (F, 503), as well as in the stories of the Knight and the Squire. But the fact remains that we do find in the Squire's performance specific details which reflect his training and personality as presented in the General Prologue, and which echo the sentiments of the Knight, under whom the Squire is serving his apprenticeship. Such details bear witness to the dramatic suitability of the tale and its teller, and we can at least hazard a guess that if other business had not prevented Chaucer's completing the story—to my mind the best explanation for its unfinished state—there would have been numerous other such details. For one can well believe that the young Squire must have brought to Chaucer many pleasant memories of his own youth.[7]

17. THE FRANKLIN

When we examine carefully the critical comment on the Franklin's Tale, we find a difficult state of affairs with regard to the suitability of this story and its teller. Earlier scholars, though they analyzed the Franklin and his performance from varying points of view, agreed that the tale was admirably suited to him;[1]

[6] *Boece*, Bk. III, pr. 2, m. 2, as presented in Robinson, *Works*, 400.

[7] Bowden, *Commentary*, 74–75.

[1] E.g., R. K. Root, *The Poetry of Chaucer* (rev. ed.), 271–77; G. L. Kittredge, *Chaucer and His Poetry*, 205–10, and *MP*, IX (1911–12), 435–67; G. H. Gerould, *PMLA*, LXI (1926), 262–79.

Epicurus owene sone

more recent writers, however, find it impossible to imagine the "son of Epicurus" as the teller of the story of Dorigen, Arveragus, and the black rocks of Brittany.[2]

Such sharp difference of opinion makes necessary a re-examination of the question in some detail. In the course of this re-examination I shall suggest (1) that Chaucer presents the Franklin as a man whose knowledge of, and regard for, the practical, everyday world are joined with a strong desire for social advancement; (2) that each of the Franklin's appearances in the *Canterbury Tales* bears out this appraisal of him; and (3) that this appraisal not only accounts for certain incongruities in the Franklin's Tale, but also makes apparent the suitability of this tale and its teller.

Before considering the sections of the *Canterbury Tales* pertinent to these three conclusions, we should review briefly the information set forth by Professor Manly in connection with Chaucer's Franklin.[3] A franklin named John Bussy was a close neighbor and associate in Lincolnshire of Thomas Pynchbek, whom Manly suggested as the possible model for Chaucer's Sergeant of the Law. Pynchbek was on the opposite side politically from Chaucer, offended Chaucer's friend William Beauchamp, and signed a writ for Chaucer's arrest. It may be, Manly argued, that the Franklin, as companion of the Lawyer, is modeled after Bussy. Chaucerian scholarship, after almost twenty-five years, is apparently willing—if we judge from Miss Bowden's *Commentary on the General Prologue*—to grant Manly all but certainty in the identification of Pynchbek, and a high degree of likelihood in the case of Bussy.[4] Thus, Chaucer's satiric treatment of the Lawyer presumably should be read in the light of Pynchbek's activities. Bussy seems to have been regarded as a man who sought to imitate the ways of the nobility, and the Franklin's conversation with the Squire indicates his ambitions for his family to join the ranks of the nobility (V, 673–94). Of course, neither the identification of Bussy as model nor the interpreta-

[2] E.g., J. R. Hulbert, *SP*, XLV (1948), 574; Nevill Coghill, *The Poet Chaucer*, 165–66.

[3] Manly, *New Light*, 157–68. A different view is held by K. L. Wood-Legh, *RES*, IV (1928), 145–51.

[4] Bowden, *Commentary*, 172, 177.

182]

tion stressing the Franklin's social aspirations can be proved absolutely. But the two points match surprisingly well and in my opinion afford sufficient reason for attempting to determine the extent to which Chaucer's Franklin exhibits his social aspirations alongside his practical concern for the everyday world.

To return to the re-examination of the Franklin, we find in Chaucer's text that four sections of the *Canterbury Tales* are concerned with him: the thirty-line sketch in the General Prologue; the conversation of the Franklin, the Squire, and the Host; the Franklin's Prologue; and the tale of Dorigen and Arveragus. These four sections present us with the following materials:

1. The Franklin accompanies the Sergeant of Law, loves food and drink, entertains lavishly, and has often held high public office (I, 331–60).

2. The Franklin is impressed with the Squire's gentilesse, in contrast with his own son's irresponsibility. But the Host says: "A straw for your gentilesse!" and the Franklin readily placates and flatters him (V, 673–708).

3. The Franklin says he will tell a Breton lay and introduces it with a "modesty prologue" (V, 709–28).

4. The Franklin's so-called "Breton lay," which includes proper names and rocks from Geoffrey of Monmouth, is concerned with generosity in marriage and sets forth a *demande d'amour* based on a section of Boccaccio's *Filocolo* (V, 729–1624).

There is one striking point about the sketch of the Franklin in the General Prologue: he is very wealthy and has epicurean tastes which he satisfies by luxurious living for pure pleasure; yet he also has often held important public offices, offices which beyond doubt were regularly held in Chaucer's day by men of outstanding ability and industry.[5] There may be many epicureans with ability, but an epicurean noted for industry is rare, especially when he has the money with which to indulge his tastes. Thus, it is possible that good hard work is more important to Chaucer's Franklin than his love of food, drink, and pleasure; if so, his lavish hospitality becomes in some respects play acting. In addition to the public offices he has earned, we find that the

[5] See the article by Gerould cited in n. 1 of this section.

Franklin is a "worthy vavasour." Although "worthy" is one of the most difficult of Chaucer's words to pin down, when we see it coming right after a list of deserved public offices a man has held, we are justified in taking it as a compliment to that man. There is also emphasis here on accomplishments, and industry is one of the Franklin's recommendations to the Squire. He says: "Fie on possessions, unless a man is also capable" (V, 686–87)—hardly a remark one would expect from the usual epicurean. Perhaps the Franklin acts the part of St. Julian in his country in an effort to imitate conduct he thinks suitable for great nobles, whose ranks he is eager to join. But before accepting or rejecting this idea, we must see how the Franklin's performance in the body of the *Canterbury Tales* fits with it.

In complimenting the Squire on his excellent performance, the Franklin expresses regret that his own son wastes his time and money and prefers to talk with a page rather than with gentle folk from whom he could learn gentilesse correctly. As noted earlier, these comments seem to indicate the Franklin's social aspirations. Professor Kittredge says:

He is . . . a rich freeholder, often sheriff in his country. Socially, he is not quite within the pale of the gentry, but he is the kind of man that may hope to found a family, the kind of man from whose ranks the English nobility has been constantly recruited. And that such is his ambition comes out naively and with a certain pathos in what he goes on to say: "I wish my son were like you. . . ."

This interpretation obviously complements the view of the Franklin as a man who has understanding of, and ability in, the routine world, and who strives to carry out his idea of noble conduct. There is further support for this argument in the Host's conversation with the Franklin.

When the Franklin states that his son will not learn gentilesse, the Host breaks in roughly:

> Straw for youre gentillesse! . . .
> What, Frankeleyn! pardee, sire, wel thou woost
> That ech of yow moot tellen atte leste
> A tale or two, or breken his beheste.   V, 695–98

Note that it is at the word "gentillesse" that the Host interrupts.

And he does not say "a straw for gentilesse"; he says "a straw for *your* gentilesse." It is not that Harry is impatient with the idea of gentilesse; he simply has no patience with *the Franklin's* holding forth on the subject. Harry Bailly, as an innkeeper, is an experienced man where questions of rank are concerned (witness his treatment of the Knight) and in his estimation, at any rate, the Franklin's station in life does not warrant such concern for gentilesse. Harry seems to feel that the Franklin is giving himself airs, and he takes immediate action to put an end to it. The Franklin's reaction to the Host's interruption also fits this reading. He meekly apologizes to the Host, as if he realizes that he has been somewhat presumptuous. Then the Host bluntly orders him to "Telle on thy tale withouten wordes mo" (V, 702), after which the Franklin shamelessly flatters Harry by saying: "I prey to God that it may plesen yow;/Thanne woot I wel that it is good ynow" (V, 708–709).

This brings us to a consideration of the Franklin's Prologue, in which he announces that his story will be a Breton lay, and apologizes for his ignorance of rhetoric. In this prologue are two points of importance to an interpretation of the dramatic interplay involved. First, the Franklin indicates immediately that he is not going to give up his interest in gentilesse just because of the Host's abrupt remarks. In fact, in the first line of his prologue he speaks of "thise olde *gentil* Britouns" and the kind of literature they liked, namely, Breton lays (V, 709–13). Such stories fit the Franklin's idea of propriety, and he points out that he is going to tell one.

The second point in this passage of interest here concerns the so-called "modesty prologue." One writer in 1927 commented on numerous parallels to this passage, showing that in the late Middle Ages, as now, it was not unusual for a speaker to begin by saying "unaccustomed as I am to public speaking," and then to talk for two hours.[6] But, as numerous eminent Chaucerians have observed, one of Chaucer's distinctive devices is putting conventional elements to functional uses; and that, I think, applies

---

[6] E. P. Hammond, *English Verse Between Chaucer and Surrey*, 392 ff. On the Franklin's inconsistency here, see B. S. Harrison, *SP*, XXXII (1935), 55–61; and C. S. Baldwin, *PMLA*, XLII (1927), 106–12.

also to the Franklin's "modesty prologue." Rather than thinking this passage accounted for by simply noting many parallels to it, we must explain it satisfactorily in its dramatic context; and the context in the present instance is furnished by the Host's preceding attack on the Franklin's interest in gentilesse, and by the succeeding Breton lay which the Franklin tells, a story in which gentilesse figures largely.

Despite the Host's attack, the Franklin indicates his determination to retell a lay made by the "gentle Bretons in their days." But he also seems eager to combat any inclination on the part of those of his listeners who are not interested in the behavior of the nobility to think that he is giving himself airs, as Harry has implied. He therefore ends his prologue with a fourteen-line section in which he states as plainly as possible that he is a "burel" man, who speaks crudely and who is ignorant of rhetoric. For the same purpose he even gets off a rather clumsy pun involving rhetorical colors and the colors of flowers and dies. But for those in his audience capable of appreciating it and of being properly impressed, he includes mention of Cicero and Mount Parnassus. He does exactly the same thing in his tale when he describes the magician's astrological preparations (V, 1261–84). He starts using technical terms, breaks off abruptly to say "I ne kan no termes of astrologye," and then proceeds to give a detailed account of the magician's activities, in which the Franklin displays impressive learning. Another similar instance is his well-known comment: "The horizon has reft the sun of his light—this is as much to say it was night" (V, 1017–18). Such remarks give evidence of his double interest: in gentilesse and the high style, but also in less elevated matters.

In each instance so far, the two sides of the Franklin's nature are apparent: on the one hand, his knowledge of, and regard for, the ordinary, practical world; on the other, his social aspirations, which lead him to conduct himself as he thinks befits the nobility. We come now to the discussion of how his tale fits into this interpretation. As preparation for this discussion we should rule out two matters: first, the idea that Chaucer had an actual Breton lay as his exact source for the Franklin's Tale, an idea in support of which one hundred years of intensive scholarship has found not the least evidence; and, second, the theory that Chaucer used the Franklin's Tale as a means of setting forth his own view of the perfect marriage. As replacement for these views, I shall attempt to show that the story Chaucer prepared especially for his Franklin evidences great originality, in that it presents an attempted combination of the two then current systems for relationships between men and women—courtly love and marriage. Further, I think that the impossibilities of such a combination cause incongruities which make evident the unworkable aspects of the Franklin's attempt to concern himself with the gentilesse he thinks proper for the nobility. These incongruities stem from the same dichotomy in the Franklin's make-up already observed. Thus his tale is not "an entirely harmonious whole": it is at the same time a courtly-love *demande d'amour* stressing gentilesse, and an attempt at defining the ideal marital situation. That such an uneasy combination does not come off successfully should surprise no one; neither should the assigning of this sort of failure to the Franklin surprise anyone who bears in mind the dramatic principle which Chaucer employed regularly in the *Canterbury Tales*. For we can be sure that Chaucer intended this tale to be read as a dramatic performance by the Franklin. In no other section of the *Tales* does a teller exhibit greater awareness of his listeners. This awareness can be observed not only in the Franklin's Prologue and at the end of his story, but also at regular intervals within the body of his tale.

Chaucer probably took the bare outline for this tale from a story told by Menedon in Boccaccio's *Filocolo*, and added to it many details similar to those used in the so-called Breton lays.[7] But although these sources contribute the atmosphere of courtly love which makes appropriate the emphasis on gentilesse, they by no means account for the Franklin's extended treatment of a happy marriage. In this connection, the opening of the Italian tale deserves attention:

In the land where I was born, I remember there being an extremely rich and a noble cavalier, who, loving a noble lady of that land with a most perfect love, took her for wife. Of which lady another cavalier,

---

[7] See the chapter by Germaine Dempster and J. S. P. Tatlock in *Sources and Analogues*, 377–97.

named Tarolfo, became enamored; and he loved her with so great love that he did not see anything except her, nor did he desire anything more. And in many ways, either by often passing in front of her house, or by tilting or by jousting or by other acts, he contrived to have her love. . . .

Although this story opens with immediate emphasis on the love triangle, at the beginning of the Franklin's Tale we have seventy-six lines devoted to Arveragus' winning Dorigen as his wife and to the arrangements they make to insure a happy marriage. The endings of the two stories also show widely differing emphasis. In the *Filocolo* we merely have each character's release of the other and then the *demande d'amour:* Who was the most generous? Near the end of the Franklin's Tale, however, Aurelius draws a moral for all wives—"every wife should be careful in her promises" (V, 1541)—and we have the Franklin's lengthy description of the happy reunion between Dorigen and Arveragus (V, 1551–56), in addition to the competition for the prize in noble conduct and the concluding question. Neither in Menedon's story nor in the Breton lays is there the constant attention which the Franklin devotes to marriage.

The details of the Franklin's attempt to combine a relationship exemplifying courtly love with an ideal marital situation can be most clearly seen from an analysis of the two chief characters in the tale—Dorigen and Arveragus—and of the asides which the Franklin inserts into their story. We learn at the opening of the tale that a knight does his "payne" to serve a lady, to please whom he carries out many a great undertaking. Because this lady is of a nobler family he scarcely dares tell her of his love. But finally she is moved by his abject humility to take pity upon him. Here is the typical courtly-love situation, described in the customary terminology. Then the knight and the lady marry, and the courtly-love relationship, in which the lady is properly supreme and the knight her servant, is replaced by the marital situation, in which the wife is considered subordinate to the husband. But the newly wed couple do not proceed according to the rules: they attempt to retain in their marital state certain aspects of their courtly-love relationship. And the passage (V, 744–52) from which we learn of this is full of a strange combination of terms from the two systems: alongside "mastery," "sover-eignty," and "humble true wife," we find "obey her and follow her will, as should any lover to his lady." Dorigen and Arveragus love each other sincerely and have all the requirements for a highly successful marriage and a happy life. Yet into their mar-riage they carry attitudes and actions from the system of courtly love.

At this point in the story the Franklin digresses from the nar-rative to comment at length on the wisdom of this arrangement. He feels that he is accomplishing both his aims: he is portraying a workable marriage acceptable to those of his listeners for whom courtly love holds no charms; and also he can still tell a tale of gentilesse and magic, ending with a *demande d'amour*. Accord-ingly, his comments here reveal his double interests. First he points out that "love will not be constrained by mastery; for when mastery appears, the God of Love at once beats his wings, and, farewell, he is gone (V, 764–65). Then he enters his com-mon-sense plea for tolerance in marriage. Finally he caps his digression with a fine example of double-talk:

> Thus hath she take hir servant and hir lord,
> Servant in love and lord in mariage.
> Thanne was he bothe in lordshipe and servage.
> Servage? nay, but in lordshipe above,
> Sith he hath bothe his lady and his love;
> His lady, certes, and his wyf also,
> The which that lawe of love acordeth to.   V, 792–98

Arveragus now takes his wife home to Pedmark and they live in great happiness. Here the Franklin in his more matter-of-fact role interrupts the story to say:

> Who koude telle, but he hadde wedded be,
> The joye, the ese, and the prosperitee
> That is bitwixe an housbonde and his wyf?   V, 803–805

This excellent state of affairs lasts more than a year until Arvera-gus goes to England for two years to seek worship and honor in arms, "For al his lust he sette in swich labour" (V, 812). A happy marriage is fine, but Arveragus has remembered that he is a courtly knight and he must go away to win honor in the tournaments. From this knightly act will stem the trouble which almost wrecks the happy marriage of Dorigen and Arveragus. We should also not overlook the fact that his leaving home is Chaucer's addition to his source; the cavalier in the *Filocolo* does not go away.

Dorigen grieves mightily over her absent husband, and her grief becomes symbolized for her in the black rocks along the coast. Thus it is that when the squire Aurelius pleads for her love, she assigns him the seemingly impossible task of removing the black rocks. But here Dorigen is not exactly the haughty lady of the courtly romances, though the way is paved for the approaching difficulties by her shifting momentarily into a courtly-love situation. She first says firmly that she will never be an unfaithful wife. Then, in jest and in the language of courtly love, she assigns the task and promises her love if Aurelius can remove the rocks. But immediately she shifts back to practical, down-to-earth considerations and tells him to put such matters out of his mind, for a man can have no pleasure in loving another man's wife (V, 1002–1005).

With Aurelius, however, the Franklin's sense of literary propriety can be indulged fully. His description of this squire includes all the conventional details: Aurelius suffers the malady of love for more than two years and utters a complaint to Apollo that would do justice to Troilus. But even with Aurelius, the Franklin is not altogether comfortable; he leaves the lovesick squire with the matter-of-fact remark: "Let him choose for me whether he will live or die" (V, 1086).

Arveragus returns, and the emphasis is placed on the happiness of the reunited husband and wife. Although Arveragus suspects nothing, the elements of courtly love which he and Dorigen have brought into their marriage—his interest in winning honor in the tournaments, and her assigning the task to Aurelius—will soon threaten their happiness.

Meanwhile, Aurelius, who has properly observed secrecy, learns from his brother that there are magicians in Orleans. He goes to Orleans, meets the magician, and strikes a bargain for the removal of the black rocks. Returning with Aurelius, the magician in due time makes the rocks disappear. Throughout this

190]

long section of his tale (V, 1101–1296), the Franklin is dealing with the kind of romance material which he thinks proper for people of breeding; yet we find injected here the same sort of matter-of-fact comments noticed earlier. When the subject of magic is introduced, the Franklin speaks of it as "such folly as in our days is not worth a fly—for our faith in Holy Church does not permit illusions to grieve us" (V, 1131–34). And later the acts of magicians are spoken of as japes, wretchedness, superstitious cursedness, and illusions which heathen folk used in those days (V, 1271–72, 1292–93). Even though magic was standard material in the Breton lays and the romances, the Franklin's practical sense prevents his acceptance of it.

When Aurelius tells Dorigen of the disappearance of the rocks, she is stunned. Arveragus is away, and she grieves alone at home. At this point in the story we have the much-debated "Complaint of Dorigen," which Chaucer took from Jerome against Jovinian, and in which Dorigen calls up as models many famous ladies of the past who chose death rather than dishonor (V, 1355–1456). Although the artistic function of this complaint has recently been skillfully defended on other grounds,[8] I feel that the presence of this lengthy passage, which so many critics have found objectionable, is most convincingly explained by reference to Dorigen's carrying over into her marriage aspects of the rules of conduct she followed when, at the beginning of the story, she was a courtly-love heroine. The "complaint" itself is a courtly-love device, as is the noble choice of suicide rather than dishonor. And the *exempla* which Dorigen cites are part and parcel of elevated literature in the Middle Ages. But even though Dorigen concludes that she should commit suicide, the tone and exaggerated nature of her complaint convince the reader that she is not going to do so. Rather, as soon as Arveragus returns, she tells him her difficulty in true wifely fashion. In other words, the "complaint" represents her testing of one aspect of courtly behavior, her discarding it, and then her adopting a more realistic and practical solution. In this connection we should note that the lady in Menedon's story in the *Filocolo* does not immediately tell her husband the cause of her grief. He has to force the facts from her.

[8] James Sledd, *MP*, XLV (1947–48), 36–45.

But Dorigen unburdens herself to her husband as soon as he asks why she weeps. In her actions here we see that, for the moment at least, the Franklin's understanding of a workable marriage overcomes his interest in what he thinks the proper behavior for noble folk.

Arveragus, however, has not yet given up the courtly principles that he brought to his marriage. Although he comforts his wife in husbandly fashion, he proclaims that she must give herself to Aurelius because "Trouthe is the hyeste thyng that man may kepe" (V, 1479). Then he instructs two servants to conduct her to Aurelius. That the Franklin realizes how strange this decision must sound to those of his listeners who put no stock in the courtly code is evident in his next comment:

> Paraventure an heep of yow, ywis,
> Wol holden hym a lewed man in this
> That he wol putte his wyf in jupartie.
> Herkneth the tale er ye upon hire crie.
> She may have bettre fortune than yow semeth;
> And whan that ye han herd the tale, demeth.
>
> V, 1493–98

The everyday listener or reader is now assured of a happy ending to the story, despite Arveragus' strange behavior, and the Franklin can proceed with his illustrations of gentilesse and the concluding *demande d'amour*. Dorigen encounters Aurelius, who asks where she is going. "To the garden, as my husband bade," she replies (V, 1512). Notice that she is here no courtly lady; she is the conventional, obedient wife. Aurelius is filled with pity and decides that to hold her to her promise would not be in accord with gentilesse. He therefore releases her, but we have difficulty praising Aurelius for noble actions when we recall that he did not hesitate to use trickery to make the rocks disappear. Even he, however, seems to realize now that the principles of courtly love do not fit well in the marital situation, and he calls Dorigen "the truest and best wife I ever knew in all my life" (V, 1539–40). Dorigen "goes home to her *husband*," not to her lord or to her knight, and they live happily ever after. If my analysis of this story is correct, we can readily suppose that their marriage was not again threatened by behavior in accord with the code of courtly love, and we note that at this point the Franklin speaks of them as "Arveragus and Dorigen his *wife*," not "Arveragus and Dorigen his *lady*," as in the earlier section of the tale.

The Franklin now presents the magician's releasing Aurelius from the debt of a thousand pounds, whereby the magician shows that he can in his actions illustrate gentilesse as well as can a knight or a squire. Then comes the Franklin's concluding question to his listeners: "Who was the most generous?" (V, 1622). It is important to observe here that whereas in the *Filocolo* the question is "Which of the three men—the cavalier, Tarolfo, or Tebano—was the most generous?" the Franklin simply asks who was the most generous. This alteration throws the competition open to Dorigen, as well as to the three men, and to my way of thinking she would win the prize by virtue of her giving up, through the immediate confession to her husband of her foolish promise, the attitudes from courtly love that she brought into her marriage.

Even so, the *demande d'amour* seems strangely out of place at the end of the Franklin's Tale. This results, I think, from the fact that the Franklin's frequent comments on the happy workability of the marriage between Dorigen and Arveragus build up a pattern which is in opposition to courtly-love elements. Thus we cannot quite accept Arveragus, whose counterpart in the *Filocolo* is judged the most generous, as a noble husband, for we have seen him send his wife to another man.

In his tale and elsewhere the Franklin tries to satisfy his two fields of interest and to appeal to his listeners of both types—the "gentils" and the less elevated folk. So far as we know, since we have no epilogue to the Franklin's Tale, his device was successful on the Canterbury pilgrimage, but most critics have been struck by the incongruities in his tale, incongruities which I think result from the ambivalence of this "worthy vavasour" so greatly concerned with gentilesse.

For gold in phisik is a cordial

18. THE PHYSICIAN

The suitability of the Physician's Tale and its teller is much debated. As I see it, there is evidence that Chaucer provided this Pilgrim with material that fits the two primary aspects of his character. The Physician is presented in the General Prologue as a "society doctor," who attempts to impress his public with his learning and skill, though he is mainly interested in collecting fat fees; in other words, he is primarily concerned with putting on an impressive show to cover his real motives. Similarly, when he performs before the Pilgrims, he tries through an allegory directed against lust to impress them with his noble defense of chastity. But Harry Bailly shrewdly explodes the bubble of his pomposity by pointed reference to the Physician's activities toward corrupting chastity.

From the sketch in the General Prologue (I, 411–44), we learn that the Physician is thoroughly familiar with the medical authorities of his time—Esculapius, Dioscorides, Rufus of Ephesus, Hippocrates, Hali, Galen, Serapion, Rhazes, Avicenna, Averroës, Constantinus Afer, Damascenus (?), Bernard Gordon, John Gaddesden, and Gilbertus Anglius. However, the numerous ironic touches in the portrait make it almost certain that Chaucer aimed at pointing up lapses in the character of this doctor, despite his learning and financial success. As early as the opening lines of the sketch, Chaucer seems to strike this satiric note. He says:

> With us ther was a Doctour of Phisik;
> In al this world ne was ther noon hym lik,
> To speke of phisik and of surgerye,
> For he was grounded in astronomye.   I, 411–14

The crucial words here are "to speke." According to one possibility, the lines mean: "If we speak generally of members of the medical profession, in all the world there was no one equal to him." The second possible reading would be: "In all the world there was no one equal to him for talking about medical matters." In my opinion, this doctor is not necessarily the world's leading practitioner of "phisik and of surgerye"; he leads the world in *speaking about* medicine.[1] In line 411 the general subject of medicine is introduced by mention of the "Doctour of Phisik" as the individual now under discussion. It would therefore seem unnecessary and clumsily out of place for Chaucer again to indicate the subject being discussed, when only one line has intervened. Moreover, although we do not know with certainty just what was Chaucer's view of astronomy as a serious part of medical science, we do know that some of his contemporaries were very dubious about it.[2] With that fact in mind, I find difficulty in accepting "For he was grounded in astronomye" as anything other than a part of a jibe at the Physician. The introductory "for" shows that we can expect to be told the reason for the Physician's pre-eminence in *talking about* medicine; and the reason is that he knew "astronomye" thoroughly.

If there is room for doubt about the presence of satire in the lines just treated, certainly in the mention of the Physician's "arrangement" with the apothecaries Chaucer is plain enough. "For ech of hem made oother for to wynne—/Hir frendshipe nas nat newe to bigynne." The same certainty is to be felt in connection with the line "His studie was but litel on the Bible." Nowadays we hardly notice that certain scientists may care little for formal religion, but that was not the case in Chaucer's day.[3]

There is one other important satiric thrust at the Physician in the portrait: he is extremely tight-fisted. Although he will spend money on fine clothes, he will use it for very little else. Indeed, one suspects that his moderate diet was dictated more by concern for expense than by considerations of health. Further, a good bit of this money which he hoards he made during times of plague—times when a doctor should have thought more of helping in an emergency than of collecting his fees. The sketch ends with an

---

[1] Curry (*Sciences*, 28) advanced this view; Manly (*Canterbury Tales by Geoffrey Chaucer*, 28) differed sharply.

[2] Bowden, *Commentary*, 204–205.

[3] G. G. Coulton, *Medieval Panorama*, 445 ff.

apt pun on "goldwasser": "For gold in phisik is a cordial,/Therefore he lovede gold in special." All in all, the Physician is not a particularly appealing individual, in that his superficial show of professional expertness is aimed principally at making money.

The story told by this fashionable medicine man[4] concerns the beautiful and innocent Virginia, whose father kills her to prevent her falling victim to the lust of an evil judge. Even though in the first line of his story the Physician refers to Livy as his source, it seems that Chaucer used the skeleton of this narrative as he found it in Jean de Meun's *Romance of the Rose*, adding to it material from Livy's Latin version.[5] One point in connection with Chaucer's use of source materials for this tale is of particular importance here. Whereas in the account of De Meun, the evil judge is the center of interest, in the Physician's Tale, Virginia is made the central figure,[6] and as such represents the ideal of virginity. The judge, Appius, on the other hand, Chaucer contrives as little more than a threat to Virginia's chastity.

The idea that the Physician intends his performance as a moral story primarily in praise of chastity is also supported by examination of the first hundred-odd lines of the tale. With the narrative economy usual in the *Canterbury Tales*, we are first introduced to a worthy knight, Virginius, who had an only daughter. But then we find a thirty-four-line description of Virginia's physical beauty; and the method of this personal description differs greatly from that employed for the sketches in the General Prologue or for such descriptions as those of Nicholas, Alison, and Absolon in the Miller's Tale. Here we have no easy, natural, gossipy, conversational tone; rather, there is the somewhat stilted, semilearned device of having Nature proudly speak of Virginia as one of her finest creations. This method seems well suited to the pompous Physician, who apparently stresses Virginia's physical beauty in order to increase his emphasis on her inner purity. In fact, he says: "And if that excellent was hire beautee,/A thousand foold moore vertuous was she" (VI, 39–40).

This statement introduces a lengthy passage in detailed praise

---

[4] The term is Miss Bowden's; see *Commentary*, 199.
[5] See the chapter by E. F. Shannon in *Sources and Analogues*, 398–408.
[6] R. K. Root, *The Poetry of Chaucer* (rev. ed.), 222.

of Virginia's admirable conduct, for "As wel in goost as body chast was she" (VI, 43); also she avoided all occasions which make young people "to soone rype and boold" (VI, 68). The Physician now inserts a long plea addressed to governesses and to parents, urging them to guard well the virtue of their young charges. Then he calls attention to the wide fame which Virginia won, both for her beauty and her virtuous behavior. At last, after 116 lines, the Physician is ready to begin his narrative, which he closes with the noble advice "Forsaketh synne, er synne yow forsake" (VI, 286).

This story is a strangely moral one for a man whose study is but little on the Bible, whose arrangements with his apothecaries are suspect, and whose main interest is in collecting and holding on to as much money as possible. The Host, in commenting on the tale, first expresses his reaction to the false judge and to the piteous death of the "sely mayde," and sententiously concludes that "Men han ful ofte moore for harm than prow" from the gifts of Nature and Fortune (VI, 287–300). Then Harry seems to be struck by the incongruity between the theme of the tale and the real character of its teller. He says:

> But trewely, myn owene maister deere,
> This is a pitous tale for to heere.
> But nathelees, passe over, is no fors.
> I pray to God so save thy gentil cors,
> And eek thyne urynals and thy jurdones,
> Thyn ypocras, and eek thy galiones,
> And every boyste ful of thy letuarie;
> God blesse hem, and oure lady Seinte Marie!
> So moot I theen, thou art a propre man,
> And lyk a prelat, by Seint Ronyan!
> Seyde I nat wel? I kan nat speke in terme;
> But wel I woot thou doost myn herte to erme,
> That I almoost have caught a cardynacle.   VI, 301–13

It seems to me that the Host is in this passage making fun of the Physician by none-too-veiled allusions to his hypocrisy in telling a story so out of keeping with his real character.[7] First, we note that Harry calls this doctor "myn owene maister deere,"

---

[7] This view was advanced by Frederick Tupper, *JEGP*, XV (1916), 61–67.

the same exaggeratedly polite title that he used in addressing the Friar (III, 1337; see also III, 1300); and we can be sure that Harry was well aware of the hypocritical practices of the "worthy lymytour." Then the Host comments again on the piteous nature of the story, but now says: "However, forget that; it doesn't matter." It is almost as if Harry is a bit ashamed of himself at this point for having been so disturbed by a story of innocence betrayed, when he reflects that this story came from the lips of a man himself not above suspicion as a betrayer in various kinds of activities. Whether or not this guess at Harry's reaction here is sound, the fact remains that he does dismiss the tale as of no importance and turns his attention to the teller.

His opening prayer for the Physician's body would seem to indicate something more than literal meaning for the line, especially when we recall how general in Chaucer's day was the assumption that doctors regularly indulged in questionable practices.[8] But Harry's ironic intent here is most clearly seen in his mention of "ypocras" and "galiones," two currently well-known love-philters widely purveyed by doctors.[9] No great interpretative straining is needed to find irony in the Host's asking God to save the aphrodisiacs sold by a man who has just completed a tale in praise of virginity. Then Harry goes on to call down the blessings of the Virgin Mary on these same items. Even this does not complete the Host's jest at the Physician's expense. He next tells the doctor that he is "a proper man, and like a prelate." The reputation of fourteenth-century prelates makes this comparison a dubious honor,[10] and Harry seems to underscore his meaning here by a lewd pun on the nickname of St. Ninian.[11]

Certainly a partial explanation for this passage is the pride the Host takes in being sufficiently learned as to address a professional man in high-sounding technical terms relating to that man's profession. We have seen this same motivation in Harry's using legal terms when addressing the Lawyer and rhetorical terms in speaking to the Clerk. Thus it is that he now proudly

[8] Bowden, *Commentary*, 209–11.

[9] See the article by Tupper cited in n. 7 of this section.

[10] See Robinson, *Works*, *CT*, VII, 1924–64, for the Host's views of the clergy's behavior.

[11] See Tupper's article cited in n. 7 of this section and Robinson, *Works*, 833.

asks the Physician: "Seyde I nat wel?" and adds with mock modesty: "I kan nat speke in terme." But, in making his transition to calling on the next storyteller, he takes one parting shot at the Physician: "But I know very well that you have caused my heart to grieve, so that I have almost caught a 'cardynacle.' "[12] Notice that it is not the sad story of Virginia which causes the Host's pain around the heart; the Physician (*thou*) causes it. In the light of Harry's preceding ironic remarks to the Physician, we have reason for suspecting that he here means that his ailment is caused by the Physician's hypocrisy in telling a moral tale which his own practices rob of any sincerity.

In conclusion, if the foregoing interpretation of the Physician's performance is tenable, the piteous story of Virginia must be regarded as his bold attempt to perpetrate on the Pilgrims a bit of moral virtuosity. When the tale is so understood, the pompous and exaggeratedly noble tone of the long introductory passage on Virginia's purity, the so-called "digressive" plea to governesses and parents, and the concluding moral do not cause baffling difficulties in the drama of this section of the *Canterbury Tales*, for they represent a part of the Physician's dramatic purpose. That the Host, in his comments upon the performance, does not allow the Physician to carry out his scheme with complete success is in keeping with Chaucer's method throughout.[13]

[12] The Host's knowledge of technical terms is a bit shaky. "Cardynacle" is his corruption of "cardiacle." See Robinson, *Works*, 834.

[13] For example, the method is almost exactly the same at the end of the performance by the Pardoner (Robinson, *Works, CT*, VI, 946–55).

19. THE PARDONER

We have now reached the actor-Pilgrim whose presentation, in my opinion, involves the greatest degree of dramatic complexity.[1] The passages pertinent to any analysis of the Pardoner's character fall into eight definite divisions: first, the portrait of the Pardoner in the General Prologue (I, 669–714); second, the interruption by the Pardoner in the Wife of Bath's Prologue (III, 163–87); third, the Introduction to the Pardoner's Tale (VI, 318–28); fourth, the Pardoner's Prologue (VI, 329–462); fifth, the sermon (VI, 463–915); sixth, the benediction (VI, 915–918); seventh, the attempted sale (VI, 919–45); eighth, the quarrel with the Host (VI, 946–68).[2]

Through a consideration of these passages in sequence, my interpretation of the Pardoner will be presented: namely, that the physically handicapped Pardoner having joined the pilgrimage with the definite purpose of extracting money from his traveling companions, most of whom he despises, by a refinement of his usual methods of salesmanship among peasants directs his actions and words throughout toward that end and fails, after almost succeeding, because he foolishly reverts to those usual methods at the crucial moment. Thus, the dramatic structure of the Pardoner's performance, which includes a tale that suits both his regular occupation and his present purpose, involves his bitter antagonism towards his physically well-adjusted companions and represents an unintentional self-revelation of his own in-

[1] The numerous studies of the Pardoner and his recital were surveyed by G. G. Sedgewick, *MLQ*, I (1940), 431–58. Subsequent references to Sedgewick throughout this section are to this article. See also C. R. Sleeth, *MLN*, LVI (1941), 138; M. P. Hamilton, *JEGP*, XL (1941), 48–72; A. L. Kellogg, *Speculum*, XXVI (1951), 465–81; A. L. Kellogg and L. A. Haselmayer, *PMLA*, LXVI (1951), 251–77; Johannes Swart, *Neophilologus*, XXXVI (1952), 45–50.

[2] See Sedgewick (p. 443), from whom I have borrowed several terms: e.g., "interruption" and "benediction." Among other of his terms, the rejection of "afterthought" for lines VI, 919–68 of the Pardoner's Tale is especially important for my analysis.

I trowe he were a geldyng or a mare

adequacies in the very field of endeavor—salesmanship—at which he feels most competent.)Here the tale proper is more completely subordinated to the whole performance than in any other instance.

There is no need here to dwell on all the familiar details of the Pardoner's portrait in the General Prologue (I, 669–714). It will suffice to note the following facts: the Pardoner has just come from Rome; he is a friend of the Summoner;(he is obviously indifferent to any adverse opinions the other Pilgrims may form concerning the moral lapses evident in his behavior; he has been a eunuch from birth; he has his relics and pardons with him; and he has been extremely successful in the past, because of his shrewdness, at extracting money from peasants.)

A close similarity exists, I think, between Chaucer's Pardoner and Shakespeare's Edmund in *King Lear*. Like Edmund, the Pardoner is subject to the scorn of society at large through no fault of his own—in fact, the Pardoner, a eunuch, has even more cause for bitterness on this score than Edmund, a bastard. Like Edmund, the Pardoner is extremely intelligent and self-reliant. We may infer that the Pardoner, like Edmund, decides that circumstances force him to find an outlet for his considerable abilities outside the sphere of normal human behavior and usual moral laws. Edmund, not feeling bound to honest dealing, outwits his family and his associates and blazes a brilliant path upward to a generalship and near kingship, until his fatal mistake of not choosing between the two evil sisters proves his undoing. The Pardoner, barred from normal satisfactions by a misfortune of birth, finds his compensation in matching wits with normal folk and coming off best in the encounter. The money he thus makes (I, 703–704) and the luxuries he can thus afford (VI, 439–53) are important to him as clear evidence to the world of his success. Perhaps he could have enjoyed even greater wealth and luxury, and some satisfaction, as a "supersalesman" in the seemingly more honest employ of some "big businessman," such as the Merchant; but the satisfaction of so obviously outwitting people born without his handicap would have been lacking.

If we assume that the Pardoner feels a bitterness against the world similar to that which characterizes Edmund, a pertinent question needs asking here: Why did the Pardoner go on the pilgrimage? It will perhaps be objected that such a question is trivial; Chaucer is presenting a fictional cross section of the society he knew, and a pardoner must needs be present. But if the enveloping plan of the *Canterbury Tales* is to deserve, as it has often received, the highest praise for literary artistry as the framework within which we meet the actors in a Human Comedy, such a question is relevant. It does not, then, seem to me too conjectural to suggest that the Pardoner, upon his return from Rome, encountered his friend the Summoner and learned of the plans for the pilgrimage, and that he therefore decided to join the company, determined to match wits with his traveling companions and, if possible, to extract money from them. Certainly his past successes among peasants filled him with confidence in his own abilities; his "walet . . ./Bretful of pardoun, comen from Rome al hoot" (I, 686–87) makes him particularly well prepared for an extraordinary effort at this time; and the hope of success among a group more sophisticated and less friendly than his usual victims, a success which would give him the greatest possible pleasure and satisfaction, would have been highly intriguing for him. It is difficult to believe that the Pardoner, just arrived in England after a long journey from Rome, would at once make the leisurely trip to Canterbury for the pleasure of a vacation. Neither are sincere devotion and desire for social approval plausible reasons for his going on the pilgrimage. Perhaps an immediate return to labors among his usual peasant victims would have brought the Pardoner more money, but his vanity and his urge "to get even with the world" would thus have been satisfied to a lesser degree than by success among the Pilgrims. In his mind, the time had come for him to advance another rung on the ladder of success.

In that light, the actions of the Pardoner mentioned in his portrait need not be dismissed simply as "broadly comic" or coolly impudent.[3] Chaucer clearly intends these actions "to be arresting," and to the Pilgrims the Pardoner's behavior must have ap-

[3] Sedgewick, 443–44.

peared shockingly different from that expected of an individual having the power of confession, no matter how widespread such abuses were.[4] But this irregular behavior by the Pardoner may have a purpose behind it, for he is not the man for aimless joking. It seems to me that the Pardoner's joining with the Summoner in a lewd secular song and his aping of the newest fashions represent his effort to test the reactions of his newly met companions from whom he had earlier decided to attempt to extract money. The big problem for him is what approach he shall employ to accomplish his end. There is, however, no necessity for his choosing his tactics at once. He will be associated with this group of people, his possible victims, for several days. Also, the Host, a man in whom the Pardoner is later to be vitally interested, has not yet become the center of attention with his proposal for the storytelling game. When this proposal is made, the Pardoner is certainly not the one to offer objections, for the storytelling presents him with the opportunity he seeks of employing his oratorical wiles before the Pilgrims.

After the General Prologue, the reader catches no further glimpse of the Pardoner until his interruption of the Wife of Bath. One imagines, however, that the Pardoner is relieved at not being called on to perform early in the game, for he now has plenty of time during the earlier tales to look about him, observing his companions closely and deciding tentatively just what methods he will use in his effort to extract money from them when his turn comes to speak. When the Wife takes the center of the stage and begins her autobiographical performance, the Pardoner, still undecided about his tactics, is probably all attention, for he recognizes a kindred spirit in the Wife and catches from her what he considers a hint as to how he can most easily accomplish his purpose when his time comes.

The Wife first regales her audience for 162 lines with arguments concerning chastity and marriage. From her speech the Pardoner realizes that here is a person who considers herself outside the governance of the usual moral laws controlling marriage

[4] Bowden, *Commentary*, 277–83.

and the sexual relationship, and who is by no means afraid of defending her position. At once the Pardoner grasps the similarity between the Wife's position with regard to marriage and his own position with regard to religion. Both are unashamedly beyond the rules by which the mass of people are governed; and each is a rebel within his sphere of human behavior.

As a result of this realization, the Pardoner is intensely interested in the reaction of the other Pilgrims to what the Wife is saying. Long before she had taken the center of the stage, while the earlier stories were in progress, the shrewd Pardoner had ample opportunity to note that many of his companions were filled with pretensions of a sort not unusual among middle-class people. Exempting for the sake of argument the truly devout members of the company, the Pardoner still saw a considerable number of individuals whose human failings were fairly marked. And, as the Wife vehemently advances her unorthodox views on the question of marriage, a question not totally unrelated to the Pardoner's closer connection with religious doctrine, it becomes apparent to him, whose previous success has resulted from his exploitation of human failings, that the most noticeable of the not unusual human failings evident in the Wife's listeners is an assuming of the "man-of-the-world" attitude toward her arguments. It is noteworthy, it seems to me, that not even the genuinely devout among the Pilgrims enter any objection to the rebellion against established morality which the Wife is preaching. Thus, as the Wife talked, the Pardoner might well have said to himself: "See how she is getting away with it; not a one of them who isn't swallowing it all." For one may easily assume that the reaction of each of the Wife's listeners—again perhaps exempting the really pious—is, in effect: "Of course, what she is saying would not do for the masses; but I am a sophisticated person, a traveler. I have seen something of the world, and I know that not everything is as one reads in the Bible or hears in church. Anyway, she is a remarkably interesting person." And who is it among the Pilgrims that is characterized to the highest degree by this affected sophistication? The Host, Harry Bailly, guide and governor for the group, who in his dealings with various Pilgrims has shown himself at times annoyingly pompous, in love with authority, convinced of his ability to handle people, and smug about his judgment as a literary critic.

It may well be, then, that the Pardoner here tentatively decides, first, that when his turn comes he can best accomplish his desired end of extracting money from his companions by an appeal to their affectation of worldliness in regard to accepted moral laws, and, second, that the Host, already bested by various Pilgrims, is probably his most likely victim. Since the Pardoner is to operate in a group more complex than his usual peasant groups, he determines to test his tentative decision by an interruption of the Wife's speech (III, 163–68), in which he protests indirectly against the doctrine she has advanced. She has just said that no matter what the clerics preach she will not be chaste; her husband shall be both her debtor and her thrall and shall have his tribulation "upon his flessh." It has been noted elsewhere that the Pardoner, an expert professional speaker, interrupts the Wife fittingly "at the conclusion of one of her numerous little homilies."[5] He directs attention to her as a "noble prechour in this cas"; the "cas" is her divergence from established behavior in marriage, and he himself is a noble preacher in a similarly divergent "cas," the matter of confession and pardon. Having emphasized for the attentive Pilgrims the Wife's pronounced divergence from established behavior, he proceeds to protest against this divergence by concrete personal application. He says: "I was about to take a wife, but your alarming description of married life has dissuaded me." This statement is directly pointed towards testing the depth of the worldliness affected by the listening Pilgrims. Had the others rallied to the support of his objection, the Pardoner would no doubt have decided that the tactics he had tentatively selected for use when his turn arrived would have to be abandoned for some likelier plan.

One critic has explained the seeming inconsistency between the Pardoner's physical handicap and his talk of his imminent marriage as an attempt to conceal his physical condition from the other Pilgrims.[6] But the Pardoner was not so foolish as to think that anyone present had doubts about his physical state, which the Narrator correctly guessed at first glance (I, 691). Nor

[5] Sedgewick, 445.   [6] Curry, *Sciences*, 68–70.

do I think that his putting himself forward as a bridegroom-to-be is mere"jocosity" and shameless impudence. As is clearly evident in his quarrel with the Host at the end of his tale, he resents having attention called to his physical lack, and would resort to such a device only for a purpose very important to him. Whatever "japes" he indulged in were for the purpose of deception which would bring him profits (I, 701–706), and his assuming the role of prospective bridegroom when he interrupts the Wife is his amazingly shrewd method of pointing to her as a breaker of established rules for behavior in marriage. Thereby he is able to determine the reaction of her listeners.

As already pointed out, not a single one of the Pilgrims joins in the Pardoner's protest against the Wife. She realizes the implications of his words and slyly attacks him on the score of his fondness for drink. Then she promises that her future remarks will reveal even more clearly the tribulations of a husband (III, 169–83). So far, the Pardoner has the answer he seeks: the worldliness which the Pilgrims affect is deep enough to allow them to accept without remonstrance the unorthodoxy which the Wife preaches. Thus, he is about ready to conclude that these same Pilgrims will not remonstrate vigorously against his own scurrilous activities if he skillfully appeals to their feigned sophistication. Remembering, however, that he is among a new element, he wants to assure himself fully before deciding finally on the tactics he will employ when his turn comes. Therefore, he tests the Pilgrims' reaction for the second time by a pretense of meekness which points even more forcibly than his earlier comment to the Wife as a rebel against accepted standards of behavior:

> Dame, I wolde praye yow, if youre wyl it were,
> ... as ye bigan,
> Telle forth youre tale, spareth for no man,
> And teche us yonge men of youre praktike.   III, 184–87

Here the Pardoner, as one of "us yonge men," presents the Wife to the Pilgrims as an older and experienced person who is misleading inexperienced youths with a dangerously unorthodox view of marriage. He as much as invites the Pilgrims to object by his "spareth for no man," and specifically calls attention to the nature of the Wife's arguments and actions by terming them "youre praktike." "Praktike" here means "immoral or dishonest dealing" rather than "customary methods." Furthermore, there is an inviting tone of ironical satire against the Wife and himself in the request that the Wife teach "us young men." But still not one of the Pilgrims suggests that the Wife should cease her shocking revelations. Therefore, the Pardoner concludes that the worldliness which the Pilgrims affect is thick enough to bear the revelation of his own gross tricks in an autobiographical confession similar to that of the Wife, another moral transgressor. He has now reached a final decision concerning the approach he will use, and it is perhaps not too farfetched to imagine him, after his interruption of the Wife, as impatient for his turn and saying under his breath: "Well, Madam, you can pat yourself on the back for your success in taking in these would-be worldly ones, but I will show you how it really should be done." Meanwhile, he casts his eye hungrily on the Host's purse.

The Pardoner's impatience is not soon satisfied, for he has to wait a considerable time before the Host calls upon him to perform. In the interval he has seen no reason to change the decision reached during the Wife of Bath's Prologue; in fact, he has had reason to become more confirmed in his early opinion that the Host is his most likely victim, for Harry's assumed sophistication has become even more evident. Now, in calling upon the Pardoner for a tale to drive away the pity he feels for Virginia, Harry uses a phrase carrying a leer and a pretense to a knowledge of French (VI, 318–19).

The Pardoner, who has waited long for this moment, replies with an immediacy so emphatic as to require more explanation than that it arises from "eager zest." He has carefully developed and tested his plan of attack, and is now fully prepared to go to work (VI, 320–22). As has been pointed out, there is in the first line of this speech "a hint of return thrust . . . in the Pardoner's echoing" of the "dubious saint" to whom Harry referred in praising the Physician.[7] The echoing is more than a hint of a thrust, I think; it is the first individual probing by the Pardoner of the Pilgrim he has picked as his most likely victim. Then, in the two

[7] Sedgewick, 447.

succeeding lines, the Pardoner demands that a halt be called in the pilgrimage so that he can have a drink and eat a cake. But the "gentils" have noted carefully the far-from-admirable traits which the Pardoner has been at no pains to hide since his first appearance, and, assuming that if such a person starts drinking he will surely tell some "ribaudye," they object to the halt for refreshments and demand "som moral thyng." The Pardoner quickly agrees to their demand, even implying in his "I graunte, ywis" (VI, 327) that they are foolish to expect other than doctrinal material from him; but he insists upon the halt. Shrewdly he inserts the idea of a bargain with the Pilgrims—"I will give you moral material if you agree to halt here"—and supports the bargain idea with a justification of the drink—it will give him time to recollect "som honest thyng"—in order to win his point.

A great deal of ink has been mixed into this draft of ale which the Pardoner demands. A usual explanation is that it is simply another touch in Chaucer's portrait of a thoroughly abandoned character who must have a drink at this point and who becomes so drunk from this one drink of ale that his later boasting confessions are to be explained thereby.[8] But the request for a drink was not then a certain indication that one was a drunkard, especially if the drink was needed to wash down a cake. Nor could the one drink result in extended intoxication. A more plausible suggestion is that the Pardoner needs a few moments to think before he can tell some moral piece creditably.[9] However, as has been indicated, it seems to me that the Pardoner long ago decided on his general plan and needs no moment's grace before beginning his speech. Thus a better explanation here is that the Pardoner first suggests the halt for refreshments and then, after the objection by the "gentils," shrewdly bargains to win agreement to that halt in order to get the Pilgrims into a group so that he can fix them with his eye and generally put on his performance with the greatest possible effect. He knew, as any experienced public speaker would have known, that most of his coming words would be lost if delivered under the casual and disrupting circumstances of traveling. To avoid that unhappy situation, he

[8] See, for example, the article by Swart cited in n. 1 of this section.
[9] Sedgewick, 447–48.

suggests, and then insists successfully upon, a halt. The Pardoner delivers his prologue and tale to a group which has halted and assembled.

This view, which approaches that advanced by a number of preceding writers, is almost what Professor Sedgewick calls "The Tavern Heresy." Although he is particularly opposed only to the view that the Pardoner's Prologue and Tale were delivered inside a tavern, he holds it "at least possible that, after a pause to suit the Pardoner's convenience, the Pilgrims rode on, their entertainer talking to the usual accompaniment of hooves and harness." To me, a pause to suit the convenience of so experienced a public speaker as the Pardoner would end only when he had finished his speech and the noise of the hooves and harness could no longer distract his audience or him. I consider the Pardoner not an "entertainer" but rather a man with definite business to accomplish, for whom an assembled audience was a necessity worth insisting upon and bargaining for. Four passages are relevant to the question, two of them in the Introduction to the Pardoner's Tale:

> . . . heere at this ale-stake
> I wol bothe drynke, and eten of a cake.   VI, 321–22

> . . . but I moot thynke
> Upon som honest thyng while that I drynke.
> VI, 327–28

One occurs in the Pardoner's Prologue:

> Now have I dronke a draughte of corny ale.   VI, 456

and one at the end of the Pardoner's Tale:

> Anon they kiste, and ryden forth hir weye.   VI, 968

The assumption that the Pardoner kept his audience halted and assembled before him throughout puts no strain upon the text.

It may well be that the "moral thyng," which the "gentils" so emphatically demanded, gives the Pardoner an important additional detail for the plan he proposes to follow in his speech, in that it suggests to him that his appeal will be much stronger if he can include a definite undertone of convincing morality within

[211

the self-revelatory harangue with which he plans to lead up to his attempted sale. How skillfully he accomplishes this combination will be indicated in the discussion which follows.

Having succeeded in halting the pilgrimage and in arranging his audience so that the fullest effect can result from his speech, the Pardoner delivers 133 lines in which he frankly and boastingly reveals his methods of extracting money from peasants (VI, 329–462). It is one of my chief contentions that these 133 lines, together with the tale that follows, are accompanied by an extremely important overtone of meaning and implication whereby the Pardoner says, in effect, to the Pilgrims: "You are sophisticated citizens of the world; you know that things cannot always be as they seem. Therefore, you will enjoy a detailed recital of the tricks I use when I am at work among ignorant peasants." The Pardoner fully intends as flattering his invitation to the Pilgrims to join with him in laughing at the gullibility of peasants. It will be recalled from the portrait in the General Prologue that "feyned flaterye" is one of the two specific methods at which the Pardoner is expert (I, 705). Also, he clearly refers in two instances (VI, 392, 437) to his usual victims as "lewd peple." The Pardoner's hope is that his acceptance of the Pilgrims into his confidence, added to the admiration for his shrewdness which the revealing of his tricks will arouse, will cause many of his listeners to desire the convenient absolution which he can sell them.

Another idea which the Pardoner may well have in mind is that frequent reference to his interest in money and to his past successes in making it will be a sure way of arousing admiration for him among such people as many of the Pilgrims are. Certainly he lays great stress on this matter (VI, 389–90, 400–406, 434–35, 439–53, 461), and such an intention would fall in neatly with his larger purpose of appealing to the pretended sophistication of his listeners. Even the Narrator sounds somewhat impressed by the Pardoner's financial success (I, 701–704).

Alongside this flattering appeal to the worldliness which the Pilgrims affect, the Pardoner carefully includes one other line of thought in his prologue. This secondary approach, artfully built into his prologue by means of several brief "defenses," can be stated as follows: "I am telling you frankly that I am a vicious man who practices the very sin he preaches against. You, as citizens of the world, understand the necessity for such methods. Notice, however, that, despite my methods, the absolution which I am fully qualified to sell and which I induce many of my usual peasant listeners to buy is as efficacious as can be found anywhere." The rather illogical insertion of a statement of his theme, *"Radix malorum est Cupiditas,"* into his opening description of his platform tricks (VI, 333–34) seems to be an introductory effort toward establishing this idea. Somewhat later, having given an example of his preaching and having stated that he is completely motivated by avarice, the Pardoner uses the age-old defense, "Others do the same or worse." He says:

> For certes, many a predicacioun
> Comth ofte tyme of yvel entencioun;
> Som for pleasance of folk and flaterye,
> To been avaunced by ypocrisye,
> And som for veyne glorie, and som for hate.
>
> VI, 407–11

Shortly thereafter, as a part of a passage in which he restates his theme and purpose, he boldly declares that though he is himself avaricious, he can make other folk repentant for having practiced that sin (VI, 429–30). To drive home his point, he inserts his fourth defense just before the last lines of his prologue: "For though myself be a ful vicious man,/A moral tale yet I yow telle can" (VI, 459–60).

It may be argued that the Pardoner accomplishes in his prologue the combination of flattery with "defense" which I have attributed to him. At least, no one stops or interrupts his performance. That the Pardoner himself, not too sure of the reaction of his audience, fears being silenced at this point is indicated by the line with which he concludes his prologue: "Now hoold youre pees! my tale I wol bigynne."

The Pardoner rushes immediately into his tale, which falls into four divisions: the sermon (VI, 463–915), the benediction (VI, 915–18), the attempted sale (VI, 919–45), and the quarrel with the Host (VI, 946–68). The next-to-last line of the Prologue, in which the Pardoner describes the "moral tale" he plans to tell as one which he uses frequently when preaching to "wynne"—that is, before his peasant audiences—has an important transitional purpose. Through this line he points out to the Pilgrims that the part of his speech still to come will be, like that part just completed, a report on his sly methods among his usual audiences. Thus, he offers to the Pilgrims a continued opportunity to laugh with him at the ignorant peasants, and he carries over to his sermon the same flattery which lay beneath his prologue.

There has been considerable discussion stressing the apparent clumsiness with which Chaucer has put together in the Pardoner's sermon incongruous materials from different sources and failed to cover up the joints. This view is based on two assumptions: first, that the "riotoures thre" (VI, 661) are awkwardly introduced because previous mention had been made only of "a compaignye/Of yonge folk that haunteden folye" (VI, 463–64); and second, that the material included concerning sins other than avarice represents Chaucer's carelessness, for the Pardoner definitely states that his preaching is always directed against avarice alone. The second of these assumptions can, I think, be easily refuted by repeating Sedgewick's wise observation that the Pardoner preaches to make money, not to appear logical, and therefore includes a wide sweep of usual sins—gluttony, drunkenness, swearing, and gambling—along with avarice, in order to thrust at as many potential victims as possible. The first assumption demands lengthier consideration.

The art of storytelling and the psychology of audiences are matters at which the Pardoner is an expert of long standing. He has been asked for, and has promised to deliver, a "moral tale." When he does fulfill his promise, his story will be one in which the sinners are the Younger Generation, a situation which has immediate appeal for his predominantly middle-aged listeners. That tale of the search for Death by the three rioters is not, however, the matter with which the Pardoner is most concerned at the moment. He wishes to give first a thorough preachment against the usual sins. But he knows from long experience that audiences love "tales olde" and are quickly bored by sermons against sin. Therefore, he decides to hook his imaginary peasant audience, as well as his present listeners, by extending the narrative bait included in the opening lines describing the wicked company of young folk in Flanders (VI, 463–79). In any age, these lines would sound like the typical opening for a good story about some interesting sinners. Then, having thus caught the close interest of his audience, he inserts his exhortation against the sins (VI, 480–660) before seriously beginning his purely narrative material. He has thereby avoided the risk of losing the interest of his audience by opening immediately with his survey of the sins. The brevity of this section (only 180 lines) bears witness to the Pardoner's realization of the danger of boredom for his audience inherent in such material, as do the brief narrative interpolations and illustrations within it. The skill of the transition from his narrative opening into his sermon is another matter not to be overlooked (VI, 477–84). There is not even the pause which would arise from the end of a sentence between the two sections.

Furthermore—looking now at the end of the Pardoner's harangue against the sins and at his introduction of the three rioters—it is perhaps beside the point to demand that the narrative-opening concerning the company in Flanders have close connection with the three rioters. From the Pardoner's point of view, that opening is connected with the sermon, and has served its purpose well by assuring him of his audience's close attention to that material. For his tale of the three rioters he provides a new introductory device, which also serves to call back the attention of any listeners who may have become bored with even so short an attack upon the sins: "But, sires, now wol I telle forth my tale." And in the following line, with which he begins the story, he does not say: "These three rioters of whom I told earlier"; he says: "These three rioters of whom I [shall] tell now." The Pardoner, at least, makes no effort at this point to recall the narrative-opening describing the company in Flanders, which, so far as he is concerned, has already served its purpose. He is far more interested in establishing continuity between his preachment and the conclusion to his sermon (VI, 895–915), in which he vigorously summarizes the sins against which he has spoken and then gives an example of his usual sales talk. The story of the three rioters is adroitly sandwiched between these two sections. It may well be that neither of the two assumptions which have been made in support of a claim that Chaucer has failed to cover up the joints is valid.

Earlier it was maintained that the Pardoner skillfully and purposely combines in his prologue an appeal to the affected worldliness of some of the Pilgrims with the idea that, in spite of his evil methods, absolution from him is thoroughly efficacious. In his prologue the latter idea stood in the background. Now, in his sermon, the Pardoner reverses their positions in the minds of his listeners; he uses the appeal to the Pilgrims' assumed worldliness as background, and moves to the fore the implication of the worth of what he has to offer as confessor.

The suggestion was also made earlier that the Pardoner, by means of line 461, carries over from his prologue to his sermon the invitation to the Pilgrims to continue laughing with him at the gullibility of his peasant audiences. This invitation establishes the background from which the Pilgrims view the whole sermon as his continued report of how he performs among peasants. Within this background the Pardoner is trying during his sermon to replace, in the minds of his listeners, the imaginary peasant audience with his present audience, the Pilgrims themselves. He is trying to do this for the same reason that he inserted the four "defenses" in his prologue: to establish in their minds the value and convenience of the absolution which he can sell them. He is slowly but surely bringing them to a receptive attitude for the sale which he has had in mind from the beginning. It is for this reason that the tone of the whole sermon (VI, 463–915) is so noticeably more solemn and serious than the excerpt (VI, 352–89) from one of the Pardoner's typical performances given in his prologue. The moving solemnity of the *exemplum* of the three rioters, noted by almost all who have had anything to say about the Pardoner, is itself an effort in that direction. He is now preaching with the same purpose he has always had—to make money, not alone for the sake of the money itself, but for the satisfaction of outwitting these normal people who have come into the world without his handicap. It also bears repeating here that he is now putting on a "superperformance" in an effort to advance from peasant audiences to middle-class groups, such as the Pilgrims.

Several other and less important details support the contention that the Pardoner is now preaching directly to the Pilgrims. Note the repetition of the form of address "lordynges," used first in the opening line of the Pardoner's Prologue, later in the midst of the harangue (VI, 329, 573). Such a form of address would not be usual in speaking to peasants. There is also an especial directness about the rhetorical question near the end of the story proper: "What nedeth it to sermone of it moore?" (VI, 879). Finally, the rapidity of the transition from the sermon to the story proper suggests that a desire for full effectiveness upon the present audience has become more important than an invitation to that audience to laugh at an imaginary gullible peasant group. When the story proper is completed and the Pardoner passes immediately to the conclusion of his sermon, he fully intends the powerful summary of the sins and the sales appeal to have almost as much effect on the Pilgrims as it would have had on his humbler audiences. No critic has denied that the Pardoner succeeds in creating that effect, not only on his listeners, but on his (or his creator's) readers also.

The next section of the Pardoner's performance is his benediction, which is quoted in full:

> And lo, sires, thus I preche.
> And Jhesu Crist, that is oure soules leche,
> So graunte yow his pardoun to receyve,
> For that is best; I wol yow nat deceyve.   VI, 915–18

A great part of the discussion by earlier writers concerning the character of the Pardoner has hinged around these four lines. Everyone agrees that the "And lo, sires, thus I preche" ends the pretense that the Pardoner is addressing any other audience than the Pilgrims. Now the imaginary audience is gone. Kittredge took this benediction as evidence of a moment of sincerity in the Pardoner;[10] Curry considered it a "preparation for his proposed masterstroke of deception";[11] Carleton Brown saw it as merely

---

[10] *Atlantic Monthly*, LXXII (1893), 831–32. See also Robinson, *Works*, 837.
[11] Curry, *Sciences*, 66–67.

the expected grave ending to the sermon;[12] and Sedgewick believed it to be a traditional and sincere farewell.[13]

Most of the critics take the lines of the benediction as meaning something about as follows: "The pardon which I hope Jesus Christ will grant you is better than mine; I will not deceive you who are my friends, as I have deceived former audiences." But perhaps the lines do not mean that at all. The assumption that the Pardoner suggests, by saying "Christ's pardon is better than mine," that he holds a position similar to Christ's but has inferior wares seems to me rather illogical. All absolution came ultimately from Christ, no matter if His agent was pardoner, friar, parish priest, or any other qualified individual. It is also difficult to believe that the Pardoner, having just worked so hard to replace, in the minds of his listening Pilgrims, the imaginary peasant audience with themselves, would intentionally toss away that advantage by recalling to them his humbler victims. Perhaps the benediction is really an even better preparation for the coming attempted sale than Curry claimed. The line "And lo, sires, thus I preche," which serves as transition between the sermon and the benediction, need not mean primarily: "There, ladies and gentlemen, I have shown you how I outwit gullible peasants." Rather, it may be aimed more at calling the Pilgrims' attention in retrospect to the good which the Pardoner accomplishes among his usual peasant audiences and can accomplish, despite his evil methods, among his present listeners. It is his preaching which he mentions specifically, not his "skinning" the gullible, and he has earlier made quite clear that much worthwhile preaching comes from "yvel entencioun," and that folk do give up their sins because of his preaching. Thus, with this one line, the Pardoner causes the picture of the peasant audience to fade entirely from the minds of his listeners, and brings fully to the foreground the value of what he has to offer. To emphasize this idea and to complete the foundation for his coming attempt to sell, he delivers the next three lines, the kind of traditional and fitting ending for his sermon that the Pilgrims would expect. The seemingly sincere devotion implied by these last three lines increases greatly their effectiveness on the Pilgrims. The Pardoner

[12] *The Pardoner's Tale, xxiv–xxv.*   [13] *Loc. cit.,* 450–51.

mentions that Christ is the true physician of "oure soules," and expresses the wish that He will grant His best-of-all pardons to the Pilgrims. The implication which stands out boldly in this traditional, expected, devout, and apparently sincere wish is that the Pilgrims should win Christ's best-of-all pardons through the medium of His agent the Pardoner, who is not only thoroughly qualified and readily available, but is also a "good fellow," the kind of spiritual guide who can "understand" such sophisticated citizens of the world as are many of the Pilgrims. Then, as a last clinching blow in his preparation for the attempted sale, he assures his listeners in the most straightforward way—not by indirection as in his earlier comments—that there will be no chicanery to have an ill effect on the value of the absolution he can sell them: "I wol yow nat deceyve." Certainly, the futurity included in this statement indicates that the Pardoner hopes to have further dealings with his listeners.

We should now recall that, as long ago as his interruption of the Wife, the Pardoner may have selected the Host, as the member of the company most filled with certain pretensions, for his most likely victim. Further, Harry's position as "gyde," "governour," "juge," and "reportour" would have suggested him to the Pardoner as the wisest choice for his first potential victim; if Harry sought absolution from the Pardoner, there would be a not inconsiderable number of the other Pilgrims who probably would follow suit.

We come now to the Pardoner's attempted sale.[14] Having skillfully maneuvered the Pilgrims into what he justly considered a receptive mood, the Pardoner offers his wares. Up to this point, if one accepts the interpretation presented above, the Pardoner has been completely successful. The attempt is, however, not a success. It is true, of course, that to a certain extent "poetic justice" dictates to Chaucer that such an individual as the Par-

[14] Sedgewick considers the attempted sale and the quarrel as a unit, which he calls the "afterthought." It may be observed that to use this term is to beg the question of what the Pardoner had in mind. Here, as in Sedgewick's earlier similar begging of the question by use of the term "Tavern Heresy," the matter is open to dispute.

doner must come to grief. But that is not an explanation of how the Pardoner fails; it is merely a demand that the Pardoner's failure be interpreted in the light of his previous words and actions. It is necessary, therefore, to examine carefully the nature of the attempted sale and to point out in detail just where the Pardoner erred.

Following the benediction, he says that he has forgotten to mention one thing: he has his relics and pardons from the Pope's hand with him (VI, 919–22). Then he issues a general invitation to the whole group to come up and buy his pardons now, or to "taketh pardoun" while traveling "at every miles ende" (VI, 922–30). Next, he stresses his qualifications and the convenience to the Pilgrims of his presence—a good appeal, he thinks, to a would-be worldly audience (VI, 931–40). Finally, he specifically invites the Host "to offre first anon" (VI, 941–45).

What methods has Chaucer used here to bring about the Pardoner's failure? An explanation lies, I think, in the fact that the Pardoner foolishly breaks the spell which his sermon and benediction have cast upon the Pilgrims; reverting in this crucial moment to his habitual methods among peasants, he establishes an atmosphere too undignified to be at all flattering in its appeal to his listeners. Note how the opening line, "But, sires, o word forgat I in my tale," with its reference to the mechanics of his speech, dispels the serious and solemn effect resulting from the sermon and the benediction. Omit that line and the spell is not broken. Second, the general invitation to take pardon at every mile's end is too jocular for acceptance by the Pilgrims. It is doubtful that the Pardoner meant for his listeners to take this invitation literally, as numerous critics have done; but he would have had more chance of success if he had changed "al newe and fressh at every miles ende" to "whenever you wish." Third, the illustration suggesting a possible fatal fall from a horse, by which the Pardoner is trying to emphasize the convenience for the Pilgrims of his presence on the pilgrimage, is too implausible and macabre to please his audience. He should have omitted that illustration altogether (VI, 935–40), for the Pilgrims surely understood by now that his services were readily available. Fourth, the whole of the specific invitation to the Host is badly done. The tone of that invitation should have been sincere and devout rather than bantering. There is no reason for him to state why the Host has been selected to offer first (VI, 941). The suggestion of kissing the relics (VI, 944), implying gullibility and superstition, should have been omitted. Also, there should have been no direct mention of money in the invitation to the Host; high regard for a "grote" is one of Harry's predominant traits.

It is here that we see the Pardoner's unintentional self-revelation of his inadequacy as a salesman. Among ignorant peasants he is a master of the psychology of supersalesmanship; but among his companions on the pilgrimage he fails. Despite a brilliant performance in laying the foundation for his attempted sale, the Pardoner fails because he reverts at the crucial moment, perhaps through force of habit or overconfidence, or perhaps through nervousness caused by the importance success in this venture had assumed in his mind, to the same crude level of appeal which he was accustomed to employ in his sales talks among peasants. Certainly the similarity in tone and structure between his benediction and attempted sale to the Pilgrims (VI, 916–45), on the one hand, and his typical sales talk to a peasant audience (VI, 904–15), on the other, is striking. The key to the dramatic structure of the Pardoner's performance lies, I think, in this explanation of his failure.

The last glimpse of the Pardoner comes in his quarrel with the Host, which follows the frustrated sale. Here Harry looses a vigorous stream of abuse upon the Pardoner. It is noteworthy that Harry's first statement in support of his refusal to "offre" is a negation (VI, 948–50) of the true worth of the Pardoner's absolution, the idea which the Pardoner had suggested indirectly in his prologue and had brought to the fore in his sermon. Then Harry makes the sharpest possible counterattack by direct reference to the Pardoner's physical misfortune. The Pardoner is speechless with anger, and the Host refuses to "pleye" any longer with him. The Knight settles the quarrel and forces the Host to kiss the Pardoner. With peace restored, the members of the company regain their usual merriment and "riden forth hir weye."

One critic saw in the Pardoner's being speechless with anger after the Host's abuse an evidence of disgust with his own evil

Ydelnesse is roten slogardye

ways. Others have set forth the likelier explanation whereby the Pardoner is quite understandably speechless with anger because of the direct references to his being a eunuch. There is, in addition to this cause for his anger, the quick realization that his own bungling of the sale brought about the failure of his carefully laid and tested plan. By stupidly reverting to his habitual level of appeal, the Pardoner robbed himself of the satisfaction of outwitting the Pilgrims and thereby progressing to a class of victims higher than his usual peasant audiences.

20. THE SECOND NUN

The Second Nun receives only brief mention in the General Prologue. At the end of the Prioress' sketch come the lines: "Another Noone with hire hadde she,/That was hir chapeleyne, and preestes thre" (I, 163–64). A traveling prioress was required to have at least one nun in attendance, and the attendant nun usually served as chaplain or secretary.[1]

Whatever characteristics Chaucer might have decided to give the Second Nun had he completed the *Canterbury Tales*, it is doubtful that he could have assigned material more suitable for her to relate to the company of Pilgrims than the prologue and tale she delivers in Fragment VIII. Her prologue begins with four stanzas on idleness, which seem to be original with Chaucer; then come eight stanzas which form the Invocation to Mary "based primarily on St. Bernard's prayer at the beginning of Canto xxxiii of Dante's *Paradiso*." The last five stanzas of the prologue present etymological interpretations of Cecilia's name and come from the *Legenda Aurea*.[2] The Second Nun says that

[1] Eileen Power, *Medieval English Nunneries c. 1275 to 1535*, pp. 62–64; F. J. Furnivall, *Anglia*, IV (1881), 238–40.
[2] My summary of sources is based on the chapter by G. H. Gerould in *Sources and Analogues*, 664–84. See also Mary-Virginia Rosenfeld, *MLN*, LV (1940), 357–59; J. S. P. Tatlock, *MLN*, XLV (1930), 296–98.

[223

she has both "the wordes and sentence/Of hym that at the sein-
tes reverence/The storie wroot" (VIII, 81–83), and a rubric
found in two manuscripts suggests that Jacobus de Voragine is
the writer of the Legend of Saint Cecilia to whom the Second
Nun refers. However, as Professor Gerould has pointed out, in
our present state of ignorance about the manuscript history of
the *Legenda Aurea* we cannot be sure just what Chaucer's copy
of the *Golden Legend* contained.[3]

This last point has important meaning for our present concern
with the workings of Chaucer's dramatic principle. Almost without exception scholars have considered the Second Nun's Tale a
translation which Chaucer did long before he had the idea for
the *Canterbury Tales*, and which he later thrust into his collection without any effort to adapt it to its teller.[4] One point regularly cited in support of this view is that Chaucer is here translat-
ing very closely from the original; therefore, since we think that
he did a number of other close translations early in his writing
career, it is argued that the Second Nun's Tale must also be an
early work. But if, as Gerould stated, we cannot be sure about the
exact make-up of Chaucer's source in this case, then we cannot
say definitely that the Second Nun's Tale is a close translation;
thus one part of the argument for Chaucer's not having adapted
the tale to its teller appears premature.

There is, however, one other claim that is always advanced to
show that Chaucer did not prepare the Legend of Saint Cecilia
especially for the Second Nun to relate to the Pilgrims. In line
62 of her prologue the Second Nun calls herself "unworthy sone
of Eve," and therefore it is regularly assumed that Chaucer assigned the story first to a man. Several scholars have even suggested that "sone" meant Chaucer himself when he translated
the legend as a part of his earlier work and that he failed to make
the necessary revision when he assigned the tale to the Second
Nun. Recently, however, W. B. Gardner has shown—convincingly, I think—that the words "sone of Eve" are not inappropriate in the mouth of the Second Nun.[5] He says:

[3] *Sources and Analogues*, 670.
[4] See, for example, Robinson, *Works*, 15, 862.
[5] University of Texas *Studies in English*, XXVI (1947), 77–83.

When Chaucer had the Second Nun refer to herself as a "sone of Eve," he was merely using a word-pattern from the *Salve Regina* which he knew every Religious actually used every day of her life in reciting the Divine Office whether in Latin or English: "Hail, quene, modir of merci, oure liyf, oure swetnesse & oure hope, hail! to thee we crien, exciled sones of eue." The most natural thing in the world was to have the Second Nun at the height of her panegyric to the Virgin use a phrase taken from a prayer with which she was most familiar. . . . To have the Second Nun at the height of her impassioned prayer revert to a familiar word-pattern, change it from the plural to the singular, and refer to herself as "unworthy sone of Eve" is another example of Chaucer's genius for molding old matter into imperishably new forms.

It seems, then, that the "sone of Eve" may as easily mean "child of Eve," and therefore the second part of the charge that Chaucer did not adapt the tale to the Second Nun is also doubtful.

Turning to the positive side of the situation, we find that Chaucer fittingly assigned to the Second Nun not just any saint's life but the life of a female saint. Legouis enumerated several other details peculiar to this particular saint's life which suit it to a nun:

The impassioned eulogy to virginity preserved even after marriage, the ironical and half hysterical outburst of the saint before a kindly judge, the intemperate virtue and holiness depicted to us—all this becomes, as it were, the expression of the fanatic Nun, and ceases to have an imperative significance outside her. It is less the truthful account of the life of a saint than the truthful revelation, by means of this account, of the feelings of a nun and of the atmosphere which reigns in a monastery.[6]

While Legouis' statement may be somewhat exaggerated, it is nevertheless true that this particular saint's life is far better suited for recital by a nun than many another saint's life would have been. And there is no reason for us, perhaps too hastily, to deprive Chaucer of credit for bringing about this dramatic suitability.[7]

[6] Émile Legouis, *Geoffrey Chaucer* (English trans.), 185.
[7] See Gardner's article cited in n. 5 of this section(pp. 82–83); Sister Mary Hostia, *College English*, XIV (1953), 351–52.

That slidynge science hath me maad so bare

21. THE CANON'S YEOMAN

When the Second Nun completes her life of St. Cecilia, there occurs one of the liveliest events of the whole pilgrimage. Two additional travelers join the company: a canon, who is an alchemist, and his yeoman, or servant. The resulting performance, which has been the subject of relatively little critical comment, is representative of Chaucer's art at its best, and no source has been discovered for either the Canon's Yeoman's autobiographical revelations or his tale proper.[1] Perhaps there is no reason to look farther than the contemporary scene as sufficient explanation for the presence of this material. Although the history of alchemy in the fourteenth century is far from clear, we do know that this "science" was widely practiced in England during Chaucer's time—in fact, strict laws prohibiting it were passed early in the fifteenth century—and there is even a record of a contemporary canon at Windsor, William Shuchirch, an alchemist, who has been named as a possible model for the canon in the Yeoman's story. These facts have led to various suggestions that Chaucer, as an afterthought, included the Canon's Yeoman's performance in the *Canterbury* collection as a satirical exposé of all alchemy, or as an attack on false alchemists and a defense of true practitioners of this science, because he was himself fleeced by Shuchirch when he invested money in a similar get-rich-quick scheme.[2]

Such speculations seem to me very tenuous, however, for there is no particular reason to believe that Chaucer did not plan the addition of the Canon and his Yeoman to the group from the time

[1] See the chapter by J. W. Spargo in *Sources and Analogues*, 685–94.

[2] Thomas Tyrwhitt, *Canterbury Tales*, IV, 181; H. G. Richardson, *Transactions of the Royal Historical Society*, Ser. 4, V (1922), 38–39; S. F. Damon, *PMLA*, XXXIX (1924), 782–88; Manly, *New Light*, 235–52.

he hit upon his general scheme for the *Tales*;[3] and the argument that *Pars Secunda* must have been written for another purpose before the Yeoman was created, and then poorly adapted to him,[4] is completely unconvincing. This argument rests on two suppositions. First, it is maintained that lines VIII, 992–1011 could be appropriately addressed only to a group of canons, of which there are none among the Canterbury company. But, as one commentator has observed,[5] these lines do not seem incongruous when viewed as a rhetorical device employed by the Yeoman to emphasize the treachery of the canon in his tale, and such a device is paralleled by the Physician's apostrophe to governesses and parents (VI, 72–104), and by the Nun's Priest's appeal to lords (VII, 3325–30). The second supposition is that the conclusion of this performance (VIII, 1388–1481) is, because of its learned nature, not acceptable as coming from an ignorant, impetuous, loquacious fool like the Yeoman. This contention is obviously dependent upon the estimate one makes of the Yeoman, and, as the most recent writer to treat the matter in detail has shown, the Yeoman is not elsewhere unacquainted with learned material.[6]

In any event, the chief necessity here is not to decide upon possible connections between the Canon's Yeoman's performance and Chaucer's biography, but to analyze the dramatic techniques which Chaucer employed in making this performance come alive. As usual, the central emphasis is steadily kept upon the character of the teller. The Canon's Yeoman's story of a treacherous alchemist inevitably fits into, and grows out of, the context provided by the dramatic antagonism that he feels against "this cursed craft" and its practitioners, in general, and against his master, in particular. Yet, by the difference between the major theme of his performance and the theme which he thinks he is emphasizing most strongly, the Yeoman unintentionally reveals more of his own state of mind than he intends. Even though he admits his own folly in continuing to work at alchemy, he seems to aim primarily at showing that alchemists are treacherous evil-

[3] G. L. Kittredge, *Transactions* of the Royal Society of Literature (London), XXX (1940), 87; O. F. Emerson, *PQ*, II (1923), 94–96.

[4] P. F. Baum, *MLN*, XL (1925), 152–54.

[5] Robinson, *Works*, 868.

[6] E. H. Duncan, *MP*, XXXVII (1939–40), 241–62.

doers who make dupes of poor innocents like himself, and little is said of the innocents' greed; but his autobiographical prologue and his narrative proper make more clearly evident the fact that anyone whose greed leads him into being victimized by alchemists is behaving in an exceedingly stupid manner. We shall now see in some detail how this disclosure is worked out.

First of all, note the skill with which Chaucer in the first twenty-seven lines builds up our interest in, and curiosity about, the two newcomers by having us view the fast-approaching Canon and his servant through the curious eyes of the Narrator as he rapidly observes each detail of their horses, baggage, and dress in an effort to decide just who and what they are. We follow this observation point by point until the Narrator concludes that the former must be "som chanoun" (VIII, 569–73). Our chief impression from these introductory lines is that the Canon and his Yeoman have had to flee pursuers, for the Canon is traveling light, and the Narrator dwells with pleasure, in his realistic, earthy description, upon the way the horses and men are sweating from hard riding.[7] But, in greeting the company, the Canon gives no hint of such flight. He explains the hard riding as the result of his desire to join such a "myrie compaignye," and his Yeoman supports this statement by remarking that the Canon "loveth daliaunce." The Host, ever eager to take advantage of an opportunity to increase the jollity of the trip, asks the Yeoman whether or not his master can tell a good tale or two. The Yeoman's answer is emphatically affirmative, but he quickly passes into his routine speech aimed at stirring up some alchemical business for the Canon. With confidential vagueness the Yeoman tells Harry that the Canon is a man of great skill, who can carry out large and important enterprises, a man from whose acquaintance Harry can profit; and, the Yeoman points out, the humility with which the Canon rides in this group should not lead Harry to underrate him.

The Host, though the first man to be interested in a profit, is impatient with such vague claims and bluntly asks whether the Canon is a cleric or what. The Yeoman continues in his previous vein and states that his master is much greater than any cleric,

[7] G. R. Coffman, *MLN*, LIX (1944), 269–71.

and, moving on to specific illustration for this point, says that the
Canon has secret skills that would enable him to turn the road
from here to Canterbury upside down and "pave it al of silver and
of gold." This extravagant assertion strains Harry's credulity,
for, in his experience, men who can command wealth dress the
part; therefore, he wants to know why the Canon's clothes are so
cheap, tattered, and dirty if he can afford better.

This question causes the Yeoman to change his tune completely, and in his answer we first glimpse his disturbed mental
state:

> Why? . . . wherto axe ye me?
> God help me so, for he shal nevere thee!
> (But I wol nat avowe that I seye,
> And therfore keepe it secree, I yow preye.)
> He is to wys, in feith, as I bileeve.
> That that is overdoon, it wol nat preeve
> Aright, as clerkes seyn; it is a vice.
> Wherfore in that I holde hym lewed and nyce.
> For whan a man hath over-greet a wit,
> Ful oft hym happeth to mysusen it.
> So dooth my lord, and that me greveth soore;
> God it amende! I kan sey yow namoore.
>
> VIII, 640–51

Obviously this yeoman is brimful of complaints against his
master, complaints which only his fear compels him to withhold.
But the Host is now sure that he has hit upon a source of good
fun, and, after flattering the Yeoman a bit, asks for further information: "Where dwelle ye, if it to telle be?" Throwing aside
all discretion, the Yeoman says that they have to hide in corners
and alleys like thieves. At once Harry is in full chase and quickly
attempts to draw more facts from the Yeoman by asking why his
face is so discolored. The latter proceeds to give details of his
work, and it becomes fully clear that the Canon is an alchemist.
The Yeoman's job has been to blow the fire, but always the experiments fail.

The Canon understandably does not like such talk and commands his servant to be silent. But the Host, delighted at the
progress of events, urges the Yeoman to take no notice of the

Canon's threats. Reassured by Harry's support, the Yeoman decides to rebel against the Canon's command. At this, the Canon "fledde awey for verray sorwe and shame." Now that he is firmly established in the center of the stage, the Yeoman promises to tell the company all that he knows about alchemy.

At the end of this introductory scene, we glimpse another important aspect of the Yeoman's state of mind (VIII, 708–19). Here we see that he is pulled by two opposing forces: he is disgusted with himself for being connected with such a bootless game as alchemy (VIII, 710); yet it holds such fascination for him that he cannot give it up (VIII, 712–14). But he does not want to accept full responsibility for his situation; in fact, he blames the alchemist who first brought him into this work (VIII, 708–709). The opposing forces have built up considerable tension within the Yeoman, tension which causes him to undertake this rebellion against his master; and the two parts of his performance can best be regarded as his method of resolving the inner conflict and releasing this tension.

In *Prima Pars* the Yeoman shows the complete hopelessness of achieving the alchemical goal and the consequent folly of staying in that game. In this autobiographical confession he combines personal details and reactions (VIII, 720–49, 830–51, 862–97, 962–71) with a chronological account of a notable failure to "multiplie" (VIII, 750–829, 852–61, 898–961). He makes easily apparent his own gullibility and seems to feel himself therefore less blameworthy than his audience may have earlier considered him. He also includes another reference to the bittersweet fascination which alchemy holds (VIII, 877–83). Consequently, by the time he reaches the end of *Prima Pars*, he is able to suggest that the blame in the chicanery he has just described should be attached not at all to him but to his lord, the Canon, who was, of course, the master of ceremonies for the experiment (VIII, 960–71). In fact, the Yeoman claims here that the Canon—who seemed wisest and truest—is in the last analysis a fool and a thief. But, most certainly, someone among the Canterbury Pilgrims must have thought to himself at this point that the Yeoman is the greater fool and an equal thief for continuing to take part in alchemical experiments.

[231

Pars Secunda, the Yeoman's Tale proper, illustrates further the perfidy of alchemists. Here a canon who, the Yeoman says, knows a hundred times more "subtiltee" than the Canon whom we saw momentarily on the pilgrimage (VIII, 1088–92), dupes a priest. The Yeoman's sympathy is wholly with the priest; he heaps an inordinate amount of invective upon the alchemist, with but slight mention of the priest's stupidity and avariciousness. Actually, however, the priest well deserves the treachery he receives. This priest is an "annueleer" who has lived in London for many years, and who is "so plesaunt and so servysable" to the woman with whom he boards that she does not charge him for his meals and clothes, and presumably furnishes him with sufficient "spendyng silver" (VIII, 1012–18). But the Yeoman, who sounds a bit envious of the cleric's situation, does not want to direct attention to the priest's shallowness and greed; he therefore says quickly: "Therof no fors" (VIII, 1019). The point, of course, is that the Yeoman is trying to impress the company with the evil represented by the canon, hoping thereby to shift attention from his own greed, which certainly matches that of the duped priest. We find little difficulty, however, in seeing the Yeoman and the priest as rogues potentially equal to the two canons.

In the last section of his performance (VIII, 1388–1481), the Canon's Yeoman rises to a climax in denouncing alchemy. "Multiplying" is the cause of great scarcity of gold; philosophers are so vague that no alchemist will ever be successful in discovering their secret. "This lusty game" makes men unhappy and poor, and all who meddle with alchemy should at once leave it. To prove these points the Yeoman says: "I wol yow tellen heere/ What philosophres seyn in this mateere." He then quotes Arnoldus de Villa Nova and Hermes Trismegistus and tells a story involving Plato, to show that the secret of the philosophers' stone cannot be discovered.

The Yeoman's familiarity here with learned material does not fit the conception of him, held by a number of critics,[8] as an ignorant, garrulous fool who on the pilgrimage holds the center of the stage for the first time in his life, and enjoys pouring forth

[8] See, for example, Manly, *New Light*, 239.

helter-skelter, without understanding them, the tags of alchemical knowledge which he has managed to pick up. As a matter of
fact, the technical talk of alchemy in *Prima Pars* is well organized and shows considerable understanding of the accepted steps
in the process.[9] Also, the Yeoman's entire performance follows a
careful pattern aimed at shifting the responsibility for his own
connection with alchemy. He is not at all the unschooled dolt
some commentators have made him out.

His performance concludes with the following lines:

> Thanne conclude I thus, sith that God of hevene
> Ne wil nat that the philosophres nevene
> How that a man shal come unto this stoon,
> I rede, as for the beste, lete it goon.
> For whoso maketh God his adversarie,
> As for to werken any thyng in contrarie
> Of his wil, certes, never shal he thryve,
> Thogh that he multiplie terme of his lyve.
> And there a poynt; for ended is my tale.
> God sende every trewe man boote of his bale! Amen.
>
> VIII, 1472–81

When we think back over the Yeoman's whole recital, this passage has a definitely uncalled-for moral smugness about it. The
Yeoman, who is not a "trewe man," has devoted his meager funds
and his constant labor to alchemy for at least seven years, and we
have had a sample of his usual method of enticing others into his
master's trap. Further, he has stated that the game so fascinates
him—presumably by its appeal to his greedy desire to get rich
quick—that he can never give it up. In addition, he has throughout his performance attempted to suggest a picture of himself as
the poor innocent led astray by him "that me broghte first unto
that game," and by his master, the Canon. The Yeoman is certainly a wonderfully entertaining fellow, who gives an excellent
performance for the Pilgrims, but a full estimate of his character
produces an individual torn between his awareness of the inevitable failure of the alchemical experiments, and his ever-present
greedy hope for success. His autobiographical confession and

---

[9] See the article by Duncan cited in n. 6 of this section.

Ay biforn and in good staat

illustrative tale represent his effort to clear himself of guilt, but Chaucer has skillfully manipulated him into revealing to the Pilgrims and to us more of his real character than he intends.

22. THE MANCIPLE

Although some critics find no indication that the tale of the talkative crow was written for the Manciple,[1] there is what seems to me good evidence here of Chaucer's usual concern for dramatic suitability.[2] In brief, the situation is this: the Manciple is given to dishonest dealings, of which the Cook is aware; by foolishly talking in such a way as to arouse the Cook's anger, he risks having his dishonesty made public by the Cook; he then tells a tale the theme of which "exalts expediency rather than morality." Thus not only is the tale a suitable one for its teller in this situation, but it also functions dramatically as a part of the Manciple's effort to smooth over his quarrel with the Cook.

From the sketch in the General Prologue (I, 567–86) we learn that the Manciple works in one of the Inns of Court in London. His job is probably "to stock the buttery; to attend the cook; to examine and keep account of the meat bought, and to see that there was no waste of it; to collect money from the lawyers and students who ate in Commons."[3] Furthermore, we have the individualizing fact that this particular Manciple makes money dishonestly by "padding" his accounts; in fact, he "sets the caps" of all his more than thirty masters, even though a dozen of them are capable of managing the largest estate in England:

[1] For example, Robinson, *Works*, 16, 870.
[2] My treatment of the Manciple and his recital depends heavily upon the essay by J. B. Severs, *JEGP*, LI (1952), 1–16, which includes references to the earlier discussions. For a different view, see Wayne Shumaker, *UTQ*, XXII (1953), 147–56.
[3] Bowden, *Commentary*, 257.

> Now is nat that of God a ful fair grace
> That swich a lewed mannes wit shal pace
> The wisdom of an heep of lerned men?   I, 573–75

Since a manciple would have regular supervisory duties over a cook, and more particularly since a manciple in Chaucer's day would have had to buy his provisions from a cookshop, neither the Cook's knowledge of the Manciple's chicanery nor the antagonism between the Manciple and the Cook, which appears in the Manciple's Prologue (IX, 1–104), is difficult to accept.[4] In that prologue the Cook is so drunk that he cannot stay awake, keep up with the group, or sit his horse securely. The Host, who also has professional reasons for seeking any opportunity to ridicule the Cook, notices his condition, calls on him to tell a tale, and then jokes at his drunken sleepiness, even suggesting that he may have spent the night with "som quene." The Cook rallies enough to say that his only desire is to sleep. At this point, the Manciple steps in with mock courtesy and humility to inform the Cook that he will be glad to tell a tale in order to do him a service. But the Manciple goes on to berate the Cook roundly for having a breath which "stynketh," and for being ridiculously drunk. Such talk can easily give rise to anger.

The Cook is still sufficiently aware of what is going on to take offense at the Manciple's jibes. In anger he swings at the Manciple but topples ingloriously from his horse: "This was a fair chyvachee of a cook!" Now comes one of the funniest scenes in the *Canterbury Tales*, when the other Pilgrims labor mightily to get the drunken Cook out of the mire and back on his horse. After this has been accomplished, Harry Bailly apparently feels that it is time to restore order. He therefore states that the Cook is too drunk to tell a decent tale and instructs the Manciple to begin his story. But the Host cannot let pass this opportunity to reprove the Manciple for talking too much. He therefore says:

> But yet, Manciple, in feith thou art to nyce,
> Thus openly repreve hym of his vice.
> Another day he wole, peraventure,

[4] Frederick Tupper, *JEGP*, XIV (1915), 261–65.

236]

> Reclayme thee and brynge thee to lure;
> I meene, he speke wole of smale thynges,
> As for to pynchen at thy rekenynges.
> That were nat honest, if it cam to preef.   IX, 69–75

Harry knows that the Manciple overcharges the lawyers whom he serves, and the Host also is aware that the Cook knows this. Here is indeed a tightly knit group of city businessmen. The Manciple, quick to realize the folly of his talking so belligerently, claims that he berated the Cook in jest only. He takes further steps to make sure that he has not permanently estranged the Cook, and, to insure peace, offers him a drink of wine, though he remarks to Harry, presumably not in the Cook's hearing, that it will be a good joke to give the drunken Cook another drink. He very willingly takes the drink and, in perfect keeping with his present state of intoxication, seems to have forgotten completely his anger at the Manciple. After the drink he thanks the Manciple as if the latter were his one true friend. At this, Harry roars with laughter, lauds the efficacy of "good drynke," and asks the Manciple to tell his tale. The Manciple, having furnished a drink for the Cook, might well have felt that the latter's ire was adequately soothed. He seems desirous, however, of making clear to the company by means of his tale that he has learned a lesson, and that he will not in the future again run the risk of exposure because of excessive talk. Thus it is that he tells the story of the crow whose talking brings on misfortunes, and that he concludes his story with an unusually long section on the advantages of keeping one's mouth shut.

For the Manciple's little tale of Phebus and the crow that talks too much, we have no certain source. Chaucer could have used almost any Ovidian text for the story proper, and the material included in the several moralizing digressions which the Manciple inserts into the tale was common property in the Middle Ages.[5] When Phebus' wife is unfaithful while he is away, the crow tells his master of her act. In anger Phebus kills his wife, and in grief

[5] See Gardiner Stillwell, *PQ*, XIX (1940), 133–38; the chapter by J. A. Work in *Sources and Analogues*, 699–722; and the article by Severs cited in n. 2 of this section.

and remorse then turns upon the crow as treacherous informer. He makes the white crow black, deprives it of speech, and slings it out of the house.

Now comes the Manciple's lengthy concluding statement stressing the moral "Kepe wel thy tonge, and thenk upon the crowe." Apparently, the Manciple has told a story the theme of which can be aptly applied to his own near disaster from talking too much in the preceding argument with the Cook. By means of the tale the Manciple as much as says: "I have learned my lesson; not holding my tongue almost led to the Cook's exposing my business activities." The story thus plays an important part in the drama of the Cook-Manciple controversy. Also such a statement in praise of expediency comes naturally from a man steadily engaged in a war of wits with his master-lawyers.

Several other aspects of this performance deserve notice here. One critic observed: "The general theme of the 'Manciple's Tale' is suitable to its narrator. But the Greek setting, the rather learned rhetorical development, and the moral disquisition are completely incongruous with the dishonest Manciple."[6] This view, it seems to me, is greatly overstated. The "Greek setting" of the tale is almost nonexistent. True, the story is about Phebus, and a number of his exploits are mentioned. But the name of his wife is not included, and the whole is cast into the form of a late medieval fabliau of cuckoldry, with the addition of an unusual amount of trite, sententious comment. Certainly the Manciple is a suitable teller for a story of cuckolding. Furthermore, the digressive comment on the folly of jealously guarding wives, on the perversity of both animal and human natural desires, on the necessity for plain speech, and on the danger of talking too much does more to mar the rhetorical development of the narrative than to give it a learned air. In fact, the Manciple's learning—represented only by his naming Plato, Solomon, David, and Seneca, by his monitory tone, by his knowledge of this story, and by his references to the "olde clerkes" and their writings—is easily explained by his steady association with lawyers, as is his glib familiarity with the phrase "noght textueel" (IX, 235, 316). A man shrewd enough to keep his financial dealings hidden from more

[6] J. R. Hulbert, *SP*, XLV (1948), 576.

than thirty lawyers could easily pick up such matters as these without any studying at all. Also, the moral disquisition, as was suggested above, results understandably from the Manciple's effort to show the company that he realizes the error of his quarreling with the Cook.

At other points in the tale we find touches perfectly suited to the "lewed" Manciple. After citing the "ensaumples" of the bird, the cat, and the she-wolf, he illogically states that he is talking only of unfaithful men, "and nothyng by wommen" (IX, 188); yet this story is of an unfaithful wife. A few lines later he indulges in a kind of exaggerated gentility when he apologizes for saying the word "lemman" (IX, 205); if this word was generally considered shocking, the Middle English audience must have been shocked with great regularity. The point is that the story does not at all have the ring of a learned teller.

23. THE PARSON

The Parson's Tale, the last[1] and longest performance in the *Canterbury* collection, is a prose sermon on penitence, into which is inserted a lengthy treatise on the seven deadly sins. For this piece, no direct source has been found.[2] That such a sermon is suited to the admirable Parish Priest permits no argument, and we are able here to see clearly just how Chaucer fitted the tale into the framework of a dramatic antagonism, which exists between the Parson and the Host. In this antagonism the tale proper functions as a whole; its very nature accomplishes its purpose in the controversy.

The Parish Priest is, of course, Chaucer's most sympathetic pic-

---

[1] On the presence and position of the Parson's Tale in the *Canterbury* collection, see W. W. Lawrence, *Chaucer and the Canterbury Tales*, chap. vi.

[2] See the chapter by Germaine Dempster in *Sources and Analogues*, 723–60.

ture of a contemporary churchman (I, 477–528). There has been extensive discussion, based in part on this sketch, as to whether or not Chaucer was a Wycliffite, and as to the extent to which he was familiar with, and sympathetic towards, the Lollard reforms widely urged during the late fourteenth century. Although this argument ranges from the claim that Chaucer's Parson is Wycliffe to the opinion that Chaucer was almost completely untouched by the religious ferment of his day, the point at issue is not of fundamental importance here. For us, the interesting aspect of the sketch is that in the character of the Parson strict observance of his duties as priest is blended with kindly tolerance and understanding. Though properly poor in material wealth, he is rich in holy thoughts and works. His wide learning he uses in devoutly teaching his parishioners, and no obstacle keeps him from visiting the most distant houses in his wide parish, "Upon his feet, and in his hand a staf," no matter whether the person visited is rich or poor. He believes firmly in setting a good example for his flock by his own actions and does not rent out his parish in order to live luxuriously in London, for "He was a shepherde and noght a mercenarie." Corruption seems to have been generally present throughout the fourteenth-century Church, but one may feel fairly confident that this parson's vigorous and exemplary devotion to duty prevented its flourishing in his parish.

Somewhat surprisingly, the Parson's absolute seriousness about his work is accompanied by unusual generosity, patience, tolerance, and humility. In an era when most parish priests seemed primarily interested in the financial benefits to be gained from their positions, the Parson is very hesitant to excommunicate his parishioners for nonpayment of tithes; instead, realizing the hard lot of the peasants who make up his flock, he often gives them a part of his own income, for "He koude in litel thyng have suffisaunce." And in times of trouble he is noted for his patient suffering. Despite his personal holiness and virtue, he does not treat sinners scornfully or speak to them in severe and haughty tones. Nor does he pretend to an overly refined conscience. On the contrary, in his handling of sinners he shows extreme consideration, in an effort to lead them by his own example to a better way

First he wroghte, and afterward he taughte

of life. Yet the Parson is no weakling when occasion demands forcefulness:

> But it were any persone obstinat,
> What so he were, of heigh or lough estat,
> Hym wolde he snybben sharply for the nonys.
>
> I, 521–23

He exhibits no trace of subservience when dealing with the rich and mighty; "But Cristes loore and his apostles twelve/He taughte, but first he folwed it hymselve." Truly the Parson's combination of active devotion with kindly tolerance merits Chaucer's emphatic statement: "A bettre preest I trowe that nowher noon ys."

Although he must not have been particularly pleased with the performances of the Miller, the Reeve, and the Cook, we hear nothing from the Parson until the Host addresses him after the Lawyer's Tale. With what seems a deliberate effort to provoke him to anger, Harry says:

> Sir Parisshe Prest, . . . for Goddes bones,
> Telle us a tale, as was thi forward yore.
> I se wel that ye lerned men in lore
> Can moche good, by Goddes dignitee!   II, 1166–69

But the Parson is too wise and experienced to furnish the Host the satisfaction of seeing him moved to anger by either his blasphemy or condescension. Instead of lecturing briskly, he briefly and skillfully throws the conversational ball back to Harry by wryly inquiring of the company at large: *"Benedicte!*/What eyleth the man, so synfully to swere?" The Host now feels that he must press on with his attack in order to stir the Parson to entertaining controversy. He therefore proclaims to the group that they shall now hear a sermon, for "This Lollere heer wil prechen us somwhat." Again the Parson refuses to rise to the bait, even though he has been called a Lollard. Instead—and probably to the Host's annoyance—the Shipman breaks in to say that he will tell a merry tale himself. The Parson-Host controversy has been set up by this scene, with the Parson winning the first round, and, although further exchange is postponed by the Shipman's intervention, neither is ready to let the matter drop. The company, however, must wait until the final performance on the pilgrimage to see the outcome of this antagonism.

When the Manciple completes his tale of the crow, the Narrator notices that the time is four in the afternoon. The Host, as manager of the group, points out that there is only one more tale to be told, and he prays that God will be good to the Pilgrim who tells the last tale. In the next line we learn, as Harry already knows, that this last teller is to be the Parson. Note that the Host, by asking God's blessing on the Parson, has completely changed his tune from the blasphemous approach he used in addressing him earlier. We assume that perhaps Harry has profited by his experience and is unwilling to risk being bested again. But immediately he reverts to the same kind of large condescension and blasphemy that characterized his earlier approach (X, 22–29). The only explanation I can see for his shift from a mild opening to his former discourtesy towards the Parson is that he suddenly decides that he has him just where he wants him: it is four o'clock in the afternoon and the journey is almost over; neither the late hour nor the probable impatience of the company to arrive at its destination favors the Parson's delivering a lengthy sermon. Harry takes further precaution against a sermon by his suggestion that the Parson tell an entertaining narrative. But "Juge" Bailly has badly misjudged the character of the Parson.

Although he could accept with tolerant good humor the Host's earlier condescension and blasphemy, the Parson feels that Harry has gone too far in suggesting that he tell a "fable." He therefore answers with noticeable immediacy—"al atones:"

> Thou getest fable noon ytoold for me;
> For Paul, that writeth unto Thymothee,
> Repreveth hem that weyven soothfastnesse,
> And tellen fables and swich wrecchednesse.
> Why sholde I sowen draf out of my fest,
> Whan I may sowen whete, if that me lest?   X, 31–36

The Parson's anger at the Host rapidly vanishes, once he has delivered this emphatic statement of his point of view, and he courteously tells the company that if they wish to hear "moralitee and vertuous mateere" and if they promise to listen to him, he will be pleased to perform as best he can. But he has one further warning: he is a Southern man and cannot recite "rum, ram, ruf" in the manner of the Northern and West Midland alliterative verse; consequently, he will speak in prose.

With considerable shrewdness the Parson seems to have guessed the reason, mentioned above, for the shift in the Host's manner toward him, and is working hard to arrange for Harry's getting his just deserts. He therefore does his best to cause the company to accept him as the last performer, and also to keep the Host, as well as the other Pilgrims, from thinking that he will deliver a lengthy technical sermon (X, 45–60). Part of the Parson's clever strategy is that he here promises a "merry tale" with which he will conclude the storytelling. Also, he remarks that he will not "glose"; "glose" is a verb with many meanings, two of which are "to comment upon a text, usually religious" and "to flatter." Although I may be giving the Parson credit for too much subtlety, it seems to me that he expects the company to understand his parenthetical remark—"I wol nat glose"—as meaning "I will not comment at length on religious texts," whereas he himself enjoys taking it as the equivalent of "I will not flatter the Host by giving the brief performance he is trying to jockey me into." Moreover, the Parson knows that the company as a whole can hardly refuse, as did the Shipman earlier, to allow him to show them the way for that "parfit glorious pilgrymage," a particularly suitable topic for this benedictory performance. Too, his assurance that he is "nat textueel" is aimed at keeping the group from thinking that he will belabor them with hair-splitting religious material, and his comment that he is interested only in the "sentence" seems to promise brevity. Finally, the humility with which he puts himself under the correction of scholars serves to suggest that he can be halted if necessary.

The company rapidly instruct the Host to ask the Parson to tell his tale, for, as he expected, they feel that a performance by him is a suitable way of bringing the storytelling and the pilgrimage to a proper conclusion. Harry therefore wishes the Parson well and commands him to begin his "meditacioun"; then, in a final effort to ensure brevity, the Host continues:

> But hasteth yow, the sonne wole adoun;
> Beth fructuous, and that in litel space,
> And to do wel God sende yow his grace!
> Sey what yow list, and we wol gladly heere.   X, 70–73

Apparently the whole company shares this hope for brevity, for the Narrator tells us that the Host in this speech "hadde the wordes for us alle." But the way is now cleared for the Parson's revenge for the treatment he has received from Harry Bailly, revenge which takes the form of the extremely long sermon called the Parson's Tale. And the Shipman must also suffer for his discourtesy. Although all readers may not be convinced that there is "solas" as well as "sentence" in the Parson's "merry tale in prose," we can hardly avoid granting him our admiration for the skill with which he repays the Host for ill-mannered behavior.

CONCLUSION

The Dramatic Principle

I

t was stated in Part I that the analyses of the twenty-three performances which make up the body of the *Canterbury Tales* lead to the conclusion that within the structure of the book as a whole Chaucer employed a principle which includes three stages of dramatic development, or three techniques of dramatic presentation. By way of summary and conclusion, I shall now restate these three steps or techniques in tabular form and arrange the various performances in their proper categories, according to the interpretations set forth in Part III.

A. Simple suiting of tale and teller.
    The Second Nun
    The Squire
    The Prioress
    The Knight
    The Franklin
    The Physician
    The Sergeant of the Law
    The Shipman
    The Cook
B. Simple suiting of tale and teller, plus an externally motivated dramatic situation.
    The Manciple
    The Monk
    The Parson
    The Friar

> The Summoner
> The Miller
> The Reeve
> The Nun's Priest
> The Pilgrim Chaucer
> The Clerk

C. Simple suiting of tale and teller, plus an externally motivated dramatic situation, plus internally motivated and
extended self-revelation of which the teller is not fully
aware.

> The Merchant
> The Canon's Yeoman
> The Wife of Bath
> The Pardoner

Although there is some minor overlapping among and within
these three categories, such an arrangement represents an ascending order of complexity in the employment of the dramatic principle involving the relationship between tales and tellers. Thus,
in the first category, the Second Nun and the Squire have a single
predominant trait, and the story each tells fits with that trait;
the Prioress, the Knight, the Franklin, and the Physician are
presented in the General Prologue as characters with double
traits or interests, and their tales mirror both sides of their characters; then, in the cases of the Sergeant of the Law, the Shipman, and the Cook—the instances in which Chaucer's dramatic
intentions are least clear and, in my opinion, least effective—we
find some appropriateness of tales and tellers, and, in addition,
a hint of the kind of controversy present in the performances
which make up the other two categories.

In the second category the Monk and the Parson deliver material aimed at discomfiting the Host; the Manciple expediently
tries to smooth over his error in dealing with the Cook; the Friar-
Summoner and Miller-Reeve pairings represent open conflict;
the Nun's Priest slyly defends the Host; the Pilgrim Chaucer exposes the Host on two counts; and the Clerk delivers a surprise
burlesque of the Wife's views.

In the four performances making up the third category, the

Merchant's remarks about his unhappy married life are cautiously brief; the Canon's Yeoman is freer in his personal revelations; and the Wife of Bath and the Pardoner give unabashed, detailed pictures of their lives, both past and present.

This study of the principle which seems to control the dramatic interplay among the Canterbury Pilgrims leads to a further important conclusion concerning Chaucer's narrative artistry in the book. There can be no doubt, I think, that upon occasion Chaucer sacrifices absolute literary criteria in favor of dramatic decorum. In plainer words, Chaucer at times purposefully includes in the *Tales* a story not possessed of consistent literary merit because a tale lacking such merit is demanded by the dramatic context. The Parson's Tale is a good example of this. We are not to assume that Chaucer thought the Parson's sermon an excellent story, or that it is present only to represent a type of late medieval literature; rather, it has its part in the dramatic interplay. A similar example is the "Melibeus." Chaucer could hardly have considered this long didactic piece a literary gem simply because the fourteenth century seems to have been fonder of such material than we are. The point is that dramatic necessity called for a long didactic piece here, and Chaucer furnished the "Melibeus." The recitals by the Franklin, the Physician, and the Manciple are among other cases in point.

Thus, though certainly we must not read medieval literature wholly in modern terms, it does not follow necessarily that the *Canterbury Tales* can be most effectively read by limiting our perspective to the conventions which governed other storytellers than Chaucer in the fourteenth century, or that "modern" is the proper term for any alleged characteristic of the *Tales* not to be found in the writings of Chaucer's contemporaries. Neither extreme—disregard of those conventions, or disregard of all else—will serve satisfactorily; for the individual tellers and tales not only exemplify contemporary persons and storytelling, but are also fashioned for a larger purpose in accord with Chaucer's dramatic principle, a principle which contributes fundamentally to the lasting greatness of the *Canterbury Tales*.

Selected Bibliography

I. BIBLIOGRAPHIES

1908 Hammond, E. P. *Chaucer: A Bibliographical Manual.* New York, Macmillan.
1926 Griffith, D. D. *A Bibliography of Chaucer, 1908–24.* Seattle, University of Washington Press.
1935 Martin, W. E., Jr. *A Chaucer Bibliography, 1925–33.* Durham, Duke University Press.
1945 Wells, J. E. *A Manual of the Writings in Middle English, 1050–1400.* New Haven, Yale University Press, 1916. Nine supplements to this manual cover to December, 1945.

II. EDITIONS

1775–78 Tyrwhitt, Thomas. *Canterbury Tales.* 5 vols. London. Printed for T. Payne.
1894–97 Skeat, W. W. *The Complete Works of Geoffrey Chaucer.* Vols. IV, V. Oxford, Clarendon Press.
1928 Manly, J. M. *Canterbury Tales by Geoffrey Chaucer.* New York, Holt.
1933 Robinson, F. N. *Complete Works of Geoffrey Chaucer.* Boston, Houghton Mifflin.
1940 Manly, J. M. and Edith Rickert. *The Text of the Canterbury Tales.* 8 vols. Chicago, University of Chicago Press.

III. TRANSLATIONS

1912 Tatlock, J. S. P. and Percy MacKaye. *The Modern Reader's Chaucer.* New York, Macmillan.
1934 Nicolson, J. U. *Canterbury Tales.* New York, Garden City; a

complete poetic version except for "Melibeus" and the Parson's Tale, which are translated in prose.

1935 Hill, F. E. *The Canterbury Tales.* London, Longmans, Green.
1948 Lumiansky, R. M. *The Canterbury Tales.* New York, Simon and Schuster. Rev. trans., New York, Rinehart, 1954. The revised translation is a complete version in prose.
1949 Morrison, Theodore. *The Portable Chaucer.* New York, Viking.
1952 Coghill, Nevill. *The Canterbury Tales.* Baltimore, Penguin.

IV. CONCORDANCE

1927 Tatlock, J. S. P. and Arthur G. Kennedy. *A Concordance to the Complete Works of Geoffrey Chaucer and to the Romaunt of the Rose.* Carnegie Institution of Washington, D.C.

V. HISTORICAL AND ANALYTICAL STUDIES

Baldwin, C. S. "Cicero on Parnassus," *PMLA,* XLII (1927), 106–12.
Baugh, A. C. "The Original Teller of the Merchant's Tale," *MP,* XXXV (1937–38), 15–26.
Baum, P. F. "The Canon's Yeoman's Tale," *MLN,* XL (1925), 152–54.
———. "Characterization in the *Knight's Tale," MLN,* XLVI (1931), 302–304.
Beichner, P. E. "Chaucer's Man of Law and *Disparitas Cultus," Speculum,* XXIII (1948), 70–75.
Block, E. A. "Originality, Controlling Purpose, and Craftsmanship in Chaucer's *Man of Law's Tale," PMLA,* LXVIII (1953), 572–616.
Bowden, Muriel. *A Commentary on the General Prologue to the Canterbury Tales.* New York, Macmillan, 1948.
Braddy, Haldeen. "The Cook's Mormal and Its Cure," *MLQ,* VII (1947), 265–67.
Brennan, M. J. "Speaking of the Prioress," *MLQ,* X (1949), 451–57.
Bressie, Ramona. " 'A Governour Wily and Wys,' " *MLN,* LIV (1939), 477–90.
———. "Chaucer's Monk Again," *MLN,* LVI (1941), 161–62.
Bronson, Bertrand. "Chaucer's Art in Relation to His Audience," *Five Studies in Literature.* Berkeley, University of California Press, 1940, 1–53.
Brown, Carleton (ed.). *The Pardoner's Tale.* New York, Oxford University Press, 1935.
Browne, W. H. "Notes on Chaucer's Astrology," *MLN,* XXIII (1908), 53–54.

Brusendorff, Aage. *The Chaucer Tradition*. London, Oxford University Press, 1925.

Bryan, W. F. and Germaine Dempster (eds.). *Sources and Analogues of Chaucer's Canterbury Tales*. Chicago, University of Chicago Press, 1941.

Caldwell, R. A. "Chaucer's *Taillynge Ynough, Canterbury Tales,* B^2 1624," *MLN,* LV (1940), 262–65.

Camden, Carroll, Jr. "Query on Chaucer's Burgesses," *PQ,* VII (1928), 314–17.

Chute, Marchette. *Geoffrey Chaucer of England*. New York, Dutton, 1946.

Coffman, G. R. "Old Age from Horace to Chaucer. Some Literary Affinities and Adventures of an Idea," *Speculum,* IX (1934), 249–77.

———. "Canon's Yeoman's Prologue, G, ll. 563–566: Horse or Man," *MLN,* LIX (1944), 269–71.

Coghill, Nevill. *The Poet Chaucer*. London, Oxford University Press, 1949.

Coulton, G. G. *Five Centuries of Religion*. 3 vols. Cambridge, Cambridge University Press, 1923–36.

———. *Medieval Panorama*. New York, Macmillan, 1938.

———. *Chaucer and His England*. 7th ed. London, Methuen, 1946.

Cowling, G. H. *Chaucer*. London, Methuen, 1927.

Cummings, H. M. *The Indebtedness of Chaucer's Works to the Italian Works of Boccaccio*. University of Cincinnati *Studies,* No. 10, Part 2 (1916).

Cunningham, J. V. "The Literary Form of the Prologue to the Canterbury Tales," *MP,* XLIX (1951–52), 172–81.

Curry, W. C. *The Middle English Ideal of Beauty*. Baltimore, Furst, 1916.

———. *Chaucer and the Mediaeval Sciences*. New York, Oxford University Press, 1926.

Damon, S. F. "Chaucer and Alchemy," *PMLA,* XXXIX (1924), 782–88.

Dempster, Germaine. *Dramatic Irony in Chaucer*. Stanford, Stanford University Press, 1932.

———. "The Original Teller of the Merchant's Tale," *MP,* XXXVI (1938–39), 1–8.

Donaldson, E. T. "Chaucer the Pilgrim," *PMLA,* LXIX (1954), 928–36.

Donovan, M. J. "The *Moralite* of the Nun's Priest's Sermon," *JEGP,* LII (1953), 498–508.

Duffey, B. I. "The Intention and Art of *The Man of Law's Tale,*" *ELH,* XIV (1947), 181–93.

Duncan, E. H. "The Yeoman's Canon's 'Silver Citrinacioun,' " *MP,* XXXVII (1939–40), 241–62.

Emerson, O. F. "Some of Chaucer's Lines on the Monk," *MP*, I (1903–1904), 105–15.

———. "Some Notes on Chaucer and Some Conjectures," *PQ*, II (1923), 81–96.

Fairchild, H. N. "Active Arcite, Contemplative Palamon," *JEGP*, XXVI (1927), 285–93.

Forehand, Brooks. "Old Age and Chaucer's Reeve," *PMLA*, LXIX (1954), 984–89.

Francis, W. N. "Chaucer Shortens a Tale," *PMLA*, LXVIII (1953), 1126–41.

French, W. H. "The Lovers in the Knight's Tale," *JEGP*, XLVIII (1949), 320–28.

Frost, G. L. "Chaucer's Man of Law at the Parvis," *MLN*, XLIV (1929), 496–501.

Frost, William. "An Interpretation of Chaucer's Knight's Tale," *RES* XXV (1949), 289–304.

Furnivall, F. J. "Chaucer's Prioress's Nun-Chaplain," *Anglia*, IV (1881), 238–40.

Galway, Margaret. "Chaucer's Shipman in Real Life," *MLR*, XXXIV (1939), 497–514.

Gardner, W. B. "Chaucer's 'Unworthy Sone of Eve,' " University of Texas *Studies in English*, XXVI (1947), 77–83.

Gerould, G. H. "The Social Status of Chaucer's Franklin," *PMLA*, XLI (1926), 262–79.

———. *Chaucerian Essays*. Princeton, Princeton University Press, 1952.

Gibbons, R. F. "Does the Nun's Priest's Epilogue Contain a Link?" *SP*, LI (1954), 21–33.

Green, A. W. "Chaucer's Clerks and the Mediaeval Scholarly Tradition as Represented by Richard de Bury's 'Philobiblon,' " *ELH*, XVIII (1951), 1–6.

Hadow, Grace. *Chaucer and His Times*. New York, Holt, 1914.

Ham, E. B. "Knight's Tale 38," *ELH*, XVII (1950), 252–61.

Hamilton, M. P. "The Credentials of Chaucer's Pardoner," *JEGP*, XL (1941), 48–72.

———. "The Convent of Chaucer's Prioress and Her Priests," *Philologica: The Malone Anniversary Studies*. Baltimore, Johns Hopkins Press, 1949, 179–90.

Hammond, E. P. *English Verse Between Chaucer and Surrey*. Durham, Duke University Press, 1927.

Harper, G. H. "Chaucer's Big Prioress," *PQ*, XII (1933), 308–10.

Harrison, B. S. "The Rhetorical Inconsistency of Chaucer's Franklin," *SP*, XXXII (1935), 55–61.

Hart, W. M. "A Note on the Interpretation of the *Canterbury Tales*,"

Transactions of the American Philological Association, XXXIX (1908), *liii–liv*.

————. "The Reeve's Tale: A Comparative Study of Chaucer's Narrative Art," *PMLA*, XXIII (1908), 1–44.

Haselmayer, L. A. "The Apparitor and Chaucer's Summoner," *Speculum*, XII (1937), 43–57.

Hemingway, S. B. "Chaucer's Monk and Nun's Priest," *MLN*, XXXI (1916), 479–83.

Hinckley, H. B. *Notes on Chaucer*. Northampton, Massachusetts, Nonotuck Press, 1908.

Hostia, Sister Mary. "The Prioress and Her Companion," *College English*, XIV (1953), 351–52.

Hotson, Leslie. "The *Tale of Melibeus* and John of Gaunt," *SP*, XVIII (1921), 429–52.

Hulbert, J. R. "What Was Chaucer's Aim in the *Knight's Tale?*" *SP*, XXVI (1929), 375–85.

————. "*The Canterbury Tales* and Their Narrators," *SP*, XLV (1948), 565–77.

Ives, D. V. "A Man of Religion," *MLR*, XXVII (1932), 144–48.

Jefferson, B. L. *Chaucer and the Consolation of Philosophy of Boethius*. Princeton, Princeton University Press, 1917.

Jones, Claude. "Chaucer's Taillynge Ynough," *MLN*, LII (1937), 570.

————. "The Monk's Tale, A Mediaeval Sermon," *MLN*, LII (1937), 570–72.

Jones, H. S. V. "The Clerk of Oxenford," *PMLA*, XXVII (1912), 106–15.

Jones, R. F. "A Conjecture on the Wife of Bath's Prologue," *JEGP*, XXIV (1925), 512–47.

Jusserand, J. J. *English Wayfaring Life in the Middle Ages*. English trans., 4th ed. New York, Putnam, 1950.

Kellogg, A. L. "An Augustinian Interpretation of Chaucer's Pardoner," *Speculum*, XXVI (1951), 465–81.

Kellogg, A. L. and L. A. Haselmayer. "Chaucer's Satire of the Pardoner," *PMLA*, LXVI (1951), 251–77.

Ker, W. P. "Chaucer," *English Prose*. Ed. Henry Craik. London, Macmillan, 1893.

Kimpel, Ben. "The Narrator of the *Canterbury Tales*," *ELH*, XX (1953), 77–86.

Kittredge, G. L. "Chaucer's Pardoner," *Atlantic Monthly*, LXXII (1893), 829–33.

————. "The Canon's Yeoman's Prologue and Tale," *Transactions* of the Royal Society of Literature (London), XXX (1910), 87.

————. "Chaucer's Discussion of Marriage," *MP*, IX (1911–12), 435–67.

————. *Chaucer and His Poetry*. Cambridge, Harvard University Press, 1915.

Knott, T. A. "A Bit of Chaucer Mythology," *MP*, VIII (1910–11), 135–39.

————. "Chaucer's Anonymous Merchant," *PQ*, I (1922), 1–16.

Knowlton, E. C. "Chaucer's Man of Law," *JEGP*, XXIII (1924), 83–93.

Kökeritz, Helge. "The Wyf of Bathe and Al Hire Secte," *PQ*, XXVI (1947), 147–51.

Kuhl, E. P. "Chaucer's Burgesses," *Transactions* of the Wisconsin Academy of Sciences, Arts, and Letters, XVIII (1916), 652–75.

————. "Notes on Chaucer's Prioress," *PQ*, II (1923), 302–309.

————. "Chaucer's Monk," *MLN*, LV (1940), 480.

Kuhl, E. P. and H. J. Webb. "Chaucer's Squire," *ELH*, VI (1939), 282–84.

Lawrence, W. W. "Satire in Sir Thopas," *PMLA*, L (1935), 81–91.

————. "The Tale of Melibeus," *Essays and Studies in Honor of Carleton Brown*. New York, New York University Press, 1940, 100–10.

————. *Chaucer and the Canterbury Tales*. New York, Columbia University Press, 1950.

Legouis, Émile. *Geoffrey Chaucer*. English trans. London, Dent, 1913.

Loomis, R. S. "Was Chaucer a Laodicean?" *Essays and Studies in Honor of Carleton Brown*. New York, New York University Press, 1940, 129–48.

Lounsbury, T. R. *Studies in Chaucer*, 3 vols. New York, Harper, 1892.

Lowes, J. L. "Simple and Coy," *Anglia*, XXXIII (1910), 440–51.

————. *Convention and Revolt in Poetry*. Boston, Houghton Mifflin, 1919.

————. *Geoffrey Chaucer and the Development of His Genius*. Boston, Houghton Mifflin, 1934.

Ludeke, Henry. *Die Funktionen der Erzählers in Chaucers epischer Dichtung*. Halle, Niemeyer, 1927.

Lyon, E. D. "Roger de Ware, Cook," *MLN*, LII (1937), 491–94.

Macauley, G. C. "Notes on Chaucer," *MLR*, IV (1910), 14–19.

McGalliard, J. C. "Chaucer's *Merchant's Tale* and Deschamps' *Miroir de Mariage*," *PQ*, XXV (1946), 193–220.

Madeleva, Sister Mary. *Chaucer's Nuns and Other Essays*. New York, Appleton, 1925.

Malone, Kemp. "Style and Structure in the Prologue to the *Canterbury Tales*," *ELH*, XIII (1946), 38–45.

————. *Chapters on Chaucer*. Baltimore, Johns Hopkins Press, 1951.

Manly, J. M. "The Stanza-Forms of Sir Thopas," *MP*, VIII (1910–11), 141–44.

————. *Some New Light on Chaucer*. New York, Holt, 1926.

Marckwardt, A. H. "Characterization in Chaucer's Knight's Tale,"

University of Michigan *Contributions in Modern Philology*, No. 5 (1947).

Mead, W. E. "The *Prologue of the Wife of Bath's Tale*," *PMLA*, XVI (1901), 388–404.

Meyer, Emil. *Die charakterzeichnung bei Chaucer*. Halle, Niemeyer, 1913.

Moffett, H. Y. "Oswald the Reeve," *PQ*, IV (1925), 208–23.

Neville, Marie. "The Function of the *Squire's Tale* in the Canterbury Scheme," *JEGP*, L (1951), 167–79.

Owen, C. A., Jr. "One Robyn or Two," *MLN*, LXVII (1952), 336–38.

———. "The Crucial Passages in Five of the *Canterbury Tales*: A Study in Irony and Symbol," *JEGP*, LII (1953), 294–311.

Owst, G. R. *Literature and Pulpit in Medieval England*. Cambridge, Cambridge University Press, 1933.

Patch, H. R. "Chaucer and Lady Fortune," *MLR*, XXII (1927), 377–88.

———. *On Rereading Chaucer*. Cambridge, Harvard University Press, 1939.

Power, Eileen. *Medieval English Nunneries c. 1275 to 1535*. Cambridge, Cambridge University Press, 1922.

Pratt, R. A. "Chaucer's Shipman's Tale and Sercambi," *MLN*, LV (1940), 142–45.

———. "Was Robyn the Miller's Youth Misspent?" *MLN*, LIX (1944), 47–49.

———. "The Order of the *Canterbury Tales*," *PMLA*, LXVI (1951), 1141–67.

Preston, Raymond. *Chaucer*. London and New York, Sheed and Ward, 1952.

Richardson, H. G. "Year Books and Plea Rolls as Sources of Historical Information," *Transactions* of the Royal Historical Society, Ser. 4, V (1922), 28–51.

Rickert, Edith. "Chaucer's 'Hodge of Ware,'" *TLS* (Oct. 20, 1932), 761.

———. *Chaucer's World*. Ed. C. C. Olson and M. M. Crow. New York, Columbia University Press, 1948.

Robertson, D. W., Jr. "Chaucerian Tragedy," *ELH*, XIX (1952), 1–37.

Robertson, Stuart. "Elements of Realism in the *Knight's Tale*," *JEGP*, XIV (1915), 226–55.

Root, R. K. *The Poetry of Chaucer*. Rev. ed. Boston, Houghton Mifflin, 1922.

Roppolo, J. P. "The Meaning of 'at erst': Prologue to *Sir Thopas*, B^2, 1884," *MLN*, LXIII (1948), 365–71.

———. "The Converted Knight in Chaucer's *Wife of Bath's Tale*," *College English*, XII (1950–51), 263–69.

Rosenfeld, Mary-Virginia. "Chaucer and the Liturgy," *MLN*, LV (1940), 357–60.

Schlauch, Margaret. *Constance and the Accused Queens*. New York, New York University Press, 1927.

———. "Chaucer's *Merchant's Tale* and Courtly Love," *ELH*, IV (1937), 201–12.

Sedgewick, G. G. "The Progress of Chaucer's Pardoner, 1880–1940," *MLQ*, I (1940), 431–58.

———. "The Structure of the *Merchant's Tale*," *UTQ*, XVII (1947–48), 337–45.

Severs, J. B. *The Literary Relationships of Chaucer's Clerkes Tale*. New Haven, Yale University Press, 1942.

———. "Chaucer's Originality in the Nun's Priest's Tale," *SP*, XLIII (1946), 22–41.

———. "Is the *Manciple's Tale* a Success?" *JEGP*, LI (1952), 1–16.

Shannon, E. F. *Chaucer and the Roman Poets*. Cambridge, Harvard University Press, 1929.

Shelly, P. V. D. *The Living Chaucer*. Philadelphia, University of Pennsylvania Press, 1940.

Sherbo, Arthur. "Chaucer's Nun's Priest Again," *PMLA*, LXIV (1949), 236–46.

Shumaker, Wayne. "Chaucer's *Manciple's Tale* as a Part of a Canterbury Group," *UTQ*, XXII (1953), 147–56.

Silverman, Albert H. "Sex and Money in Chaucer's *Shipman's Tale*," *PQ*, XXXII (1953), 329–36.

Slaughter, E. E. "Clerk Jankyn's Motive," *MLN*, LXV (1950), 530–34.

Sledd, James. "Dorigen's Complaint," *MP*, XLV (1947–48), 36–45.

———. "The *Clerk's Tale:* The Monsters and the Critics," *MP*, LI (1953–54), 73–82.

Sleeth, C. R. "The Friendship of Chaucer's Summoner and Pardoner," *MLN*, LVI (1941), 138.

Spurgeon, C. F. E. *Five Hundred Years of Chaucer Criticism and Allusion*. 3 vols. Cambridge, Cambridge University Press, 1925.

Stillwell, Gardiner. "Analogues to Chaucer's *Manciple's Tale* in the *Ovide Moralisé* and Machaut's *Voir-dit*," *PQ*, XIX (1940), 133–38.

———. "The Political Meaning of Chaucer's *Tale of Melibee*," *Speculum*, XIX (1944), 433–44.

———. "Chaucer's 'Sad' Merchant," *RES*, XX (1944), 1–18.

———. "Chaucer in Tartary," *RES*, XXIV (1948), 177–88.

Stobie, M. R. "Chaucer's Shipman and the Wine," *PMLA*, LXIV (1949), 565–69.

Stokoe, W. C., Jr. "Structure and Intention in the First Fragment of *The Canterbury Tales*," *UTQ*, XXI (1951–52), 120–27.

Swart, Johannes. "Chaucer's Pardoner," *Neophilologus*, XXXVI (1952), 45–50.

Tatlock, J. S. P. *The Development and Chronology of Chaucer's Works.* London, Chaucer Society, 1907.
———. "Chaucer and Wyclif," *MP*, XIV (1916–17), 257–68.
———. "Chaucer and the *Legenda Aurea*," *MLN*, XLV (1930), 296–98.
———. "The *Canterbury Tales* in 1400," *PMLA*, L (1935), 100–39.
———. "Chaucer's *Merchant's Tale*," *MP*, XXXIII (1935–36), 367–81.
———. "Chaucer's Monk," *MLN*, LV (1940), 350–54.
———. "Is Chaucer's Monk a Monk?" *MLN*, LVI (1941), 80.
ten Brink, Bernhard. *History of English Literature.* English trans. New York, Holt, 1889–96.
Trevelyan, G. M. *England in the Age of Wyckliffe.* 4th ed. London, Longmans, Green, 1909.
Tupper, Frederick. "The Quarrels of the Canterbury Pilgrims," *JEGP*, XIV (1915), 256–70.
———. "Chaucer's Sinners and Sins," *JEGP*, XV (1916), 56–106.
———. *Types of Society in Medieval Literature.* New York, Holt, 1926.
———. "The Bearings of the Shipman's Prologue," *JEGP*, XXXIII (1934), 352–71.
Utley, F. L. *The Crooked Rib.* Columbus, Ohio State University Press, 1944.
Watt, Francis. *Canterbury Pilgrims and Their Ways.* London, Methuen, 1917.
White, F. E. "Chaucer's Shipman," *MP*, XXVI (1928–29), 249–55, 379–84, and XXVII (1929–30), 123–28.
Willard, Rudolph. "Chaucer's 'Text That Seith That Hunters Ben Nat Hooly Men,'" University of Texas *Studies in English*, XXVI (1947), 209–51.
Williams, Arnold. "Chaucer and the Friars," *Speculum*, XXVIII (1953), 499–513.
Wilson, H. S. "The *Knight's Tale* and the *Teseida* Again," *UTQ*, XVIII, (1948–49), 131–46.
Wood-Legh, K. L. "The Franklin," *RES*, IV (1928), 145–51.
Woolf, H. B. "The Summoner and His Concubine," *MLN*, LXVIII (1953), 118–21.
Worcester, David. *The Art of Satire.* Cambridge, Harvard University Press, 1940.
Work, J. A. "Echoes of Anathema in Chaucer," *PMLA*, XLVII (1932), 419–30.
Young, Karl. "A Note on Chaucer's Friar," *MLN*, L (1935), 83–85.

Index

Afer, Constantinus: author of *De Coitu*, 163

Africanus (in *Parlement of Foules*): analogous to Arcite in Knight's Tale, 44

Albertano of Brescia: author of *Liber Consolationis et Consilii*, 93

Alchemist: the Canon, 227

Alchemy: in fourteenth century, 227

Alliteration: referred to by Parson, 244

Alopicia: Summoner's disease, 137

Anglo-Norman Chronicle: source for Lawyer's Tale, 68

Antifeminism: attitude of Monk towards, 102; in Nun's Priest's Tale, 114–15, 116; in Jenkin's anthology, 123–24; in Merchant's Tale, 170

Apothecaries: Physician's arrangement with, 196

Appius (judge in Physician's Tale), 197

Arcite (character in Knight's Tale): analysis of, 38–49; earlier studies of, 39 n.; prays to Mars, 46; final puzzlement, 47; speech from *Boece*, 180

Argus: Mercury's visit to, 44–45

Artifice: in composition of *CT*, 11–12

Artistry in *CT*: relative criteria, 249; convention and originality, 249

Arveragus (character in Franklin's Tale), 182–93 *passim*

"At erst": meaning of, in Prologue to "Sir Thopas," 88–89

Attempted sale: by Pardoner, 219–23

Aurelius (character in Franklin's Tale), 190–92

Bailly, Harry. *See* Host

Beauchamp, William, 64, 182

Benediction: by Pardoner, 217–19

Black rocks of Brittany (in Franklin's Tale), 190–91

Blindness: as symbol in Merchant's Tale, 168–71

Boccaccio, Giovanni: author of source for Knight's Tale, 32, 34, 39; author of source for Franklin's Tale, 183, 187

Boece: used in Squire's Tale, 180

Boothius: influence on Knight's Tale, 32, 34–38, 39

Bowden, Muriel: on Prioress, 80, 82; on Pynchbck and Bussy, 182

Breton lay: Franklin's Tale as, 183; Franklin's choice of, 185, 186

Brown, Carleton: on Pardoner's benediction, 217–18

Bussy, John: possible model for Franklin, 182

Cambuscan (character in Squire's Tale), 178–80 *passim*

Canacee (character in Squire's Tale), 177–80 *passim*

Canon: his flight, 230–31. *See also* Alchemist

[261